The Fragility of Freedom

The Fragility

Joshua Mitchell

# of Freedom

Tocqueville on

Religion, Democracy,

and the American

Future

The University of Chicago Press
Chicago and London

The University of Chicago Press, Chicago 60637
The University of Chicago Press, Ltd., London
© 1995 by The University of Chicago
All rights reserved. Published 1995
Paperback edition 1999
Printed in the United States of America

04 03 02 01 00 99   5 4 3 2

ISBN: 0-226-53208-9 (cloth)
ISBN: 0-226-53209-7 (paperback)

Library of Congress Cataloging—in—Publication Data

Mitchell, Joshua.
    The fragility of freedom : Tocqueville on religion, democ-
racy, and the American future / Joshua Mitchell.
        p.   cm.
    Includes bibliographical references (p. 245) and index.
    1. Democracy.   2. Democracy—Religious aspects—
Christianity.   3. Tocqueville, Alexis de, 1805–1859—Contributions in democracy.   I. Title.
    JC423.M627   1995   94-48763
    324.6′3′0973—dc20   CIP

FOR PAUL AND ANDREW
inheritors of a future less ours to fashion than we sometimes wish,
but more ours to forge than we often acknowledge

[The spirit of man], unable to hold firmly to what is true and just, is generally reduced to choosing between two excesses.
Tocqueville

It was religion that gave birth to the English colonies in America. One must never forget that.
Tocqueville

And I have given you a land for which ye did not labour, and cities which ye built not, and ye dwell in them; of the vineyards and olive yards which ye planted not do ye eat.

Now therefore fear the Lord, and serve him in sincerity and in truth: and put away the gods which your fathers served on the other side of the flood, and in Egypt; and serve ye the LORD.
Joshua 24:13–14

Contents

Preface

This is at once a study of Tocqueville and an exposition of sorts about the present American situation. No patient reading of Tocqueville will allow us to return peaceably to our received views about America; and conversely, no sincere effort to comprehend the American situation today can long avoid a confrontation with Tocqueville's thinking. The juxtaposition of Tocqueville's "story book truth" about America, and the bewildering array of problems about which so much is presently written, does not, I think, compel us to conclude that the text of life cannot be oriented by the written word. Nor, happily, must we concede that the written word—that is, *Democracy in America*—remains stolidly intransitive to the vicissitudes of concrete experience, purveying a procrustean vision in which only apologists for an America gone by (if not wholly ethereal) may find solace. Tocqueville was, if I may use the phrase, a moral historian, that is, a historian (of the sort Rousseau and Hegel were) for whom history is less an objective record of the past than a profound disclosure of the very trajectory of the human spirit. The history of which Tocqueville speaks is more than an account of America in the Jacksonian era, as his calmly confident remark at the end of the Author's Introduction to this prophetic work suggests.

> I have tried to see not differently but further than any party; while they are busy with tomorrow, I have wished to consider the whole future.

As a moral historian his intention was to situate the kind of soul that has come to dominate in the present age—what I will throughout this book call the *democratic soul*—in the grand sweep of providential history in order to specify its strengths and weaknesses, its advantages and disadvantages, what must be done to save democratic freedom and what traps must be scrupulously avoided. *This* project of orienting the soul outstrips the snapshot moment in time about which it speaks. America in the 1830s is the occasion for *Democracy in America*, but the book speaks to the prospects and instabilities of democracy itself; it speaks to the distant future when the fortunate coincidence of historical accidents that have, perhaps inadvertently, maintained a fragile American democracy may no longer hold sway. The *logic* of equality concerned Tocqueville; its historical articulation in America was but an informative instance.

We are, nevertheless, permitted to wonder why his analysis is especially pertinent *just now*. The anomic drift of the present moment, which seems to call out for guidance and clarity, seems reason enough. Yet this drift is not peculiar to the present age. Tocqueville himself, writing in the 1830s, could already say that he was living in a world "where nothing any longer seems either forbidden or permitted, honest or dishonorable, true or false." For Tocqueville, however, there were mechanisms that forestalled the full implications of this anomic drift, mechanisms that are less robust in these times.

This, in fact, is precisely why Tocqueville is pertinent just now, in the wake of the cold war. For what Tocqueville tells us is that while instability, unhappiness, restiveness, envy, unbounded ambition, isolation—the list is not exhaustive—are verities eternally linked to democracy, there are what I will throughout this book call institutional mechanisms that can moderate the excesses, the immoderations, of the democratic soul. Without these, democracy will falter; with them, the fragile freedom democracy offers may endure. America in the 1830s provided Tocqueville with a glimpse of the institutional mechanisms that forestall the immoderations of the democratic soul. He wrote extensively about them. America in the 1990s ignores them at its peril.

This may sound overly harsh, yet it seems to me that the conceptual horizon of policymakers, economists, politicians, and (regrettably) even political theorists has been largely established by the cold war alternatives of Karl Marx and Adam Smith. Bipolarity is not just a geopolitical fact; it has been an academic one as well. That there might be another genuine alternative, one that is confirmed by what has *actually occurred* in American democracy rather that by what our cold war defenders have earnestly and honestly invoked for the purpose of opposing Karl Marx, has largely gone unconsidered. And now that a certain rendition of Adam Smith seems to have won, there appears to be even less reason to wonder whether the either-or of intellectual bipolarity exhausts the possibilities. This book is dedicated to the proposition that the possibilities for human freedom are not exhausted by intellectual currents that have mimicked the geopolitical struggle of our times. There is another alternative; and that alternative is Tocqueville.

By this I mean to suggest that Tocqueville understood the extraordinary fragility of freedom in the modern world, and that neither the efforts to defend the "market solution to the problem of social order" nor the many disastrous experiments with socialism comprehend this fragility; nor do they understand the real threats to which freedom in the modern world is exposed.

More specifically, Tocqueville understood that human beings are not, essentially, rational maximizers; nor are they agencies of a dialectic of history that will lead to the New Kingdom. Rather, they are beings capable of moderation provided that certain institutional mechanisms are in place to assist them; they are, as well, beings capable of bearing the responsibilities of living in a history the contours of which are defined by the movement toward equality. In this history humankind has been granted the opportunity either to live freely or amid servility. We may freely choose—at least for a time.

This view of the situation is neither oblivious to the movement toward equality that has and will increasingly shape us, nor does it celebrate the ineluctable historical logic that will take the chosen few to the Promised Land and bury the rest. It responsibly takes stock of the undeniable movement of history and soberly propounds a way of contending with the more ominous aspects of that movement—for they do exist.

While the details must await a more thorough introduction, Tocqueville focuses upon three institutional mechanisms that moderate the democratic soul: family, religion, and associational life—of which local politics plays an important part. (His thinking about the law's capacity to moderate, important as it surely is, I have considered here only in passing.) I should note, however, that what I have done in my exposition of these institutions is to place them within the larger context of Tocqueville's thinking about the instabilities of the democratic soul, rather than evaluate them in abstraction. Thus, for example, I have explored his thinking about women in the framework of his understanding of the immoderation of restiveness (among men) for which there must be an antidote if democracy is to thrive, and also as an aspect of his understanding of the need for the preeminence of the invisible over the visible—a view that can be traced back through Rousseau, Augustine, and even Plato. To pull his thoughts about women out of these larger contexts does a disservice to his vision; we may capture *what* he said, but we will fail to comprehend the valence of his thought. I have adopted the same approach with his thinking about religion and associational life. His isolated thoughts on this or that matter, eloquent as they surely are, must not be abstracted from the context in which they find themselves. I have, moreover, in accordance with my intention to grasp the whole of his thinking, been a sympathetic reader, less concerned with criticizing the parts than with showing the coherence and power of the *way* Tocqueville thought. It is this way of thinking from which we can learn most in the post–cold war era. On Tocqueville's reading, the prospects for saving democratic freedom are not strong; the time of irretrievable errors, however, has not yet passed. Until it has, Tocqueville's way of thinking offers hope for those willing to think beyond the contemporary categories that have so gripped us.

The origin, but not necessarily the substance, of this project can be traced to a class taught by David Tracy of the University of Chicago Divinity School, in the late 1980s, in which he suggested that Tocqueville's thinking about democracy could not be disentangled from certain theological suppositions, one of which pertained to the relationship between humankind and God in history. This proposition, by happy coincidence, corroborated the main theme of my dissertation research on Luther, Hobbes, Locke, and Rousseau, which was subsequently published under the title, *Not by Reason Alone*. In certain respects this project continues the investigation begun there, though with the following difference. Where *Not by Reason Alone* was concerned with specifying the historical horizon within which identity was construed by certain early modern thinkers, *Fragile Freedom* focuses more on the institutional mechanisms and habits that constitute identity, and on the relationship between constituted identity and the logic of history that conspires to bring about conditions of equality—theoretical matters that remain indecipherable without attending to certain theological suppositions embedded in Tocqueville's thinking (which suppositions, I add, are traceable to Augustine—that luminous Father whose mark is still upon us today). Both books are concerned with what might be called the logic of equality; here that logic is explored in a different idiom. This is a rather compact way of formulating the matter, I recognize; reading what follows will, I hope, render this formulation less opaque.

On a more practical level, this project could not have been completed in a timely manner without the extraordinarily generous support of the Earhart Foundation during the summers of 1992 and 1993, the George Washington University for a Dilthey Faculty Fellowship in 1992, the Liberty Fund for an invitation to attend a Tocqueville conference in January 1993, Georgetown University for summer support in 1993, and the students who enrolled in my many courses on Tocqueville's *Democracy in America*, initially in the University of Chicago's Common Core, subsequently at the George Washington University, and more recently at Georgetown University. The urgency about the future that was registered in their voices—and in their sometimes pregnant silence—is reluctantly though faithfully reproduced here. To them, and to the many colleagues who have helped me think through democracy in America, I am deeply indebted. Above all, in the course of thinking, teaching, writing, and talking I have learned that the sober-minded hope that Tocqueville proffers can sustain us as we move into an uncertain future. If I have conveyed that much in these pages, I will count this work a success.

I
Introduction

The Delphic injunction, "Know thyself," seems nowhere to have been more happily violated than in the American context. It was, after all, Tocqueville the Frenchman, the stranger in America,[1] who was able to grasp the multiple valences of the democratic soul in this country as no American author had done before or has done since. "The majority lives in a state of perpetual self-adoration," Tocqueville says; "only strangers or experience may be able to bring certain truths to the Americans' attention."[2] And elsewhere,

> A foreigner does, it is true, sometimes meet Americans who are not strict slaves of slogans . . . but no one, except yourself, listens to them, and you, to whom they confide these secret thoughts, are only a stranger and will pass on. To you they will disclose truths that have no use for you, but when they go down into the *marketplace* they use quite a different language.[3]

The language of the marketplace, its limitation, as it were, is doubly pertinent to this study of Tocqueville's social and political thought. Philosophically, the stranger whose currency is not easily exchanged in the market is able to grasp its significance from afar more thoroughly than were he uncritically involved with it. "Know thyself" is for the

1. See Alexis de Tocqueville, *Democracy in America*, ed. J. P. Mayer (New York: Harper and Row, 1968), Author's Introduction, p. 20: "[A] stranger often hears important truths at his host's fireside, truths which he might not divulge to his friends; it is a relief to break a constrained silence with a stranger whose short stay guarantees his discretion." See also vol. 1, part 2, chap. 9, pp. 285–86.

2. Tocqueville, *Democracy in America*, vol. 1, part 2, chap. 7, p. 256.

3. Tocqueville, *Democracy in America*, vol. 1, part 2, chap. 7, p. 258 (emphasis added). The French, *place publique*, Lawrence translates as *marketplace*—a rendition that is occasionally overly narrow. Notwithstanding this shortcoming, the thought is to be found already in Plato: the Piraeus is never the place of truth. See Plato, *Republic*, trans. Paul Shorey, in *The Collected Dialogues of Plato*, ed. Edith Hamilton and Huntington Cairns (New York: Bollingen Books, 1961), bk. 1, 327a.

market-wary. Notwithstanding Tocqueville's admiration of the American commercial spirit, he well knew that its boldness, the awesome scale of its entire enterprise, was a profoundly unstable one, susceptible to disintegration by two conflicting dispositions that dwarf the seemingly ubiquitous disposition to "truck, barter, and exchange."[4] The economic impulse, the commercial spirit, *can* be a driving force, but only if dispositions that would unravel it are kept in abeyance. What Tocqueville found wondrous about America was not simply its commercial spirit, but also the institutional mechanisms that counteracted the tendency of rationality to come undone. The marketplace is the most immediately visible thing, yet it is made possible by institutional mechanisms that are, strictly speaking, invisible to the market.[5]

To know the democratic soul in America, then, one must stand back from the marketplace, from the supposition that the commercial can be understood wholly on its own terms.[6] To speak somewhat cryptically for now, Tocqueville's view supposes that the commercial spirit must be understood through the eyes of Saint Augustine rather than Adam Smith. Had it been otherwise, had Tocqueville thought that human beings were rational maximizers of the sort Smith at times seemed to have had in mind, the content of his book would have been quite different. He did not, after all, return from his voyage to America and write an update to *The Wealth of Nations*. The pertinence of local government, family, and Christian religion to the commercial spirit is not immediately obvious—and received no significant treatment by Adam Smith. Yet these are carefully considered by Tocqueville, not simply because they are interesting, but because they bear upon the commercial spirit that rules the American soul. Local government, family, and Christian

4. Adam Smith, *The Wealth of Nations* (Chicago: University of Chicago Press, 1976), bk. 1, chap. 2, p. 17.

5. See Jean-Jacques Rousseau, "Has the Restoration of the Sciences and Arts Tended to Purify Morals" (hereafter, *First Discourse*) in *The First and Second Discourses*, trans. Roger D. Masters (New York: St. Martin's Press, 1964), p. 51: "[A]ccording to [economists] a man is worth no more to the state than the value of his domestic consumption." Rousseau, like Tocqueville who follows, thought that the visible measures to which the economists resort are not an adequate measure of the vitality of a society.

6. See Amitai Etzioni, *The Moral Dimension: Toward a New Economics* (New York: Free Press, 1988), p. 250: "[A] paradox arises to the extent that it is true that the market is dependent on normative underpinning (to provide the pre-contractual foundation such as trust, cooperation, and honesty) which all contractual relations require: *The more people accept the neoclassical paradigm as a guide for their behavior, the more the ability to sustain a market economy is undermined*" (emphasis in original).

religion attenuate certain problems that attend what I will here call the *Augustinian self.* Absent a remedy to these problems, the commercial spirit cannot long endure.

1. THE AUGUSTINIAN SELF

What, then, is meant by the Augustinian self, and why is it not disposed toward the moderate disposition so necessary for commercial success?

By the Augustinian self I mean the kind of self that is prone to move in two opposite directions: either *inward,* in which case it tends to get wholly shut up within itself and abandon the world; or *outward,* in which case it tends to be restive, overly active, and lost amid the world, searching at a frenzied pace for a satisfaction it can never wholly find there.[7] Neither of these two opposing tendencies can bring happiness in its wake; and they are liable to succeed one another in turn as the vacuity of each is dimly intuited.[8] Human health is not captured by either alter-

7. See Tocqueville, *Democracy in America,* vol. 2, part 2, chap. 13, pp. 535–38. Absent the prospect of eternal life, the temporal horizon extends only as far as the span of a person's life; so oriented, reward will be construed in worldly terms that will always be transitory. "A man who has set his heart on nothing but the good things of this world," Tocqueville says, "is always in a hurry" (p. 536). See Blaise Pascal, *Pensées,* trans. A. J. Krailsheimer (New York: Penguin Books, 1966), sec. 73, p. 49: "[W]hat causes inconstancy is the realization that present pleasures are false, together with the failure to realize that absent pleasures are vain." For a provocative treatment of Tocqueville's indebtedness to Pascal for his psychological insights, see Peter Augustine Lawler, *The Restless Mind: Alexis de Tocqueville on the Origin and Perpetuation of Human Liberty* (Lanham, Md.: Rowan and Littlefield, 1993).

8. Thus, for example, it is possible—indeed likely—to find a culture self-absorbed in the solipsism of popular psychology and at the same time searching with abandon for material success. Not inconsistent with this analysis are the historical cycles about which Schlesinger writes. See Arthur M. Schlesinger, Jr., *The Cycles of American History* (Boston: Houghton Mifflin, 1986), pp. 23–48. The twin tendencies about which Tocqueville speaks are treated in his work as a series of successive moments that oscillate between activity and passivity. See also Hannah Arendt, *Between Past and Future* (New York: Viking Press, 1961), pp. 100–101: "[F]or more than a hundred and fifty years [public opinion] has swung at regular intervals from one extreme to the other, from a liberal mood to a conservative one and back to a more liberal again, at times attempting to reassert authority and at others to reassert freedom, [all of which has] resulted only in further undermining both, confusing the issues, blurring the distinctive lines between authority and freedom, and eventually destroying the political meaning of both." Not grasping the right relationship between freedom and authority yields either the too-fast (where pseudofreedom for a time reigns) or the

native, as tempting as one may be in the face of the insufficiency of the other. The necessary relationship between the two I will treat in due course.

While the more quantitatively minded may scoff at the idea, the first disposition can be characterized by a lack of motion (or, rather, insufficient motion); the second, by hypermotion. (I will offer an account of the importance of motion in Tocqueville's thinking in section 6, below). In either case, a careful, moderate, and farsighted course of action is unlikely, if not impossible.[9]

This way of thinking about the two immoderate dispositions is not scientific, to be sure; it is, nevertheless, justified for two reasons: first, Tocqueville's analysis of the democratic soul and American situation would remain opaque without invoking the concept of motion; and second, while these terms may be unscientific, like the pornography about which Justice Stewart has spoken, "[W]e know [moderation and immoderation] when we see it."[10] I will unabashedly resort to this usage throughout. Other ways of conveying the twin dispositions of the Augustinian self could no doubt be found, but Tocqueville's method is adequate for our purpose here.

In chapter 2, these twin dispositions and their interrelationship will be worked through in some detail; there, I will provide from the works of Augustine, Hobbes, and Rousseau evidence demonstrating that in the past the self has been thought of in these terms, as well as a preliminary exposition of the theoretical stance of Tocqueville's *Democracy in America* confirming that he, too, ascribes to this view of the self—and, more importantly, believes the democratic soul *must* be understood in this way. Here, I merely wish to comment briefly upon Tocqueville's

---

too-slow (where pseudoauthority reigns.) Arendt believes that this oscillation is an unstable equilibrium.

9. On Tocqueville's view, certain kinds of actions and understandings will be meaningful only to certain kinds of human beings; democratic souls are capable of certain efforts and thoughts, while aristocratic souls are capable of others. People are formed in certain ways that dispose them to act and think this way rather than that; so formed, the efforts of reason to change people through argument alone are often mocked. See also Jean-Jacques Rousseau, "Discourse on the Origin and Foundations of Inequality among Men" (hereafter, *Second Discourse*), in *First and Second Discourses*," p. 165: "[I]t does not behoove slaves to reason about freedom." Tocqueville thought, as I have said, that the temporal horizon of the democratic soul was short-term; institutions, not arguments, could palliate this disposition.

10. In *Jacobellis* v. *Ohio.*, 378 U.S. (1964), p. 184.

reading of the immense political and social implications of this twin tendency.

To put the matter succinctly: if the self is inclined either to fall quietly into itself—Tocqueville's term for this phenomenon is "individualism"—or to be anxiously carried away, then the more moderate, intermediate disposition is not given in the nature of things but rather must be achieved over and over again. And since I mean here, by the moderate disposition, a rational disposition, which is neither broodingly enclosed from the world nor anxiously carried away by it, I mean to suggest that rationality is an unstable intermediate in human life that must be achieved through human effort and, more precisely, through institutional support. To express the matter in terms of figures in the history of political thought again, where Adam Smith would have come perilously close to insisting that human beings are rational (or more accurately that what we might call market rationality may be observed in all cultures at all times),[11] and that distortions upon the market *stand in the way* of our becoming rational; Tocqueville would have it that human rationality, and so the commercial spirit, is made possible at all by institutions that draw human beings toward a more moderate disposition— away, that is, from the too-slow or the too-fast.

2. ANTIDOTES TO THE IRRATIONALITIES OF THE AUGUSTINIAN SELF

The theoretical problem for Tocqueville, then, is how to assure that human beings be drawn out of individualism (too little motion) and kept from restiveness (too much motion). What does this, in addition to the unprecedented availability of land for expansion (the significance of

11. See Smith, *The Wealth of Nations*, bk. 1, chap. 2, p. 19, where even primitive people are said to be engaged in market rationality; and those who are not remain steeped in barbarism and squalor (chap. 21, p. 25). Cf. Marshall Sahlins, *Stone Age Economics* (Chicago: Aldine-Atherton, 1972), p. 4: "The market-industrial system *institutes scarcity*, in a manner completely unparalleled and to a degree nowhere else approximated. Where production and distribution are arranged through the behavior of prices, and all livelihoods depend upon getting and spending, insufficiency of material means becomes the explicit, calculable starting point of all economic activity" (emphasis added). Scarcity, for Sahlins, is not an objective condition, but rather a relationship; as with Rousseau in *Emile*, scarcity is overcome solely by assuring that one's desires do not exceed one's capacity to fulfill them. See also John Kenneth Galbraith, *The Affluent Society* (Boston: Houghton Mifflin, 1984), pp. 126–33.

which will be considered section 6 of chapter 3), is a certain set of institutional arrangements that he finds most firmly established in America.

The corrosive effects of individualism, for example, which "[shuts a man up] in the solitude of his own heart,"[12] can be counteracted by political participation at the local level. By giving people a stake in their own affairs, individualism can be averted and a healthy political and civil society produced. Centralized administration, while perhaps efficient along one parameter, is grossly inefficient along another; we misapprehend the function of government if we endorse it. Government's purpose is to draw human beings out of themselves, to avert individualism. If it does not do this, no matter how "efficient," it has failed.

On this reading, of course, the contemporary fixation upon the question of whether government is descriptively representative betrays a misconception about what government must do. Note Tocqueville's pregnant remark:

> It is certainly not the elected magistrate who makes the American democracy prosper, but the fact *that* the magistrates are elected.[13]

---

12. Tocqueville, *Democracy in America*, vol. 2, part 2, chap. 2, p. 508. See also Tocqueville's letter of January 1, 1856, to Madame Swetchine: "You could not imagine, Madame, the pain and often cruelty I experience in living in this moral isolation, to feel myself outside the intellectual community of my time and my country. Solitude in a desert would seem to me less harsh than this sort of solitude among men. Because, I confess my weakness to you, isolation has always frightened me, and to be happy and even calm, I have always needed, more than is wise, to find a certain concourse around myself and to count on the sympathy of a certain number of my fellows. This profound saying could be applied especially to me: it is not good to be alone" (Alexis de Tocqueville, *Selected Letters on Politics and Society*, ed. Roger Boesche [Berkeley and Los Angeles: University of California Press, 1985], p. 326). Also see Wilhelm Hennis, "In Search of the 'New Science of Politics,'" in *Interpreting Tocqueville's "Democracy in America,"* ed. Ken Masugi (Savage, Md.: Rowan and Littlefield, 1991), p. 49: "Tocqueville radicalizes the experience [of loneliness] suffered so much more prevalently in modern society by making this oldest pronouncement of our Judeo-Christian conception of human history the basis of his entire political thought. It is not only oppressive and sad, it is *not good*—it weakens and destroys spiritual strength and the soul of man if he is not torn from behind the walls of his ego into constant social and brotherly responsibility" (emphasis in original). The Masugi compilation as a whole is quite good, though some of the essays convey a general unease with respect to the historical claims about the inevitability of equality, as well as a dubiety about Tocqueville's lack of attention to the American founding.

13. Tocqueville, *Democracy in America*, vol. 2, part 2, chap. 4, p. 512 (emphasis added).

As the concern about difference becomes ever more acute—a democratic phenomenon through and through!—the contemporary mind becomes increasingly concerned with whether various ethnic, racial, or religious identities are represented; yet assuring proper representation will in no way insure the success of democracy. The purpose of representation in a democracy is not to guarantee that all different identities have their say, but rather that the universal disposition toward worldly passivity be countered.[14] Representation, if not a means to this, is vacuous.

That Tocqueville writes about local government so early on in *Democracy in America* serves to confirm the importance of participation; there, at the local level, passivity, the too-little of individualism, can be countered. (There is, in fact, very little mention of representation throughout his book!) Unless human beings are drawn out of themselves, no amount of fine tuning of the market will generate or maintain a healthy civil society. A healthy civil society can be sustained only when the prior problem of individualism has been averted. On this reading, politics is logically prior to economy.[15] Politics helps to *form* the soul capable of rationally participating in the economy.

The problem of too little motion (individualism), then, can be absolved with the assistance of face-to-face political life. The second problem—the debilitating effects of restiveness, of too much motion—can be attenuated by the institutions of family and of religion.

With respect to family, Tocqueville's scant references belie his assessment of its importance—perhaps because he thought that institution far less susceptible to disruption than, say, religion. Family, or more precisely women's role in the family, cannot be abrogated without debilitating consequences.[16] Notwithstanding their necessary though by

14. See J. S. Mill, "Considerations on Representative Government," in *Three Essays* (Oxford: Oxford University Press, 1975), pp. 179–98.

15. Aristotle, too, claims that politics is more important than economics, though the basis of his conclusion is different than Tocqueville's. For Aristotle, politics is the highest form of human association, that toward which all lesser forms of association aim. (See Aristotle, *Nicomachean Ethics*, trans. Martin Ostwald [New York: Macmillan, 1986], bk. 1, chap. 2, 1094a18–1094b12.) Economics, therefore, is subsumed by politics. Tocqueville reaches the same conclusion, but for different reasons. Politics is not, for him, the arena in which we express the highest human attributes, but rather an antidote to the individualism that is the plague of the modern world. Politics draws the self out of itself; that is its primary purpose.

16. Wilson notes that *the* social problem is male socialization. Where the family is no longer intact, there must be other social institutions (boarding schools, churches, etc.) that teach certain habits capable of arresting "pointless

no means unequivocal deference to men, women have a peculiarly important place in the moral economy, just as Augustine would have it.[17] (That women were the first to witness the Resurrection suggests their important standing in the New Testament.)[18] Rousseau, too, notes in *Emile* that women have a special position in the moral economy and insists that, should they abandon their peculiar virtues, all will be lost:

> Do you wish to bring everyone back to his first duties? Begin with mothers. You will be surprised by the changes you will produce. [Degeneracy] follows from this first depravity [of women].[19]

---

masculine display" (James Q. Wilson, "Human Nature and Social Progress," Bradley Lecture, American Enterprise Institute, May 9, 1991, p. 20). Rousseau, in his own way, would have agreed. See Jean-Jacques Rousseau, *Emile*, trans. Allan Bloom (New York: Basic Books, 1979), bk. 5, p. 363: "[T]he more women want to resemble [men] the less women will govern them, and then men will truly be masters." In a different key, Stephen Holmes, in his introduction to Hobbes's *Behemoth*, comments on Christianity's capacity to arrest pride (the Hobbesian equivalent to the problem of male socialization). In his words, "[T]he greatest source of anarchy is pride; and (as Pascal showed) there is no mythology more effective in attacking pride than the mythology of sin and redemption. Society would certainly be more peaceful if both 'glory' and 'vengeance' could be reserved to God, as Scripture says they should be. It is no accident that Hobbes lifted his central metaphor, the state as the king of the children of pride, from the Bible" (Thomas Hobbes, *Behemoth*, ed. Ferdinand Tönnies [Chicago: University of Chicago Press, 1990], p. xlvi).

17. It was Augustine's mother who, in his estimation, spoke not her own words of chastisement of his errancy from God, but rather God's words. Augustine's father only wished that he become a prominent figure in the world; it was his mother who brought him back to God. See Augustine, *Confessions*, trans. Henry Chadwick (New York: Oxford University Press, 1991), bk. 2, chap. 3, p. 46: "[My mother's solicitation not to commit fornication and the like] seemed to me womanish advice which I would have blushed to take notice of. But they were your warnings and I did not realize it. I believed you were silent and that it was only she who was speaking when you [God] were speaking to me through her." See also bk. 21, chap. 11, pp. 49–50. Woman brings the soul of man back to God from its errancy in the world. See also Tocqueville's letter to Sophie Swetchine of February 11, 1857: "I lack the greatest of all conditions of happiness: the tranquil enjoyment of present good. I live, however, beside a person [my wife] whose contact should long ago have sufficed to cure me of this great and ridiculous misery; and indeed this contact has been very salutary for me for twenty years, enough to fortify my mind in my present condition, not enough to produce regular and complete equilibrium" (*Selected Letters*, pp. 348–49).

18. Matt. 28:5–10; Mark 16:5–13; Luke 24:3–11; John 20:1.

19. Rousseau, *Emile*, bk. 1, p. 46. Bloom's assessment of the importance of recognizing the natural differences and peculiar purviews of men and women is

Tocqueville follows both of them, in his own way, in this view; he is, at any rate, certainly no less sanguine than they that the restiveness of life cannot be ameliorated without a woman's central place in the family.

> [In America] religion is often powerless to restrain men in the midst of innumerable temptations which fortune offers. It cannot moderate their eagerness to enrich themselves, which everything contributes to arouse, but [religion] reigns supreme in the souls of the women, and it is women who shape mores. . . . When the American returns from the turmoil of politics to the bosom of the family, he immediately finds a perfect picture of order and peace. There all his pleasures are simple and natural and his joys innocent and quiet, and as the regularity of life brings him happiness, he easily forms the habit of regulating his opinions as well as his tastes.[20]

I have no interest in quarreling about the picture of domestic tranquility Tocqueville offers. Rather, I only point out that the tendency *of men* to get caught up in worldly affairs must, in his view, be moderated by the institution of the family. Excess motion must be bridled in order to have a healthy society. "The attraction of domestic life is the best counterpoison for bad morals," Rousseau says.[21] Tocqueville agrees.

On this view, if you wish to have a healthy civil society (one that is robust but not frantic—that is, capable of sustained attention to an enterprise), then you must somehow assure that the institution of the family not be undermined. While you may, for a time, increase the aggregate wealth of society by increasing the number of workers who participate in its production, if such an increase is achieved by undermining the family, the long-term consequences can only prove disastrous. Because the point of moderate equilibrium between the too-slow and the

---

no less forgiving than Rousseau's of the impulse to level all differences between the sexes. See Allan Bloom, *The Closing of the American Mind* (New York: Simon and Schuster, 1987), pp. 122–32.

20. Tocqueville, *Democracy in America*, vol. 1, part 2, chap. 9, p. 291. See also vol. 2, part 3, chap. 9, p. 590: "[T]here have never been free societies without mores, and as I have observed in the first part of this book, it is woman who shapes these mores. Therefore everything which has a bearing on the status of woman, their habits, and their thoughts is, in my view, of great political importance."

21. Rousseau, *Emile*, bk. 1, p. 49. See also Rousseau, *Second Discourse*, p. 89: "[A]miable and virtuous countrywomen, the fate of your sex will always be to govern ours. . . . What barbarous man could resist the voice of honor and reason in the mouth of a tender wife? And who would not despise vain luxury seeing your simple and modest attire which, from the luster it derives from you, seems the most favorable to beauty?"

too-fast (which allows civil society to be robust) is achieved only with institutional support, the undermining of the family ultimately undermines civil society.

Put yet another way, economic rationality—where actors calmly calculate their interests—*supposes already* an institutional arrangement on the basis of which such rational and calm calculation becomes possible; rationality is an achievement made possible only by prolonged effort in other arenas of human life. Failing to attend to those institutional supports, making public policy on the basis of market efficiency alone—or rather, a *narrow* view of market efficiency—is ultimately counterproductive.[22] The psychological acuity of Tocqueville, not the more formal aspects of Smith's *The Wealth of Nations*, must be our guide. Human beings have a tendency to be irrational; it is only with the aid of certain institutional supports that they become capable of rationality at all![23]

With respect to religion, here I can only begin to articulate Tocqueville's position that Christianity provides an invaluable institutional support for democracy. This is a massive issue that will be considered throughout chapter 4, and elsewhere. To introduce the matter, consider his observation:

> When a people's religion is destroyed, doubt invades the highest faculties of the mind and half paralyzes all the rest; [then] in despair of solving unaided the greatest problems of human destiny, men ignobly give up thinking about them.

22. See Karl Brunner, "The Perception of Man and the Conception of Society: Two Approaches to Understanding Society," *Economic Inquiry* 25, no. 3 (1987): 388: "[O]f particular importance for our times is a deep understanding of the attrition of *social capital*. One suspects that the range of conflicts will grow and that pervasive uncertainty will increase, with further consequences for economic affairs and social coherence" (emphasis added). Brunner's intention is to extend economic analysis so that it may be able to account for invisible social capital; that is, so that it, too, may become visible to economic analysis.

23. This, incidentally, is a variant of what Locke argues in his famous vindication of representative government. Children are not born reasonable; it is only by the education within the family that they become so. See John Locke, *An Essay concerning the True Original, Extent, and End of Civil Government* (hereafter, *Second Treatise*), in *Two Treatises of Government*, ed. Peter Laslett (Cambridge: Cambridge University Press, 1988), chap. 6, secs. 55–63, pp. 304–9. See also Nathan Tarcov, *Locke's Education for Liberty* (Chicago: University of Chicago Press, 1984), p. 209: "[I]f government by consent [of reasonable beings] is to be meaningful, the formation of that consent or dissent must be entrusted to other agencies. For Locke, the family was the natural and safest agency for these crucial purposes."

> Such a state inevitably enervates the soul, and relaxing the springs of the will, prepares them for bondage.
>
> Then not only will they let their freedom be taken from them, but often they actually hand it over themselves.[24]

These are portentous remarks, to be sure. Religion rebinds the soul, orients it toward a transcendent unity it longs for but can never wholly grasp in this world. So oriented and bound by something otherworldly, so fixed to a horizon seen only by the eyes of hope and promise amid the mystery of mediation, the soul does not fall into the temptation of idolatry, or into worshiping a tyrant in this world who would offer the false security of a unity that can only be held together (if at all) by isolation and passivity. Almost like Hobbes, there must be obedience to a sovereign in order for there to be peace[25]—only for Tocqueville, we make our choice: we may obey and be bound by God or by a tyrant. Human beings are only capable of so much uncertainty and the unboundedness that it occasions. Religion offers a vital antidote that is ignored at our peril. *Something* must calm the soul—and either religion or a tyrant can do this. The secret longing for repose, which can never be truly satisfied in the world, must be directed toward the realm where alone it is promised. Absent this realm that can dwell in the heart only as hope, the soul seeks solace through a worldly power most nearly having the attributes it has forsaken in the realm it has renounced. There will always be a God, Tocqueville intimates; the crucial question is whether we will seek him in the right place!

3. OF THE EMBODIMENT AND DISEMBODIMENT OF THOUGHT

Underpinning Tocqueville's analysis of the institutional mechanisms that moderate the irrationalities of the soul is an understanding of the relationship between practice and thought—between being and consciousness, if you will—that warrants some attention here. Already in the Author's Introduction we are presented with a worry about the Europe of his day: moderation of thought and emotion was no longer possible; the old order had fallen away, and with it the constraints upon

24. Tocqueville, *Democracy in America*, vol. 2, part 1, chap. 5, p. 444.
25. See Thomas Hobbes, *Leviathan*, ed. Michael Oakeshott (New York: Macmillan, 1962). Without a sovereign we are condemned to remain in the state of nature. There, life is lived in "continual fear, and danger of violent death; [there] the life of man [is] solitary, poor, nasty, brutish, and short" (part 1, chap. 13, p. 100).

thinking that institutions inexorably impose upon those who are its members. Ideas may shape the world, but the reverse is no less true.[26] They are both cause and consequence. Disembody thought, eliminate the institutions within which thought "becomes flesh," as it were, and the ideas that come to mind will themselves be unfettered.

> In the *heat* of the struggle each partisan is driven beyond the *natural limits* of his own views by the views and excesses of his adversaries, loses sight of the very aim he was pursuing, and uses language which ill corresponds to his real feelings and his secret instincts.[27]

An escalating conflict of ideas that may lead to violence is the inevitable outcome of thought's labor when it is no longer embodied in viable institutions.[28]

Of particular interest, for Tocqueville, were the defenders and detractors of religion. By historical accident the Roman Catholic Church had come to be identified with transient political powers, which themselves are always "shaken by the shifting winds of time," as Augustine

26. Marx was not the first to suggest that being precedes consciousness. See Karl Marx, "German Ideology," in *Marx's Concept of Man*, ed. Erich Fromm, trans. T. B. Bottomore (New York: Frederick Ungar, 1978), p. 198. See also the letter from Marx to Engels of August 2, 1862, in *Marx-Engels Correspondence* (Moscow: Progress Publishers, 1955), p. 120, where Marx remarks that "it is remarkable how Darwin recognizes among beasts and plants his English society." Elsewhere he remarks, "[N]ature, as it develops in human history, in the act of genesis of human society, is the *actual* nature of man; thus nature as it develops through industry, though in an *alienated* form, is truly *anthropological* nature" ("Private Property and Communism," in *Marx's Concept of Man*, p. 136). While for Marx the directionality is preeminently from being to consciousness, Engels (and no doubt Marx) recognized that it may go the other way as well. See, for example, the letter from Engels to Schmidt of October 27, 1890, in *Correspondence*, p. 400: "[While the ideological outlook is really only an economic reflection, it] influences in its turn the economic basis and may, within certain limits, modify it."

27. Tocqueville, *Democracy in America*, Author's Introduction, p. 16 (emphasis added). The worry that underlies Clifford Orwin's "Civility," in *American Scholar* 60 (Autumn 1991): 553–64, is that the natural limits about which Tocqueville speaks are being overstepped in contemporary debates. Hobbes, too, seems to have worried about this problem. "The secret thoughts of a man," he says, "run over all things, holy, profane, clean, obscene, grave, and light, without shame, or blame; which verbal discourse cannot do, farther than the judgment shall approve of the time, place, and persons" (*Leviathan*, part 1, chap. 8, p. 61).

28. For an instance of this ill correspondence from the ancient world, see Thucydides' discussion of the civil war in Corcyra in *History of the Peloponnesian War*, trans. Rex Warner (New York: Penguin Books, 1972), bk. 21, pp. 236–45.

put it.[29] God's ordination that the aristocratic age should be supplanted by the age of equality meant, consequently, that the Church, too, would be a casualty of this movement. Here was a great irony: Christianity, "which [had] declared all men equal in the sight of God, [and could not] hesitate to acknowledge all citizens equal before the law,"[30] stood opposed by the Christian Church. Christianity declared one thing, Christians another; Christianity conduced toward democracy, the Church opposed it.[31] Because the Church was now disestablished from the verities of the democratic age, the thought that emerged from it was zealous, unbalanced, and disengaged. As the institution ceased to comport with emerging democratic sentiments, so, too, did the thought that issued from it.

29. Saint Augustine, *City of God*, trans. Demetrius B. Zema, S.J., and Gerald G. Walsh, S.J., in *The Fathers of the Church*, ed. Roy Joseph Deferrari (New York: Fathers of the Church, 1950), vol. 6, bk. 1, preface, p. 18. The Henry Bettenson translation of Augustine's *City of God* (New York: Penguin Books, 1972) has: "which sway in their temporal instability" (p. 5). Throughout this work I will first cite the more authoritative Deferrari edition (as *City of God*), and subsequently cite the page or pages to which it corresponds in the more readily available Bettenson translation (as *CG*).

30. Tocqueville, *Democracy in America*, Author's Introduction, p. 16. Cf. Ralph Waldo Emerson, "Politics," in *Emerson's Essays* (New York: Harper and Row, 1951), p. 409: "[D]emocracy is better for us, because the religious sentiment of the present time accords better with it."

31. See Reinhold Niebuhr, "The Tower of Babel," in *Beyond Tragedy: Essays on the Christian Interpretation of History* (New York: Charles Scribner's Sons, 1951), p. 32: "[The civilization of the Middle Ages was a] 'Christian' civilization in its own estimation. But it was also a Tower of Babel. It failed to realize that it was also primarily a landlord's civilization which had carefully woven the peculiar economic interests of feudal aristocrats into the fabric of Christian idealism. Its theory of the 'just price' sought to set a religiomoral check upon economic greed. But the theory of the just price was the expression of a consumer's economy at the expense of producers, the aristocrats being the consumers and the city artisans the producers. In the same way its rigorous prohibition of usury was ostensibly the application of a scriptural ideal to the problem of borrowing and lending. It was enforced only as long as the landed gentry were primarily borrowers and not lenders of money." Niebuhr's distinction between "biblical religion" and "culture religions" (p. 44) is helpful in clarifying the problem about which Tocqueville worries. On Niebuhr's view, biblical religion warns against the construction of totalities that purport to grasp the whole. (The story of the Tower of Babel conveys precisely this message.) Culture religions, on the other hand, succumb too readily to this temptation. Tocqueville thought that the American genius was to have rejected cultural religion in favor of biblical religion.

The sincere proponents of democracy, in turn, had seen the institutional connection between aristocracy and Christianity and so moved away from both. To defend democracy, their "eyes had turned more to earth than to heaven."[32] Christianity itself, rather than its particular affiliation at that moment in history, was an affront to democratic sentiments, it seemed. These sentiments, they opined, could only be nurtured through abstract and disembodied philosophical investigations. There alone could the foundation of democracy be secured. Tocqueville clearly saw the futility, if not the danger, of trying to build democracy on this foundation. Religion will always be necessary; "[only] by doing moral violence to their nature [can] men detach themselves from religious beliefs," he says.[33] The Americans, not having linked their religion with politics as had been done in Europe's aristocratic age, could see more clearly than the Europeans that Christianity supports rather than detracts from democracy. Able to think within the confines of a viable religious forum, it was not necessary for them to embark upon the task of constructing from first principles an abstruse philosophical defense of democracy.

I am informed that on the [European] side of the ocean freedom and human happiness lack nothing but Spinoza's belief in the eternity of the world and Cabinas' contention that thought is a secretion of the brain. To that I have really no answer to give, except that those who talk like that have never seen either religious peoples or free ones. . . . Despotism may be able to do without faith, but freedom cannot.[34]

32. Tocqueville, *Democracy in America*, Author's Introduction, p. 17. Perhaps Tocqueville is here thinking of the utilitarian basis of democracy—which *is* democratic at least in the sense that it supposes that everyone can or should act on the basis of perceived utility. But like Augustine before him, Tocqueville insists that belief in God is the source of human comfort and stability. See Augustine, *City of God*, vol. 7, bk. 8, chap. 8, pp. 35–36 (*CG*, p. 310), where, against all the other philosophers of antiquity with the possible exception of the Platonists, he says: "[T]hose who sought for human good either in man's body or in his mind or in both did not think they had to search outside of man himself to find it. . . . From this we infer that the pursuer of wisdom, that is, the philosopher, will only be truly happy when he begins to rejoice in God." If God has ordained that there will be equality, then humankind cannot, without dire consequences, turn away from God and hope to institute the equality of freedom that it is its responsibility to secure. About this Tocqueville was certain.

33. Tocqueville, *Democracy in America*, vol. 1, part 2, chap. 9, p. 297. See also p. 300: "[W]ith us [Europeans] there must be some accidental and particular cause preventing the human spirit from following its inclinations and driving it beyond those limits within which it should naturally remain."

34. Tocqueville, *Democracy in America*, vol. 1, part 2, chap. 9, p. 294.

The rejection of the institutional forum that can most nurture freedom condemns thinking that wishes to defend democracy against the embodied prejudices of an age to an impotence that belies the grandeur of its vision. It takes flight, but its wings are weak.[35]

The significance of thought's embodiment will emerge in the course of this study as a central theme in Tocqueville's thinking. By way of further introduction consider his remarks, not about why Christianity was being rejected in the Europe of his day, but rather why was it accepted in the Roman world in the first place. Here, as before, Tocqueville is not satisfied with a purely philosophical account; for if thought is to make sense it must in some way accord with the real-life conditions that it articulates.

> At the time when Christianity appeared on earth, Providence, which no doubt *was preparing* the world for its reception, had united a great part of mankind, like an immense flock, under the Caesars. The men composing this multitude were of many different sorts, but they all had this in common, that they obeyed the same laws, and each of them was so small and weak compared to the greatness of the emperor that they all seemed equal in comparison to him. One must recognize that this new and singular condition of humanity *disposed* men to receive the general truths preached by Christianity, and this serves to explain the quick and easy way in which it then penetrated the human spirit.[36]

35. Tocqueville is temptingly close in his thinking here to Hegel. Abstract thought, while powerful, cannot sustain a living community. Theologically, the word must become flesh. See G. W. F. Hegel, *The Phenomenology of Spirit*, trans. A. V. Miller (London: Oxford University Press, 1977), sec. 590, p. 359: "[When self-consciousness] has completed the destruction of the actual organization of the world, and exists now just for itself, [universal freedom] is its sole object, an object that no longer has any content, possession, existence, or outer extension, but is merely this knowledge of itself as an absolutely pure and free individual self." For both Tocqueville and Hegel, the perverse drive toward universalism is coincident with the emergence of the solitary, disembodied soul. For both, as well, mediation is necessary to absolve this dilemma.

36. Tocqueville, *Democracy in America*, vol. 2, part 1, chap. 5, p. 446 (emphasis added). The French, *particulier,* is better translated as *particular* or *special,* rather than *singular.* See also Alexis de Tocqueville, *The Old Régime and the French Revolution*, trans. Stuart Gilbert (Garden City, N.Y.: Doubleday, 1955), p. 13, where the idea of equality could not take hold of Europe prior to the eighteenth century because the real-life conditions did not yet accord with it. Also see Paul Tillich, *Systematic Theology* (Chicago: University of Chicago Press, 1951), 1:61: "[T]he divine-human relation, and therefore God as well as man within this relation, changes with the stages of history of revelation and with the stages of every personal development." Tillich's "method of correlation," like Tocque-

The real-life condition of the Romans (where, as in Roman Catholicism, all are equal under the pope/emperor) "disposed" the people toward a religious idea that recapitulates what their lived experience avowed. They could easily come to *think* Christianity because the life they lived already evinced the Christian pattern. Being precedes consciousness; real-life conditions of equality dispose thought to accept certain religious notions.

But there is more: the breakdown of the Roman Empire into its numerous fragments had precisely the opposite effect on thought than did the unification of Rome under the caesars.

> There soon developed within these nations an infinite hierarchy of ranks. Racial differences became marked, and castes divided each nation into several peoples. In the midst of this communal effort, which seemed bent on subdividing humanity into as many fragments as it is possible to conceive, Christianity did not lose sight of the principal general ideas which it had brought to light. . . . Unable [then] to subdivide the Deity, they could at least multiply and aggrandize his agents beyond measure.[37]

There is an account of why Roman Catholics worshiped the saints! The real-life fragmentation of the Roman Empire disposed persons to accept the idea of particular mediaries who were God's agents.

As I have said, the relationship between the teachings of Christianity and the real-life conditions in a democracy will be considered in depth in chapter 4. There, too, I will consider the problem of slavery, which also cannot be comprehended without grasping Tocqueville's understanding of the relationship between thought and real life. About that, some initial remarks should be made here.

The problem is twofold. On the one hand, the difficulty is that the real-life conditions of the slaves have disposed them toward certain ways of thinking and foreclosed others.

> For [the slave's] *life* has taught him to submit to everything, except the dictates of reason; and when reason becomes his only guide, he cannot hear its voice. [38]

---

ville's sociology of knowledge, insists that the *whatness* of God for humankind can never be other than historically bound and can only be comprehended in terms of lived experience at any given moment of history.

37. Tocqueville, *Democracy in America*, vol. 2, part 1, chap. 5, p. 446.

38. Tocqueville, *Democracy in America*, vol. 1, part 2, chap. 10, p. 318 (emphasis added).

A people long accustomed to this debilitating relationship will have profound difficulty extricating themselves from it: here is a thought that can be traced back to the Exodus narrative in which the central lesson is the perpetual backsliding of a people who longed for freedom. The Egyptian bondage of the soul has its appeal, even—perhaps especially—when on the way to the promised land.[39] Tocqueville may, in fact, have had this lesson in mind when he referred to the slaves as a "wandering tribe."[40] On the other hand, Pharaoh, the master who only yields when finally convinced that God himself opposes him, is no less incapable of renouncing his own place in the dialectic of mastery and servitude. Combined, these two aspects have massive implications for how America is to confront the problem of slavery. On Tocqueville's view, notwithstanding the perennial efforts to rename it, the crisis we face remains the crisis of the *memory* of slavery. Racism, I will suggest, is as much an effect as a cause of our problem.[41]

There is another less somber and bleak aspect of the relationship between thought and real life that deserves mention here. Tocqueville's defense of democracy, as any reader knows, is not unequivocal. Democracy has been foreordained by God, but it can only work well under a certain set of institutional arrangements that human beings must fortify. Tocqueville is not, as I have said, sanguine about the prospects for the democratic soul left to its own devices. In particular, he has no great faith in the ideas of democratic lawmakers. The aristocratic lawmaker has the advantage of being farsighted and patient; the democratic lawmaker is shortsighted and fickle. How, then, can a democratic polity be successful at all?

His answer, briefly, is that while at the level of ideas the aristocrat is a superior lawmaker, democratic lawmakers' interests are essentially democratic. That is, democracy benefits from democratic lawmakers because of who they are rather than because of what they think. Deeper than what they *think* is who they *are*. Their laws are good because democratic lawmakers are democratic souls:

39. See Michael Walzer, *Exodus and Revolution* (New York: Basic Books, 1985), pp. 33–55.

40. Tocqueville, *Democracy in America*, vol. 1, part 2, chap. 10, p. 351.

41. By way of anticipation, see Tocqueville, *Democracy in America*, vol. 1, part 2, chap. 10, p. 341: "[M]emories of slavery disgrace the race, and race perpetuates memories of slavery." The French, *le souvenir*, is better translated as *recollection* rather than *memory*. This deficiency aside, there is, here, a circularity of cause and effect. Unlike ancient slavery, where differences in appearance did not coincide with differences in social standing, modern slavery directs attention to race. Color difference serves as a reminder of slavery.

> In general, the laws of a democracy tend toward the good of the great-
> est number, for they spring from the majority of all the citizens, which
> may be *mistaken* but which cannot have an *interest* contrary to its
> own.[42]

Their inadequacies as lawmakers are undisputed; in spite of their ideas, however, the general tendency of their laws is salutary.[43]

What is to be feared is not their inefficiency, or the ineptitude of their ideas, but rather that their interests might cease to be democratic. Were this to change, then any "improvement" in their capacity as lawmakers would work to the detriment of democracy!

These examples are not exhaustive. They do serve, however, to highlight the profoundly important matter of the embodiment (or disembodiment) of thinking. Tocqueville does not dissever thinking from the conditions that give rise to it and that, in turn, it reflects upon. Any effort to comprehend the identity of a people must seek to grasp the real-life conditions that have given rise to certain stable patterns of thinking, patterns about which we may occasionally rejoice and mourn.

4. CIRCULARITY OF CAUSE AND EFFECT

For the purpose of introducing the importance of the relationship between thought and its embodiment in the discussion above, I have given the impression, on several occasions, that Tocqueville was a rather linear thinker: being determines consciousness, and seldom the other way around. Such a straightforward account does not, however, grasp the subtleties of his thinking about causality. What is at one moment the cause is at the next moment also an effect. For Tocqueville, there is no such thing as unilinear in the social world. One factor may be predominantly a cause, it is true; but it is also then affected by what it causes.

Consider, for example, Tocqueville's thinking about the relationship between civil and political associations. His question, as I have already suggested, is how to draw people out of their self-enclosed worlds, how

42. Tocqueville, *Democracy in America*, vol. 1, part 2, chap. 6, p. 232 (emphasis added). Cf. Jean-Jacques Rousseau, *The Social Contract*, trans. Maurice Cranston (New York: Penguin Books, 1968), bk. 2, chap. 3, pp. 72–74.

43. See Edmund Burke, "Thoughts on the Cause of the Present Discontents," in *Burke's Politics*, ed. Ross J. S. Hoffman and Paul Levack (New York: A. A. Knopf, 1949), p. 28: "the virtue, spirit and essence" of a nation's representatives lies "in its being the express image of the feelings of the nation." Here, as in Tocqueville, to be well represented is a more ephemeral matter, not subject to empirical test. See also Robert Wiessberg, "Collective vs. Dyadic Representation in Congress," *American Political Science Review* 72, no. 2 (1978): 535–47.

to redraw the boundaries around the self, in order that the threat of individualism be averted. The way to do this is through participation at
the local political level. Healthy civil society, in turn, arises once the self
has been drawn out of itself in local politics. This much has been posited already. But that is not the end of the matter.

> The more there are . . . little business concerns in common, the more
> do men, without conscious effort, acquire the capacity to pursue great
> aims in common.
>   Thus civil associations pave the way for political ones, but on the
> other hand, the art of political associations *singularly develops* and im-
> proves this technique for civil purpose.[44]

Each kind of activity affects the other; one (political participation) is,
nevertheless, more of a cause than the other (civil association). The sub-
tlety of this interaffective relationship, in which one element nevertheless predominates, will be examined in section 3 of chapter 3. I bring it
up here only to illustrate the nuanced view of causality that Tocqueville
embraces.

Consider, as well, Tocqueville's observations about the relationship
between Christian religion and long-term worldly goals. In the democratic soul, Christianity singularly facilitates long-term thinking, which,
unlike the aristocratic soul, it is not by nature disposed toward.

Unlike Nietzsche, for whom the inner kernel of Christianity is the
will to truth that "finally forbids the *lie involved in the belief in God*,"[45]
here the inner kernel of Christianity is more akin to Pascal's wager.[46]
Nietzsche's will to truth, which must responsibly bear the truth it unconceals, is displaced by an even-tempered assessment of the habits of
thinking that Christianity instills—the most socially pertinent being the
careful and deliberate calculation about what must be forgone in a world
of ephemeral pleasures in order to attain salvation at the end of this life.
Here habits of thinking about the next world devolve into habits of
thinking and acting in this one.

The capacity of Christianity to bring about long-term thinking I will
consider in section 5 of chapter 4; here I only wish to rehearse Tocqueville's argument about what happens when Christianity's hold on the
soul is loosened and long-term thinking gives way to a dangerous sort of

44. Tocqueville, *Democracy in America*, vol. 2, part 2, chap. 7, pp. 520–21
(emphasis added).

45. Friedrich Nietzsche, *On the Genealogy of Morals*, trans. Walter Kaufman
(New York: Random House, 1967), third essay, sec. 27, p. 160 (emphasis in
original).

46. See Pascal, *Pensées*, sec. 418, pp. 149–53; Tocqueville, *Democracy in America*, vol. 2, part 2, chap. 9, p. 529.

immediacy of thought. We should be clear about this: for Tocqueville, without some mechanism that extends the temporal horizon of the democratic soul into the future, it will stumble through and over the present; for its natural disposition is to think only of the moment.

> As soon as they have lost the way of relying chiefly on distant hopes, they are naturally led to want to satisfy their least desires at once; and it would seem that as soon as they despair of living forever, they are inclined to act as if they could not live for more than a day.[47]

When the power of Christianity over the soul diminishes, another means of instilling long-term thinking must be found. What can best do this is government, more precisely, the long-term projects of a government that capture the imagination of the people. In an age of skepticism, Tocqueville suggests, this is government's "most important business."[48] Such projects are not to be justified on the basis of dollar return on direct investment, but rather on the fact that they help form the democratic soul and countermand one of its deficiencies; such projects dispose it toward long-term thinking—the "return" on which cannot be measured directly in dollars.

The matter cannot be left at that, however. Should the natural temporal horizon of the democratic soul be modified in such a way that it does become capable of long-term thinking, and should the habits it acquires by virtue of governmental programs of a certain sort be developed, then, Tocqueville argues, religion will begin to make sense once again.

> I have therefore no doubt that, *in accustoming* the citizens to think of the future in this world, they will gradually be led without noticing it themselves toward religious beliefs.[49]

Here, again, is the mutual causation that makes Tocqueville's thinking so subtle. Now worldly habits dispose persons to accept Christianity! It is accepted, not because the doctrine of Christianity is any more true

---

47. Tocqueville, *Democracy in America*, vol. 2, part 3, chap. 17, p. 548. The shortening of the temporal horizon that coincides with the abandonment of religion does not occasion the abandonment of deep longing; it merely shifts it toward the massive temporal power in a democratic society: the government. When religion is no longer the sphere of deep longing, that *habit of thinking* merely seeks its object in another sphere. I will consider this matter further in section 2 of the chapter 5.

48. Tocqueville, *Democracy in America*, vol. 2, part 3, chap. 17, p. 548.

49. Tocqueville, *Democracy in America*, vol. 2, part 2, chap. 17, p. 549 (emphasis added).

than it was before, but because it comes to comport with the lived experience of persons now oriented by long-term goals.

> Thus the same means that, *up to a certain point*, enable men to manage without religion are perhaps after all the only means we still possess for bringing mankind back, by a long and roundabout path, to a state of faith. [50]

Religion develops certain worldly habits; the development of certain worldly habits by governmental programs makes it more likely that religion will be accepted. Like the relationship between political and civil society, while the causation is mutual, the predominant movement is one way (in this case, from religion to worldly habits). Were a prediction to be made on the basis of these remarks, it would be that should this decade face the sober task of beginning to pay for the excesses of the previous one, then the long-term habit of thinking necessary to do so is likely to produce a return to Christianity of the sort that occasionally sweeps the country.[51]

Finally, let me speak here about the reciprocal relation between family and the spirit of democratic equality. Recall, first, that for Tocqueville women are the guardians of mores. Second, like Sophie, in Rousseau's *Emile*, women have need of their reputation.[52] Yet neither the vastness of the country, the English origin of its inhabitants, nor religion is sufficient to maintain women's morals and, thus, moderate democratic sentiments.[53] What helps to do this is the destruction of the barriers between people, so characteristic of the democratic age.

When such barriers exist, natural passions between men and women of different social standing are scorned; yet, ironically, the very distance

50. Tocqueville, *Democracy in America*, vol. 2, part 3, chap. 17, p. 549 (emphasis added). Note that while government may be partially effective in bringing about the long-term thinking that the democratic soul lacks, ultimately it is religion that must do this.

51. See Jerald C. Brauer, *Protestantism in America* (Philadelphia: Westminster Press, 1965) for a narrative account of these cycles of spiritual renewal. In his words, "it is not easy to characterize Protestantism in America, but two characteristics seem to mark it. One is the constant free experimentation and search for a fuller manifestation of God's truth and will, and the other is the sustained effort to avoid going beyond the truth and light already known in the Bible and codified in certain basis beliefs and confessions. Thus Protestantism in America can be characterized in terms of a full, free experimentation and an enduring Biblicism" (p. 7). Both of these moments accord with Tocqueville's view, though Tocqueville clearly emphasizes the latter.

52. Rousseau, *Emile*, bk. 5, p. 417.

53. Tocqueville, *Democracy in America*, vol. 2, part 3, chap. 11, p. 595.

between one another makes the illicit nature of their affair all the more tempting. Knowing that they shall never be truly united in the public eye, their temptations are unhinged in private. The greater the public distance, the more the unfettered personal intimacy, the easier moral transgression becomes.

When no obstacles stand in the way, however, this perverse proportionality is broken. When conditions are equal,

> no girl feels that she cannot become the wife of the man who likes her best, and that makes irregular morals before marriage very difficult. For however credulous passion may make us, there is hardly a way of persuading a girl that you love her when you are perfectly free to marry her but will not do so.[54]

The equality of conditions erases boundaries that isolate passion from social standing and person from person; the morality of women is abetted by an equality that repudiates the hidden forum capable of debilitating it. A hidden space is made possible only by high fences.

Here, women's morality is both cause and effect of the equality of conditions. This equality buttresses women's morality, which, in turn, is a driving force in the maintenance of a beneficent form of democratic equality. Without the equality of conditions, women's morality would be undercut by that hidden forum which makes women the object of "malicious gossip" in Europe.[55] Its absence makes possible a respect for woman that the aristocratic order was incapable of generating. Intrigue being foreclosed, nature's passions must now be kept under the wing of reason rather than allowed to take flight.

5. OF THE SPILLOVER EFFECTS OF ONE SPHERE UPON ANOTHER

A distinction of sorts can be made between the circularity of cause and effect and what Tocqueville calls the "spillover effect" of one sphere upon another.[56] They are clearly related. I note their difference more for heuristic purposes than for theoretical reasons. The language of cause and effect is one more familiar to social theorist of the present day. As a

54. Tocqueville, *Democracy in America*, vol. 2, part 3, chap. 11, p. 595. See also vol. 1, part 2, chap. 10, p. 344: "perhaps the northern American might have allowed some Negro woman to be the passing companion of his pleasures, had the legislators declared that she could not hope to share his nuptial bed; but she can become his wife, and he recoils in horror from her."

55. Tocqueville, *Democracy in America*, vol. 2, part 3, chap. 11, p. 595.

56. Tocqueville's first use of this term occurs in *Democracy in America*, vol. 1, part 2, chap. 6, p. 242.

whole, however, Tocqueville is not taken with that predictive enterprise; his concern again and again is with the character formed by involvement in one institutional forum and the beneficent effects such
character formation has in another domain. The spillover effect is a key
entrée into the inner citadel of Tocqueville's thinking about character
formation and so ought to be introduced here in a general way.

The theoretical matter at issue here can be found already in the
highly charged seventeenth-century debate between Locke and Filmer
about the affinity between paternal and monarchal power, though it can
be traced back to Aristotle's teleological view of the relationship between the lower and higher forms of association. For Aristotle, the lower
forms aimed at the higher ones and were not only completed by them
but also were likened to them as well.[57] The household is like the polis;
nevertheless, the polis is a higher form of association than the household.

Locke's argument in the *Second Treatise*, recall, is that paternal and
political power are "perfectly distinct."[58] Against Filmer, Adam's power
of dominion over his children, granted by God in the beginning, is paternal and not political power.[59] The matter that Aristotle treated teleo-
logically is transposed, to be sure, into a biblical key.[60] Nevertheless, the
question of the relationship between these two domains (paternal/
household, political/polis) remains—and against Aristotle's analogical
vision, Locke argues that they are decisively different.

Tocqueville's sympathies are not with Aristotle on this matter; yet
Locke's disjunction—explosive in its political import—was too abrupt

57. See Aristotle, *Nicomachean Ethics*, bk. 1, chap. 2, 1094a18–1094b12; and
bk. 8, chap. 10, 1160b22: "*resemblances* to [the three forms of government and
their corruptions] can be found in the household" (emphasis added).

58. Locke, *Second Treatise*, chap. 6, sec. 71, p. 314: "these two *Powers, Political and Paternal, are . . . perfectly distinct and separate*" (emphasis in original).
Locke, unlike Aristotle, insists that the key to linking political and paternal
power is historical, not analogical. While there is no likeness, paternal power
becomes political power as history moves forward; indeed, even when paternal
power has been superseded (in true dialectical fashion), a residual of it remains.
See also Hegel, *Philosophy of Right*, secs. 255–56, pp. 154–55.

59. Cf. Sir Robert Filmer, *Patriarcha*, in *Patriarcha and Other Writings*, ed.
Johann P. Sommerville (Cambridge: Cambridge University Press, 1991), chap. 1,
secs. 6–10, pp. 8–12.

60. The most thorough treatments of the importance of biblical history in
early modern thought remain Eldon Eisenach's *Two Worlds of Liberalism: Religion
and Politics in Hobbes, Locke, and Mill* (Chicago: University of Chicago Press,
1981); and Henning Graf Reventlow's *The Authority of the Bible and the Rise of the
Modern World* (Philadelphia: Fortress Press, 1985). On their reading, Hobbes and
Locke are not wholly secular figures but rather are involved in ongoing debates
about the meaning, political and otherwise, of biblical history.

for an observer of Tocqueville's acumen to endorse. The subtle interplay between family and politics could not be captured as the distinction stood.[61] One of Tocqueville's important contributions was to have
incorporated into social and political theory, perhaps more than anyone
else, the insight that while the spheres of life may be distinct, habits of
thinking in one realm spill over onto another without regard to the borders that logic might wish to impose. This insight is to be found in Rousseau's thinking, to be sure; in Tocqueville's thought it is much more
systematically applied.

I have briefly spoken of family in the previous section. Consider, for
a moment, Tocqueville's remark about the spillover effect of habits
learned within the family upon political life:

> In Europe almost all the disorders of society are born around the do-
> mestic hearth and not far from the nuptial bed. It is there that men
> come to feel a scorn for natural ties and legitimate pleasures and de-
> velop a taste for disorder, restlessness of spirit, and instability of de-
> sires. Shaken by the tumultuous passions which have often troubled
> his own house, the European finds it hard to submit to the authority
> of the state's legislators.[62]

The character formed in one arena of life affects the dispositions, capacities, and thoughts exhibited in another. While there may be a logical
separation between the two spheres, family and polity, there is a real-
life spillover; habits of thought produced in one domain dispose persons
to behave in certain ways in another domain. There are, on this view,
prepolitical foundations of politics.

The spillover effect from family to polity, important though it may
be, is eclipsed, however, by the spillover effect from religion to polity.
What must not be forgotten is that Tocqueville the Catholic,[63] who had

61. This is perhaps too strong. Locke is aware of the power of habit, but is
intent upon demonstrating the insufficiency of habit for politics. Government
must be based upon principles knowable to reason, not on habit, custom, and so
forth. Nevertheless, he does acknowledge that the first governments were paternal because the "children" citizens were accustomed to it from their infancy
within the family (see *Second Treatise*, chap. 6, sec. 67; chap. 8, sec. 107). The
task, now, is for reasonable beings to establish government upon its true, and
principled, foundation. While a liberal, Tocqueville does not believe that reason
alone is sufficient.

62. Tocqueville, *Democracy in America*, vol. 1, part 2, chap. 9, p. 291. See also
Rousseau, *Emile*, bk. 5, p. 363: "[It is] by means of the small fatherland which is
the family that the heart attaches itself to the large one."

63. Tocqueville, *Democracy in America*, vol. 1, part 2, chap. 9, p. 295: "as a
practicing Catholic I was particularly close to the Catholic priests, with some of
whom I soon established a certain intimacy." For a subtle treatment of the

etched in his mind the painful memory of the temporal prerogatives usurped by the Roman Church in Europe, recognized both the danger and need of Christian religion within a democracy. The grave failure of the Roman Church was to have aligned itself with transient powers— not out of a conviction of its strength, but out of the gnawing suspicion of its own weakness:

> When a religion makes a [worldly alliance], I am not afraid to say that it makes the same mistake as any man might; it sacrifices the future for the present, and by gaining a power to which it has no claim, it risks its legitimate authority.[64]

Religion must hold sway in a democratic society; without it—we shall come to this in a moment—mores are not fortified and the menacing natural dispositions of the democratic soul more readily emerge.

Religion may not, however, enter directly into matters of politics. This insight was, in Tocqueville's estimation, a large part of the American genius. *The political effects of religion must be indirect;* habits of thought produced by religion spill over into other arenas of life, that is all. Given the extraordinary power of religion in its proper sphere, that is enough:

> One cannot say, therefore, that in the United States religion influences the laws or political opinion in detail, but it does direct mores, and by regulating domestic life it helps to regulate the state.[65]

There are clear implications of this way of thinking for what seems to be a growing debate about the right role of religion in a democratic polity. For Tocqueville, any proclamation of the need to bring God into politics betrays the belief, not in God's power, but rather in His weakness. About this I will have more to say in chapter 4.

The spillover effect suggests the image of different domains, or spheres of activity, each offering its bounty to the other. While perhaps logically distinct, in practice they can be mutually reinforcing. Religion supports family; family bolsters religion; both encourage democratic freedom; local politics nourishes civil society, and so on. The priority of one over any other is not readily apparent; their relations are, if you will, horizontal rather than vertical. No one domain is preeminent.

There is another set of relations that accords with Tocqueville's

---

equivocal nature of Tocqueville's faith, see Doris S. Goldstein, *Trial of Faith: Religion and Politics in Tocqueville's Thought* (New York: Elsevier Press, 1975), pp. 5–11.

64. Tocqueville, *Democracy in America*, vol. 1, part 2, chap. 9, p. 297.
65. Tocqueville, *Democracy in America*, vol. 1, part 2, chap. 9, p. 291.

thinking about the different domains of life yet that cannot be fully comprehended in terms of them. These relations—between religion, mores, and laws—are, if I may, vertical rather than horizontal; they pertain to the relative weight of certain factors that shape character, rather than to the internal logic and effect of a particular domain upon the democratic soul.

The relationship between religion, mores, and laws, I suggest, must be grasped if we are to understand the subtle policy implications of Tocqueville's thinking. To disregard the relative sway each has over the soul is to misunderstand the real basis of the stability of the democratic soul in America; it is to build upon a foundation of sand. While these implications will be considered in chapter 5, introductory remarks about this relationship are warranted here.

Stated baldly, deeper than laws are mores, and deeper than mores is religion:

> Religion is considered the guardian of mores, and mores are regarded as the guarantee of the laws and the pledge for the maintenance of freedom itself.[66]

By themselves, Tocqueville argues, laws cannot be salutary unless a people have habits of thinking that make them able to bear laws with equanimity.[67] Law is not an adequate foundation. Neither, however, is

66. Tocqueville, *Democracy in America*, vol. 1, part 1, chap. 2, p. 47.

67. See Rousseau, *The Social Contract*, bk. 2, chap. 8, p. 88: "just as an architect who puts up a large building first surveys and tests the ground to see if it can bear the weight, so the wise lawgiver begins not by laying down laws good in themselves, but by finding out whether the people for whom the laws are intended are able to support them." See also bk. 4 chap. 4, p. 167: "one should not try to give a corrupt people the same laws which suit a virtuous people." See also Rousseau, *Second Discourse*, p. 80: "I would not have wished to live in a newly instituted republic, however good its laws might be, for fear that . . . the State would be subject to be disturbed and destroyed almost from its birth. For freedom is like those solid and rich foods or those healthy wines, which are proper to nourish and fortify robust constitutions habituated to them, but which overpower, ruin, and intoxicate the weak who are delicate and unsuited for them."

Also see Baron de Montesquieu, *The Spirit of the Laws*, trans. and ed. Anne M. Cohler, Basia Carolyn Miller, Harold Samuel Stone (Cambridge: Cambridge University Press, 1989), part 3, bk. 19, pp. 308–333. Tocqueville comments: "I am convinced that the luckiest of geographical circumstances and the best of laws cannot maintain a constitution in despite of mores, whereas the latter can turn even the most unfavorable circumstances and the worst laws to advantage. The importance of mores is the universal truth to which study and experience

habit; for habit itself is subject to atrophy and a loss of vitality. To remedy this—I am following Rousseau here—there must be "an authority of another order."[68] However construed (whether as a ruse,[69] or as a way of installing politics at the site it may rightly occupy from the vantage of eternity)[70] religion, which imbues "that *salutary fear* which makes men keep watch and ward for freedom,"[71] must be called upon to do what habit alone cannot.[72]

In Tocqueville's case, unlike Machiavelli, Montesquieu, and perhaps Rousseau, there is little reason to suspect that he was being disingenuous in his appraisal of Christianity.[73] There are simply too many pas-

---

continually bring us back. I find that it occupies the central position in my thoughts; all my ideas come back to it in the end" (*Democracy in America*, vol. 1, part 2, chap. 9, p. 308). See also Mill, "Representative Government," in *Three Essays*, pp. 148–53.

68. Rousseau, *The Social Contract*, bk. 2, chap. 7, p. 87.

69. Cf. Niccolò Machiavelli, *The Prince*, trans. Harvey Mansfield (Chicago: University of Chicago Press, 1985), chap. 6, pp. 22–24, where Moses is subtly portrayed as a political founder like any other. See also Niccolò Machiavelli, *The Discourses*, ed. Bernard Crick (New York: Penguin Books, 1970), bk. 1, discourses 11–12, pp. 139–46, on the political importance of religion.

70. Augustine's *City of God*—and, more controversially, Hobbes's *Leviathan* and Locke's *Second Treatise*—are examples of this attempt.

71. Tocqueville, *Democracy in America*, vol. 2, part 4, chap. 7, p. 702 (emphasis added). The French edition does not contain "for freedom." Cf. Montesquieu, *Spirit of the Laws*, part 1, bk. 21, chap. 9, p. 28: "[In a despotism] fear must beat down everyone's courage and extinguish even the slightest feeling of ambition." There is a difference, for Tocqueville, between this kind of fear and the *salutary* fear of God that is necessary for a healthy democracy.

72. See Augustine, *Confessions*, bk. 8, chap. 5, pp. 139–41, where the contrast is made between the empire of habit, which tends toward degeneracy, and the domain of spirit, which awakens the soul to life and alone is capable of circumventing the empire of habit.

73. Cf. Ralph Hancock, "The Uses and Hazards of Christianity," in Masugi, *Interpreting Tocqueville's "Democracy in America*," pp. 348–93. Hancock correctly sees the possible fate of the democratic soul: that "[he] destroys the secondary powers of aristocratic worlds until he is left with only the pantheistic god of 'continual flux,' a god who can manifest himself only as a destroyer of all that is unequal or distinct, all that stands up for itself" (pp. 390–91). The logic of equality, about which Tocqueville is concerned, especially in volume 2, moves in precisely this direction. This logic, moreover, is linked to Christianity, as Hancock suggests. Nevertheless, as I will argue in subsequent chapters, Christianity can ameliorate the logic of equality that it is instrumental in implementing. Hancock is less certain about this claim and so wishes to demonstrate Tocqueville's profound ambivalence toward Christianity.

sages where his admiration, indeed reverence, seems sincere. Religion, rebinds the soul to its Ground; the passivity demanded by obedience attenuates the ceaseless worldly activity into which the soul wishes to throw itself and, at the same time, in which the soul dimly intuits it can never find happiness.

> The soul has needs which must be satisfied. Whatever pains are taken to distract it from itself, it soon grows bored, restless, and anxious amid the pleasures of the senses. If ever the thoughts of the great majority of mankind came to be concentrated solely on the search for material blessings, one can anticipate that there would be a colossal reaction in the souls of men.[74]

Laws may provide certainty and eliminate obstacles to the pursuit of worldly success, and mores may grant persons the proficiency to acquire what the world may offer; but religion opens upon the ineffable domain and *commands* that the persons adopt certain habits that, without the benefit of higher authority, would not be embraced. It is religion, not as dogma but rather as command in the face of the ineffable,[75] that is capable of shaping habits. Laws, as it turns out, can shape habit only so much; religion, because deeper than habit, is much more effective. Tocqueville notes that it was "talk about religion [that] led to chaster mores [in England]."[76] Talk about the laws of a nation cannot have this effect—an insight often lost or deliberately disregarded in the contemporary fray but well known in the past.[77]

74. Tocqueville, *Democracy in America*, vol. 2, part 2, chap. 12, p. 535.

75. Here I mean to follow Levinas, for whom there is the possibility of "a *signification without a context*" (Emmanuel Levinas, *Totality and Infinity*, trans. Alphonso Lingis [Pittsburgh: Duquesne University Press, 1969], p. 23 [emphasis in original]). That is, there is the possibility of an opening unto infinity that can be proclaimed, notwithstanding the context of the totality in which that opening must be voiced. In Tocqueville's language: "the short space of sixty years can never shut in the whole of man's imagination; the incomplete joys of this world will never satisfy his heart" (*Democracy in America*, vol. 1, part 2, chap. 9, p. 296). Religion must exist in the world to answer to the hopes of being so constituted that it is forever called beyond the world; religion violates its charge if it aligns itself with worldly power and becomes, in Levinas's idiom, a *totality*. See Tocqueville, ibid., pp. 296–97.

76. Tocqueville, *Democracy in America*, vol. 1, part 1, chap. 2, p. 33.

77. See the 1794 sermon of Jonathan Edwards, the younger, "The Necessity of the Belief of Christianity by the Citizens of the State, in Order to Our Political Prosperity," in *Political Sermons of the American Founding Era, 1730–1805*, ed. Elis Sandoz (Indianapolis, Ind.: Liberty Press, 1991), pp. 1187–1216.

6. OF MOTION AND BOUNDARIES

I mention here the well-known influence of Montesquieu upon Tocqueville's thinking.[78] This is nowhere more confirmed than in the attention Tocqueville pays to the interplay of motion and boundaries, a consideration of which can be found throughout Montesquieu's *Spirit of the Laws*. This may fairly be said to be an aristocratic fascination; the aristocratic soul, as Tocqueville observes, was the moderate soul—the one that did not overstep the boundaries of propriety. For Montesquieu, as for Tocqueville, boundaries (or fences) enclose space, order it, and render it possible to establish the speed and direction of the motions most felicitous to the preservation of that space.[79] Montesquieu observes, for example, that there is a danger of having too many slaves within one political community because "[they find] security established for others and not for [themselves]." Such slaves, he says, "are the natural enemies of society, and it would be dangerous for them to be numerous."[80] This state of affairs generates too much motion within the community and can only engender great disorder—a thought not lost to Tocqueville when he wrote of the potentially explosive situation involving blacks and whites in the South.[81] Not to be overlooked, as well, is Montesquieu's fascination with the unfenced peoples of the north (notably the Tartars) who possess the kind of virtuous frugality and self-renunciation that enabled them to conquer the fenced peoples—the more servile, voluptuous cultivators—of the southern regions below them.[82] The ana-

78. "There are three men in whose company I find myself for a while each day: Pascal, Montesquieu and Rousseau" (letter to Kergolay on Nov. 10, 1836, in *Oeuvres complètes*, ed. J. P. Mayer [Paris: Gallimard, 1977], 13:418).

79. The fence metaphor is to be found, as well, in Locke's *Second Treatise*. There, the fence around the self that *is* property secures the self from transgression, so that reason's light may be enkindled. The fence separates light from darkness (rational and industrious labor from the unregenerate; reason's rule of law from the arbitrary will of the sovereign). With Montesquieu and Tocqueville, the boundary, the fence, orders motion and makes moderation possible. Locke's focus upon light and darkness can, I think, be attributed to his reading of biblical history as a narrative that reveals the progressive unconcealment of Christ's light, which itself revealed the foundation of moral duty still obscured to the Jews of the Old Testament. This had immense political implications, in his view. See Joshua Mitchell, "John Locke and the Theological Foundation of Liberal Toleration: A Christian Dialectic of History," *Review of Politics* 52, no. 1 (1990):64–83.

80. Montesquieu, *Spirit of the Laws*, part 3, bk. 15, chap. 13, p. 256.

81. Tocqueville, *Democracy in America*, vol. 1, part 2, chap. 10, pp. 353–55.

82. Montesquieu, *Spirit of the Laws*, part 3, bk. 17, chaps. 3–6, pp. 279–84; bk. 18, chap. 20, pp. 295–96.

logue for Tocqueville may well be the unfenced and uncouth wester-
ners for whom society did not yet exist.[83]

The unfenced land of the West, in fact, offered an *empty* space into
which the excess motion of the Americans could be diverted,[84] and so
defuse the tensions that inevitably attend the close-quartered life in cities.[85] What in Europe would be called excess motion is, in America, appropriate motion—simply because the space that could contain it was
so much larger than in Europe.[86]

The great irony, for Tocqueville, was that the very boundlessness of
America (an ever-expansive land without fences), which could embrace
both extraordinary industriousness and excess, would be peopled by inhabitants who would "enclose thought within a formidable fence,"[87]
and so make free thinking difficult. The boundlessness of the physical

83. Tocqueville, *Democracy in America*, vol. 1, part 1, chap. 3, p. 55; part 2,
chap. 9, pp. 307–8. Of significance, for Tocqueville, were the moderate and
religious easterners who migrated westward and restrained the excesses found
in the Western territories (p. 293).

84. On Tocqueville's view, land is "empty" even if occupied (periodically)
by hunters. See *Democracy in America*, vol. 1, part 1, chap. 1, p. 30: "the Indians
occupied but did not possess the land. It is by agriculture that man wins the soil,
and the first inhabitants of North America lived by hunting." Later, Tocqueville
notes that the Indians did indeed have a relationship to the land, one based
upon the ancestors who were buried there (part 2, chap. 10, p. 338). Interestingly enough, the temporal horizon of the Indian, like the aristocrat but unlike
the democrat, extends into the past several generations. Tocqueville does note
the similarity: "in the manners [of the Indians]," he says, "[there is] a habitual
reserve and a sort of aristocratic courtesy" (part 1, chap. 1, p. 28).

85. Cf. Frederick Jackson Turner, "The Significance of the Frontier in
American History," in American Historical Association, *Annual Report for the
Year 1893* (Washington, 1894), pp. 199–227. For Turner the diffusion of tension
was only part of the story. Unlike Tocqueville, Turner suggests that while
chronologically subsequent, the logical origins of democracy are displayed most
vividly in the comparatively primitive conditions of the frontier. New England
may have come before the West, but American democracy would be inconceivable without the kind of character formed by the confrontation with the primitive frontier. For Tocqueville, on the other hand, origin and subsequent identity
are linked; what is there at the beginning, in the Puritan mind, shapes the future
course of American identity.

86. See Tocqueville, *Democracy in America*, vol. 1, part 2, chap. 9, p. 284: "in
Europe we habitually regard a restless spirit, immoderate desire for wealth, and
an extreme love of independence as great social dangers. But precisely those
things assure a long a peaceful future for the American republics." Elsewhere
he notes that the French who populated Canada and who retained their old ways
did not exhibit the motion requisite to occupy the space they inhabited (p. 306).

87. Tocqueville, *Democracy in America*, vol. 1, part 2, chap. 8, p. 255.

space is inversely proportionate to the self-imposed constraints upon the American mind.

Ironic though it may be, however, this paradox confirms a psychological principle that, while distasteful in the democratic age, is not to be ignored without peril. There must always be boundaries; where they do not exist in the material world, they must exist in the mind. Human beings are not constituted to be able to bear chaos from all quarters. Laws may allow, even encourage, the full development of a world ever in motion and without boundaries; yet this unremitting movement must be countervailed by a stasis of the imagination if the American soul (or any other) is not to fall into terror or tyranny. Religion, which channels the mind down certain paths so that the unrelenting terror of the unbounded imagination may be averted, singularly accomplishes this:

> Thus while the law allows the American people to do everything, there are things which religion prevents them from imagining and forbids them to dare. [88]

The great paradox—and success—of the Americans is that they hold all things firm within the moral boundaries established by religion and therefore are able to experiment boldly in a world that is ever in motion. The terror of a world that unrelentingly "comes at one" [89] is averted by

---

88. Tocqueville, *Democracy in America*, vol. 1, part 2, chap. 9, p. 292. This tendency of imagination to overstep its boundaries was an especial concern for Rousseau in *Emile*, and is to be found in Deut. 31:21 ("for I know their imagination which they go about, even now, before I have brought them into the land which I swear"). There, the imagination of the Jews becomes active when Moses, their mediator, withdraws from them to speak with God. Religion in America, on this reading, is like Moses standing before the Jews: a reminder of the singular importance of God, which keeps the mind's restless tendencies in check.

89. Hans Blumenberg (*Work on Myth*, trans. Robert M. Wallace [Cambridge, Mass.: MIT Press, 1985]), suggests that the achievement of upright posture so extended the horizon from which reality can "come at one" (p. 5) that it became necessary for the imagination to arrest the "existential anxiety" (p. 6) that ensued when the human being nakedly faced the unoccupied, unnamed horizon. Myth fills that horizon and arrests anxiety. On this reading myth is a permanent need of human beings, diminished perhaps, but never overcome, by the machinations of logos, which would tame "the world." Tocqueville, before Blumenberg, recognized this need of "the human spirit never [to see] an *unlimited* field before itself" (*Democracy in America*, vol. 1, part 2, chap. 2, p. 292 [emphasis added]). See also Rousseau, *Emile*, bk. 4, p. 268: "doubt about the things it is important for us to know is too violent a state for the human mind, which does not hold out in this state for long. It decides in spite of itself one way or the other and prefers to be deceived rather than believe in nothing."

a religious enclosure that quells the imagination forever prompted toward paroxysm by the boundlessness of the world. Rousseau notes in
Emile that the imagination must be arrested if there is to be happiness;[90]
Tocqueville found in the religion of the Americans precisely the device
to do so. Where Rousseau structured Emile's world in order to keep his
imagination from awakening, Tocqueville happily finds the equivalent
to Emile's ever-mindful mentor in the unadorned commands of Christian religion. Without it, the mind would become as precipitous as the
world that it faces, and this simply cannot be endured:

> It is therefore of immense importance to men to have *fixed ideas* about
> God, their souls, and their duties toward their Creator and their fel-
> lows, for doubt about these principles would leave all their actions to
> chance and condemn them, more or less, to anarchy and impotence.[91]

The palpable danger, however, is not anarchy; for human beings cannot
long suffer even the prospect of disarray. Antedating general disorder is
too often the plaintive cry for the demagogue who would set the material world in order.[92] Absent an ordered mind, the soul will demand order
in the only other place it can be secured. This is what prompted
Tocqueville to observe:

> When there is no authority in religion or in politics, men are soon
> frightened by the *limitless* independence with which they are faced.
> They are worried and worn out by the constant restlessness of every-
> thing. With everything on the move in the realm of the mind, they
> want the material world at least to be firm and stable. . . . For my part,
> I doubt whether man can support complete religious independence

90. Rousseau, *Emile*, bk. 2, pp. 80–81.

91. Tocqueville, *Democracy in America*, vol. 2, part 1, chap. 5, p. 443 (emphasis
added). See also David Hume, "Of Superstition and Enthusiasm," in *Essays,
Moral, Political, and Literary* (Indianapolis, Ind.: Liberty Press, 1985), pp. 72–
73: "the mind of man is subject to certain unaccountable terrors and apprehensions. . . . In such a state of mind, infinite unknown evils are dreaded from
unknown agents; and where real objects of terror are wanting, the soul active to
its own prejudice, and fostering its predominant inclination, finds imaginary
ones, to whose power and malevolence it *sets no limits*" (emphasis added).

92. Schlesinger, in *Cycles of American History*, offers another alternative. Periods of activity and excess motion are succeeded by periods of passivity and
withdrawal (p. 28). The two poles of the Augustinian self here manifest themselves sequentially, in the cycles of American history. The threat of tyranny is
averted by a self-protective psychological mechanism rather than by a demagogue who would set the world in order to offset the general chaos attributable
to imagination that has run rampant.

and entire political liberty at the same time. I am led to think that if he has no faith he must obey, and if he is free he must believe.[93]

I should add, here, that Tocqueville was not unequivocal in his thinking about the sway of religion over the American mind. While it restrained the imagination, in the very act of directing its possessor toward the infinite it preempted the prospect for the development of thinking along novel lines in the moral domain. The Puritan "invasion of conscience"[94] had not abated, and this prompted Tocqueville to worry whether the very medium through which the infinite was divulged, the mind propitiated, and the heart opened might not also carry with it the risk that it would be transposed into a force that promulgated a self-enclosed totality whose yield would only be a sluggishness and mediocrity at the end of history.[95] And in our day we might add: the atavism of Christianity's settlement of everything in the moral world comes to haunt a people now needful but perhaps incapable of either returning to faith or wholly jettisoning it. Here is the contemporary situation: a world proceeding at breakneck speed counterposed to the American mind obstinately clinging to a residuum that is only tenuously its own— yet which it cannot disown.

7. OF NEW BEGINNINGS AND AMERICAN EXCEPTIONALISM

"There is," Emerson said, "a genius of a nation, which is not to be found in the numerical citizens, but which characterizes the society."[96] No reading of *Democracy in America* can avoid confronting this same sentiment throughout. The American character is a new one; one disposed toward courses of action and thought absent in Europe; one attributable to the Puritan pilgrimage here in the beginning;[97] one indisposed to the

---

93. Tocqueville, *Democracy in America*, vol. 2, part 1, chap. 5, p. 444 (emphasis added).

94. Tocqueville, *Democracy in America*, vol. 1, part 1, chap. 2, p. 42.

95. Tocqueville, *Democracy in America*, vol. 2, part 3, chap. 21, pp. 640–45.

96. Emerson, "Nominalist and Realist," in *Emerson's Essays*, p. 424.

97. See Tocqueville, *Democracy in America*, vol. 1, part 2, chap. 9, p. 279: "I have said before that I regarded the origin of the Americans, what I have called their point of departure, as the first and most effective of all the elements leading to their present prosperity. . . . When I consider all that has resulted from this first fact, I think I can see the whole destiny of America contained in the first Puritan who landed on those shores, as that of the whole human race in the first man." See also vol. 2, part 1, chap. 1, p. 432: "it was religion that gave birth to the English colonies in America. One must never forget that."

categories of class that could—and did—capture the European mind. While in the twentieth century, three hundred years after the pilgrimage, Marx conquered a Europe still in the throes of working through its own inherited categories,[98] it was Freud who conquered America. The past does not wholly retract:[99] inner perspicuity, not class, preoccupied the Pilgrims, and this has never changed. We may bemoan the present morass of solipsism into which the post-Freudian therapeutic understanding has brought us,[100] but even in this we stand as we have for so long: as one pilgrim charging another with pridefulness that masquerades as salvation.

[Only when you look at the baby in his mother's arms] will you understand the origin of the prejudices, habits, and passions which are

98. See Tocqueville, *Democracy in America*, vol. 2, part 3, chap. 21, p. 634: "when a people has lived for centuries under a system of castes and classes, it can only reach a democratic state of society through a long series of more or less painful transformations."

Marcuse's effort to explain the failure of the Revolution in America by recourse to an arrest upon the dialect of history that American capitalism accomplishes (Herbert Marcuse, *One-Dimensional Man* [Boston: Beacon Press, 1964], pp. 247–57) is a study in the failure to comprehend the meaning of the self-enclosure of the American mind. The dialectic of history, as Marx conceived it—that is, driven forward by class antagonisms—cannot *make sense* here, as Hartz has argued. See Louis Hartz, *The Liberal Tradition in America* (New York: Harcourt Brace Jovanovich, 1955), p. 6: "the hidden origin of socialist thought everywhere in the West is to be found in the feudal ethos. The *ancien régime* inspires Rousseau; both inspire Marx." Hartz understands the importance of America's new beginning, but would link it to "Lockean Liberalism"—that is, to property alone. This is only part of Tocqueville's answer to why there will be no revolution in America. (See *Democracy in America*, vol. 2, part 3, chap. 3, p. 636.)

99. Hence, to alter the valence of this thought slightly, Tocqueville's praise of Washington and Jefferson for not entering America onto the scene of world history, where wars confirm and reaffirm identities and conflicts long ago constituted. That past, about which wars are fought, ought to be kept at a distance. See Tocqueville, *Democracy in America*, vol. 1, part 2, chap. 5, pp. 226–28.

100. See Robert Bellah et al., *Habits of the Heart* (New York: Harper and Row, 1985), pp. 121–38. See also Ernst Troeltsch, *The Social Teachings of the Christian Churches*, trans. Oliver Wyon (New York: Harper and Row, 1960), 2:1004–5: "the Christian Ethos alone possessed, in virtue of its personalistic Theism, a conviction of personality and individuality, based on metaphysics, which no Naturalism and no Pessimism can disturb. That personality which, rising above the natural order, is only achieved through a union of will and the depths of being with God, alone transcends the finite, and alone can defy it. Without this support, however, every kind of individualism evaporates into thin air."

to dominate his life. The whole man is there, if one may put it so, in the cradle. Something analogous happens with nations. People always bear some marks of their origin. Circumstances of birth and growth affect all the rest of their career.[101]

What Tocqueville does suppose, and what we (as thoroughgoing Americans) find so difficult to accept, is the resilience and depth of identity, the stability of an originary past that does not wholly recede in the face of an ongoing present. Contemporary social science has renamed this phenomenon "socialization," but it has come no closer to understanding the mystery of the stability of identity over time, or the persistence of atavisms of a past now disavowed. I do not seek here to comprehend this mystery, only to enlist its assistance, to educe conclusions about the present impasse in America before the "chance to make mistakes that can be retrieved" has, paradoxically, passed by.[102]

About the point of departure of the Americans, about its "founding," something must be said. While we are accustomed to thinking that the founding of America pertains to the so-called Revolutionary period, to the "founding fathers," nothing could be further from the truth. I do not quite mean here that this proposition is an error; rather, that the Declaration of Independence, the Constitution, and the Bill of Rights, important as these surely are, are mere proclamations and laws that, on Tocqueville's view, must be underlaid by mores and, deeper still, by religion.[103] The profound articulations of the founding fathers are ephemeral musings unless conjoined to a people whose austere mores make them capable of bearing the burden and responsibility that such articulations impose.[104]

101. Tocqueville, *Democracy in America*, vol. 1, part 1, chap. 2, p. 31. See also p. 32: "there is not an opinion, custom, or law, nor, one might add, an event, which the point of departure will not easily explain."

102. Tocqueville, *Democracy in America*, vol. 1, part 2, chap. 5, p. 225.

103. See Thomas G. West, "Misunderstanding the American Founding," in Masugi, *Interpreting Tocqueville's "Democracy in America,"* pp. 155–77. In Tocqueville's view, he argues, "what occurs in the subpolitical realm is more important than—and actually determines—what happens in politics. In contrast to Tocqueville's approach, the political science of the Founders maintains that government forms society" (p. 159). This is only partly true. Tocqueville only argues that the *preeminent* force is "subpolitical." Laws can affect the formation of the soul (see, for example, *Democracy in America*, vol. 1, part 2, chap. 8, pp. 263–70, on the legal profession), yet they are comparatively weak.

104. Hence, Tocqueville's worry about future democratic revolutions in other parts of the world: that they should "[take] place in a society without those changes in laws, ideas, customs and mores which [are] needed to make that revolution profitable" (Tocqueville, *Democracy in America*, author's introduction,

The insecurity of academic social science, however, which is still in search of its own scientific underpinnings, cannot easily admit the vagary of mores or, more importantly, their relationship to origin. This has prompted social theorists largely to ignore Tocqueville's claim about identity, and political theorists compromisingly to grasp that portion of the insight which best comports with its own long-established tradition of thinking about political foundings.[105] The notion of the founding is accepted, but the founding of which Tocqueville spoke is spurned, perhaps because of the disturbing implication this has for the prospect of the survival of democratic freedom in America without religion.

Tocqueville is quite clear on this matter. While there are allusions to the founding fathers scattered throughout, their real significance seems only to have been that they unconcealed at the national level what had lain hidden at a local level for more than a century: the principle of sovereignty of the people. Indeed Tocqueville dedicates only three sustained pages to the significance of the Revolution.[106] His treatment there, moreover, follows a long chapter on the Puritan originaries.[107] The revolutionary war, in a word, was not a revolution, and hence not a real founding.[108]

---

p. 13). I leave it for the reader to see the stark implications this has for the prospect that the spirit of democracy that is sweeping now discredited and oppressive regimes will end in freedom or servitude.

105. Think here of Plato's discussion of the fall of the ideal state in the *Republic*, bk. 8, 534a–568c; Rousseau's claim that "the right of laying down rules of society belongs only to those who form a society" (*The Social Contract*, bk. 2, chap. 6, p. 83); and Machiavelli's assertion that the maintenance of any institution requires that it periodically return to its originating principles (*The Discourses*, bk. 3, discourse 1, pp. 385–90). More recently, think of the arguments of Robert Bork ("Neutral Principles and Some First Amendment Problems," *Indiana Law Journal* 47, no. 1 (1971): 1–35) and Henry Monaghan ("Our Perfect Constitution," *New York University Law Review*, 56, nos. 2–3 (1981): 353–96).

106. Tocqueville, *Democracy in America*, vol. 1, part 1, chap. 4, pp. 58–60.

107. Tocqueville, *Democracy in America*, vol. 1, part 1, chap. 2, pp. 31–49.

108. See Nathan O. Hatch, *The Democratization of American Christianity* (New Haven: Yale University Press, 1989), for the claim that the religious consequence of the American Revolution was the "rise of democratic Christianity" (p. 16). Here is an analysis consistent with the "spillover" effect about which Tocqueville spoke (see *Democracy in America*, vol. 1, part 1, chap. 3, p. 51: "at the time of the Revolutionary War] a taste for every form of independence grew"). On this account, the Revolution was not a new beginning; but it did transform the character of American Christianity by bringing out its more independent aspects.

The efforts made by the Americans to throw off the English yoke have been much exaggerated. With twenty-eight hundred miles of ocean between them and their enemies, aided by a powerful ally, the United States owed their victory much more to their position than to the valor of their armies or the patriotism of their citizens.[109]

And elsewhere:

[America] sees the result of the democratic revolution taking place [in Europe] without experiencing the revolution itself.[110]

The founding fathers, it is true, threw off the yoke of George III, but this patricide obscured the ongoing allegiance to the sovereign Father that was not forsaken.[111] Having one, they were more easily disposed to rejecting the burdensome other. The Puritans acted and enacted laws, Tocqueville reminds us, "as if they were dependent upon God alone."[112] The slogan "No King but King Jesus" during the Revolutionary period certainly does not approach the grandeur of the Declaration of Independence, but it did comport with the Gospel injunction to subordinate the earthly to the heavenly Father,[113] and in this respect it confirms the deep allegiance of the Americans to the Father not of this world. Notwithstanding the importance of the political regime in which we live, Tocqueville reminds us, they are all, by nature, unstable.

Like our years upon earth, the powers of society are all more or less transitory; they follow one another quickly, like the various cares of life; and there has never been a government supported by some invariable disposition of the human heart or one founded upon some interest that is immortal.[114]

Nothing endures for all time; indissoluble allegiances cannot be offered to the contrivances of worldly fathers—be they kings who would dominate colonies or citizens who would rightly renounce the disregard of their liberty. Those who would make sacrosanct the principles of the

---

109. Tocqueville, *Democracy in America*, vol. 1, part 1, chap. 8, p. 113.

110. Tocqueville, *Democracy in America*, author's introduction, p. 18.

111. Tocqueville speaks of the two fathers of the Americans when he considers the conditions that sustain democracy in America. In his words, "[The Puritans' fathers] gave them a love of equality and liberty, but it was God who, by handing a limitless continent over to them, gave them the means of long remaining free and equal" (*Democracy in America*, vol. 1, part 2, chap. 9, p. 279).

112. Tocqueville, *Democracy in America*, vol. 1, part 1, chap. 2, p. 41.

113. Luke 14:26; Matt. 19:29.

114. Tocqueville, *Democracy in America*, vol. 1, part 2, chap. 9, p. 297.

founding fathers of the American system of government have failed to grasp this.[115]

The real founding was not political. Moreover, while it can be given a spatiotemporal location (Plymouth, 1620), the power and endurance of that founding emanates precisely from what cannot be found in the spatiotemporal record of the event.

> This rock [Plymouth rock] has become an object of veneration in the United States. I have seen fragments carefully preserved in several American cities. Does not that clearly prove that man's power and greatness resides entirely in his soul? A few poor souls trod for an instant on this rock, and it has become famous; it is prized by a great nation; fragments are venerated, and tiny pieces distributed far and wide. What has become of the doorsteps of a thousand palaces? Who cares about them?[116]

Paradoxically, an opening unto the Transcendent establishes the American founding in space and time. The rock is both historical and transhistorical event; the solemn crossing of its threshold establishes and sustains the American identity forever as both pilgrim and chosen entrant, Nazarene and savior, misunderstood of the world and liberator of it. The founding is in time and beyond it.

This second aspect, this opening unto the Transcendent, Tocqueville found especially pertinent to the American situation; for without such an opening, eternally available to the human heart and made possible by the separation of religious and political life, the democratic soul could not long endure. Its transient impulses are underlaid by a deeper, and unmoved, Ground—traceable *in time and space* to the Pilgrims, yet outstripping any effort to find it wholly there.[117]

115. See, for example, Thomas Pangle, who in *The Spirit of Modern Republicanism* (Chicago: University of Chicago Press, 1988) argues that the founding fathers, drawing on Locke, "attempted to exploit and transform Christianity in the direction of Liberal rationalism" (p. 21). While it is true that the founders were deeply committed to reason, Tocqueville's point nevertheless stands: political existence is preeminently a bottom-up affair in America, made possible by stringent mores rooted in Christianity, not by a (top-down) national founding based upon reason (*Democracy in America*, vol. 1, part 1, chap. 2, p. 44).

116. Tocqueville, *Democracy in America*, vol. 1, part 1, chap. 2, p. 38n.

117. See Ralph Waldo Emerson, "The Over-Soul," in *Emerson's Essays*, p. 209: "our religion vulgarly stands on numbers of believers. Whenever the appeal is made,—no matter how indirectly,—to numbers, proclamation is then and there made that religion is not. He that finds God a sweet enveloping thought to him never counts his company." On this reading, religion is ineffable; empirical techniques can nevery fully capture it nor make accurate predictions about it.

Here, finally, is a memory of a different and deeper sort. The past, forever forgotten by the American soul that is unwilling to remember, recedes breathlessly;[118] and yet, ironically, there is a deeper memory that may be *eternally* drawn upon, which undergirds the enduring *arrest* of identity called the American soul, and which is crucial for the survival of the *form* of democratic freedom with which America has been familiar. To a consideration of this deeper Ground, which we all too frequently forget, and which originates long before the arrival of the Pilgrims, I now turn.

118. Consider, for example, Tocqueville, *Democracy in America*, vol. 1, part 2, chap. 9, p. 285: "to flee from the paternal hearth and the fields where his ancestors rest, and to leave both living and dead to chase after fortune are all things most praiseworthy in [the Americans'] eyes."

2
The Augustinian Self

Let us begin here with a simple yet somewhat unorthodox proposition, whose root can be found already in Augustine's thinking about the soul and its dispositions. It is not the distortions upon the system of the exchange of goods and services that constitute the preeminent hazard for a society of rational human beings, but rather the absence of institutional forums that attenuate the twin perils of self-enclosed solipsism and restive overreaching. Distortions in the market, the recalcitrant arrangements that conspire to keep prices from reaching their natural level,[1] are ever less a threat than distortions, if you will, in the souls of citizens. Once moderation has been achieved, careful efforts may be undertaken to correct the distortions in the market that call out for remedy; but if no attempt is made first to bring forth moderate souls (moderate citizens, if you wish), then attempts to remove whatever distortions in the market are present may not yield beneficent results. Without care, such efforts, often undertaken with the best of intentions, may well undermine the institutions that draw the self-enclosed soul outside of itself or that arrest its overreaching.

Fully understood, the implication of the investigation undertaken in this chapter is that the economic model of human rationality is blind to the foundation upon which rational action—and hence the entire com-

---

1. See Smith, *Wealth of Nations*, bk. 1, chap. 7, p. 62. For Smith, the market is always and only correlative with the division of labor (chap. 3, p. 21). Scarcity is reduced (but never eliminated) by a maximum articulation of the division of labor, which itself is encouraged to the extent that market price gravitates toward natural price. Smith does note that the natural price is contingent upon, among other things, "the general circumstances of the society" (chap. 7, p. 62) but proceeds to offer an account that supposes a system of incentives and responses to lags and disturbances of natural price that are plausible to an *already rational* person. He takes for granted what Tocqueville thought necessary to carefully ascertain, namely, the precondition of rationality itself. On Tocqueville's view, rationality is made possible with the assistance of the institutions that make up the "general circumstances of the society."

mercial enterprise—is possible. To be sure, *homo economicus* does exist, but only as a subspecies, a moderate intermediate (robust *yet achieved* rather than given in the nature of things),[2] who bridges that vast expanse between those souls who are wholly drawn in upon themselves, without motion; and the prideful, overly active, overreaching souls, the souls that would "[ascend] the throne of the world without any power being able to resist [them]."[3]

It is both an easy temptation and an egregious error to conclude from the vast range of possible variation that the two ends of the spectrum represent nothing but limit cases, helpful in defining the (predominant) mean, but of little theoretical or practical consequence. From Augustine to Tocqueville and beyond, thinkers have concluded otherwise: the *universal* human tendency is to gravitate toward one of these two limits— and back again. Where the moderate course has prevailed, it has been attributable to institutions rather than to any *innate* human propensity for balance—I am tempted to say, for rationality. Should there be a wish to sustain a commercial republic, the implications are as clear as they are sobering.

Indeed, if Augustine, Tocqueville, and others have grasped the truth about the soul's predilection for irrationality, then the real problem underlying certain contemporary intractabilities stands still before us— unconfronted because unconceived in the light of the half-century historical antinomy generated by the cold war and its continually rever-berating aftershocks that have darkened our vision. The ceaseless quest for, or consuming battle against, political utopias of the sort witnessed during the last half-century has yielded an intractable polarization,

2. Cf. Smith, *Wealth of Nations*, bk. 1, chap. 2, p. 17. Smith assumes there that the division of labor arises from a *universal* disposition, a "certain propensity," to "truck, barter, and exchange." Consider, in this light, Friedrich Nietzsche: "[I]f we possess our *why* of life we can put up with almost any *how*. Man does *not* strive after happiness; only the Englishman does that" ("Maxims and Ar-rows," in *Twilight of the Idols*, trans. R. J. Hollingdale [New York: Penguin Books, 1968], p. 23; emphasis in original). Contrary to Smith, Nietzsche would have it that "reason" was achieved at great cost. For a sobering view of just how ex-traordinary is the *achievement* of rationality, of forward-looking calculation, see Nietzsche, *Genealogy of Morals*, second essay, sec. 3, p. 62: "[W]ith the aid of [gruesome bodily tortures and the memory it produces] one at last came 'to reason.' Ah, reason, seriousness, mastery over the affects, the whole somber thing called reflection, all these prerogatives and showpieces of man: how dearly they have been bought! how much blood and cruelty lie at the bottom of all 'good things.' "

3. Hegel, *The Phenomenology of Spirit*, sec. 585, p. 357. See also Rousseau, *Emile*, bk. 4, p. 292.

which has supposed that the analytical categories are exhausted by the alternatives of either a command or free market economy. Yet this vicious polarization does not exhaust the possibilities of understanding. The ideological struggle of the cold war has crippled both warriors. Marx has lost; we should be hesitant, however, to conclude that Smith can win.

The real problem now that the cold war has receded and we fumble forward into the future is not, as it would appear, how to insure world-around free markets; rather, it is how—in America, at least—to arrest the twin phenomenon of a narrow egoism that would oversee only the world within its immediate purview and an overstepping franticness that is forever unsatisfied with itself and the whole world. The victory of "the free market" over the recently fallen socialist utopias, I suggest, indicates *relative* and not absolute strength, as the events of history will subsequently confirm should the real institutional supports for it (which alone can avert the twin irrationalities of the democratic soul) continue to be ignored. For some time, for example, the foreign threat posed by these socialist utopias has served to arrest the fall into solipsism.[4] What now?

It is, of course, Tocqueville's thinking about America with which I am expressly concerned. His suppositions about the democratic soul in America, however, originate with Augustine. In this chapter, therefore,

4. See Augustine, *City of God*, vol. 6, bk. 1, chap. 30, p. 67 (*CG*, p. 42): "[The great Scipio] refused to consent to the destruction of Carthage, then challenging Rome's bid for power. He stood out against Cato, who was all for it. For, Scipio *feared complacent security* as the enemy of feeble spirits, and believed that a vigilant fear would be a better, and a badly needed, teacher for the Romans" (emphasis added). See also chap. 33, p. 71 (*CG*, p. 45): "Scipio wanted you to have a salutary fear of the enemy, lest you should rot into debauchery"; and bk. 5, chap. 13, p. 273 (*CG*, p. 201). (Hobbes, in his own way, agrees. See *Leviathan*, part 2, chap. 17, pp. 130–31.) Tocqueville does not move in this direction because he recognizes the *frailty* of democracy and its weakness relative to undemocratic foreign powers. Better that democracies *not* have a foreign enemy to keep them virtuous. See Tocqueville, *Democracy in America*, vol. 1, part 2, chap. 5, p. 224: "[F]or a democratic republic to survive without trouble in a European nation, it would be necessary for republics to be established in all the others at the same time. . . . If for a century a democratic country were to remain under a republican government, one can believe that at the end of that time it would be richer, more populated, and more prosperous than neighboring despotic states; but during that century it would often have run the risk of being conquered by them." Tocqueville would, nevertheless, have agreed with Augustine that fear may be salutary. Rather than have it provided by a foreign threat, however, he thought it better conferred by God.

I will consider the attributes of the Augustinian self. This will involve, first, an exposition of Augustine's thinking, followed by a consideration of Hobbes and Rousseau. The divergences, significant though they certainly are, will concern us only in passing; I am more intent upon establishing the profile of the self that Tocqueville invokes in his social and political theory. These achieve their clarity and poignancy, I suggest, only in the light of what I am here calling the Augustinian self. Whatever their differences, Augustine, Hobbes, Rousseau, and Tocqueville are unanimous in their concern with the *instability* of human life, with its tendency to get wholly and broodingly caught up in itself or pridefully and explosively to overstep its bounds.

First, then, I will consider Augustine, followed by Hobbes and Rousseau. In each exposition I will consider four aspects: (1) the nature of human errancy; (2) the inevitable oscillations in the soul between self-enclosed inwardness and restive outwardness that such errancy occasions; (3) how the love of, as it were, *merely* human liberty conceals within itself certain tendencies that predispose the soul toward misery; and, (4) how only a return to the Source—the content of which is, of course, construed differently for Augustine, Hobbes, and Rousseau—can absolve human life of its unrelenting oscillation. By virtue of the complexities of each author's thinking, certain other issues will be considered along the way; these four I have mentioned, are, nevertheless, the central ones. After having worked through these aspects of their thinking, I will indicate how Tocqueville conceives of the matter. This will provide the groundwork for a subsequent discussion of, among other things, the significance of local politics, the family, and religion for the democratic soul. Finally, I will make some remarks on Nietzsche and the endurance of the Augustinian self.

1. AUGUSTINE AND THE ERRANCY FROM GOD

The great paradox of the Augustinian self is that without God, it conceives of itself in its aloneness as supremely powerful and self-sufficient and yet intimates at the same time that it is utterly impotent. Its proclamations belie its inner secret; its self-understanding is tortured by what it perennially and loudly seeks to deny—hence the din of human affairs in "the world." How this anguished paradox presents itself in Tocqueville's analysis will become clear in due course. I state it here at the outset so that it may serve as a point of orientation throughout the entire discussion.

The source of the paradox of apparent (and articulated) power and intimated powerlessness, for Augustine, can be traced to Adam's errancy from God in the beginning. Adam, while created in the likeness of God,[5] nevertheless falls away from God through disobedience.[6] Once having disobeyed the injunction not to eat of the tree of knowledge, Adam *hides* from God,[7] and the opening of his eyes unto knowledge coincides with Adam's distancing from God.[8] That "he should be like us,"[9] that he should he eat from the tree of knowledge, is conjoined with Adam's eviction from the Edenic paradise; and the two aspects together—the presence of God in intimate proximity[10] and the hiddenness of God due

5. Gen. 1:26.

6. Gen. 3:6. See Augustine, *City of God*, vol. 7, bk. 12, chap. 7, p. 257 (*CG*, pp. 479–80): "[N]o one, therefore, need seek for an efficient cause of an evil will. Since the 'effect' is, in fact, a deficiency, the cause should be called 'deficient.' The fault of an evil will begins when one falls from Supreme Being to some being which is less than absolute." As in Plato, there is, properly speaking, no agency until the soul is rightly oriented to and by what veritably is. See Plato, *Republic*, bk. 9, 588e–589a, where, until the soul is oriented by the Good, it is a multiheaded beast who only *appears* to be a unitary being and so cannot act coherently as a *single* agent.

7. Gen. 3:8. Luther and the other Reformers would later read this to mean that the image of God in which humans partake was completely corrupted by virtue of disobedience. In Luther's words, "[S]ince the loss of this image through sin we cannot understand it to any extent" ("Lectures on Genesis," in *Luther's Works*, ed. Jaroslav Pelikan [Saint Louis: Concordia Publishing House, 1958], 1:61). Furthermore, "[N]ot only have we no experience of [this likeness to God], but we continually experience the opposite; and so we hear nothing except bare words" (1:63). While Augustine reads Gen. 3:8 to mean that human beings "sew together fine words without the fruit of good works, in order while living badly to cover up their baseness by speaking well" (*The Trinity*, trans. Edmund Hill [New York: New City Press, 1991], bk. 12, chap. 3, sec. 13, p. 330), he, unlike Luther, was willing to speculate about the divine image in human-kind—which his fifteen years of work on *The Trinity* confirms.

8. G. W. F. Hegel notes that "the Fall is . . . the eternal Mythus of Man" (*Philosophy of History*, trans. J. Sibree [New York: Dover Publications, 1956], part 3, sec. 3, chap. 2, p. 321). Knowing always involves a standing-away-from. Hence, his observation that the owl of Minerva always "spread[s] its wings only with the falling of the dusk" (*Philosophy of Right*, trans. T. M. Knox [Oxford: Oxford University Press, 1967], preface, p. 13). See also Augustine, *City of God*, vol. 7, bk. 13, chap. 3, pp. 302–3 (*CG*, p. 512), citing Ps. 49, 12:20: "Man when he was in honor, *did not understand:* he is compared to senseless beasts, and is become like to them" (emphasis added).

9. Gen. 3:5.

10. See Augustine, *City of God*, vol. 7, bk. 11, chap. 26, p. 228 (*CG*, p. 459): "[W]e ourselves can recognize in ourselves an image of God, in the sense of an image of the Trinity. . . . [For we resemble the divine Trinity in that] we are, and we know that we are, and we love to be and know that we are." Notwith-

to sin[11]—establish an extraordinary tension in the human soul, one that must be ameliorated, not by returning to the first innocence for which we so long,[12] but rather by meriting a second,[13] assisted by sincere obedience yet, in the final analysis, made possible only by virtue the gift that is God the Son.[14]

The problem, however, is that while it is to the advantage of human beings to be subject to God, this verity is forever being forgotten.[15] It is,

---

standing the hiddenness of God, his trace resides in us. Note Augustine's pre-Cartesian assertions throughout chap. 26 (pp. 228–29, [*CG*, pp. 459–60]).

11. See, for example, Exod. 20:19 ("speak thou to us [Moses], and we will hear: but let not God speak with us, lest we die"); and Isa. 59:1–2 ("your iniquities have separated you from your God; and your sins have hidden His face from you, so that He will not hear"). The sinfulness of the Israelites and the hidden face of God are linked.

12. See Augustine, *The Trinity*, bk. 4, chap. 1, sec. 2, p. 153: "[W]e were exiled from this unchanging joy, *yet not so broken and cut off from it* that we stopped seeking eternity, truth, and happiness even in this changeable time-bound situation of ours" (emphasis added). Cf. Hobbes, for whom the problem of human existence in history before the end time stems from this fact. In his words, "[W]hereupon having both eaten, [Adam and Eve] did indeed take upon them God's office, which is judicature of good and evil; *but acquired no new ability to distinguish between them aright*" (*Leviathan*, part 2, chap. 20, p. 157 [emphasis added]). For Hobbes, the problem for which the Leviathan is the remedy stems from the human unwillingness to admit that the relationship really was broken off!

13. See Augustine, *City of God*, vol. 7, bk. 13, chap. 23, pp. 333–34 (*CG*, pp. 536–37): "[T]he first man of the earth, earthly, became a living soul, but not life-giving spirit. That was reserved for him as a reward for obedience." Theologically, the primitive unity that was maintained by the tree of life was dirempted by eating of the tree of knowledge. Eternal life, a higher unity, entails a falling away, an errancy, and then a return made possible for the meritorious—for those who *could* fall away but do not. Not incidentally, this *pattern* of primitive unity/diremption/higher unity is recapitulated in the dialectics of Hegel and Marx, though (arguably) there is little place for merit in their constructions.

14. See Augustine, *Confessions*, bk. 3, chap. 11, p. 50: "[D]espite my frequent efforts to climb out of [darkness and falsehood], I was the more heavily plunged back into the filth and wallowed in it." By virtue of God's gift of his Son alone, and not by mortal effort, may human beings be saved—as Augustine argued during the Pelagian controversy. See also Augustine, *The Trinity*, bk. 13, chap. 3, sec. 12, p. 353: "[F]or it is in [God the Son] alone and thanks to him alone that [the sons of man] can be happy, by sharing in his immortality; it was to persuade us of this that the Son of God came to share in our mortality."

15. See Augustine, *Confessions*, bk. 7, chap. 17, pp. 127–28. It is the *gravity* of the body, the weight of *habit*, that pulls the soul back from its vision of God/

in fact, human nature *to* forget. Rather than submit to God, human beings hide from God, think themselves to be without the need of God,
forget that the purview of the created does not include acting as only
the Creator may.

The difficulty does not arise simply because human beings are created. More than this, they carry the *trace* of the Creator in them, as they
must, for they are made in God's image.[16] This trace, it is, that *tempts*
human beings to act like a God, to create a world, as God alone did and
can. Madness, it is, to wish to be a creator; Nietzsche's reward for his call
unto creation was well deserved.[17]

It is the simultaneous presence and hiddenness of God, then, that
makes human life gravitate toward certain polarities. Had human beings
not defected from God, their eyes would not have been opened; they
would not have known of God. Had human beings completely fallen
away from God, not thought themselves bound by God's call to come
out of hiding,[18] then, too, there would be no difficulty. The God who is
utterly hidden from view cannot disturb beings who are wholly unto
themselves.

For Augustine, the drama of the soul is established by the tension
between an eye-opening distantiation from God and the forever regnant
boundedness by him. Human pathology develops because we are unable to find a path that respects the *boundary* between God and hu-

---

the Good. See also Simone Weil, "Gravity and Grace," in *Gravity and Grace*
(London: Routledge and Kegan Paul, 1963), p. 1: "[A]ll the *natural* movements
of the soul are controlled by laws analogous to those of physical gravity. Grace is
the only exception" (emphasis in original). Without grace, without the gift, "all
faults are possible" (p. 4).

16. Gen. 1:26. Graham Walker notes that "according to Augustine [human
nature] though fallen, is not effaced. As a result, [human beings] cannot simply
let the void be. Proclaiming that nature fails to stock itself with moral content,
they license themselves to do the job—even though their own account of reality
makes this ultimately impossible to defend" (*Moral Foundations of Constitutional
Thought: Current Problems, Augustinian Prospects* [Princeton: Princeton University
Press, 1990], chap. 4, p. 117).

17. See Nietzsche, *Thus Spoke Zarathustra*, trans. Walter Kaufman (New
York: Penguin Books, 1978), first part, "On the Way of the Creator," pp. 62–65.
Augustine earlier insisted on distinguishing between "God creating and forming from within and created agents working from without" (*The Trinity*, bk. 3,
chap. 2, sec. 14, p. 135). See also Augustine, *City of God*, vol. 7, bk. 12, chap. 26,
p. 291 (*CG*, pp. 505–6), the title of which reads: "That the nature and the form
of every living thing created are entirely due to the work of God alone."

18. Gen. 3:8.

manity while at the same time honoring the God who rules the world[19] and who knows the innermost recesses of the human heart.[20] The tendency is either, boldly and with hubris, to suppose oneself to be *like* God (in doing so "[we] end up becoming like beasts"),[21] or else to withdraw into hiding from him—to harden one's heart against God in the lonely security of isolation that sometimes masquerades as the search for God within.

Both trajectories, into the world with abandon and away from it in seclusion, are, to be sure, ways of evading God; moving in those very directions, however, is made possible—indeed, likely—by virtue of the human affinity *with* God. "In their perverted way all humanity imitates you," Augustine says.[22] The illusion of freedom in the world, and rulership over it, betrays our likeness as much as does the withdrawal from the world and into the recesses of the heart. God is self-sufficient and free *and* is known only in that "secret hidden place" within. Human errancy, the trajectory of its evasion from God, recapitulates the mystery of God, though this mystery is now only seen "through glass, darkly."[23]

Human eyesight, then, is dim; yet it is illuminated by enough light to see that there are two tendencies, two poles between which the human soul oscillates. Consider, first, the frantic activity in, and love of, the world that masquerades as self-sufficiency and freedom. As Augustine recounts it,

> [In this confession] I shall remind myself of my past foulness and carnal corruptions, not because I love them but so that I may love you, my God. . . . You gathered me together from the state of disintegration in which I had been fruitlessly divided. I turned from unity in you to be divided in multiplicity. At one time in adolescence I was *burning* to find satisfaction in hellish pleasures. I *ran wild* in the shadowy jungle of erotic adventures. "My beauty wasted away and in your

19. Consider Job 38:4 ("where wast thou when I laid the foundations of the earth? declare, if thou hast understanding").

20. See 1 Kings 8:39 ("for thou, even thou only, knowest the hearts of all the children of men").

21. Augustine, *The Trinity*, bk. 12, chap. 3, sec. 16, p. 331.

22. Augustine, *Confessions*, bk. 2, chap. 6, p. 32.

23. 1 Cor. 13:12. Augustine's efforts in *The Trinity* are, by his own admission (bk. 15, chap. 2, sec. 10, pp. 401–2), a failure. Human beings cannot directly grasp the Trinitarian structure of God in the image of which they partake. Nevertheless, Augustine proceeds in the remaining chapters to suggest that notwithstanding the inadequacies of the image trinity by which we may see the divine Trinity "through a glass darkly," the latter is translucent, not wholly opaque, to the mortal soul.

sight I became putrid" (Dan. 10:8), by pleasing myself and by being ambitious to win human approval.[24]

Already here is the claim—to be investigated shortly—that envy and the "passion to gain distinction"[25] is necessarily linked to errancy from God. More to the point for present purposes, however, is the characterization Augustine offers of the kind of *motion* that attends the lost soul immersed in the world.

> [Those who desire] to find delight in things outside themselves easily become empty and expend their energies on "the things that are seen and temporal" (2 Cor. 4:18). With starving minds they can only lick the images of these things. . . . In you is repose which forgets all toil because there is none besides you, nor are we to look for the multiplicity of other things that are not what you are.[26]

And elsewhere,

> This is the outcome when you are abandoned, font of life and the one true Creator and Ruler of the entire universe, when from a self-concerned pride a false unity is loved in the part. . . . [But] you hear the groans of the prisoners and release us from the chains we have forged for ourselves, on the condition that we do not erect against you the horns (Ps. 75:5) of a false liberty by avaricious desire to possess more and, at the risk of losing everything, through loving our private interest more than you, the good of all that is.[27]

The human tendency is to get caught up in the visible, ever shifting, created world, to be tossed about upon the surface of a sea ever fearful of the *calm depths* beneath. Think here of Jonah.[28]

---

24. Augustine, *Confessions*, bk. 2, chap. 1, p. 43 (emphasis added).

25. Rousseau invokes this phrase (*First Discourse*, p. 50), with a view to pointing out the temptation of most people to misuse scientific knowledge. Only the virtuous few who insularly dwell within the boundary of famed societies are not subject to this misuse. Notwithstanding some rather obvious differences between the two, Rousseau seems to be heavily indebted to Augustine for his analysis of envy and the temptations of the world.

26. Augustine, *Confessions*, bk. 9, chap. 4, p. 161–62.

27. Augustine, *Confessions*, bk. 3, chap. 8, pp. 47–48.

28. Jonah is swallowed by the depths and then descends further still into the deep (into the belly of the whale [Jon. 1:15–17]). Only in this doubly deep place—deeper still than the (surface) world can fathom—does Jonah remember his obligation to God and cease to frantically evade God's call. Cf. Friedrich Nietzsche, *Thus Spoke Zarathustra*, fourth part, "The Drunken Song," p. 324:

One of the manifestations of getting caught up in the surface agitations of the world is the temptation to become, so to speak, a vendor of words.[29] The danger of language, which would become a preoccupation for Hobbes in *Leviathan*,[30] and for Rousseau in *Emile*,[31] stems from the power words have to order the world. That Adam was granted the power to *name* creation so near to the beginning is suggestive of its awesome significance.[32] More than this power to order, however, is the power of words to charm us, as Plato might say.[33] Words fill up the darkness with light—like God did in the beginning.[34] Only here, the light cast is not the Creator's light and bears only a pale resemblance to it. Human beings are tempted to warm themselves by this light that brings no true

---

> O man, take
> What does the deep midnight declare?
> "I was asleep—
> From a deep dream I woke and swear:
> The world is deep, Deeper than day had been aware.
> Deep is its woe;
> Joy—deeper yet than agony:
> Woe implores: Go!
> But all joy wants eternity—
> Wants deep, wants deep eternity."

29. See Augustine, *Confessions*, bk. 2, chap. 3, pp. 26–28. Augustine here speaks of his father's wish that he "possess a cultured tongue." He continues: "though my culture really meant a desert uncultivated by you, God" (p. 26). In place of "a cultured tongue," the F. J. Sheed translation of the *Confessions* (New York: Sheed & Ward, 1943) has "copious in speech" (p. 26).

30. See, for example, Hobbes, *Leviathan*, part 1, chaps. 4–7, pp. 33–58. Hobbes's natural science is meant to keep language from becoming "absurd." That is, all words must ultimately have an empirical referent for them to be admitted into legitimate discourse.

31. See Rousseau, *Emile*, bk. 4, p. 251: "I do not tire of repeating it: put all the lessons of young people in actions rather than in speeches. Let them learn nothing in books which experience can teach them." In order for words not to *go astray* they must have experiential referents.

32. Gen. 2:19–20.

33. See Plato, *Republic*, bk. 10, 607e–608a: "[S]o long as [poetry] is unable to make good her defense we shall chant over to ourselves as we listen the reasons that we have given as a countercharm to her spell, to preserve us from slipping back into the childish loves of the multitude." Elsewhere, the suggestion is made that the antidote for the art that *imitates* is the art that *uses* (601e–602b).

34. Gen. 1:2–3.

comfort.[35] *Their* words fill up the world (and so "[divide] the light from the darkness")[36]—not with true light, but rather with noise.

> Do not be vain, my soul. Do not deafen your heart's ear with the tumult of vanity. Even you have to listen. The Word himself cries to you to return.[37]

The soul, however, does not return. Confronted increasingly with the dim knowledge of its own emptiness, it throws itself with greater abandon into the world. Its eyes focus with ever greater precision and longing on "Rome."

Occasionally, it is true, the vacuity of the world, which no mortal utterance can alleviate, overwhelms the soul; and finding the world barren, the soul looks, *vainly*, in that other place where the trace of God is present. "I was seeking for you outside myself," Augustine says, "and I failed to find the God of my own heart."[38]

> From a hidden depth a profound self-examination had dredged up a heap of all my misery and set it in the sight of my heart. That precipitated a vast storm bearing a massive downpour of tears.[39]

The remorseful soul, which longs for respite and repose, looks inward in the face of the futility of the world.

> Grief darkened my heart. Everything on which I set my gaze was death. My home town became a torture to me; my father's house a strange world of unhappiness.[40]

35. See Simone Weil, "Imagination Which Fills the Void," in *Gravity and Grace*, p. 16: "[T]he imagination is continually at work filling up all the fissures through which grace may pass." That is, human imagination hastens to keep God at bay, to assist the soul in its desire to remain in the totality of its created, mediated world.

36. Gen. 1:4.

37. Augustine, *Confessions*, bk. 4, chap. 11, p. 62.

38. Augustine, *Confessions*, bk. 6, chap. 1, p. 90. See also Hegel, *Phenomenology of Spirit*, sec. 668, p. 407: "[The] 'beautiful soul,' then, being conscious of this contradiction in its unreconciled immediacy, is disordered to the point of madness, wastes itself in yearning and pines away in consumption. Thereby it does in fact surrender the *being-for-self* to which it so stubbornly clings; but what it brings forth is only the non-spiritual unity of [mere] being" (emphasis in original). Without further elaboration, I suggest here that the dialectical achievements of the spirit in the *Phenomenology* entail the movement back and forth between a bold and apparent sufficiency in the world and a brooding withdrawal occasioned by the negativity lurking in every achievement. Hegel's spirit is the Augustinian self that not only finds itself *in time*, but also *finds* itself—in time.

39. Augustine, *Confessions*, bk. 8, chap. 12, p. 152.

40. Augustine, *Confessions*, bk. 4, chap. 4, p. 57.

And elsewhere,

> My lacerated and bloody soul . . . [found] no rest in pleasant groves,
> nor in games or songs, nor in sweet-scented places, nor in exquisite
> places, nor in the pleasures of the bedroom and bed, nor, finally, in
> books and poetry.[41]

This repudiation of the world is not sustained, however. The world has
its enticements. And so the soul traverses back and forth, leaping between the too-fast of worldly involvement and the too-slow of the self-
enclosed search within, moving from one domain to another, neither of
which nourishes. Here is a chasm "that a very Achilles of a free spirit
would not venture to leap without a shudder."[42]

This at once self-confident and forlorn movement between restiveness and self-enclosure is the *inner* secret of the love of the world, of the
City of Man.

The avowed proclamation, of course, is that the world is sufficient
unto itself, that time does not need Eternity, that the light of worldly
happiness cannot be overwhelmed by the void. Yet melancholy lurks
in the shadow of all alacrity; the burden of time *unfilled* intervenes.
Silenced despair forever intercedes. As Kierkegaard would put it:

> the more spiritual despair becomes, and the more the inwardness be-
> comes a peculiar world of its own in inclosing reserve, the more incon-
> sequential are the externalities under which the despair conceals
> itself. But the more spiritual the despair becomes, the more attention
> it pays with demonic cleverness to keeping despair closed up in in-
> closing reserve. . . . [T]he more spiritual [despair] is, the more urgent
> it is to dwell in an externality behind which no one would ordinarily
> think of looking for it. . . . [This provides] a world *ex*-clusively for
> itself, a world where the self in despair is restlessly and tormentedly
> engaged in willing to be itself.[43]

Carving out a reserve far from the world where the silent brooding of
one's precious heart may toil without interruption, however, offers no
real consolation, no enduring substance, no antidote to boredom—that
onerous intrusion of Eternity into the totality of the world. Neither the
warm comforts of life nor the long sleep of death are genuine possibili-

41. Augustine, *Confessions*, bk. 4, chap. 7, p. 59.

42. Nietzsche, *Genealogy of Morals*, first essay, sec. 6, p. 32. I will consider
Nietzsche in section 5 below. Achilles, representative of the ethic of nobility, is
not capable of such oscillation; only the spiritualization of human life (by the
priests) makes such massive swings possible. Augustine would agree.

43. Søren Kierkegaard, *The Sickness unto Death*, trans. and ed. Howard V.
Hong and Adna H. Hong (Princeton: Princeton University Press, 1980), p. 73
(emphasis in original).

ties here; the surface of expectation is penetrated by the deep suspicion that for all its joy this life is but a "lingering death."[44]

So tormented, the soul longs to establish to its own satisfaction that it is, in fact, alive. The cheery enchantments of the world, however, are not enough. "Happiness" alone has never been enough—except, again, for Englishman and other single-minded purveyors of the market.[45] Not happiness, but rather suffering and pity: these, more than happiness ever could, avow that life is not but a lingering death.[46] Suffering and pity: those sweet reminders that "graze the skin" but cause no real wound.[47] To *watch* suffering, even one's own!—here is the ecstatic tes-

44. Plato, *Republic*, bk. 3, 406b. The condition Plato describes is that of a patient who "[struggles] against death, [and] by reason of his science [wins] the prize of a doting old age." The science is the science of medicine that sustains physical life but fails to gently guide us toward the Good. It offers antidotes to bodily afflictions but not antidotes to the lies harbored in our soul that keep us from the Good. This condition of life stands existentially, between living the true life and death; and, epistemologically, between truly knowing and ignorance. In either case, it corresponds to the condition of the cave dwellers in bk. 7, 514a–517c. Only by dying to this life that is not yet life, can there be happiness—hence Socrates' summons to "prepare [ourselves] for dying and death" in the *Phaedo* (trans. Hugh Tredennick, in *Collected Dialogues of Plato*, 64a).

45. Again, see Nietzsche, "Maxims and Arrows," in *Twilight of the Idols*, p. 23: "[M]an does not strive after happiness; only the Englishman does that" (emphasis in original).

46. About the appeal of suffering, about its capacity to kill time, see John Glen Gray, *The Warriors* (New York: Harper and Row, 1970), p. 216: "[The secret love of war] cannot be disregarded. The ways of peace have not found—perhaps cannot find—substitutes for the communal enthusiasms and ecstasies of war. Unless we find a way to change men's hearts, there appears to be small chance that they will fall out of love with destructive violence. In 1955 I talked with a Frenchwoman who had suffered cruelly during the war from lack of food and anxieties for her family, but was now living in comfortable bourgeois fashion with her husband and son. We reviewed the misadventures of those war days, and then she confessed to me with great earnestness that, despite everything, those times had been more satisfying than the present. 'My life is so unutterably boring nowadays!' she cried out. 'Anything is better than to have nothing at all happen day after day. You know that I do not love war or want it to return. But at least it made me feel alive, as I have not felt alive before or since.' "

47. The Chadwick translation, to which I have resorted almost exclusively here, has, "scratched me on the surface" (Augustine, *Confessions*, bk. 3, chap. 2, p. 37). The R. S. Pine-Coffin translation of the *Confessions* (New York: Penguin Books, 1961), while less authoritative, is occasionally more lyrical. Here I cite the Pine-Coffin, which has "graze the skin" (p. 57). Cf. Rousseau, *Emile*, bk. 4,

timony that the Augustinian self is not really dead. That Rome loved the theater: did this not confirm its errancy from God?[48]

The melancholy delight in suffering and pity that is succored in the recesses of the heart is a largely hidden secret within the Augustinian self. There are, however, other and more visible aspects of the love of the world that the Augustinian self displays. Consider the entire constellation of envy, the passion to gain distinction, pride, and the desire for honor—all of which hopelessly ensnared Augustine while on his way to becoming a "vendor of words" prior to his conversion. These other-related passions, which wrack the soul distracted by the offerings of the City of Man, are not only the consequence of an evasion from God; more than this, what must be remembered here is that these deficien-

---

pp. 221–27. Rousseau's three maxims are designed to direct the amour propre that *will* emerge, away from envy and toward pity, the other-related passion that does not fan the flames of pride. Yet Augustine would wonder whether *this* pity adds *spice* to the life of the soul that is lost to God. Oddly, perhaps, Nietzsche and Augustine are narrowly in accord: "[T]his overestimation of and predilection for pity on the part of modern philosophers is something new: hitherto philosophers have been at one as to the *worthlessness* of pity" (*Genealogy of Morals*, preface, sec. 5, p. 19 [emphasis added]). Pity is, for Nietzsche, the *final sin*. See *Thus Spoke Zarathustra*, fourth part, p. 327: "[Pity] has had its time. My suffering and my pity for suffering—what does it matter? Am I concerned with *happiness*? I am concerned with my *work*" (emphasis in original).

48. See Augustine, *Confessions*, bk. 3, chap. 2, pp. 35–36: "[The theater] fueled my fire. Why is it that a person should wish to experience suffering by watching grievous and tragic events which he himself would not wish to endure? Nevertheless he wants to suffer the pain given by being a spectator of these sufferings, and the pain itself in his pleasure. What is this but amazing folly?" See also Augustine, *City of God*, vol. 6, bk. 1, chap. 33, p. 70 (*CG*, p. 44): "[A]re your minds bereft of reason? You are not merely mistaken; this is madness. Here are people in the East bewailing Rome's humiliation, and great states in remote regions of the earth holding public mournings and lamentations—and you Romans are searching for theaters, pouring into them, filling them, behaving more irresponsibly than ever before. It was just this spiritual disease, degeneration, decline into immorality and indecency that Scipio feared when he opposed the erection of theaters.... He did not think that the republic could be happy while walls were standing, yet morals were collapsing." Augustine also praises Plato (bk. 2, chap. 14, pp. 93–95 [*CG*, pp. 63–64]) for wishing to keep citizens away from the theater. For Plato, the soul enthralled by "lingering death" is drawn to theater because it satisfies the lower part of the soul (which cannot know true life), that "part of the soul . . . that has hungered for tears and a good cry and satisfaction, because it is its nature to desire these things" (*Republic*, bk. 10, 606a).

cies of the human soul are themselves perverse *imitations* of God—as Augustine's recollection of the incident at the pear tree suggests:

> [My theft as a youth was not even beautiful] in the way that specious vices have a flawed reflection of beauty. Pride imitates what is lofty; but you alone are God most high above all things. What does ambition seek but honour and glory? Yet you alone are worthy of honour and are glorious for Eternity.[49]

The human soul, after all, bears *witness* to the light, but is not itself the light.[50] Envy, the passion to gain distinction, pride, and the desire for honor: each of these is but a pale imitation of the God of Israel, who time and again demanded that he be worshiped, attended to, and put first above all others. "For thou shalt worship no other god: for the LORD, whose name *is* Jealous, *is* a jealous God."[51]

This pale imitation, however, is by no means a shadowy apparition that does little. On the contrary, the entire imitative constellation would demand that the world attend singularly to the soul made in the image of God if it could.

Yet why, it may be asked, is this visible imitation of God by a creature estranged from him such a danger? The answer can be found by looking at how that imitative complex shows itself in the world. For God is not just a Jealous God, but also a creator God.

Consider, for example, Jeremiah 23:24 ("Do I not fill heaven and earth?"). Insofar as human beings imitate God they, too, will try to "fill heaven and earth." Because human beings are made in the image of God, they will tend to act like God—unless, as Augustine would wish and Christianity would countenance, they recognize the boundary between Creator and created.

Not recognizing this boundary is the perennial tendency, to be sure; yet on this reading the turning away from God evinced by the (modern?) Baconian project, which would have it that

> if a man endeavor to establish and extend the power and dominion of the human race itself over the universe, his ambition (if ambition it can be called) is without a doubt [noble],[52]

49. Augustine, *Confessions*, bk. 2, chap. 6, p. 31.

50. John 1:8; Augustine, *Confessions*, bk. 7, chap. 9, p. 121.

51. Exod. 34:14.

52. Francis Bacon, *The New Organon*, ed. Fulton H. Anderson (New York: Macmillan, 1960), bk. 1, sec. 129, p. 118). In fairness to Bacon, he did not conclude that the kingdom of nature over which the machinations of human reason would have dominion is the only kingdom to which allegiance is owed. There is, additionally, the Kingdom of God and the political kingdom. "Filling up

can only end in filling up heaven and earth—to their detriment. It is not simply that the natural world cannot accommodate envy, the passion to gain distinction, pride, and the desire for honor. Rather, when these are conjoined with the desire to fill up heaven and earth—and they *will* be in the Augustinian self—then the finite, natural, world must bear a burden that it cannot. Creation, after all, occurred only once! The corrupted image of God proceeds to fill up heaven and earth—for the purpose (no doubt hidden to itself) of elevating itself above all others. Lurking behind or within the Baconian project, which *is* authorized by God, is the imitative constellation of envy, the passion to gain distinction, pride, and the desire for honor. And this claim about the relationship between science and moral disposition, as the careful reader of the *First Discourse* will have already grasped, is at the center of Rousseau's much later argument—to which I will turn in section 3 below.

How, then, can the secret and ominous tendencies that arise be averted when human beings, in their errancy from God, suppose that the totality of the world is sufficient unto itself? How can the dark brooding of the wounded soul that holds itself "in reserve" from the world it purports to love so dearly be redirected so that the world from which it suffers does not become an *externality* to its incessant injury? How can the soul that would frenziedly fill up the world in order to conceal and sustain its envy, passion to gain distinction, pride, and desire for honor, be countermanded? Augustine's answer is to grant what is due to God and not confuse the boundary between the Creator and created, between the City of God and the City of Man:

> [W]hat is really involved in God's prohibition is obedience, the virtue which is, so to speak, the mother and guardian of all the virtues of a rational creature. The fact is that a rational creature is so constituted

---

heaven and earth" could not become the singular concern for Bacon, that it (arguably) has become in the contemporary world. See also Martin Heidegger, *The Question concerning Technology*, trans. William Lovitt (New York: Harper and Row, 1977). Heidegger is not unaware of the "totality" that technology may portend. Yet he remains hopeful that the totality that is "enframing" may be disrupted by the gift that is the revealing of technology. In his terms, "[I]t is precisely Enframing, which threatens to sweep man away into ordering as the supposed single way of revealing, and so thrusts man into the danger of the surrender of his free essence—it is precisely in this extreme danger that the innermost indestructible belongingness of man within granting may come to light, provided that we, for our part, begin to pay heed to the coming to presence of technology" (p. 32). Heidegger's theological stance here is akin to Augustine's: the totality of the world can only be overcome by the *gift!*—and the gift is given *only* in the face of the totality of the world.

that submission is good for it while yielding to its own rather than its Creator's will is, on the contrary, disastrous.[53]

The City of Man is not sufficient unto itself; the human gaze must be directed beyond that totality if life is not to be ravaged by a restiveness that is driven forward by God-like jealousies that purport to "so love the world"—or no less destructively, if it is not to succumb with pathetic delusion to the temptations that are offered in the solitary desert of the soul.[54] Only by honoring God (and, therefore, the *boundary* between Creator and created), only by granting what is due to the City of God, can mortal life be accorded whatever fullness it may possess—and may *suffering* have a meaning that deepens human life rather than destroys it.[55]

> My sin consisted in this, that I sought pleasure, sublimity, and truth not in God but in his creatures, in myself and other created beings.[56]

For Augustine, unless the human gaze is averted from the City of Man, there can only be the oscillation between brooding and activity without rest:

> There is no rest to be found where you seek it. Seek for what you seek, but it is not where you are looking for. You seek the happy life in the region of death; it is not there. How can there be a happy life where there is not even life.[57]

2. HOBBES AND THE PROBLEM OF PRIDE

Hobbes may be said to have the psychological acuity of Augustine about the pridefulness of human beings, but without the bosom of Christ in which to rest when weary. There are, to be sure, decisive respects in which he is unlike Augustine—think, for example, of his insistence that Christianity's greatest error was to posit the existence of *two* cities,[58] and

53. Augustine, *City of God*, vol. 7, bk. 14, chap. 12, pp. 379–80 (CG, p. 571).

54. Matt. 4: 1–10.

55. See Nietzsche, *Genealogy of Morals*, third essay, sec. 28, p. 162: "[T]his interpretation—there is no doubt of it—brought fresh suffering with it, deeper, more inward, more poisonous, more life destructive suffering: it placed all suffering under the perspective of guilt. But all this notwithstanding—man was saved thereby, he possessed a meaning" (emphasis in original).

56. Augustine, *Confessions*, bk. 1, chap. 20, pp. 222–23.

57. Augustine, *Confessions*, bk. 4, chap. 12, p. 64.

58. For Hobbes, political and religious sovereignty must be unified. Wishing even to supersede this false opposition in words, Hobbes remarks, "[T]here is therefore no other government in this life, neither of state, nor religion, but *temporal*" (*Leviathan*, part 3, chap. 39, p. 340; emphasis in original).

of his peculiar reading of who Christ is.[59] Yet it can be truly said that it was precisely because his psychology was Augustinian that he moved in the direction that he did. Calvin, it can be said, radicalized Augustine.[60] So, too, in his own inimitable way, did Hobbes.

The central dilemma for Hobbes (as for Augustine) was, I suggest, human pridefulness. More precisely, Hobbes was concerned to show that human pridefulness was so overwhelming that it required the extraordinary measure of establishing a powerful Leviathan who would, as it were, take in upon himself the pridefulness of the citizens in order that they might "live."[61] Long before Heidegger's final tenebrous proclamation that "only a God can save us,"[62] Augustine had insisted that human pridefulness was so monumental, that human beings were so prone to derelicting their duty to God and seeking refuge in the world, that it was necessary for God himself to take human form in order that the *totality* of the world might be overcome.[63] Hobbes, no less than Au-

59. See Joshua Mitchell, "Luther and Hobbes on the Question, Who Was Moses, Who Was Christ?" *Journal of Politics* 53 (August 1991): 676–700. Hobbes insists that Christ did not set a spiritual kingdom next to the earthly kingdom; rather, he renewed the Mosaic covenant (abandoned by the Jews under the reign of Saul when they wished to be ruled like other earthly kingdoms) according to which citizens owe obedience to whoever is the rightful sovereign. See also A. P. Martinich, *The Two Gods of Leviathan* (Cambridge: Cambridge University Press, 1992), for whom Hobbes's Christology may be peculiar but can nevertheless be traced to existing orthodox understandings available to him at the time he wrote.

60. See, for example, John Calvin, *Institutes of Christian Religion*, ed. John T. McNeill, trans. Ford Lewis Battles (Philadelphia: Westminster Press, 1960), vol. 2, bk. 3, chaps. 21–23, pp. 920–64, on predestination. While Calvin consistently cites Augustine as an authority, the somber theme of predestination in Augustine is attenuated by God's presence and partial comprehensibility. The logic of predestination, for Calvin, necessitated that such comprehensibility be relinquished.

61. This is a venerable Reformation pattern of thinking. The One Sovereign (Christ) takes in upon himself the pridefulness of the many (Christians). See, for example, Luther, "Freedom of a Christian" in *Works*, 31:357: "[A]ll sin is swallowed up by the righteousness of Christ." What Augustine earlier says of God—"[by yielding to You] my mind was free of the biting cares of place seeking, [and] of desire for gain" (*Confessions*, bk. 9, chap. 1, p. 155)—Hobbes would say of the Leviathan.

62. See Martin Heidegger, "Nur ein Gott Kann Uns Retten," *Der Spiegel*, May 31, 1976, p. 209.

63. About the totality of the world, the claim made by the City of Man of its own self-sufficiency, see Augustine, *City of God*, vol. 7, bk. 14, chap. 28, (*CG*, p. 593): "[W]orldly society has flowered from a selfish love which dared to despise even God, whereas the communion of saints is rooted in the love of God

gustine, saw the temptation of pride. His deep suspicion of democracy may be attributable to his view that human beings (like God, Augustine would say!) invariably try to make themselves the center of the world, and that their cry for freedom was, when disencumbered from the conceit of self-understanding, a ruse behind which lay the desire to be unbound from a legitimate authority, who alone can assure peace and ameliorate their own impotence. Better it is that the most important political matters not be subject to

> the persuasion and advice of private men, but [to the] laws of the realm, [and having done this] you will no longer suffer ambitious men through the streams of your blood to wade to their own power.[64]

As with Augustine, the corrupted will predisposes human beings to go astray even while they think their motives pure. *Obedience* to the will of the sovereign, therefore, is necessary. Obedience is, to repeat Augustine's words, "the mother and guardian of all the other virtues in a rational

---

that is ready to trample on self. In a word, this latter relies on the Lord, whereas the other boasts that it can get along by itself." So powerful is the propensity to turn from God, to glory in the totality of the City of Man, that God had to take mortal form. Were he *merely* human he could not have averted the temptation; had God remained God and not taken human form, he could not have mediated (bk. 9, chap. 15, pp. 99–101 [*CG*, pp. 359–61]). He must have taken on the poison of mortal life, in order to provide the antidote to the sin that characterizes it. See Augustine, *The Trinity*, bk. 4, chap. 4, sec. 24, p. 169: "[H]ealth is the opposite pole from sickness, but the cure should be half-way between the two, and unless it has some affinity with sickness it will not lead to health." Also see bk. 8, chap. 3, sec. 7, p. 247: "[T]his indeed it is useful for us to believe and to hold firm and unshaken in our hearts, that the humility thanks to which God was born of a woman, and led through such abuse at the hands of mortal men to his death, is a medicine to heal the tumor of our pride and a high sacrament to break the chains of our sin." Christ is the *pharmakon*. In this light, consider the verses added by the early Church fathers to the Gospel of Mark (Mark 16:8–20), notably 16:18 ("They shall take up serpents; and if they drink any deadly thing, it shall not hurt them; they shall lay hands on the sick, and they shall recover.") Mortal poisons receive their antidote through the resurrected Christ. Cf. Jacques Derrida, "Plato's Pharmacy," in *Dissemination*, trans. Barbara Johnson (Chicago: University of Chicago Press, 1981), pp. 62–171.

64. Thomas Hobbes, *De cive*, in *Man and Citizen*, trans. Bernard Gert (Gloucester, Mass.: Humanities Press, 1978), preface, p. 103. See 1 Pet. 2:13–16 ("Submit yourselves to every ordinance of man for the Lord's sake. . . . For so is the will of God, that with well doing ye may put to silence the ignorance of foolish men. As free, and not using *your* liberty for a cloke of maliciousness, but as the servants of God").

creature."[65] The structure of *Leviathan*, it should be noted, recapitulates this insight: the politics of reason (parts 1 and 2) must be supplemented by the politics of obedience (parts 3 and 4).

The condition that best describes the absence of obedience is, of course, the state of nature. Not surprisingly, in that condition—which lurks forever under the surface of all forms of civil society,[66] but especially of democracy—human beings are prone to move in two different directions: on the one hand, the well-known restless struggle for goods of the world that ends only in death,[67] and on the other hand, the less well explored disposition to *brood* over the injury that results from humiliation, competition for honor, etc. Here is a recapitulation of the Augustinian self: the self is disposed toward the too-little of brooding or the too-much of never ending struggle—from which only a (mortal) God can save us![68]

Consider, first, the dangers of the human use of language:

> [Men use words] to grieve one another; for seeing nature hath armed living creatures, some with teeth, some with horns, and some with hands, to grieve an enemy, it is but an abuse of speech, to grieve him

65. Augustine, *City of God*, vol. 7, bk. 14, chap. 12, p. 379 (CG, p. 571).

66. See Hobbes, *Leviathan*, part 1, chap. 13, p. 101: "[B]ut though there had never been any time, wherein particular men were in a condition of war against one another, yet at all times [there is evidence of this] posture of war" (emphasis added). Just under the veneer of lawful civil society lies the brooding beast. This thought anticipates Nietzsche's later insight that "the criteria of prehistory [of the love of violence are] . . . in any case present in all ages or may always reappear" (*Genealogy of Morals*, second essay, sec. 9, p. 71). Both Hobbes and Nietzsche, I suggest, were addressing the discord that attends the same (Augustinian) soul: Hobbes attempted to orient it toward the sovereign; Nietzsche struggled to *reorient* it in the face of the death of the Sovereign (see *Thus Spoke Zarathustra*, prologue, p. 12). About Hobbes's efforts to quell pride by recurring to the theological pattern that is itself the root of the disease, consider Nietzsche's observation: "A legal order thought of as sovereign and universal, not as a means in a struggle between power-complexes but as a means of *preventing* all struggle in general . . . would be a principle *hostile to life*, an agent in the dissolution and destruction of man, an attempt to assassinate the future of man, a sign of weariness, a secret path to nothingness" (*Genealogy of Morals*, second essay, sec. 11, p. 76 [emphasis in original]).

67. See Hobbes, *Leviathan*, part 1, chap. 13, pp. 98–102. The equality of all produces diffidence, which in turn yields war. This, in turn, can only be arrested by an awesome sovereign to which all defer. Diffidence can only proceed from equality, however, if the desires of all are acute. In Hobbes's view, they are. There is, he suggests, "a restless desire for power in all men" (chap. 11, p. 80).

68. Hobbes, *Leviathan*, part 2, chap. 17, p. 132.

with the tongue, unless it be one whom we are obliged to govern; and then it is not to grieve, but to correct and amend.[69]

So dangerous is this "grieving with words," it would seem, that the sovereign alone is to have the privilege of using it. Augustine noted that "the human tongue is our daily furnace."[70] Hobbes would say no less. Human beings enjoy liberty only when they enjoy "an exemption from the constraint *and insolence* of their neighbor," he says.[71] "The art of words," it is, that troubles the peace.[72] Owing to the "privilege of absurdity"[73] that language bestows, human beings injure each other in ways no other animal can—hence the need for a science that disallows certain kinds of speech. To keep the soul from withdrawing into itself and brooding, language must be disarmed.

Aside from science of the sort Hobbes has in mind, the antidote to the immoderation of withdrawal due to injury is the polity Hobbes sets forth: right rulership under and by the Leviathan. One of his principal arguments against the democratic soul who would resist his proposal, in fact, pertains to this matter of verbal injury. Consider the following remark:

> To see his opinion, whom we scorn, preferred to ours; to have our wisdom undervalued before our own faces; by an uncertain trial of a little vain-glory, to undergo most certain enmities . . . to hate and to be hated, by reason of the disagreement of opinions; to lay open our secret councils and advices to all, to no purpose and without any benefit; to neglect the affairs of our own family: these, I say, are the grievances [of democracy].[74]

The soul, it would seem, opens itself up to perpetual injury within a democracy. (Nietzsche would agree!) The "temper of our souls" cannot

---

69. Hobbes, *Leviathan*, part 1, chap. 4, p. 34. See also Rousseau, *Second Discourse*, p. 149, where physical injury is of lesser danger than the injury wrought by words.

70. Augustine, *Confessions*, bk. 10, chap. 27, p. 214. See James 3:5–8.

71. Hobbes, *Behemoth*, dialogue 1, p. 59 (emphasis added).

72. Hobbes, *Leviathan*, part 2, chap. 17, p. 131; *De cive*, chap. 5, pp. 168–69. See also Holmes's introduction to *Behemoth*, pp. xxii–xxv.

73. Hobbes, *Leviathan*, part 1, chap. 5, p. 43.

74. Hobbes, *De cive*, chap. 10, pp. 229–30. See also Rousseau, *Second Discourse*, p. 156: "[C]onsuming ambition, the fervor to raise one's relative fortune less out of true need than in order to place oneself above others, inspires in all men a base inclination to harm each other, a *secret jealousy* all the more dangerous because, in order to strike its blow in greater safety, it often assumes the mask of benevolence: [here, there is] always the *hidden desire* to profit at the expense of others" (emphasis added).

withstand the injury from language when *all* are free to speak in the face-to-face of democratic politics. The "privilege of absurdity" requires an antidote—which the Leviathan can provide.

About that other aspect of the Augustinian self in Hobbes's thinking, about the tendency of the soul to throw itself into the world, we need only briefly rehearse here what is already well known. There is no *Summum Bonum* in which human beings may rest when the animations of desire reveal their insufficiency. There are, in fact, *only* desires—which never cease *despite* (or rather, *because of*) their insufficiency.

> The felicity of this life, consisteth not in the repose of the mind satisfied. For there is no such thing as *finis ultimus* . . . as is spoken of in the books of the old moral philosophers. Nor can a man any more live, whose desires are at an end, than he, whose sense and imagination are at a stand. *Felicity is a continual progress of the desire, from one object to another; the attaining of the former, being still but a way to the latter.*[75]

Desire knows no bounds.[76] Plato, too, knew this[77]—yet he never would have acceded to the view that only a mortal God could save us. Hobbes, however, bears little resemblance to Plato. The lack of a *finis ultimus*, the equality of all which conspires to assure that the objects of desire will be the same (and hence scarce), the pridefulness of a being that itself is without bounds—all these make life in the state of nature "solitary, poor, nasty, brutish, and short."[78]

75. Hobbes, *Leviathan*, part 1, chap. 11, p. 80 (emphasis added).

76. As Hobbes points out, in the state of nature (where desire is not limited by the awful One who stands over the many) "there be no propriety, no dominion, no *mine* and *thine* distinct; but only that to be every man's, that he can get: and for so long, as he can keep it" (*Leviathan*, part 1, chap. 13, p. 101 [emphasis in original]).

77. See Plato, *Republic*, bk. 2, 372d–373e. When the frugal city, the city not ruled by the appetites, allows the appetites to have their way, it expands outward, poses a threat to its neighbors, and requires a guardian class to protect it. Construed as a verity about the soul rather than the city, the implication is that only through the unboundedness of desire does the differentiation of the soul into its constituent elements occur. Cephalus's proclamation at the outset that "justice is granting each its due" (bk. 1, 331b) turns out to be true, but only when construed within the context of the fully differentiated soul—the articulation of which is accomplished in the unfolding of the argument of the *Republic*. Justice construed as "granting each its due" has not yet achieved its truth for the one who is Cephalus—mere "head" without desire!

78. Hobbes, *Leviathan*, part 1, chap. 13, p. 100. Theologically, the state of nature is akin to the desert of the soul in which the Israelites are condemned to dwell without a king. See Judg. 21:25 ("In those days there was no king in Israel: every man did *that which was* right in his own eyes").

Entering into a covenant with others upon the realization that without a verbal assent to the sovereign there can be only death,[79] however, atones for the immoderations human beings are, without constraint, prone to exhibit. By obeying the powerful one, whose injunctions human beings would not *naturally* wish to obey (think here of the hiding of Adam and Eve from God),[80] conditions under which boundaries are not violated are established and the tendency to fall into the immoderations of brooding and restiveness is countered. Now citizens are protected from the consequences of language misused and desire ungoverned. Now, through assent and obedience, there can be peace.

On Hobbes's view, human beings naturally want to show themselves off with words and grant their desires free reign—hence their ostensible love of democracy and of liberty. Yet what, Hobbes asks, does this love countenance? What does the liberty that rejects obedience really amount to? In Augustinian terms the love of democratic liberty is akin to the love of the City of Man. For here, in this City, human self-glorification succumbs to temptations that promise freedom and power even while they yield misery. When the love of the City of Man rules, then *all* persons aspire to be Ixion.[81] As Tocqueville would later point out:

79. The valence of assent in Hobbes must be understood as a religious articulation comprehensible only in the context of the inadequacy of human will in the face of a world that confronts the soul with the prospect of death (in the state of nature). The social contract entered into by virtue of assent reiterates the proclamation of rebirth of the natural man (Adam) unto the body of Christ; once reborn through a covenant, there is stability and genuine human health. Assent here is *not* the voicing of a "preference" of an "autonomous individual."

80. Gen 3:10. By nature Adam and Eve would wish to continue to hide, yet they know that they are not simply natural and on their own. They are thrown into nature, to be sure; yet they recognize that the Ground of their being is not the world into which they are thrown. The Old Testament again and again coveys the consequences of not recognizing the deeper Ground, of the lapse from God; and again and again the consequence is made clear: "death"—the respite from which is the renewal of the covenant with the awful One who stands over all.

81. Ixion, the myth goes, was invited by Jupiter to a banquet, at which he fell in love with Juno. Attempting to embrace her, he clasped a cloud, from whence the centaurs, in Hobbes's words, "a fierce, fighting, and unquiet generation [proceeded]" (*De cive*, preface, p. 98). In Hobbes's interpretation of the myth, Ixion represents the private man who was invited into the court of politics to consider matters of Justice. He fell in love, not with Justice but with his wife and sister instead; and, embracing Justice's shadow thus, gave birth to "those hermaphrodite opinions of moral philosophers, partly right and comely, partly brutal and wild; the causes of all contention and bloodshed" (p. 98). The myth of Ixion suggests to Hobbes that the private person was incapable of embracing

It is true that American courtiers never say "Sire" or "Your Majesty," as if the difference mattered; but they are constantly talking of their master's natural brilliance . . . they do not give him their wives or their daughters hoping that he will raise them to the rank of his mistress, but they do sacrifice their opinions to him *and so prostitute themselves.*[82]

Tocqueville, to be sure, thought this not an insurmountable objection to democracy. Yet the point here is that while democracy promises liberty, for a being constituted in such a way that it must obey, such promises only "masquerade as fullness," as Augustine would say.[83] All was lost for the Jews, Hobbes reminds us, when the people of Israel rejected God and instituted a succession of kings "to judge [them] like all other nations."[84] What appears to be the ground of true freedom turns out to be the ground of abiding servitude. The liberty that is loved carries with it the burden of envy, hatred, brooding, restiveness, instability, and sorrow—in secret, of course. The ebullient celebration of liberty is attended by that brooding aspect which is held in reserve.[85] To forestall

---

justice itself; that its shadow was the most that could be possessed, the consequence of which was that "none but those to whom the supreme hath committed to the interpretation of his laws [should deliberate over such matters]" (p. 98).

82. Tocqueville, *Democracy in America*, vol. 1, part 2, chap. 7, pp. 258–59 (emphasis added).

83. The phrase comes from the Pine-Coffin translation of Augustine's *Confessions* (bk. 2, chap. 6, p. 50). The entirety of bk. 2, chap. 6 (in the Chadwick translation, pp. 30–32) illustrates the way in which human beings search for the right thing, but look in the wrong *place.*

84. Hobbes, *Leviathan*, part 3, chap. 40, p. 348. Hobbes's citation, quoted in part, is from 1 Sam. 3:5. The covenant ends with the election of Saul (see chap. 41, p. 354). The difference between Hobbes and Augustine is nowhere made more clear than on their readings of Saul. See Augustine, *City of God*, vol. 8, bk. 17, chap. 7, p. 44 (*CG*, p. 731): "[The Greek (rather than Latin) version of 1 Samuel 15:23–28 reads]: 'The Lord has rent the kingdom from Israel from thy hand,—the expression 'from Israel' being equivalent to 'from thy hand.' In this way, Samuel stood figuratively for the people of Israel which was to lose he kingdom when our Lord Jesus Christ would come to reign—spiritually, not carnally—in the New Testament." Hobbes insisted that the covenant lost with Saul was renewed through Christ; Augustine insisted that Christ brought about a *new,* spiritual, kingdom.

85. Plato, too, seems to have understood that the soul that glories in the City of Man has its hiding places where alone its misery can be seen. "Let us not be dazzled by fixing our eyes on that one man, the tyrant, or a few of his court," he says, "but let us enter into and survey the entire city, as is right, and declare our opinion only after we have so dived to its uttermost recesses and contemplated its life as a whole" (*Republic*, bk. 9, 576d–e [emphasis added]).

Ixion's euphoria (and secret sorrow), better it is that he be kept away from Jupiter's banquet. Better that he obey than yield to the liberty that enslaves him. Rightful obedience is the only palliative for the soul that would go astray in the City of Man. The love of *merely* human liberty conceals within itself a secret that predisposes the soul toward misery, if not violence. This must be averted—and only obedience can do this.

It is possible, of course, to see in this repudiation of the liberty in a democracy a purely political motive: Hobbes simply wished to defend monarchy against democracy. Obedience, he is often inferred to have concluded, was more precious than liberty, notwithstanding his ostensible argument that "in the act of our *submission*, consisteth both our *obligation*, and our *liberty*." [86] This latter claim is not, however, simply a piece of political rhetoric. It may just as easily be viewed as an integral part of his entire argument about how pride may be attenuated. As with many other Christian thinkers, human beings are so corrupted by pride that *any* effort on their part to will their own salvation—here broadly conceived to include salvation from the death that awaits them in the state of nature—cannot succeed. Prideful creatures acting in freedom always succumb to greater errancy. Only by resisting their pridefulness, by *obeying* the One Sovereign and not believing in the sufficiency of their own efforts, can their undertakings be fruitful. Obedience is the precondition of *genuine* human liberty.

This is, as I have said, a very old thought, not one peculiar to Hobbes's purported defense of absolute government. It is to be found, for example, in the Old Testament in the narrative of Sarah's barren womb.[87] Abraham and Sarah, by themselves, could not bring forth God's chosen people. Their efforts would have only come to naught without the intervention of God. But Abraham *obeys* God's commands, and this obedience is the precondition of the beneficence that follows.

In Augustine, too, as we have seen, obedience is crucial as well. Deference before the Sovereign (God) arrests the pridefulness of human beings who would think their own efforts sufficient. As with Hobbes, acting in accordance with one's own will can result only in "death." Obeying the sovereign is the only way for humankind to avoid calamity.

During the Reformation, Hobbes was not alone in taking this view. Consider, for example, Luther's insistence that obedience to the commandments of God is the precondition for the attainment of true righ-

86. Hobbes, *Leviathan*, part 2, chap. 21, p. 163 (emphasis in original). While the terms of the debate are somewhat different in Rousseau, he, too, would agree. See Rousseau, *Emile*, bk. 5, p. 461: "[E]ach man who obeys the sovereign obeys only himself, and . . . one is more free under the social pact than in the state of nature."

87. Gen. 16:1.

teousness *and freedom* under Christ.[88] His sentiment, too, comports with Hobbes's position about the need for obedience to the sovereign. No less can be said of Calvin:

> For, as consulting our self-interest is the pestilence that most effectively leads to our destruction, so the sole haven of salvation is to be wise in nothing and to will nothing through ourselves but to follow the leading of the Lord alone.[89]

The point here is that within Reformation Christianity there are good *religious reasons* for asserting that obedience to the sovereign is the only way to establish true freedom, and that the liberty that withdraws itself from under the sovereign, that claims itself sufficient unto itself, is a species of pridefulness that cannot be countenanced. Without obedience, errancy is inevitable; the prideful longing for liberty can lead only to death unless it is linked to obedience.[90]

Hobbes, I suggest, is not simply being rhetorical when he subsumes liberty to obedience; he is voicing an axiom of the Reformation—only here, because he understands Christianity *not* to have brought about a spiritual kingdom that stands *next to* the City of Man, the insight that other Reformers applied only to the Christian's relationship to God the Son here applies to the citizen's relationship to the sovereign, who, for Hobbes, is the only rightful *personator* of God.[91]

Notwithstanding the peculiarities of Hobbes's formulation as it has

88. See, for example, Martin Luther, "Freedom of a Christian," 31:333–77. The paradox of Christianity, for Luther, can be summed up in the observation: "[A] Christian is a perfectly free lord of all, subject to none. A Christian is a perfectly dutiful servant to all" (31:343). That is, only through obedience can there be freedom; only through the (Jewish) Law can there be (Christian) freedom.

89. Calvin, *Institutes of Christian Religion*, vol. 1, bk. 3, chap. 7, sec. 1, p. 690.

90. See F. C. Hood, *The Divine Politics of Thomas Hobbes* (Oxford: Clarendon Press, 1964), pp. 174–75: "[M]an's mistaken confidence in his own ability to judge between good and evil is that original sin of pride, in which all men participate. In disobeying his sovereign, the subject repeats the sin of Adam, for he disobeys God." Completely off the mark is Strauss, for whom "the whole scheme suggested by Hobbes [is made possible by] the disenchantment of the world, by the diffusion of scientific knowledge, or by popular enlightenment." Strauss continues, "Hobbes's is the first doctrine that necessarily and unmistakably points to a thoroughly 'enlightened,' that is, a-religious or atheistic society as the solution of the social or political problem" (Leo Strauss, *Natural Right and History* [Chicago: University of Chicago Press, 1953], p. 198).

91. See *Leviathan*, part 1, chap. 12, p. 127. Unlike Augustine, Hobbes does not speak of the Trinity. *Trinity* is a word without a referent (chap. 8, p. 68). Rather, he speaks of the personations of God.

been traced out here, however, the crucial claim found already in Augustine remains: only by turning away from the seeming self-sufficiency of human liberty—which carries in its wake the immoderations of self-enclosure and restiveness—can there be a measure of human happiness. Only by deferring to the awful One can human life be absolved of its unrelenting oscillation.

3. ROUSSEAU AND THE ERRANCY FROM NATURE

The prima facie case for the affinity between Augustine and Rousseau is not immediately obvious. They both write *Confessions*, it is true; but not far into Rousseau's version the suspicion dawns that he is contriving to supersede Augustine's chronicle of the soul, to supplant a view according to which human beings are born corrupt by virtue of Adam's stain, with one that implores that they are naturally good, though *corruptible.* "I am really the innocent one," is the herald throughout. Where Augustine confesses to God his errancy from God, Rousseau avows to us his own natural goodness and the outrages he has endured in the cauldron of a corrupt society. An aspect of the contemporary mind is already here in place: society, not the soul, must be reoriented in order that human beings may live with whatever measure of mortal happiness they are due. Augustine, of course, would never have acceded to this opinion. We must endure suffering in patience and in faith, and may be made happy in mortal measure by a right relationship to God.[92] To seek solace, joy, or repose in any other place—it does not matter how earnestly—is to countenance solipsism.

Along this line of inquiry the contrast between Augustine and Rousseau is stark. The authentic self for whom Rousseau longs may be

92. See Augustine, *City of God*, vol. 6, bk. 4, chap. 25, p. 225 (*CG*, p. 166): "[H]uman weakness has become aware that only a god has the power to bestow felicity." See also bk. 5, preface, p. 241 (*CG*, p. 179). Locke, in his Censor's Valedictory Speech of 1664, concurs: "[P]hilosophy holds out many riches, but they all are mere words rather than the property of men. Those pointed and shrewd discourses concerning the highest good do not heal human misfortunes any more than fist and sword cure wounds. . . . Philosophers in their search for happiness have not accomplished more than to tell us that it cannot be found" ("Can Anyone by Nature Be Happy in This Life? No," in *Essays on the Law of Nature*, ed. W. von Leydon [Oxford: Clarendon Press, 1954], pp. 221–23). Human effort alone cannot bring happiness. In his view, "[Prior to Christianity, it was] too hard a task for unassisted reason, to establish morality, in all its parts, upon its true foundation; with a clear and convincing light" (*The Reasonableness of Christianity*, ed. George W. Ewing [Washington: Regnery Gateway, 1965], sec. 241, p. 170). Christianity dispelled the darkness that philosophy alone could not.

deeper than the self that is exhibited amid the cloud of social conformity; for Augustine, however, the so-called *deeper* self is no less of
a shadowy image than the unauthentic self. Without God, the self
(whether socially constituted and deformed, or purportedly authentic
and unhampered by a stain of its own making) lacks a ground. All
searching for the self must be directed toward God. Without that, there
can be only "hell"—unauthentic or otherwise. About this, the New
Testament is unequivocal, though evidence from the Old Testament,
too, would not be difficult to adduce:

> Enter ye in at the strait gate: for wide *is* the gate, and wide *is* the way,
> that leadeth to destruction, and many there will be that go in
> thereat. [93]

Yet the matter is complicated and cannot be left to rest with these remarks. Perhaps most to the point, Rousseau, like Augustine, would have
it that the soul's errancy is the occasion of its disease in "the world," and
that the extent to which we turn away from the Source marks the extent
to which we are liable to fall easily into tyranny.

This is, to be sure, is an insight of ancient pedigree, and not original
with Augustine. Book 8 of Plato's *Republic*, for example, traces the decline of the just city and the soul as it falls of its own gravity into tyranny. [94] There, what all souls harbor [95] that are not oriented (as if by

---

93. Matt. 7:13. See also Calvin, *Institutes of Christian Religion*, vol. 1, bk. 1,
chap. 4, sec. 1, p. 47–48: "[V]anity joined with pride can be detected in the fact
that, in seeking God, miserable men do not rise above themselves as they
should, but measure him by the yardstick of their own carnal stupidity, and
neglect sound investigation; thus out of curiosity they fly off into empty speculations. They do not therefore apprehend God as he offers himself, but imagine
him as they have fashioned him in their own presumption. When this gulf
opens, in whatever direction they move their feet, they cannot but plunge head-
long into ruin. Indeed, whatever they afterward attempt by way of worship or
service to God, they cannot bring as tribute to him, *for they are worshiping not
God, but a figment and a dream of their own heart*" (emphasis added). Also see
Hegel's critique of the romantic impulse in the *Phenomenology*, preface, sec. 10:
"[W]hen this non-conceptual, substantial knowledge professes to have sunk the
idiosyncrasy of the self in essential being, and philosophize in a true and holy
manner, it hides the truth from itself: by spurning measure and definition, instead of being devoted to God, it merely gives itself free rein both to the contingency of the content within, and to its own caprice. . . . [What] they bring to
birth in their sleep [are] nothing but dreams."

94. Plato, *Republic*, bk. 8, 543b–569c.

95. What the soul harbors is first alluded to by Plato in the *Republic*, bk. 5,
449a. The entirety of book 8 is about the unconcealment of what is harbored; it
ends with "tyranny *open* and avowed" (569b [emphasis added]).

Grace)[96] toward the Good is incrementally unconcealed until the tyrant within is revealed. Without the *love* of the Source, of the good, human beings become enthralled by the charms of the world; and in doing so they move away from the True Homeland of the soul and toward the unconcealment of the beast within. (What Freud purported to have discovered about the wellsprings of the id, Plato had already long before articulated in the *Republic*.)[97] Without a knowledge of the good, the cause of all that is, as well as of our ethical and moral judgments, human beings drift about aimlessly in a shadow world tempted by the lure of injustice which can never fulfill—and finally suffer the awful consequences of tyranny unconcealed. What profit can there be, Plato asks,

> in possessing everything except that which is good, or in understanding all things else apart from the good while understanding and knowing nothing that is fair and good?[98]

Without the love of the good there can be no real happiness; the pursuit of illusory happiness ends, inexorably, in the misery of tyranny—with all its charms.

Augustine, as I have said, grasps this insight, though through biblical eyes. Already in the preface to the book 1 of *City of God*, for example, there is the paradoxical relationship between the City of God and the City of Man,

96. Plato's allusions to divine gifts are too numerous to ignore (see *Republic*, bk. 4, 425e, 443b–c; bk. 6, 492a, 492e, 496c, 499b; bk. 8, 558b; bk. 9, 592a). Even the dialectic, that enterprise in which the philosopher must be engaged in order to come unto a vision of the Good, is a gift of the gods (see Plato, *Philebus*, trans. R. Hackforth, in *Collected Dialogues of Plato*, 16c). Reason, it would seem, is not without divine support. In Christian theology the gift comes only through God the Son. See Acts 2:38 ("Repent, and be baptized every one of you in the name of Jesus Christ for the remission of sins, and you shall receive the gift of the Holy Spirit").

97. See Plato, *Republic*, bk. 9, 571c–d.

98. Plato, *Republic*, bk. 6, 505b. See also Augustine, *City of God*, vol. 7, bk. 8, chaps. 8–11, pp. 35–42 (*CG*, pp. 309–15). Notwithstanding their differences, both Plato and Augustine can be understood as twice-born souls. See William James, *The Varieties of Religious Experience* (New York: Vintage Books, 1990), lecture 8, p. 155: "[For the twice-born soul] the world is a double-storied mystery. Peace cannot be reached by the simple addition of pluses and elimination of minuses from life. Natural good is not simply insufficient in amount and transient, there lurks a falsity in its very being. . . . It keeps us from our real good [and] renunciation and despair of it are our first step in the direction of the truth."

that city which lusts to dominate the world and which, though nations bend to its yoke, *is itself dominated by its passion for dominion.*[99]

The City of God is the pristine city; the City of Man—and this is the crucial psychological insight that Plato perhaps only dimly anticipated—oscillates back and forth between mastery of the world and servitude.[100] Each is an aspect of a complex that *invariably* emerges provided the soul's allegiance is not toward the City of God. To transpose Plato's idiom slightly, not grasping the transcendent unity of all things condemns us to wander amid the realm where those things are alternatively "this" then "that."[101] To put it otherwise, the condition to which all who dwell in the cave aspire (though mostly in secret)—to be a tyrant, a ruler over all—turns out to be the supreme form of enslavement.[102] This way of thinking is not at all foreign to Rousseau. For him, of course, nature (not God or the Good) is the Source; this insight about the final consequence of errancy, its temptation and vacuity, is, however, deeply embedded in Rousseau's thinking.

I will consider the matter of errancy and tyranny in due course. First,

99. Augustine, *City of God*, vol. 6, bk. 1, preface, p. 18 (emphasis added) [*CG*, p. 5].

100. Consider Augustine, *City of God*, vol. 6, bk. 5, chap. 19, pp. 287–88: "[Nero] was so cruel, that only those who knew him could believe he had any tenderness in him." The Bettenson translation is more forthright: "[S]uch was [Nero's] cruelty that no one would have suspected anything effeminate in his nature, if one had not known about it" (*CG*, p. 213). I do not explore the sexual dimensions of the relationship between mastery and servitude that are intimated by Augustine's comment here. Shortly I will consider Nietzsche's claim that the *oscillations* of the soul are a consequence of the spiritualization of man that biblical religion occasions. Plato—a preamble to the Christian soul (*Genealogy of Morals*, third essay, sec. 24, p. 152)—intimates this psychological profile, but it remained for the "priests" of Judea to fully develop it. See also Friedrich Nietzsche, *Beyond Good and Evil*, trans. Walter Kaufman (New York: Random House, 1966), preface, p. 3: "Christianity is Platonism for 'the people.' "

101. Plato, *Republic*, bk. 9, 583b–587a. At that place Plato offers a third argument for the superiority of justice: only the just soul is able to distinguish relative from absolute pleasures. Not grasping the transcendent Ground of pleasure, the soul will first be allured by the appearance of relative pleasures and then, in time, become disillusioned with them. There is in this understanding the *possibility* of throwing oneself into the world in pursuit of a pleasure and then withdrawing from the world amid the realization of its emptiness, yet Plato does not move in this direction. As I have already intimated, Nietzsche may have been correct in suggesting that the *spiritualization* of human life drives the soul into the pattern of immoderate oscillation I have been considering here.

102. Plato, *Republic*, bk. 9, 579d–e.

however, something must be said about the inevitable oscillations between self-enclosed inwardness and restive outwardness that such errancy occasions. Consider, in this light, the early lessons in *Emile*.

A glance at the frontispieces of books 1, 2, and 3, respectively, of
Emile serves to reveal the trajectory of Rousseau's thinking as a whole:
for children to grow into adults capable of using their faculties well
they must be immersed initially into nature, then develop their bodies
in such a way that nascent reason does not awaken, and only later
'approach the temple' of knowledge—as the frontispiece to book 3
suggests.

What Rousseau seems most concerned to arrest is the independent
development of the higher faculties without the experiential referents
that practice alone can provide. Should this occur, children sound like
adults, to be sure; but they overstep their true capacities. No longer
subject to nature's lessons, they graduate unprepared into the moral
world of adulthood, and so suffer from what might be called bad infinity.

This has a familiar pedigree. Hobbes, too, attempted to foreclose the
possibility of thought overstepping its capacities; he, however, sought
redress through an adequate scientific method rather than through education of a certain sort. Words tend to go astray; language carries with it
"the privilege of absurdity."[103] With this Rousseau would agree. Rousseau would have insisted, however, that the scientific enterprise Hobbes
propounds delivers its antidote too late: the disease has already fully run
its course by the time of adulthood and university education.[104] (For that
reason, in Rousseau's view, science must fall only within the purview of
the *uncorrupted ones* who are insularly ensconced in "famed societies"—
hence the argument of the *First Discourse*.)

The theology ought to be clear here as well. Rousseau's thinking recapitulates one of the fundamental axioms of Reformation thinking,
namely, that human beings must be "Jews" before they can be "Christians."[105] The childhood of the soul must precede the adulthood of the

103. Hobbes, *Leviathan*, part 1, chap. 5, p. 43.

104. See Hobbes, *Behemoth*, dialogue 1, p. 58: "[T]he core of the
rebellion . . . [is in] the Universities." See also Hobbes, *Leviathan*, Review and
Conclusion, pp. 510–11.

105. Much of the tension in Luther's thought, for example, derives from his
view that, in effect, Christians—he has in mind the Roman Church—are still
"Jews," who search for salvation through the active righteousness of works
rather than the passive righteousness of faith. Like John the Baptist in Matthew
3:1, Luther thought himself to be a "preach[er] in the wilderness of Judea."
This self-understanding in the German world that would call the soul beyond
its native "Jewishness" is not unique to Luther. Hegel understands Kant in this
way in his "The Spirit of Christianity and Its Fate"; Nietzsche charges us all of

soul.[106] If it doesn't, then all is lost. Rousseau's articulation, to be sure, is clearly different in content, but the form is identical. The child must first be subject to the necessity of *things* before coming unto the level of moral development. Theologically, nature cannot comprehend spirit; but to come unto spirit, nature must be passed through—Rousseau's *Emile* and Hegel's *Phenomenology* articulate the much the same understanding.[107]

> Keep the child in dependence only on things. You will have followed the order of nature in the progress of his education. Never present to his undiscriminating will anything but physical obstacles.[108]

What happens, however, when this education that relies upon, yet supplements, nature is abandoned? More precisely, how does this errancy

---

this in the *Genealogy of Morals*; and Heidegger wonders about the soul's propensity to be caught up in the everyday world of "works" in *Being and Time*, and about the authenticity made possible by his equivalent of Luther's *passive* righteousness!

106. Following Luther's lead, Hegel would further develop this distinction and claim that even the person of faith is still a child if grounded on the authority of Christ's miracles. Unless faith is given oneself by oneself, one is as a slave is to a lord: faith based on the authority of God has not yet attained its truth. In Hegel's words, "[Human nature] is too dignified to be placed at this level of nonage where it would always need a guardian and could never enter its status of manhood" ("The Positivity of Christian Religion," in *Early Theological Writings*, ed. Richard Kroner [Philadelphia: University of Pennsylvania Press. 1971], part 1, sec. 9, p. 80, emphasis added). Compare this to the master-slave dialectic of the *Phenomenology*, sec. 194, p. 117: "[S]ervitude has the lord for its essential reality; . . . its whole being has been seized with dread; for it has experienced the fear of death, the absolute Lord. In that experience it has been quite *unmanned*" (emphasis added). In both its theological and philosophical expression the movement toward manhood is a movement beyond *fear* (by the Jews/the slave) of a Lord. This step is a necessary one, in much the same way as for Luther the Christian must pass through the Old Law (the Jews) in order to attain Christian freedom. The Old Law portends but does not disclose the truth of the New Testament. The argument of Rousseau's *Emile* is analogous: the soul must pass through childhood, must be a child, *before* it is possible to be an adult—to unite with Sophie. Finally, with Freud (*Civilization and Its Discontents*, ed. and trans. James Strachey (New York: W. W. Norton, 1989), chap. 2, p. 22, passim), there is a reluctant resignation to the fact that most human beings will be unable to face reality and so remain in *perpetual* childhood. Here is monotheistic religion!

107. While Bloom would not have put it this way, he suggests in his introduction to *Emile* that it is "a *Phenomenology of Mind* posing as Dr. Spock" (p. 3).

108. Rousseau, *Emile*, bk. 2, p. 85.

that *we bequeath*[109] to our children manifest itself? Consider the baby's cry, that first occasion for errancy from nature.

> A child cries at birth. . . . At one time we bustle about, we caress him in order to pacify him; at another, we threaten him, we strike him in order to make him keep quiet. Either we do what pleases him, or we exact from him what pleases us. . . . Thus his first ideas of are those of *domination and servitude.* Before knowing how to speak, he commands; before being able to act, he obeys. . . . It is thus that we fill up his young heart at the outset with the passions which we later impute to nature and that, after taken efforts to make him wicked, we complain about making him so.[110]

This is, I suggest, a trenchant criticism of both Augustine and Hobbes. Where Augustine thought the baby's cry to be evidence of original sin,[111] Rousseau retorts that "sin" is a repercussion of the betrayal of our charge to our children; where Hobbes thought human beings to be naturally prideful, Rousseau responds that they are, indeed, prideful only after we have already led them astray. And to both Augustine and Hobbes, Rousseau rejoins: no mere theologico-political solution will do. Because the problem is prelinguistic, covenantal assent in any form—whether in the blood and body of the New Covenant (Augustine) or in the deferential obedience to the Leviathan that forestalls bloodletting and further violations of the body (Hobbes)—is a hopelessly superficial antidote!

I do not intend to assess the adequacy of Rousseau's provocation against much of the edifice that Augustine and Hobbes build. Instead, I wish to move in a different direction and suggest here that the manifestation of human errancy, for Rousseau, looks remarkably like the portrait Augustine and Hobbes offer. The cause may be different, but the attributes the psyche evinces once errancy has befallen it are virtually

---

109. See Rousseau, *Emile,* bk. 2, p. 86: "[W]hen children's wills are not spoiled *by our fault,* children want nothing uselessly" (emphasis added).

110. Rousseau, *Emile,* bk. 1, p. 48 (emphasis added).

111. See Augustine, *Confessions,* bk. 1, chap. 6, p. 7: "[As an infant I] wanted to manifest my wishes to those who could fulfill them as I could not. For my desires were internal; adults were external to me and had no means of entering into my soul. So I threw my limbs about and uttered sounds, signs resembling my wishes. . . . When I did not get my way, either because I was not understood or lest it be harmful to me, I used to be indignant with my seniors for their disobedience, and with free people who were not slaves to my interests; and I would revenge myself upon them by weeping." Cf. Freud, *Civilization and Its Discontents,* chap. 1, p. 14. There, the cry gives birth only to the separation of the ego and the external world.

the same. For my purpose here, *what* relation the soul has broken off is less important than *how* it subsequently acts.

For Rousseau (like Augustine and Hobbes), human life too often is involved in the onerous oscillation back and forth between dominion and servitude, between feeling no constraint whatsoever and feeling utterly impotent before a hostile world.

> If these ideas of dominion and tyranny make them miserable already in their childhood, what will it be when they grow up and their relations with men begin to extend and multiply? Accustomed to seeing everything give way before them, what a surprise on entering into the world to feel everything resists them and to find themselves crushed by the weight of the universe they thought they moved to their pleasure! . . . Not omnipotent, they believe they are impotent.[112]

As if this perennial theme of *Emile* were not enough to confirm the affinity, consider also the related matter of the immoderations to which the soul is prone if inattentive to the Source (in Rousseau's idiom, to nature), and the *necessary* relationship between each immoderate moment when the subversion (of nature) occurs.

> True satisfaction is neither gay nor wild. . . . A truly happy man hardly speaks and hardly laughs. He draws, so to speak, the happiness around his heart. Boisterous games and turbulent joy veil disgust and boredom. But *melancholy is the friend of delight.*[113]

This observation bears pondering for a moment. A "delight" in the world—with the trappings of society, of science, of the whole expansive domain filled out by human effort—bears with it a melancholy that cannot be purged. Bemused by the world, for example, the (bourgeois) soul scoffs at bread and water—nature's offering[114]—in preferment of more elegant fare.[115] Indeed these are seen as the wages of dereliction from civil society, of crime against it. Yet evermore elegant fare, understood more broadly now to include "progress" in all its aspects, belies its su-

---

112. Rousseau, *Emile*, bk. 2, p. 88. If they had been subjected to *things* right from the beginning, subsequently they would neither feel wholly immune from the world or wholly subject to it. The two go together. See also bk. 1, p. 66: "[T]he first tears of children are prayers. If one is not careful, they soon become orders. . . . [By these are] subsequently born the idea of empire and domination."

113. Rousseau, *Emile*, bk. 4, p. 229 (emphasis added).

114. Rousseau, *Emile*, bk. 2, p. 151.

115. Rousseau, *Second Discourse*, pp. 109–10. Hobbes has his equivalent claim. The soul that in its errancy wishes for democracy "has a continual torment of thirst, and yet abhorreth water" (*Leviathan*, part 2, chap. 29, p. 242).

periority over the simplicity of nature, the evidence of which is the intruding melancholy it wishes to mask.

The soul *repulsed* by bread and water, by the simplicity of nature, however, fails to see this necessary relationship between delight and melancholy and so unwittingly revels in the world with alacrity in proportion to the melancholy it would wish to keep at bay. The relationship between the two is unseen, yet the desire for more elegant fare is animated by the occasionally obtruding abyss of melancholy that seems unrelated. Appearances to the contrary, human beings wholly involved in society and oblivious to nature are not merely rational maximizers; in conjunction, they are (always unsuccessful) melancholy averters who hold their anguished heart in reserve! Again, think of Kierkegaard—or, more conventionally, of the Smith of *The Wealth of Nations*.[116]

We are here beginning to consider how the love of the world, if I may use this shorthand, conceals within itself a secret that pilots the soul unwittingly toward woe. The *First Discourse*, as I have intimated, offers precisely this view. Enlightenment, that promise to fill up the darkness and fill out the world, turns out to be the occasion, not of fullness, but rather of *loss*. The happy self-confidence of the soul enamored of light, of articulation in all its various guises, is confronted with the vacuity that is Enlightenment's hidden secret. Augustine's succinct phrase, "[A]bundance masquerades as fullness,"[117] somewhat transposed, directs us to what Rousseau wishes to convey.

> Since learned men have begun to appear among us, [Seneca tells us], good men have disappeared. Until then, the Romans had been content to practice virtue; all was lost when they began to study it.[118]

116. The division of labor, the development of markets, the threat of scarcity that harnesses industry and enterprise: these fill out the world yet yield a melancholy that will now and again obtrude in the midst of every success. It is worth pondering whether the business cycle can at all be illuminated by this insight about the necessary relationship between melancholy and delight. In Tocqueville's words: "I believe that the recurrence of these industrial crises is an endemic disease among all democratic nations in our day. It can be made less dangerous, but not cured, for it is not due to accident but to *the essential temperament* of these peoples" (*Democracy in America*, vol. 2, part 2, chap. 19, p. 554 [emphasis added]).

117. Augustine, *Confessions*, Pine-Coffin trans., bk. 2, chap. 6, p. 50. Unlike Rousseau, for whom fullness is to be found in the soul who *is* much rather than *has* much, for Augustine, only God is the fullness for which we seek. Rousseau's musings would erroneously locate plenitude in an historical place rather than outside of time altogether.

118. Rousseau, *First Discourse*, p. 45. Smith, on the other hand, argues that the Romans were a virtuous people because students could demand of their

Rome here represents a kind of pivot point of history, where substance gave way to superfluity. Modern society (or rather what followed early Roman society) privileges the brilliant superfluities it can produce but fails to grasp that all great things move in silence.[119] The proclamation of greatness already betrays what has been lost. When it is said, it is already dead.

> [When] living conveniences multiply, arts are perfected and luxury spreads, true courage is enervated, military virtues disappear, and this too is the work of the sciences and of all those arts which are exercised in the shade of the study.[120]

And further on,

> The Romans admitted that military virtue died out among them to the degree that they became connoisseurs of painting, engravings, jeweled vessels, and began to cultivate the fine arts.[121]

Historical examples could be multiplied, and not just about Rome. The *actual events* of history, however, are not really at issue.[122] The crucial proposition throughout is that the more we are charmed by what appears to be substantive, the more what is really substantial withdraws from us.

---

teachers that they teach virtue. "The demand for instruction produced," he says, "what it always produces, the talent for giving it; and the emulation which an unrestrained competition never fails to excite, appears to have brought that talent to a very high degree of perfection" (*The Wealth of Nations*, vol. 2, bk. 5, chap. 1, p. 300). All was lost, not when they began to study virtue, but when teachers were no longer accountable to the student's demands, as they would have been if education, like other commodities, had been subject to the market.

119. See Nietzsche, *Thus Spoke Zarathustra*, second part, p. 146: "[I]t is the stillest words that bring on the storm. Thoughts that come on doves' feet guide the world."

120. Rousseau, *First Discourse*, p. 54

121. Rousseau, *First Discourse*, p. 55. See also Plato, *Phaedrus*, trans. R. Hackforth, in *Collected Dialogues of Plato*, 275a-b: "[Writing offers only a] semblance, for by telling [human beings] of many things without teaching them you will make them seem to know much, while for the most part they know nothing, and as men filled, not with wisdom, but with the conceit of wisdom, they will be a burden to their fellows."

122. See Rousseau, *Emile*, bk. 2, p. 156 (note): "[C]ritical erudition absorbs everything, as if it were important whether a fact were true, provided that a useful teaching can be drawn from it. Sensible men ought to regard history as *a tissue of fables* whose moral is very appropriate to the human heart" (emphasis added). The truth can be found in the heart, not in the realm of historical facts.

> Precisely what, then, is at issue [here]? To know whether it is more
> important for Empires to be *brilliant and transitory or virtuous and
> durable*. [123]

The inner logic of the errant soul, it would seem, is to be drawn toward
an Enlightenment that fills out the world, and be debilitated by the
ostensible benefits in purveys.

Then there is the matter of envy. The argument requires scant re-
hearsal. Whether in *Emile*, or in either of the *Discourses*, errancy involves
casting one's gaze toward the other.

In the state of nature, recall, the other, though *there*, is not yet *for* the
natural human being in the way that he or she is for the civilized. Not
having entered into a certain kind of relationship with an other, there is
no possibility of enslaving or being enslaved. Dominion and servitude
(which Augustine thought to be evidence of *sin*) are unknown to the
savage. [124] The savage is still innocent and without stain:

> It is impossible to enslave a man without first putting him in the po-
> sition of being unable to do without another; a situation which, as it
> did not exist in the state of nature, leaves each man there free of the
> yoke, and renders vain the law of the stronger. [125]

Because the self in *this* epoch cannot do without the other, cannot
conceive of itself except in relation to an other, Rousseau (like Augustine and Hobbes) is suspicious about the claim that human beings can
use their reason well. What masquerades as reason, what looks like a
love of the world, of science, turns out to be little more than the "passion to gain distinction." [126] Beneath the appearance of a healthy motive
lies a more portentous one.

For that reason, if there is to be science and the arts at all, a *boundary*
must be placed between those whose virtue makes them immune from
this passion and those without the antidote: hence, the famed societies
about which Rousseau speaks at the close of the *First Discourse*. [127]
Where Hobbes thought it necessary to cordon off sovereignty from the
people but encourage them to develop their capacity for science, for
reason toward circumscribed ends; Rousseau thought it necessary to cordon off science from the people but encourage them to invest sover-

123. Rousseau, *First Discourse*, p. 52 (emphasis added).

124. Rousseau, *Second Discourse*, p. 139.

125. Rousseau, *Second Discourse*, p. 140. See p. 151 for the same thought. See
also p. 173: "[I]t is . . . difficult to reduce to obedience one who does not seek to
command."

126. Rousseau, *First Discourse*, p. 50.

127. See Rousseau, *First Discourse*, pp. 59–64.

eignty wholly in the people. Both of them efface one boundary (science for Hobbes, sovereignty for Rousseau) and fortify another (science for Rousseau, sovereignty for Hobbes). In either case, however, a boundary must be instantiated if all is to go well. And in both cases the boundary is instantiated at the site where human proclamations of good intention are least to be trusted.

(There is also another forum where Rousseau considers the good intentions of the errant ones: his *Second Discourse*. The motive not to be trusted there is the love of wealth rather than the love of science. Indeed, the latter portions of it could appropriately be subtitled, "What the Love of Wealth Conceals."[128] The original equality of man in the state of nature, he argues, has given way to a gross inequality in civil society, an inequality that *will* lead to a new form of equality where all are now equal *under a tyrant*.[129] The consequence of the errancy from nature can only be tyranny for the soul who erroneously believes that wealth is the highest good.)

How, then, is the soul to find release from oscillating between "melancholy and delight," from envy, from the power of science that brings impotence in its wake, from the love of wealth that unwittingly delivers tyranny—from the travail and ebullient tears shed by the errant ones on their way in the world?

All of Rousseau's varied articulations point in one way or another

128. Rousseau's argument anticipates Marx's dialectic of history and refutes it. For Marx, the original opposition between humankind and nature occurs because nature provided the wherewithal for human life only reluctantly. The dialectic of history is the means by which that initial scarcity is overcome, though not without considerable suffering (especially in the penultimate, capitalist, stage of history). Rousseau argues that while the desire to secure the necessities of life is prior to the desire for power after power, this latter desire superimposes itself upon natural *amour de soi*. In Marx's terms, while scarcity may have been present from the beginning (thus making it appear to be the original problem), the present and predominant problem is the desire for power after power. The dialectic of history may, in other words, proceed up to the point where scarcity is almost overcome, only to reveal the predominant motive behind even the struggle to overcome scarcity: the desire for power. We end, then, not with communism, but rather with Orwell's 1984. Errancy from nature leads to the tyranny of power: the master theme of the *Second Discourse*.

129. Tocqueville offers the same alternatives that Rousseau does: either the equality of all in freedom (found in the state of nature) or the equality of all under a tyrant. See Tocqueville, *Democracy in America*, vol. 1, part 1, chap. 3, p. 57: "[F]or a people who have reached the Anglo-American's social state, it is hard to see any middle course between the sovereignty of all and the absolute power of one man."

back to nature. From gently listening to the voice of nature with the heart[130] to submitting vigorously to the general will in order that the soul be subject to the necessity of things anew,[131] the soul must attend to verities it is not prone to heed. Disencumbered from nature, the soul intimates a ground of its freedom that proves to be illusory and sorrow laden. Here again, as with Augustine and Hobbes (and with Tocqueville as well) there must be obedience (in this case, to nature or to contrived necessity) if there is to be genuine freedom.

4. TOCQUEVILLE AND THE DEMOCRATIC SOUL

[Certain austere puritanical codes] undoubtedly bring shame on the spirit of man; they attest to *the inferiority of our nature*, which, unable to hold firmly to what is true and just, is generally reduced to choosing between two excesses.[132]

The democratic soul, like democracy itself, is fundamentally unstable. These instabilities, moreover, unless redressed, dispose the democratic soul toward servitude under a powerful tyrant. The *inner secret* of the democratic soul, to put it forcefully, is tyranny.[133]

130. See Rousseau, *Emile*, bk. 3, p. 169: "[I]t is in man's heart that the life of nature exists. To see it one must *feel* it" (emphasis added).

131. See Rousseau, *The Social Contract*, bk. 1, chap. 2, p. 50: "[A]s soon as [a person] reaches the age of reason . . . he becomes his own master." Reason liberates the child from the binding power of amour propre. The general will spoken of in *The Social Contract* can be understood as a mechanism by which amour propre is constrained and freedom and servitude are reconciled. See *Emile*, bk. 2, p. 85: "[What is necessary is to] substitute law for man and to arm the general wills with a real strength superior to the action of every particular will. If the laws of nations could, like those of nature, have an inflexibility that no human force could ever conquer, dependence on men would become dependence on *things* again" (emphasis in original). Connolly is correct, I think, in suggesting that "the general will redeems the purity lost through the original fall from the innocence of nature. It is a condition where reason, sociality and complex emotions develop in harmony with virtue, where we are finally at one with ourselves and at home in the civil society in which we reside" (William E. Connolly, *Political Theory and Modernity* [New York: Basil Blackwell, 1988], p. 62).

132. Tocqueville, *Democracy in America*, vol. 1, part 1, chap. 2, p. 43 (emphasis added).

133. Characterized in this way, the temptation is to construe Tocqueville's suggestion here in the light of Plato's examination of the democratic and tyrannical soul in books 8 and 9 of the *Republic* (558c–580a). Where Aristotle would

This thought will be developed at length in subsequent chapters, and more briefly after a few preparatory comments on Tocqueville's claim about human errancy: that we are "generally reduced to choosing between two excesses."

It is important to note, first, that in Tocqueville's view, while human nature does not change, social conditions in the aristocratic age are more likely to assuage the soul's tendencies toward excess than are conditions in the democratic age. Being *bounded* in a way democratic society does not, the soul in aristocratic society finds institutional supports of which democratic society is bereft. God, however, has ordained that democracy—or rather, equality—shall reign. Not inconsequentially, the task of new political science, which I shall consider again in chapter 5, is to discover what conditions within the New World democratic order serve to avert these excesses. Aristocracy itself no longer offers the antidote; now humanity must *consciously construct* an inoculate. Again, there is a *universal* human tendency toward immoderation, toward drawing boundaries in the wrong places, but the dawning democratic age exacts of us new responsibilities, which Tocqueville is uncertain we will be willing to bear.

As with Augustine, Hobbes, and Rousseau, the excesses to which the soul is prone are self-enclosed inwardness and restive outwardness. Consider first the restlessness of the American soul, its tendency to throw itself into the world in search of a happiness it longs to find there yet dimly intimates it cannot. As Rousseau anticipated it:

> The man who sets the greatest store in life is he who knows least how to enjoy it. And the one who aspires most avidly to happiness is always the most miserable.[134]

---

have it that polity gives way to democracy, that a healthy form of rule by the many gives way to the corrupted form of rule by the many (*Politics*, trans. Ernest Barker [New York: Oxford University Press, 1958], bk. 3, chap. 7, pp. 113–15); Plato knows that because the democratic soul is reluctant to draw *boundaries* at all (*Republic*, bk. 8, 557b–558c), let alone in the appropriate places, it is incapable of justice, of "granting each its due." Without justice, tyranny (where all boundaries are transgressed) is inevitable. The "boundary problem," if I may, remains intractable without the Good. Just where the Good, or God, is necessary in Aristotle's political thought is unclear. For Plato and Tocqueville the Good and God, respectively, are essential for the health of a polity. For Tocqueville, the democratic soul *naturally* tends to draw its boundaries in the wrong place; and it is these incorrectly drawn boundaries that conduce toward tyranny.

134. Rousseau, *Emile*, bk. 4, p. 265.

And in Tocqueville's words:

> Americans cleave to the things of this world as if assured that they will
> never die, and yet are in such a rush to snatch any that come within
> their reach, as if expecting to stop living before they have relished
> them. They clutch everything but hold nothing fast, and so lose grip
> as they hurry after some new delight.[135]

This observation bears further examination. Implicit in the unrelenting and energetic motion of the Americans, which changes everything
but yields *nothing different*,[136] is a particular relationship to "the world,"
Tocqueville's understanding of which could easily have come from the
pages of Augustine's *Confessions*.

There is, here, in the democratic soul, an avowal about the sufficiency of the world that is belied by the very franticness of the claim.
"All that I could possibly love is in the world," the soul says. Yet
attempting to *grasp it all* with unyielding hunger betrays a shaken confidence (Oh, how Americans have this!) that wants, above all else, to fill
up the void that lurks in all things—with more things! Theologically,
the soul terrified by the sting of God's call beyond the world, throws
itself evermore ardently into the world, into activities and works, in order to evade the call. Not wishing to journey to Nineveh (as it should),
it flees to Tarshish.[137]

The *sleep* of Jonah that keeps God at bay is a deep one, to be sure; it
is not, however, sustainable.[138] The sleep that declares the sufficiency of
"the world" is never too far from wakefulness, and it is precisely this
knowledge (which does not wish to be *acknowledged*) that drives the soul
to "clutch everything but hold nothing fast, and so lose grip as [it hur-
ries] after some new delight." The restiveness of the American soul, its
turbulent and unending motion, is one aspect of a disregard for God—
as it was for Augustine.[139]

135. Tocqueville, *Democracy in America*, vol. 2, part 2, chap. 13, p. 536. See
also Tocqueville's letter to Eugène Stoffels of June 28, 1831: "[T]he bad [side
of America] is the immoderate desire to make a fortune and to do it quickly, the
perpetual instability of desires, the continual need for change, the absolute absence of old traditions and old mores, the commercial and mercantile spirit that
is applied to everything, even to what least admits of it. Such at least is the
external appearance of New York" (*Selected Letters*, p. 44).

136. See Tocqueville, *Democracy in America*, vol. 2, part 3, chap. 17, p. 614:
"[In an aristocratic society] nothing changes, but everything differs." In democratic society, on the other hand, everything changes but nothing differs.

137. Jon. 1:2-3, 10.

138. Jon. 1:5-6.

139. Consider, for example, Tocqueville's chapter, "Why Some Americans
Display Enthusiastic Forms of Spirituality" (*Democracy in America*, vol. 2, part 2,

[The democratic soul has] petty aims, but the soul cleaves to them; it dwells on them every day and in great detail; in the end they shut out the rest of the world and sometimes come between the soul and God.[140]

That other aspect is, of course, the too-slow of self-enclosure. It should be noted here that Tocqueville, the great theorist of associations, the theorist for whom human greatness was only possible in the concert of community, did not believe, as Aristotle did, that "man is by nature a political animal."[141] By nature, human beings are immoderate; without institutional arrangements that draw them out of themselves or slow down their excess motion, tyranny looms just over the horizon.[142] Aristocracy, as I have said, offers its own antidotes; the problem of self-enclosure is resolved by the indelible *links* that are forged between persons.

> In aristocratic societies men have no need to unite for action, since they are held firmly together. . . . But among democratic peoples all

---

chap. 12, pp. 534–35). There he argues that the attempt to *deny* the spiritual dimension, to throw oneself into the world, leads to explosive reactions against it. Human beings have both and material and spiritual existence, neither of which can be denied.

140. Tocqueville, *Democracy in America*, vol. 2, part 2, chap. 11, p. 533.

141. Aristotle, *Nicomachean Ethics*, bk. 1, chap. 7, 1097b12; *Politics*, bk. 1, chap. 2, 1253a3. This contrast, I admit, obscures the matter somewhat. Tocqueville notes, for example, that "as the extent of political society expands, one must expect the sphere of private life to contract. Far from supposing that the members of our new societies will ultimately come to live in public, I am more afraid that they will in the end only form very small coteries" (*Democracy in America*, vol. 2, part 2, chap. 13, p. 604). Human beings under democracy will tend to break into *small* social groups. Unlike Aristotle, the political forum of the polity *as a whole* was not the predominant locus for Tocqueville. It is largely in the immediacy of the face-to-face that human life achieves what greatness it may. While this does not, precisely speaking, contradict Aristotle, the emergence of the modern state renders Aristotle's analysis oblique to the present situation. The politics of the face-to-face is no longer the politics of the whole.

142. Aristotle is quite concerned with moderation and immoderation as well. He, however, would not have thought through the problem in the way Tocqueville does. Moderation is something the mature man possesses by virtue of the inculcation of certain habits. (See *Nicomachean Ethics*, bk. 2, chap. 1, 1103b21: "[C]haracteristics develop from corresponding activities. For that reason, we must see to it that our activities are of a certain kind, since any variations in them will be reflected in our characteristics.") Aristotle offers no institutional analysis of the sort Tocqueville provides. Rather, he is concerned with a habituation unto the virtues. Aristotle is working within a different theoretical landscape than is Tocqueville.

the citizens are independent and weak. . . . They would all therefore find themselves helpless if they did not *learn* to help each other
voluntarily.[143]

In democratic society the bonds that unite people must be daily constructed. Without continual effort, the boundary around the self closes
in, and the soul flounders in the security of its seclusion.

[In a democracy] each man is forever thrown back on himself alone,
and there is danger that he may be shut up in the solitude of his own
heart.[144]

I will consider associational life in greater detail in sections 2–5 of chapter 3. Here I only note in passing the problem of self-enclosure to which
the democratic soul is naturally prone, and for which associational life is
a powerful antidote. There must be a way to draw the self out of itself,
to enliven it, to roust it from its lethargy.[145] In what well might be the
credo for the entire work, Tocqueville remarks:

Feelings and ideas and renewed, the heart enlarged, and the understanding developed only by the reciprocal action of men *one upon
another*.[146]

Associational life can facilitate what neither "top-down"—that is, national—government nor solitary individuals who purport to love their
liberty (by behaving, for example, as rational maximizers in the market)
can produce: enlivened citizens. In the idiom of the recent American
political debate, neither the liberal nor so-called conservative agenda
will serve democracy well.

Tocqueville, then (like Augustine, Hobbes, and Rousseau), dis-
cerned that there were two excesses toward which the soul gravitates:
either the too-much of restiveness or the too-little of self-enclosure.
Like them, too, he understood that the love of *merely* human liberty
conceals within itself secrets that predispose the soul toward anguish, if
not tyranny. To this matter I now turn.

In Tocqueville's case, these secrets are twofold: on the one hand, the

143. Tocqueville, *Democracy in America*, vol. 2, part 2, chap. 5, p. 514 (emphasis added). The French, *librement*, is perhaps more accurately rendered as
freely, rather than as *voluntarily*, here.

144. Tocqueville, *Democracy in America*, vol. 2, part 2, chap. 2, p. 508.

145. See Tocqueville, *Democracy in America*, vol. 1, part 2, chap. 6, pp. 243–
44: "It is incontestable that the people often manage public affairs very badly,
but their concern therewith is bound to extend their mental horizon and shake
them out of the rut of ordinary routine."

146. Tocqueville, *Democracy in America*, vol. 2, part 2, chap. 5, p. 515 (emphasis added).

hidden love of the powerful state that lurks in the hearts of the solitary souls who *purport* to love their freedom; on the other hand, the taint of envy that lurks in the hearts of the souls who love equality.

With regard to the former secret, we may pick up where we left off a short while ago—with the soul who advocates top-down government and the soul who purports to love liberty above all else. These two attitudes, which seem opposed to one another, are actually aspects of a single phenomenon, namely the inevitable impotence that attends independence. (The impotence attending the independence that masquerades as freedom is, it should be noted, the central concern in part 4 of volume 2 of *Democracy in America*—Tocqueville's last word on the democratic soul and its precarious future.)

> [The democratic soul] is both independent and weak. These two conditions . . . give the citizen of a democracy extremely contradictory instincts. He is full of confidence and pride in his independence among his equals, but from time to time his weakness makes him feel the need for some outside help which he cannot expect from his fellow citizens, for they are both impotent and cold. In this extremity he *naturally* turns his eyes toward that huge entity which alone stands above the universal level of abasement. [147]

The inner secret of the love of independence, it would seem, is top-down government. The so-called freedom to be independent—that is, freedom not linked to others through associational life—leads to tyranny. The logic is inexorable. Indeed, at the place where Tocqueville describes the omnipotence of the majority in America, where he proclaims that no one and everyone rules, he quotes Jefferson in warning that while the people now rule absolutely, "[the age of] the executive will come in its turn, but it will be at a remote period." [148] The theology implicit in this thought must be made clear: the impotent freedom possessed by the soul that wanders through the City of Man is consummated by servitude—perhaps kinder and gentler, [149] but servitude nevertheless. In this respect, Tocqueville and Augustine agree.

The other secret of the democratic soul that lurks under a love of equality that purports to redress the injustices of the world is envy. This will receive considerable treatment in sections 2–3 of chapter 4. Here I

---

147. Tocqueville, *Democracy in America*, vol. 2, part 4, chap. 3, p. 672 (emphasis added).

148. Tocqueville, *Democracy in America*, vol. 1, part 2, chap. 7, p. 261.

149. Tocqueville, *Democracy in America*, vol. 2, part 4, chap. 6, p. 691: "[I]f a despotism should be established among the democratic nations of our day, it would probably have a different character [than in the past]. It would be more widespread and milder; it would degrade men rather than torment them."

wish only to delineate briefly the logic of envy, why it derives from the very conditions of equality that are so coveted in the democratic age; and why it, too, leads by a secret path to tyranny.

> [The] ever-fiercer fire of endless hatred felt by democracies against the slightest privileges singularly favors the gradual concentration of all political rights in those hands that alone represent the state.[150]

While the gentleness of mores that democracy encourages shall not concern us, it is appropriate to begin with this thought here; for the condition under which envy becomes possible at all, ironically, is identical to that under which sympathy may emerge, namely that "we are shown ourselves under a different guise."[151] And in order for that to occur, the boundary that insulates the self from an other, which aristocratic societies are singularly effective at producing and maintaining, must be abrogated so that the other may be recognized as the same:

> Have we more sensibility than our fathers? I do not know, but it is certain that our sensibility embraces more objects. When ranks are almost equal, as all men think and feel in nearly the same manner, each instantaneously can judge the feelings of all the others; he just casts a rapid glance at himself, and that is enough. So there is no misery that he cannot readily understand, and a secret instinct tells him its extent. It makes no difference if strangers or enemies are in question.[152]

Human beings are no less *cruel* now than they ever have been; rather, when the pathos of distance is dissolved by the conditions of equality in the democratic age, the other ceases to be radically Other. Cruelty occurs only at a distance.[153]

---

150. Tocqueville, *Democracy in America*, vol. 2, part 4, chap. 3, p. 673.

151. Tocqueville, *Democracy in America*, vol. 2, part 3, chap. 1, p. 561.

152. Tocqueville, *Democracy in America*, vol. 2, part 3, chap. 1, p. 564.

153. Cf. Nietzsche, *Genealogy of Morals*, second essay, sec. 6, p. 66: "It seems to me that the delicacy and even more the tartuffery of tame domestic animals (which is to say modern men, which is to say us) resists a vivid comprehension of the degree to which *cruelty* constituted a great festival pleasure of more primitive men and was indeed an ingredient of almost every one of their pleasures; and how naively, how innocently their thirst for cruelty manifested itself, how, as a matter of principle, they posited 'disinterested malice'" (emphasis in original). Tocqueville would perhaps agree with aspects of his analysis, though he would not find it necessary, as Nietzsche does elsewhere, to invoke the distinction between Athens and Jerusalem in order to make the point. Merely consult the seventeenth-century letters of Madame de Sévigné he excerpts (*Democracy in America*, vol. 2, part 3, chap. 1, p. 563).

As I have intimated, the diminution of distance produces an extraordinary tension: on the one hand, an unparalleled and universal sympathy for the suffering of others; and on the other hand, the proliferation of envy. Envy is not possible, after all, when an other is radically Other. Only when an other is *like us* can we be comparative—can we want what they have. Only when the "distinctions of rank [begin] to get confused, and the barriers separating men [get] lower"[154] does envy in the democratic age proliferate.

> In America I never met a citizen too poor to cast a glance of hope *and envy* toward the pleasures of the rich or whose imagination did not snatch in anticipation good things that fate obstinately refused to him.[155]

A full account of the problem of envy must be deferred; yet the characterization that emerges already from these preliminary remarks is disquieting. The conditions of equality conspire to produce the gentle soul capable of unabashed sympathy—but also the soul that seethes with envy under the thin veneer of moral decency and concern. It is, to reiterate, the condition of equality *that is so loved* that gives rise to the envy that is so debilitating.

There is, indeed, reason to be somber here, for the condition to which Tocqueville suspects envy will give rise comes perilously close to the politico-theological ordering Hobbes would sanction—where the envy of the many is averted by the powerful one who overawes the rest. After the centuries-long travail of souls who mistakenly believe they are capable of using their freedom well—remember the myth of Ixion!—we finally, unwittingly, adopt the pattern of the equality of all under the one. Hobbes, that scandal to democratic sensibility, was not wrong after all, only premature. Remember, too, Rousseau's prognostications at the close of the *Second Discourse*—and, indeed, his characterization of the brooding discontent beneath the veneer of civility, progress, and happiness in the *First Discourse*. There is a remarkable consonance across the centuries.

The antidotes to the immoderations of the Augustinian soul and to the secret tendencies that emerge amid the love of the world are, for Tocqueville, institutional. Without laboring over the details, some of which have already been briefly considered in the chapter 1, I note here that these institutions serve to instantiate or redraw boundaries of the democratic soul in such a way that its excessive motion is diminished

154. Tocqueville, *Democracy in America*, Author's Introduction, p. 14.
155. Tocqueville, *Democracy in America*, vol. 2, part 2, chap. 10, p. 531 (emphasis added).

(family and religion do this), or its insufficient motion counteracted (local politics in particular, and associational life in general).

These institutions, it is true, can never be wholly successful in counteracting the natural tendencies of the democratic soul; yet without them affairs would go much worse. Transposed into a religious idiom, while humankind will forever sin, without the institution of the Church in the world the consequences of sin would be far greater. Consider, in this light, Tocqueville's remarks on religion:

> The main business of religions is to purify, control, and *restrain that excessive and exclusive* taste for well-being which men acquire in times of equality, but I think it would be a mistake for them to attempt to conquer it entirely or abolish it. They will never succeed in preventing men from loving wealth, but they may be able to induce them to use only honest means to enrich themselves.[156]

The analogue in the domain of social and political theory to the *belief*—Tocqueville's Catholicism, fragile though it may have been, cannot be ignored here!—that there must always be a Church to deflect (but never wholly absolve) sin is, I suggest, that there must always be institutions that keep human beings from "choosing between two excesses," from missing the mark of moderation that *is* sin.[157] Not being capable of choosing their own salvation, of using the light of reason well, human beings must be bounded by institutions that light the way for them. Here is the task of the new political science! Without understanding the importance of nurturing mediating institutions that stand between the many and the one—how this is more Catholic than Protestant should be clear!—tyranny is the likely outcome.

In a perverse way, it should be added, Nietzsche, too, recognized this logic, this need for intermediaries.

> The advance toward universal empires is always also an advance toward universal divinities; despotism with its triumph over the *independent nobility* always prepares the way for some kind of monotheism.[158]

---

156. Tocqueville, *Democracy in America*, vol. 1, part 1, chap. 5, p. 448 (emphasis added).

157. The Greek word *harmartia*, meaning "to miss the mark," is the word commonly used in the Greek New Testament for sin.

158. Nietzsche, *Genealogy of Morals*, second essay, sec. 20, p. 90 (emphasis added). Nietzsche, like Tocqueville, wanted to keep modern despotism at bay. Not mediating *institutions*, but rather creators, were the way to accomplish this. They alone can keep history from ending in the tedium of the utilitarian reverie, in the tame future about which Tocqueville worries.

Yet in Tocqueville's view (departing significantly from Nietzsche), even these institutional arrangements, which we have yet to ponder seriously, cannot be efficacious standing alone. "What greater impotence than that of institutions, when ideas and mores do not nourish them,"[159] he observes. Deeper still than institutions are the ideas and mores that religion alone may instill. Put another way, religion, because it instills a salutary fear, because its "Thou shalt not's" countenance freedom within *bounds*,[160] is the principal institution, without which no other institution may succeed:

> There is hardly any human action, however private it may be, which does not result from some very general conception men have of God. . . . Nothing can prevent such ideas from being the common spring from which *all else* originates.[161]

Theologically, unless the boundary between Creator and created is respected, all other boundaries will be transgressed—perhaps the central motif in the entirety of Augustine's work!

5. THE ENDURING POWER OF THE AUGUSTINIAN SELF: NIETZSCHE AND THE DEMOCRATIC AGE

Nietzsche once observed that, like all things truly learned, Christianity had *burned* itself into the European soul.[162] Notwithstanding the brilliance of the Greeks, and even in our own sophisticated protestations against it, Christianity is still with us.[163]

There are a variety of ways in which Nietzsche understood this: the

159. Tocqueville, letter to Gustave de Beaumont, February 27, 1858, in *Selected Letters*, p. 366.

160. See Tocqueville, *Democracy in America*, vol. 1, part 2, chap. 9, p. 294: "[W]hat can be done with a people master of itself if it is not subject to God?" Henning observes, "[I]n the name of freedom and human dignity Tocqueville rehabilitates prejudice" ("In Search Of," p. 55).

161. Tocqueville, *Democracy in America*, vol. 2, part 1, chap. 5, p. 442 (emphasis added).

162. Nietzsche, *Genealogy of Morals*, second essay, sec. 3, p. 61.

163. See Nietzsche, *Genealogy of Morals*, first essay, sec. 9, p. 36: "Which of us would be a free spirit if the church did not exist? It is the church, and not its poison, that offends us." It would take some time to plumb the depth of this insight. Briefly, just as Christianity is the *victory* of Judaism, so, too, is democracy the victory of Christianity. As with the victory of Judaism, what changes is the guise that the victor wears, not the substance it encapsulates.

will to truth will forever yield nihilism until the soul finally gathers together the necessary fortitude to uncover the joy beneath its woe over the death of God; humanity now stands at a historical precipice characterized by the will's weariness to utter itself; precisely morality now stands in the way of the future—the list is not exhaustive.

Needless to say, each of these articulations treats Christianity as a deception, as an obstacle, which only strength enough for a new beginning that dares to overcome the weariness of the world, the habits of thinking engendered by the ethic of resentment, can accomplish. And that task is for the Napoleon of some future epoch:

> But some day, in a stronger age than this decaying, self-doubting present, he must come to us, the *redeeming* man . . . this victor over God and nothingness—*he must come one day*. [164]

The magnitude of the problem that Nietzsche thought he confronted can be illuminated by considering his understanding of the burden of habit, to which I will first turn. Nietzsche is well aware of the enduring power of habit—think, for example, of the camel of the "Three Metamorphoses." [165] In contrast to Tocqueville, habit as Nietzsche understood it is akin to *gravity*. Because "every good thing on earth [ends] by *overcoming itself*," [166] all things that endure come to embody the dead weight of history. Dialectically, habit precluded the emergence of the antithesis and, consequently, the irruption of the synthesis. Theologically, the dead weight of the letter is a burden to the living spirit that once gave rise to it. [167] (In this latter light, notwithstanding his contempt

---

164. Nietzsche, *Genealogy of Morals*, second essay, sec. 24, p. 96 (emphasis in original).

165. See Nietzsche, *Thus Spoke Zarathustra*, prologue, pp. 25–28.

166. Nietzsche, *Genealogy of Morals*, second essay, sec. 10, p. 73 (emphasis in original).

167. Mill offers a variant of this insight (see "On Liberty," in *Three Essays*, chap. 2, pp. 53–54). Without an earnest confrontation with different understandings, living truth becomes dead letter. Emerson takes this insight in a different direction. "All religious error," he says, "[consists] in making the symbol too stark and solid, and, at last, nothing but an excess of the organ of language" (Ralph Waldo Emerson, "The Poet," in *Emerson's Essays*, pp. 285–86). The poet is capable of renewing the once vital and now ossified language of religion. Language is forever in the process of dying to its living referents, and so must be renewed by the poet. More recently, Rorty makes the same move. See Richard Rorty, *Contingency, Irony, and Solidarity* (New York: Cambridge University Press, 1989), p. 20: "[T]he poet, in the generic sense of the maker of new words, the shaper of new languages, [is] the vanguard of the species." The present moves

for Luther,[168] both call humanity unto life beyond the letter, unto a life of struggle, dialectical change,[169] and a life unsatisfied with the self as it presently stands. For both, though for different reasons, habit can yield only ossification and *death*.)

Habit, the way of the camel, does, however, have its place. For Nietzsche, the burden of habit "speeds [the soul] into . . . the loneliest desert [where] the second metamorphosis occurs."[170] Here the camel becomes a lion, becomes a destroyer before it creates anew—before it becomes a child. The desert must be passed through, for only by bearing the weight of the world can it be cast off. (This, too, as I have said above, is more than vaguely reminiscent of Luther's understanding of the necessary burden of the Old Law, and of the liberation only subsequently offered by Christian righteousness.)

This understanding of habit is quite different than what is to be found in Tocqueville. For Tocqueville, habit is not unequivocally linked to gravity, and so to death. Indeed, the case for American exceptionalism rests firmly on the beneficent reverberations of the habits of the first Puritans down to the present day. Habit may produce malignancies— arrests upon the spirit—that only war may cure,[171] but such conditions are exceptional conditions. Tocqueville would agree that the lion has its

---

forward into a *living* future out of the mouth of the poet. Finally, Tocqueville, too, seems to have grasped this relationship. Those who would be satisfied with the world use prose; while those who would change the world use poetry, he says (*Democracy in America*, vol. 2, part 3 chap. 21, p. 634). See also Tocqueville's letter to Mary Mottley of August 26, 1833: "[P]oetry is encountered only by chance in this life [and] the essence of existence is only vile prose" (*Selected Letters*, p. 88).

168. See Nietzsche, *Genealogy of Morals*, first essay, sec. 16, p. 54: "[B]ut Judea immediately triumphed again, thanks to that thoroughly plebeian (German and English) *ressentiment* movement called the Reformation." Cf. Friedrich Nietzsche, *Daybreak: Thoughts on the Prejudices of Morality*, trans. R. J. Hollingdale (Cambridge: Cambridge University Press, 1982), bk. 1, sec. 88, p. 51: "Luther's most significant achievement was the mistrust he aroused for the saints and the whole Christian *vita contemplativa*: only since then has the way again become open to an unchristian *vita contemplativa* in Europe and a limit set to contempt for worldly activity and the laity."

169. See Joshua Mitchell, *Not by Reason Alone: Religion, History and Identity in Early Modern Political Thought* (Chicago: University of Chicago Press, 1993), pp. 19–45.

170. Nietzsche, *Thus Spoke Zarathustra*, prologue, p. 26.

171. Tocqueville, *Democracy in America*, vol. 2, part 3, chap. 22, p. 649.

place from time to time;[172] only a tortured soul, however, would decipher in the lion a key to all of history.[173]

Habit, in Tocqueville's view, stabilizes human life amid the turbulence it is our charge to bear with equanimity. The world, the burden of history, will be overcome, but in God's good time.[174] Until then, habit will endure, peoples will endure—and to this it must be added: *it may be good.* To believe that human creation of the sort Nietzsche had in mind, an act of "merely" mortal redemption, can and must overcome habit underestimates both its durability and value. Nietzsche, like the American soul so carried away by his thinking, thought that the burden of history was surmountable,[175] thought "salvation" was within human purview.[176] Tocqueville was under no such illusion.

This is not to say that Nietzsche labored under the delusion that mere thinking can change habit. Habit is deeper than thought and often gives rise to it. That Christianity had burned itself into the European soul, for example, meant more than that Europeans believed; it meant

172. See Tocqueville's letter to Gustave de Beaumont, of August 9, 1840, where, considering the prospect for war, he remarks: "[Y]ou know what a taste I have for great events and how tired I am of our little democratic and bourgeois pot of soup" (*Selected Letters,* p. 143). More forceful is Tocqueville's letter to Mill, of March 18, 1841: "I do not have to tell you, my dear Mill, that the greatest malady that threatens a people organized as we are is the gradual softening of mores, the abasement of the mind, the mediocrity of tastes; that is where the greatest dangers of the future lie. . . . One cannot let this nation take up easily the habit of sacrificing what it believes to be its grandeur to its repose, great matters to petty ones" (pp. 150–51).

173. In Nietzsche's *Genealogy of Morals,* the lion—the blond beast—is the protagonist in the history of the species (phylogenetic history); in *Zarathustra* the lion transports the soul forward on its journey (ontogenetic history).

174. Matt. 24:36, 42–43; Mark 13:32; Acts 1:7.

175. See Tocqueville, *Democracy in America,* vol. 1, part 1, chap. 2, p. 47: "[In America] old views which have ruled [Europe] for centuries vanish; almost limitless opportunities lie open in a world without horizon; the spirit of man rushes forward to explore it in every direction." See also Bloom, *Closing of American Mind,* part 2, pp. 141–56, on how Nietzsche has captured the American soul.

176. The theological analogue here is Pelagius's doctrine that human beings have free will, condemned at the Councils of Carthage in 416 and 418 upon the insistence of Augustine. Pelagius held that grace merely helps the Christian accomplish what is already in his own power. Neither Augustine nor Luther believed that the Christian could achieve salvation without the divine gift. See Augustine, *City of God,* vol. 7, bk. 9, chaps. 14–15, pp. 98–101 (*CG,* pp. 359–61); Martin Luther, "The Bondage of the Will," in *Luther's Works,* 33:107, passim. There is, however, no place for the gift in Nietzsche's thinking; it is not needed.

that they *were* Christians, perhaps in spite of their beliefs. The Augustinian self has not receded. Its constitution is of durable stock and cannot be obliterated or abandoned by the *mere absence of belief*. Tocqueville remarks, in a prescient observation that may well haunt the next century, that

> incoherent opinions still [can be] found here and there in society that hang like broken chains still occasionally dangling from the ceiling of an old building but carrying nothing.[177]

Both Tocqueville and Nietzsche well knew that atavisms, habits, remain even when the thoughts that once attended them have long since vanished.

In the context of Nietzsche's world, this meant that to change the Europeans, to turn them decisively away from their pseudoliberation from the Church that is belied by a deeper, visceral, and habitual craving for equality (the inner truth of Christianity!), would require more than a German revolution in the thought, customary since the days of Kant. Struggle and chaos would be necessary. The democratic soul, however, wants security, freedom from fear,[178] a calculable "life course," above all else. Being tame, its thoughts gravitate toward peace—only to be disturbed intermittently.

> A little poison now and then: that makes for agreeable dreams. And much poison in the end, for an agreeable death.[179]

This conjunction, it is, of the need to overcome the habitual world of the Jewish-Christian-democratic soul, and the meager prospect that in the midst of the soothing comforts offered to the "last man" such an self-overcoming *can* occur, accounts for the frenzied and foreboding tone—even in its humor—of nearly the entirety of Nietzsche's corpus. The near insurmountability of habit is the somber background against which the exhortation to "hold holy your highest hope"[180] amid the awesome forces of gravity and mediocrity is heard.

Disentangle Nietzsche's observations about the attributes of the "last man," of the Jewish-Christian-democratic soul, from a theory of history that purports that all things that endure become *unendurable*, however, and the extraordinary tension dissipates somewhat. The envy,

177. Tocqueville, *Democracy in America*, vol. 1, part 1, chap. 2, p. 32. See also Tocqueville's letter to Gobineau of September 5, 1843: "[S]ociety is much more alienated from the theology than it is from the philosophy of Christianity" (*Oeuvres complètes*, 9:46).

178. See Nietzsche, *Genealogy of Morals*, first essay, sec. 12, pp. 43–44.

179. Nietzsche, *Thus Spoke Zarathustra*, prologue, pp. 17–18.

180. Nietzsche, *Thus Spoke Zarathustra*, first part, "On the Tree on the Mountainside," p. 44.

the substitution of interest for passions, the great leveling, the desire for equality, the taming of the human soul, the nearly exclusive search of material comfort—in short, the entire disquieting depiction of the democratic soul does not fade, to be sure. Yet the *valence* of this portrayal is altered. This portrait, of the Augustinian self absent a theory of history in which habit and the absence of dialectical change is correlated with death itself, is, if I may suggest, remarkably close to the one that Tocqueville himself offers! Their differing theories of history I shall consider shortly. First, however, more must be said about Nietzsche's view of the Judaic/Christian—that is, the thoroughly democratic—soul.

Nietzsche does not speak explicitly of the Augustinian self; yet his characterization of the priest as a *type* is apace with what I have here described as the Augustinian self. Consider, for example, the consequence of impotence, of inaction, of self-enclosure:

> As is well known, the priests are the *most evil enemies*—but why? Because they are the most impotent. It is because of their impotence that in them hatred grows to monstrous and uncanny proportions, to the most spiritual and poisonous kind of hatred.[181]

Here is a caustic portrayal of the soul *incapable* of uttering itself, of the soul for whom only a self-enclosed brooding is possible.

But there is more. The soul who at once is incapable of action in society *explodes*, unconceals the beast, when given the opportunity to step outside of society. The veneer of civility is able to overlay and turn the will inward so completely and with debilitating effects in one domain; but in the other—where an enemy may be constituted without recrimination—all restraint is abandoned.

This back-and-forth between self-enclosure and frenzy is to be found, as I have said, in Augustine, Hobbes, Rousseau, and Tocqueville; yet here there is a significant difference. Where Augustine, Rousseau, and Tocqueville conceived that the entire complex occurred within society, Nietzsche locates a separate site for each moment. (Hobbes is more akin to Nietzsche in this regard. The state of nature is that place which lurks just under the surface of the veneer of civil society where the beast is most likely to utter itself.) Nietzsche's "last man" is tame—indeed, placid—only within society; once outside of the domain within which calm interest reigns, the passion for violence invariably emerges.[182]

---

181. Nietzsche, *Genealogy of Morals*, first essay, sec. 7, p. 33.

182. Tocqueville, too, has this insight. He notes, for example, that while democratic citizens are the most pacific, democratic armies are not. Warfare is the site outside of the civil sphere where their ambition may be kindled. See Tocqueville, *Democracy in America*, vol. 2, part 3, chap. 22, pp. 647–48. I will

To overstate the matter somewhat: where Augustine, Rousseau, and Tocqueville understand the oscillation within society to occur because of a distorted relationship to what undergirds the human soul (God or nature), Hobbes and Nietzsche—not as prone to thinking in terms of dualisms as are the others—relegate each polar moment of the Augustinian self to a different *immanent* location: temporally, prior to civil society; or spatially, outside of civil society.

This distinction is not, I repeat, exhaustive. Rousseau, for example, is equivocal about just where nature is to be found; sometimes hidden deep within, sometimes outside of the borders of civil society. Tocqueville, too, seemed to have been peculiarly fascinated by the "homesickness for the wild"[183] that lies just outside of the border of civilization that Nietzsche insists afflicts the modern soul—as his treatment of the American Indians attests.[184]

To further complicate the distinction I have been making, consider the matter of the spiritualization of human life about which Nietzsche is so equivocal. In Nietzsche's view, while the soul has been deepened as a result of the "world-historic mission [of the Jews],"[185] such deepening has been purchased at great cost. The natural consciousness of the ancient was, after all, less dangerous than the spiritualized consciousness of the modern. Tocqueville, too, seems to have grasped this insight, though by no means does his theory of history hinge upon the

---

discuss this matter further in section 7 of chapter 3. Tocqueville's argument for this paradox is sociological; Nietzsche's is psychological.

183. Nietzsche, *Genealogy of Morals*, second essay, sec. 16, p. 85.

184. See Tocqueville, *Democracy in America*, vol. 1, part 2, chap. 10, p. 331n: "[T]here is something in the adventurous life of a hunting people which seizes the heart of man and carries him away in spite of reason and experience. . . . When [a man returns after such adventures] to civilized society, he confesses that the existence whose afflictions he has described has *secret charms which he cannot define*" (emphasis added). See also Tocqueville's letter to Louis de Kergorlay of September 21, 1834: "I do not know what I will become; but I feel very strongly that it would be easier for me to leave for China, to enlist as a soldier, or to gamble my life in I know not what hazardous and poorly conceived venture, than to condemn myself to leading the life of a potato, like the decent people I have [met]" (*Selected Letters*, p. 93).

185. Nietzsche, *Genealogy of Morals*, first essay, sec. 9, p. 36. Cf. Hegel, *Philosophy of History*, part 3, sec. 3, chap. 2, p. 321: for a higher condition to emerge, man "must feel himself as the negation of himself. . . . This state of mind, this self-chastening, this pain occasioned by our individual nothingness—the wretchedness of our [isolated] self, and the longing to transcend this condition of soul—must be looked for elsewhere than in the properly Roman World. It is this which gives to the *Jewish people* their World-Historical importance and weight. . . . [In this people] is the thirst of the soul after God" (emphasis in original).

austere and unremitting dichotomy between nature and spirit—a Protestant fascination since Luther. Tocqueville's remarks about ancient and modern slavery are informative:

> The ancients only knew the fetters of death as means to maintain slavery; the Americans of the South of the Union have found guarantees of a more intellectual nature to assure the permanence of their power. They have, if I may put it in this way, spiritualized despotism and violence. In antiquity men sought to prevent the slave from breaking his bonds; nowadays the attempt is made to stop him from wishing to do so. [186]

Notwithstanding these two exceptions (one pertaining to space, another to time), however, Nietzsche offers a rather dissimilar reading of *where* the two moments of the Augustinian self display themselves. For Tocqueville, both occur largely within society; for Nietzsche, one is within, and the other without.

These quite significant differences between Nietzsche and Tocqueville aside, both thinkers well know the afflictions that plague the Augustinian soul—and are in remarkable agreement about the narrowness of its aptitude and the magnitude of the resentment it harbors. They do, after all, go together. [187]

Consider, now, Nietzsche's understanding of the Augustinian soul. There is, first, that place held in reserve, that site where the dark brooding of the impotent one is concealed from view. "His spirit loves hiding places, secret paths and back doors," [188] Nietzsche says of the man of resentment. The resentful soul, the one who seemingly loves the world, harbors a secret:

> Would anyone like to take a look at [this sick soul]? Who has the courage?—Very well! Here is a point we can see through into this dark workshop. But wait a moment or two, Mr. Rash and Curious: your eyes must first get used to this false iridescent light.—All right! Now speak! What is going on down there? Say what you see, man of the most perilous kind of inquisitiveness. [189]

This secret place is, of course, the place of brooding, where cleverness plots its revenge against the natural—not spiritual—consciousness of

---

186. Tocqueville, *Democracy in America*, vol. 1, part 2, chap. 10, p. 361.

187. Consider, for example, an observation Tocqueville makes about the slaves. While slavery fosters a kind of vacancy of soul, there is an "energy of despair" that attends it (*Democracy in America*, vol. 1, part 2, chap. 10, p. 358). In Nietzsche's idiom, the inability of the will to utter itself in *action* carries with it an explosive energy of resentment.

188. Nietzsche, *Genealogy of Morals*, first essay, sec. 10, p. 38.

189. Nietzsche, *Genealogy of Morals*, first essay, sec. 14, p. 46.

the noble one. The human soul wants action, a little beastliness; unable to accomplish this, it turns upon itself. There will always be injury, it would seem; if not directed outward, then it will be directed inward toward the self.[190]

Nietzsche has clearly grasped, here, a massive tension within the Augustinian self. On the one hand, the resounding call of the "last man" is for the comforts of the world. In the daylight of the marketplace, where the "last man" is most pretentious and seemingly on solid ground, Zarathustra's overture to the future is received only with derision.[191] "What more *could* there be beside the marketplace comforts of the world," asks the "last man"—but not too inquisitively.

> "Formerly all the world was mad," say the most refined, and they blink. . . . "We have invented happiness," say the last men, and they blink.[192]

There is, however, another place that is belied by the very din of the market and the cackle about its sufficiency. Beneath the marketplace, which wants all doors open, lies that secret place (its doors closed), where the "last man" is inured to the perpetual injury that morality, civility, calculability, and all the other things that he professes deeply to love cause him. Amid the bustle of life in the marketplace that promises comfort and security is a place "held in reserve" in proportion to the announced sufficiency of the world. The marketplace and the secret place *must* go together.[193] The more the one is loved, the more the other is painfully and unremorsefully carved out—in seclusion.

There is another paradox as well. The "last man," for whom great-

---

190. If the action of the beast within is denied, violence is not simply relinquished; rather, human beings will oscillate between an inward-turning violence and transgressions against others on the margin in reaction to being hideously bound up in the first place. The modern—that is, tame—soul wants only peace and passivity. Yet the "prehistory [of the beast] is in any case present in all ages or may always reappear" (*Genealogy of Morals*, second essay, sec. 9, p. 71), and for this reason peace will always be fleeting. Peace is a *denial* of the essential nature of the human soul. Consider also Rousseau's less vivid indictment of civilized peace: "[N]atural man prefers the most turbulent freedom to tranquil subjection" (*Second Discourse*, p. 165).

191. Nietzsche, *Thus Spoke Zarathustra*, prologue, p. 18.

192. Nietzsche, *Thus Spoke Zarathustra*, prologue, p. 18.

193. Plato, too, grasped this insight. The transition from the oligarchic to the democratic soul is marked by the emergence of the secret appetites. "In the absence of transcendent natural gifts" (*Republic*, bk. 8, 558b) or without a training that keeps the secret appetites at bay, the oligarchic soul (and regime) is bound to decay into the democratic soul (558d–561d).

ness and marks of distinction evince a "pathos of distance" that must be overcome,[194] is plagued by a sense of impotence that exhibits itself as envy. It is, in fact, precisely because of the "last man's" perceived impotence that there is a wish to obliterate all boundaries, to be secure in the knowledge that differences must be overcome—to believe that all of history conspires to subsume difference within identity.[195] Yet hidden beneath the ostensible love of the other is an implacable wariness that is animated in proportion to the extent that barriers between different peoples are obliterated.

> The reverse side of Christian compassion for the suffering of one's neighbors is a profound suspicion of all the joy of one's neighbor, of his joy in all that he wants to do and can.[196]

The greater the extent of equality, the greater the envy and hidden mistrust of the neighbor. The call of the people is for equality to reign supreme; yet in that place held in reserve, hatred and enmity flourish.

Nietzsche's claim, which cannot developed here, was that the entire complex of the Augustinian self must be overcome, that humanity stands on a dangerous historical precipice where the human spirit itself is on the verge of succumbing to the terminal illness we call democracy.

Tocqueville, as I have said, observes many of the same symptoms that Nietzsche does but prescribes only a palliative—for nothing more is truly needed. The envy, for example, that arises from the lack of distance in the age of equality does gnaw away at the Augustinian soul, dissipate its energy, and reduce it to pettiness. The *reestablishment of distance* that alone may reduce the scope of envy—about the need for this, both Tocqueville and Nietzsche are in agreement—cannot be accomplished, however, by overcoming equality in the world. That equality is here to stay. Aristocracy is over:

> [In *Democracy in America*] I tried to show that . . . perhaps, after all, the will of God was to diffuse a mediocre happiness on the totality of men, and not to concentrate a large amount of felicity on some and

194. Nietzsche, *Genealogy of Morals*, first essay, sec. 2, p. 26.

195. On this reading, Hegel's dialectic in the *Phenomenology* and the transcendentalism of Emerson's *Essays* are the crowning achievement of the democratic spirit. For a brief consideration of history, identity, and difference in Emerson, see Mitchell, *Not by Reason Alone*, pp. 147–52.

196. Nietzsche, *Daybreak*, bk. 1, sec. 80, p. 48. See also *Genealogy of Morals*, first essay, sec. 8, pp. 34–35, where the tree of universal (Christian) love is nourished by the subterranean soil of (Jewish) hatred, envy, resentment, and the like.

allow only a small number to approach perfection. I intended to demonstrate to them that, whatever their opinion might be in this regard, there was no longer time to deliberate; that society was every day proceeding and dragging them along toward equality of conditions.[197]

For Tocqueville, a powerful remedy for this extraordinary dilemma of the Augustinian soul is to avert the gaze toward God, away from the City of Man and toward the Transcendent, away from the many who have been *made visible* by the obliteration of boundaries that the march of equality accomplishes. (I will consider this matter in some detail in sections 2 and 3 of chapter 4.)

For Nietzsche, on the contrary, envy could not be averted by turning one's gaze toward God; only the noble soul whose gaze is not directed toward the other in the first place can be free of envy. Not having constituted identity in relation to another, no antidote is needed:

> [The noble man] conceives the basic concept "good" in advance and spontaneously out of himself and only then creates for himself an idea of "bad." This "bad" of noble origin and that "evil" out of the cauldron of unsatisfied hatred—the former an after-production, a side issue, a contrasting shade, the latter on the contrary the original thing, the beginning, the distinctive *deed* in the conception of slave morality—how different these words "bad" and "evil" are.[198]

The pathos of distance, it is, that makes freedom from envy possible; and only the noble soul—an atavism from the past incapable of thriving in this democratic age—possesses a character capable of innocently displaying it.

Tocqueville did recognize that the pathos of distance that characterizes the aristocratic age is receding.[199] Yet unlike Nietzsche, whose protestations amount to nothing less than the call for the self-overcoming of a two-thousand-year epoch of human history, Tocqueville sought rather to buttress institutions that could avert but not wholly absolve the problem. New beginnings are not possible except with God's assistance. Habits endure; the "splendid *blond beast* prowling about avidly in search

197. Tocqueville, letter to Eugène Stoffels, February 21, 1835, in *Selected Letters*, p. 99.

198. Nietzsche, *Genealogy of Morals*, first essay, sec. 11, pp. 39–40.

199. For Tocqueville, it should be noted, the aristocratic age corresponds to the age of Christianity. In contrast, the Nietzsche of the *Genealogy* identifies the ancient Greeks with aristocracy and the Jews/Christians with democracy. See Tocqueville, *Democracy in America*, vol. 2, part 2, chap. 15, p. 544: "[W]hen any religion has taken deep root in a democracy, be very careful not to shake it, but rather guard it as the most precious heritage from aristocratic times."

of spoil and victory"[200] has no place in an age that juxtaposes both an unprecedented novelty that the very lion of the soul would find difficult to comprehend let alone imitate, and ancient memories that are not easily expunged—and which may be good *in spite of* their persistence. God alone creates and destroys on a world-historical scale; in the face of the unfathomable mystery of his purpose, human beings must confine themselves to the more circumscribed task of maintaining institutions that nurture the measure of freedom granted to them within "the short space of [our] sixty years."[201]

We come, then, to the crucial dissimilarity between Tocqueville and Nietzsche, from which many of their divergences follow: their differing theories of history and the understanding of the relationship between God and humankind with which those theories are inextricably bound.

For Nietzsche, God is the projection of a wounded animal, a perilous invention through which "man first became . . . *interesting.*"[202] The wound itself, he suggests, occurred when the beast within was renounced (by the weak ones) and the trappings of society, peace and tranquility, were embraced. The lamentable consequence was that human beings were left with no other choice but to rely upon "their 'consciousness,' their weakest and most fallible organ."[203]

On this view, reason is not essential to human identity; rather, the action of the beast within us makes human health possible. Having renounced that possibility, however, reason tries futilely to comprehend the hostile world that the self-immolated soul who possesses it has fashioned.[204] "What *bestiality of thought* erupts as soon as [man] is prevented just a little from being a *beast indeed*," Nietzsche says.[205] Reason cannot save us; only the willful act of a creator who redeems us from the present burden of history—of the self-confident though ultimately grotesque machinations of the Jewish/Christian/democratic soul—can do that.

---

200. Nietzsche, *Genealogy of Morals*, first essay, sec. 11, pp. 40–41 (emphasis in original).

201. Tocqueville, *Democracy in America*, vol. 1, part 2, chap. 9, p. 296.

202. Nietzsche, *Genealogy of Morals*, first essay, sec. 6, p. 33 (emphasis in original).

203. Nietzsche, *Genealogy of Morals*, second essay, sec. 16, p. 84. See also *Thus Spoke Zarathustra*, first part, pp. 34–35: "[T]here is more reason in your body than in your best wisdom."

204. Think, for example, of the inventions of classical economics and Darwinian biology: scarcity and adaptation, respectively. For Nietzsche's judgment upon the social applications of Darwinian biology, see *Genealogy of Morals*, second essay, sec. 12, pp. 78–79.

205. Nietzsche, *Genealogy of Morals*, second essay, sec. 22, p. 93 (emphasis in original).

The soul's call to God in this age of democracy does not lighten the burden and assuage the (hidden) suffering and unhappiness of the beast; rather, it exacerbates it, drives it to ever wider oscillations between brooding and restiveness—and to ever-higher levels of recrimination toward itself and others on the margin.

And when God *is* renounced, the enlightened defenders of democracy who are biblical religion's heirs do not slacken in their pilgrim's quest to bring about what the love of God conceals: a condition of equality that mollifies the impotent soul and solemnizes its slumber.

This argument is not to be taken lightly. It is a bristling condemnation of the democratic soul, which demands nothing less than a New Beginning. Wounded animals can endure entrapment for only so long before they succumb. God and democracy: these belong together. (Tocqueville would agree!) The Christian antidote the suffering democratic soul administers to itself turns out to be harsh poison, one that makes a New Beginning impossible.

Tocqueville, like Nietzsche, grasps the intimate link between Christianity and democracy, yet sees neither as an obstacle to the future. The reason, as I have suggested, is that, in his view, the horizon of human existence is *given to* humankind rather than *created by* it. An wholly immanent historical horizon will never be sufficient to grasp the verities of this age or any other.

Tocqueville's disaffection with the materialism that is countenanced by an wholly immanent historical horizon is well known.[206] Human beings are not, essentially, animals—wounded or otherwise. Nor is God, consequently, the projection of a wounded animal. Had Tocqueville adopted the theological stance that Nietzsche did, it is difficult to imagine, in the light of their roughly comparable assessment of the psychological instabilities of the democratic soul, the grounds on which his conclusions could be so unlike Nietzsche's own.

To state their essential difference boldly: for Tocqueville, God is God, and not a projection. The morass of subjectivity, of "Pelagianism," into which Nietzsche falls, consequently, ensnares the impotent democratic soul with a promise that scrambles boundaries and fails to grasp the rather circumscribed, though important, human task in history.

Following Augustine, if God is God, then the injunction to grant what is due to the Creator and the created, respectively, is the foremost injunction from which flows the measure of happiness due in mortal life.

If God is God, then the structure and meaning of history, which Nie-

---

206. See Tocqueville, *Democracy in America*, Author's Introduction, p. 17; and vol. 2, part 2, chaps. 15–16, pp. 542–47. See also Goldstein, *Trial of Faith*, chap. 1, p. 4.

tzsche claims so assuredly to have grasped in his archaeological excavations of the etymological record,[207] is not fully transparent. We may perhaps discern its direction, "through glass, darkly,"[208] but not its meaning. God's plan for creation is not within human purview to know.

If God is God, then contingency and hope are linked in a manner to which Nietzsche could never accede, yet with which Tocqueville seems quite comfortable. For only if Tocqueville took seriously the claim that God is God can we make sense of the "religious dread," about which he writes when referring to the unknown future.

> This whole book [*Democracy in America*] has been written under the impulse of a kind of religious dread inspired by contemplation of this irresistible revolution advancing century by century over every obstacle and even now going forward amid the ruins it has itself created.[209]

The "terror of history" can be borne, to be sure;[210] yet in Tocqueville's case it becomes bearable at all only by dwelling in God's *promise*, by dwelling in faith:

> Am I to believe that the Creator made man in order to let him struggle endlessly through the intellectual squalor now surrounding us? I cannot believe that; God intends a calmer and more stable future for the peoples of Europe; I do not know His designs but shall not give up

207. See Nietzsche, *Genealogy of Morals*, preface, sec. 7, p. 21: "[I]t must be obvious which color is a hundred times more vital for the genealogist of morals than blue: namely *gray*, that is, what is documented, what can actually be confirmed and has actually existed, in short the entire long hieroglyphic record, so hard to decipher, of the moral past of humankind!" (emphasis in original).

208. 1 Cor. 13:12.

209. Tocqueville, *Democracy in America*, Author's Introduction, p. 12.

210. See Mircea Eliade, *The Myth of the Eternal Return* (Princeton: Princeton University Press, 1954), pp. 139–62. Eliade argues that religious faith in the God of the Bible "constitutes a new formula for man's collaboration with the creation—the first, but also the only such formula accorded to him since the traditional horizon of archetypes and repetition was transgressed. Only such a freedom . . . is able to defend modern man from the terror of history—a freedom, that is, which has its source and finds its guaranty and support in God" (p. 161). See also Kierkegaard, *The Sickness unto Death*, p. 39: "[The believer] leaves it entirely to God how he is to be helped, but he believes that for God everything is possible." That is, the believer is the person for whom the possibility of redemption from despair no longer exists by mortal effort. In this abyss, *and only here*, can there be the avowal that the radically new confirms the transcendence of God rather than the contingency of Fate. Rather than terror, the yield is a frail comfort that submits to new verities.

believing therein because I cannot fathom them, and should prefer to doubt my own understanding rather than His justice.[211]

Without this faith there can be no hope with which to confront the sometimes horrific contingencies of the future. The meaning of history may have been the incessant struggle to shoot the arrow of longing beyond oneself for Nietzsche; for Tocqueville, however, humanity has a more circumscribed task in this history *not of its making*: to accept that the democratic soul, cast firmly as it is in the mold of the Augustinian self, has won.

The human task is not to create the soul anew, but to educe its beneficent dispositions and counter its more egregious ones. For this task, there is but one course of action: to use the light of reason to nurture institutions of the sort that alone can secure a measure of human freedom in this unstable age whose future cannot be foretold.

To Tocqueville's analysis of these institutions we now turn.

211. Tocqueville, *Democracy in America*, Author's Introduction, p. 18.

3
The Politics of Competition

1. THE PURPOSE OF POLITICS

Tocqueville's prose, although always well crafted, is often punctuated with poetic insights of extraordinary clarity. For our purpose here, consider a simple observation from which so much else follows:

> It is certainly not the elected magistrate who makes the American democracy prosper, but rather the fact that the magistrates are elected.[1]

The purpose of politics is less to represent than to educe, to draw the self out of its self-enclosed world. Problems of representation (which so tangle the contemporary debate about democracy) are, on this reading, secondary problems: to put it succinctly, the purpose of political *institutions*—and here Tocqueville's Catholic habit of thinking shines through—is to attenuate the disposition of the soul to fall into errancy of a certain sort. Political representation, it is true, receives some attention in *Democracy in America*,[2] but nowhere is the matter treated as an acute problem. The remarkable attentiveness to the problem and meaning of representation located first in Hobbes,[3] then again, with

1. Tocqueville, *Democracy in America*, vol. 2, part 2, chap. 4, p. 512.
2. Tocqueville, *Democracy in America*, vol. 1, part 2, chap. 6, pp. 231–45; chap. 7, pp. 246–47. In these places what is represented are not *fundamentally* different interests, but rather the ubiquitous American soul that tacitly accords with itself—in spite of its different interests. There is reason to suspect here that Rousseau's thinking about the general will plays some part in Tocqueville's argument. See Rousseau, *The Social Contract*, bk. 2, chap. 3, pp. 72–74.
3. Pitkin notes that Hobbes is the first political theorist to give a systematic account of the meaning of representation (Hanna Fenichel Pitkin, *The Concept of Representation* [Berkeley and Los Angeles: University of California Press, 1972], p. 4). Her analysis fails, however, to comprehend the bearing of the Old Testament upon Hobbes's thinking about representation. For Hobbes, whoever holds the place of Moses in a Christian commonwealth represents God to the people and is thereby authorized to interpret his word. (See Hobbes, *Leviathan*, part 3,

startlingly different conclusions, in Locke,[4] and later (in a form whose
contours are fashioned largely by the notion of progress) in Mill,[5] is

chap. 40, p. 346.) For Hobbes, representation must be understood to extend in
two different directions: on the one hand, the sovereign represents God to the
people; and on the other, the sovereign represents the people. Hobbes mentions
both of these kinds of representation in *Leviathan*, part 1, chap. 18, pp. 134–35.
To be sure, this twofold representation in which the citizen is represented, yet
must accede to the sovereign's laws and interpretation, does not accord with
contemporary and common-sense view of representation. In Pitkin's words,
"[W]hen we see the final result of the definition [of representation] embodied
in a Hobbesian political system with an absolute sovereign, we feel that something has gone wrong, that representation has somehow disappeared while our
backs were turned" (p. 37). The difficulty of Hobbes's concept of representation
for the contemporary mind is that it is biblical and, for that reason, a stumbling
block. Citizens are represented by the Leviathan in the way God's chosen
people were represented by Moses. In Pauline Christianity, in contrast, it is
Christ who represents, who *stands in* for all humankind. The great interest in
the Old Testament (which Hobbes displays) was linked to the efflorescence of
Protestant thought in England. See David S. Katz, *Philo-Semitism and the Readmission of the Jews to England, 1603–1655* (Oxford: Clarendon Press, 1982),
p. 9: "[There was an] interest in Hebrew studies which blossomed in England
during the late sixteenth and early seventeenth centuries as a consequence of
the emphasis that Reformation theologians placed on the reading and understanding of the text which recorded the word of God. The validity of the Old
Testament commandments for Christians was an issue of crucial importance
during the Reformation."

4. The theologico-political nature of representation is different in Locke
than in Hobbes. Because human beings partake of God's grant to Adam of reason and property in the beginning (see John Locke, *First Treatise of Government*,
in *Two Treatises of Government*, chap. 4, sec. 29, p. 161), government's charge is to
insure that the *fence* around reason and property be secure. Here *all* reasonable
human beings are sacrosanct; government not ruled by reason's law cannot be
representative. On this reading, Hobbes's sovereign—his Moses to whom the
citizens/sons of Levi (Exod. 32:26) defer because their power of reason cannot
vanquish the irrationality of their passions—appears as an arbitrary and *therefore*
unrepresentative ruler. For Hobbes, representation hinges upon the unity of the
will of the representative to whom deference is given; for Locke, representation
hinges upon the unity of the *reason* of those represented.

5. For Mill, the task of government is to assist in the development of human
faculties: intellectual, practical, and moral. The only way this can be done is to
encourage the activity of citizens—which representative government facilitates.
Intellectual, practical, and moral life are developed only through such activity
(see Mill, "Considerations on Representative Government," pp. 190–92, passim). This accords with Tocqueville, with one massive exception (which I will
consider more fully in sections 4 and 6 of chapter 4). Briefly, for Tocqueville,

oddly absent in Tocqueville. In this treatise on democracy, paradoxically enough, his gaze is directed elsewhere.

To be sure, politics is an arena for the felicitous representation and mediation of different interests.[6] That, however, is more a convenient result than a singular goal. The interplay of interests serves a higher purpose than the accommodation and dissemination such interplay produces. More important than *what* is done is *that* something is being done—inefficient as it may be.[7] Coincident with the mediation of interests is an activity utterly indispensable for the soul that, in one of its prominent valences, tends to withdraw into itself. Interest is less important than the more moderate soul formed *by attending to* its interest in a certain forum:

> Taking everything into consideration, that is the greatest advantage of democratic government, and I praise it much more on account of what it *causes* to be done than for what it does.[8]

The distinction here between interest and the activity that embodies it is not trivial. While much conventional thinking would have it that all human beings have interests, that politics is concerned with the interplay of interests, and that democratic politics involves the representation of those interests, for Tocqueville these measures do not fully articulate the conditions under which democratic politics may serve the purpose for which it is so well suited in this age of equality.

The conditions just described could, for example, describe a system of national representation where the forum through which interests are mediated does not entail the activity of those whose interests are represented. There may, in a word, be an interplay of interests—even fren-

---

intellectual and practical activity is made possible because all things are settled in the moral realm. The Americans are morally passive; they defer before the Christian God—and so *can* be active in the realm of politics. A passivity before Eternity confers the possibility of beneficent activity in the world.

6. In Dahl's words, "[Democracy] is a political system one of the characteristics of which is the quality of being completely or almost completely responsive to its citizens" (Robert A. Dahl, *Polyarchy* [New Haven: Yale University Press, 1971], p. 2). Democracy, for Dahl, is the forum in which interests are mediated and where "all full citizens must have unimpaired opportunities [to] formulate their preferences, [to] signify their preferences to their fellow citizens and the government by individual and collective action, [and to] have their preferences weighed equally in the conduct of the government" (p. 2).

7. See Tocqueville, *Democracy in America*, vol. 1, part 2, chap. 6, pp. 231–35.

8. Tocqueville, *Democracy in America*, vol. 1, part 2, chap. 6, p. 243 (emphasis added). See also p. 244: "[With democratic government] each thing is less well done, but more things are done."

zied interplay—without activity; activity at the national level may well betray passivity at the local level. (This will be considered more fully in section 2 below.) Representation of interests is not enough—not enough, that is, until we specify the proper *site* where its interplay yields activity of the sort Tocqueville thought necessary. It cannot be said too often: democracy cannot be salutary simply by virtue of the (rainbow) spectrum of representation it exhibits; it confers its blessings only through the participation it arouses, the motion it generates.

2. OF SCALE AND PARTICIPATION

> How is it that in the United States, where the inhabitants arrived but yesterday in the land they occupy . . . [that] each man is as interested in the affairs of his township, of his canton, and of the whole state as he is in his own affairs? It is because each man *in his sphere* takes an *active* part in the government of society.[9]

We must begin here with a secret; more precisely, with that secret longing in the human heart about which Tocqueville speaks, which disposes democratic souls, perhaps especially those who ostensibly oppose big government most vehemently,[10] to venerate the powerful state that stands over them. Important theological questions are raised by this secret tendency; these, however, must be deferred until chapter 4 (especially in sec. 4). Here it may be treated in another light.

Recall, for a moment, the argument of Rousseau's *Second Discourse*. The original unity found in the state of nature, where human beings were, like the Indians about which Tocqueville spoke,[11] sufficient unto

9. Tocqueville, *Democracy in America*, vol. 1, part 2, chap. 6, pp. 236–37 (emphasis added).

10. Tocqueville seems to have anticipated the paradox of American government in the 1980s: the call for the reduction in the size of government is quite consistent with the burgeoning influence of special-interest groups. In his words, "[D]emocratic ages are times of experiment, innovation, and adventure. There are always a lot of men engaged in some difficult or new undertaking which they pursue apart, unencumbered by assistants. Such men will freely admit the general principle that the power of the state should not interfere in private affairs, but as an exception, each one of the wants the state to help in the special matter with which he is occupied" (*Democracy in America*, vol. 2, part 5, chap. 3, p. 672n).

11. Tocqueville, *Democracy in America*, vol. 1, part 2, chap. 10, p. 318: "[T]he Europeans have not been able to change the character of the Indians entirely, and although they can destroy them, they have not been able to establish order or to subdue them." See also Rousseau, *Second Discourse*, p. 173: "[I]t is . . . difficult to reduce to obedience one who does not seek to command."

themselves, gives way to civil society. The original freedom in the state of nature is dirempted (for reasons never fully clear); and this marks the fall into history, into that time in which human beings are preeminently *other-related*. After that long and silent prehistory that precedes the word, the relationship of dominion and servitude that is history is established.[12]

This is not, however, the end of the story. The condition of primitive unity, wherein all were equal on account of never needing others, does not merely give way to the necessary inequality that dominion and servitude denote; more than that, at the end of history the initial condition of the equality of all is reinstituted, now in a malevolent form. Here, at the end, when human errancy from nature has reached its apogee, the fruit of that errancy finally becomes visible. What was latent is now revealed.[13] Original equality gives way to the inequality prevalent in civil society—which in turn yields an equality in servitude at the end of history.

There is, for our purpose, a crucial point to note about this threefold movement: inequality is an unstable equilibrium. Attending to the voice of nature, living the simple life, allows us to be equal and free; but once we have left this condition, the incessant quest to satisfy adulterated desires that can never be truly fulfilled leads us toward servitude *even as we profess freedom*. Having defected from nature, we are subject to

> excesses of all kinds, immoderate ecstasies of the passions, fatigues and exhaustion of the mind; numberless sorrows and afflictions which are felt in all conditions and by which souls are perpetually tormented [that] are the fatal proofs that most of our ills are our own work . . .

12. In *Emile*, the concern is not phylogenetic history, but rather the ontogenetic history that evinces the relationship of dominion and servitude which is instilled by adults into (still) uncorrupted children. The cause of the dialectic of dominion and servitude is not original sin, as it was for Augustine; rather, an education that does not accord nature its due is to blame. See Rousseau, *Emile*, bk. 1, p. 48.

13. Rousseau's articulation of the unconcealment in civil society of its inner truth (servitude) prefigures Marx's argument that the inner truth of capitalism, eventually unconcealed, is servitude and immiseration. Long before either Rousseau or Marx articulated their claims, however, Plato had come to a similar conclusion in the *Republic*. There, what is concealed within the oligarchic soul is the tyrant who aspires to power and dominion. See Plato, *Republic*, bks. 8–9, 550d–580c. See also Tocqueville, *Democracy in America*, vol. 1, part 1, chap. 5, p. 63: "[W]ithout local institutions . . . the despotic tendencies which have been driven into the interior of the social body will sooner or later break out on the surface."

[We] would have avoided almost all of them by preserving the simple, uniform, and solitary way of life prescribed to us by nature.[14]

The simple life to which Rousseau is referring, as I have said, is the life of the savage who lives "within himself," in contrast to "the sociable man, [who always lives] outside himself."[15] Not being other-related, the savage knows nothing of the dialectic of dominion and servitude.[16] This dialectic is only for the fallen soul. We deceive ourselves that the inequalities of civil society are justified by the call to diminish scarcity and to increase aggregate wealth; the true motive that underlies this subterfuge is the desire to have dominion over others.[17] The restless and insatiable pursuit of wealth produces only greater and greater disparity once we no longer want simplicity.[18] Theologically, once we no longer want the unity of God, once our desires have been adulterated, we gravitate (unwittingly, to be sure) toward "Rome," toward that worldly equality of all under the one caesar.[19]

There are, to conclude this prolegomenon, only two alternatives for Rousseau in the *Second Discourse:* either an equality in freedom (nature) or an equality in servitude (the end of history); and it is an errancy in the soul, *not the material conditions of life*, that drives the engine of history toward its grim conclusion.

These two alternatives, equality in freedom and equality in servitude, are, not incidentally I think, the alternatives that Tocqueville offers early on in *Democracy in America*.[20] In his view, these are the ones

14. Rousseau, *Second Discourse*, p. 110.
15. Rousseau, *Second Discourse*, p. 179.
16. Rousseau, *Second Discourse*, p. 139.
17. With this, as I have just said, Plato agrees. The love of wealth conceals a deeper motive, as book 8 of the *Republic* attests. Marx's dialectic, which supposes that history is driven forward by economic forces, is only part of the picture. Deeper than the love of wealth is the love of power—which is revealed, perhaps, only after the love of wealth dominates a period of human history.
18. See Rousseau, *Second Discourse*, p. 145. The beginning of the fall into servitude is private property.
19. Augustine, recall, was drawn to Rome by the temptations of worldly power, as his *Confessions* amply attests. Tocqueville maintained that Rome was the worldly pattern that prefigured the spiritual pattern (of the equality of all under the One) established through Christ. See *Democracy in America*, vol. 2, part 1, chap. 5, p. 446.
20. Tocqueville, *Democracy in America*, vol. 1, part 1, chap. 3, p. 57. Hegel, too, dwelled upon these two kinds of equality. See G. W. F. Hegel, "The Spirit of Christianity and Its Fate," in *Early Theological Writings*, sec. 1, p. 198: "[T]he Greeks were to be equal because all were free, self-subsistent; the Jews equal because they were incapable of self-subsistence." For Tocqueville, as I shall

toward which the Americans, now this way, now that, gravitate. While the *inexorability* of the march toward the equality in servitude is perhaps absent in Tocqueville, its prospect is no less threatening. As with Rousseau, the engine that drives history toward this outcome is not a material one:

> [The human heart] nourishes a debased taste for equality, which leads the weak to want to drag the strong down to their own level and which induces men to prefer equality in servitude to inequality in freedom. [For] freedom is not the chief and continual object of their desires; *it is equality for which they feel an eternal love.*[21]

The thought here, in Nietzsche's idiom (which, as I noted in chapter 2, is in certain respects frighteningly compatible with Tocqueville's own), is that the age of equality, of democracy, has as its inner secret the ethic of resentment.[22] Slave morality (Nietzsche), the *love* of equality (Tocqueville), amour propre (Rousseau): however this is understood, a secret force that the modern soul would not wish to avow is the real engine of history. To put it succinctly, notwithstanding all of our talk of freedom, deeper still lies the envy that secretly would dispose us to settle for a powerful sovereign who keeps the other at our level. In our heart of hearts, in the silence masked by our vehement objections, we all yearn for a Leviathan to rule!

Rousseau and Nietzsche's palliative for the disease of envy cannot detain us here.[23] Tocqueville's prescription, in turn, will wait until section 3 of chapter 4. Christianity, I will nevertheless intimate, plays a crucial role in attenuating the envy that drives the love of equality to ever more feverish heights. In the absence of an antidote, the power of the state seemingly offers a remedy for this affliction in the modern soul:

---

show in section 4 of chapter 4, it was by virtue of the Americans' *denial* of their subsistence in moral matters—by virtue of their being Jews before God—that they became *capable* of exercising their political freedom well.

21. Tocqueville, *Democracy in America*, vol. 1, part 1, chap. 3, p. 57 (emphasis added).

22. See Nietzsche, *Genealogy of Morals*, first essay, secs. 9–10, pp. 35–39.

23. Rousseau, who comes at the problem from several different directions, offers, alternatively, nature *(Second Discourse)*, the general will *(The Social Contract)* or education of a certain sort *(Emile)*. Friedrich Nietzsche, on the other hand, offers the ethic of nobility *(Genealogy of Morals)* and the *Übermensch (Thus Spoke Zarathustra)*. For all of Nietzsche's vitriolic condemnation of those philosophers who are unable to come down to earth, his antidotes are no less chimerical than are Rousseau's.

This ever-fiercer fire of endless hatred felt by democracies against the slightest privileges singularly favors the gradual concentration of all political rights in those hands which alone represent the state. The sovereign, being of necessity and incontestably above all the citizens, does not excite their envy, and each thinks that he is depriving his equals of all those privileges which he concedes to the state.[24]

What is important to stress, in light of the hidden and seemingly inexorable logic of the fall into servitude, is that investing the state with a measure of power incompatible with the freedom of its citizens *will* occur unless there are mechanisms available to defuse the odious and formidable threat that envy poses. In Tocqueville's view, religion is a crucial aspect of the antidote.

Let us suppose, however, that envy is abrogated by prepolitical (religious) means, as Tocqueville seems to suggest is possible. This problem having been disposed of, what, then, may politics possibly bring forth, and at what *site* does this appear?

> Local liberties, then, which induce a great number of citizens to value the affection of their kindred and neighbors, bring men constantly into contact, despite *instincts* which separate them, and force them to help one another.[25]

Politics at the local level, small-scale politics, combats the disposition of the Augustinian soul to withdraw into itself. "Local liberties" have, in a word, a psychological purpose more than a political one. The reflex of the Augustinian soul is to shun local politics and to long secretly to defer to a powerful state. While religion is singularly suited to combat the secret longing, only local politics can revitalize human life in the interplay of the *face-to-face*. Religion may reorient thought away from the immanent unity promised by the powerful state, but without a site that draws the self out of itself, that thought remains abstract, disembodied,

---

24. Tocqueville, *Democracy in America*, vol. 2, part 5, chap. 3, p. 673. Hobbes, recall, endorsed what Tocqueville worried would befall democratic peoples in the future. Envy and pride were, for Hobbes, the greatest threat to domestic peace; for that reason he insisted that the gaze of the demos be averted by deflecting its gaze toward the awesome Leviathan. If envy is the inner secret of the democratic soul, then the political structure offered by Hobbes in *Leviathan* is the most accurate depiction in the history of political thought of the political structure that will be found at the end of the democratic age! While boisterous human pride may revolt against such an arrangement, secretive envy draws us toward it.

25. Tocqueville, *Democracy in America*, vol. 2, part 2, chap. 4, p. 511 (emphasis added).

and impotent; and the soul retrenches into its solitude. Without the mediation of the face-to-face, human life is incapable of being revitalized; without a real-life site, even right thinking is of no avail:

> The morals and intelligence of a democratic people would be in as much danger as its commerce and industry if ever a government usurped the place of private associations.[26]

What occurs in the face-to-face of local politics and private associations can best be considered by addressing the significance of participation, or *experience*, in Tocqueville's thinking. Experience is, for him, the largely invisible attribute of a healthy society; and one that cannot be ignored without grave consequences.

In the case for rights, for example, Tocqueville notes that in order for the idea to make sense, it is necessary that "[citizens] be given the peaceful *use* [of them]."[27] Here, properly speaking, the idea means nothing without the experience of its use. It is the long experience of the Americans that disposes them to be able to manage certain ideas that the Europeans, to their detriment, have only grasped in abstract thought.[28] "Experience," as Emerson says, "is the hands and feet of every enterprise."[29] Saying is mute without the activity that goes with it. *Focal knowledge*, the entirety of mediated knowledge, rests upon the silent foundation of *tacit knowledge* and can never be dissevered from it.[30]

---

26. Tocqueville, *Democracy in America*, vol. 2, part 2, chap. 5, p. 515.

27. Tocqueville, *Democracy in America*, vol. 1, part 2, chap. 6, p. 238 (emphasis added).

28. Hegel's remark, "[W]hat is rational is actual and what is actual is rational" (*Philosophy of Right*, preface, p. 10; emphasis in original), captures his opposition to the philosophy of his day, which would dissever thought from concrete life. Theologically, he is more interested in the *incarnation* of spirit than in the Kantian dualism that is based upon the (Lutheran) separation between "the world" and spirit. The politicophilosophical implication of the Incarnation is that thought must be institutionally embodied in order for it to be real—the central proposition of the *Philosophy of Right*.

29. Ralph Waldo Emerson, "Experience," in *Emerson's Essays*, p. 309.

30. Tacit knowledge is that knowledge which is dwelt in rather than focally apparent. This "invisible" knowledge is essential to the development of all higher theoretical knowledge. See Michael Polanyi, *Personal Knowledge* (Chicago: University of Chicago Press, 1958), pp. 49–202. In Rousseau's words, "[W]e work in collaboration with nature, and while it forms the physical man, we try to form the moral man. But we do not make the same progress. The body is already robust and strong while the soul is still languorous and weak, *and no matter what human art does, temperament always precedes reason*" (*Emile*, bk. 4, p. 314 [emphasis added]).

There is good reason to suspect that Rousseau is lurking behind Tocqueville's awareness of the primacy of unmediated knowledge.[31] The education of the European, Rousseau says,

> [burdens the child's] memory either with words he cannot understand or with things that are good for nothing to him; after having stifled his nature by passions that one has caused to be born in him—this factitious being is put in the hands of a preceptor who completes the development of the artificial seeds that he finds already all formed and teaches him everything, except how to know himself, except to take advantage of himself, except to know how to live and to make himself happy.[32]

In a word, the premature awakening of thinking, of the adult, of focal knowledge, of verbal utterance, subverts the necessary development of the practical, tacit knowledge, of the child. Without this period of silence (where rather than doing we must "prevent anything from being done"),[33] focal knowledge, verbal utterance that finally breaks the silence, has no substantial referent. The soul thus formed is impaired; its words are *sophisticated*—think of Tocqueville's reservations about the entire European philosophical enterprise—but it lacks the concrete experience that is a precondition of using words, of using focal knowledge, well.[34]

31. Rousseau's position on the matter is not unequivocal. While the content of *Emile* would suggest that doing must precede saying—see, for example, the frontispiece of book 2 (p. 76), where the first education is the education of the body—the *form* suggests a more subtle relationship. See, for example, *Emile*, bk. 1, p. 50: "I shall put my hand not to the work but to the pen; and instead of doing what is necessary, I shall endeavor to say it." Here writing is, as Derrida has pointed out, a necessary supplement to the deed. See Jacques Derrida, *Of Grammatology*, trans. Gayatri Spivak (Baltimore: Johns Hopkins University Press, 1976), part 2, chap. 2, pp. 141–64. For Rousseau *doing* must precede saying if all is to go well; yet *saying* of the sort that offers an antidote to *doing* done incorrectly is a necessary supplement. While education must accord with nature, nature needs its supplement if all is to go well.

32. Rousseau, *Emile*, bk. 1, p. 48.

33. Rousseau, *Emile*, bk. 1, p. 41.

34. On this reading Hegel's insistence that philosophy is the concrete manifestation of the Idea only takes us part way toward the truth. In principle he is correct. The philosophical enterprise alone, however, will not allow us to grasp this truth, for *prior* to philosophy—and essential for the concretization of thought—is the education that develops the soul *capable* of grasping this truth. The phylogenetic history of the *Phenomenology*, while chronologically prior, is logically subsequent to the ontogenetic history of the soul offered by Rousseau in *Emile*!

The Americans, however, have the practical experience that the Europeans do not. Where Rousseau pathetically searched his imagination for the soul well formed by practice, Tocqueville encounters living examples of such souls in his journey through America—and is unequivocal about the superiority of the practical knowledge of the Americans over the merely intellectual knowledge of the Europeans. The Americans

> prefer the good sense which creates fortunes to the genius which often dissipates them; their minds, accustomed to definite calculations, are frightened by general ideas; and they hold practice in greater honor than theory.[35]

Practical experience, while it appears to be less substantial than intellectual knowledge, is actually the wellspring of all focal knowledge. As Rousseau put it, "If one divided all of human science into two parts—the one common to all men, the other particular to the *learned*—the latter would be quite small in comparison to the former. But we are hardly *aware* of what is attained, because it is attained *without thought* and before the age of reason."[36] The Americans, in Tocqueville's estimation, possess an extraordinary wealth of (prearticulate) experience, which makes possible the good use of their good fortune. Not being a particularly learned people does not work to their detriment; for not thought, but rather practical experience, is the foundation upon which the Americans build. The American *is* Emile—at the early stage of his education, at any rate!

> [I] am very far from thinking, as many people in Europe think, that to teach men to read and write is enough to make them good citizens immediately. True enlightenment is in the main born of experience, and if the Americans had not gradually grown accustom to rule themselves, *their literary attainments would not now help them much toward their success.*[37]

There are important policy implications of this claim about the relationship between learned knowledge and practical experience. These,

35. Tocqueville, *Democracy in America*, vol. 1, part 2, chap. 9, p. 285. See also pp. 301–5; vol. 2, part 1, chap. 4, pp. 441–42; chap. 10, pp. 459–65.

36. Rousseau, *Emile*, bk. 1, p. 62.

37. Tocqueville, *Democracy in America*, vol. 1, part 2, chap. 9, p. 304 (emphasis added). Here, the literary *word* may not act as a necessary supplement without the requisite practical experience. With the requisite experience, however, words can be beneficent. Unlike Rousseau, for Tocqueville there are certain words that are not to be understood as necessary supplements: the words of the Bible that instill a *salutary fear* in the minds of the hearer. I will discuss salutary fear in section 7 of chapter 4.

however, will have to wait until section 3 of chapter 5. My purpose here in diverting attention to the relationship between practical experience and focal, learned, knowledge has been to introduce the argument for the primacy of unseen, unvoiced, practical knowledge in Tocqueville (and in Rousseau). That *women*, who are almost unseen and unvoiced in *Democracy in America*, turn out to be critical to the success of America is also profoundly suggestive. This at once epistemological and metaphysical position about the primacy of the invisible, if you will, shall be developed further in section 6 below (and in secs. 4 and 6 in chap. 4). In light and in anticipation of this argument having been made, the extraordinary emphasis Tocqueville places on the sites where practical knowledge may be nurtured becomes intelligible:

> I do say that the most powerful way, and perhaps the only way remaining, in which to interest men in their country's fate is to make them *take a share* in its government.[38]

Participation at the level of local politics gives citizens the practical experience so necessary for the development of the kind of knowledge they truly need: not learned knowledge, but rather the knowledge that is, again in Emerson's words, "the hands and feet of any enterprise."[39] Local politics provides the site where this development may occur.

Should this site be subverted by the secret longing for a powerful state, the consequence is not simply the relocation of the locus of political power from the local to the national level, but also the destruction of the site where practical experience may be nurtured. The poverty produced by that transference is concealed by the only apparently increased efficiency of national politics. What is lost by the destruction of the site of local politics can never be compensated by the greater effi-

38. Tocqueville, *Democracy in America*, vol. 1, part 2, chap. 6, p. 236 (emphasis added).

39. See also Michael Oakeshott, "Political Education," in *Rationalism in Politics* (London: Methuen, 1962), pp. 43–69. The ideological style of politics, he argues (p. 54), fails to recognize that practical experience forever undergirds the knowledge that can be articulated as abstract political principles. His comments about Locke's *Second Treatise* confirm Emerson's claim and offer a rejoinder to those whose would have it that political regimes are founded by philosophers. "Locke's *Second Treatise of Government*, read in America and in France in the eighteenth century as a statement of abstract principles to be put into practice, [was] regarded there as a preface to political activity. But far from being a preface, it has all the marks of a postscript, and its power to guide derived from its roots in actual political practice. Here, set down in abstract terms, is a brief conspectus of the manner in which Englishmen were accustomed to go about the business of attending to their arrangements—a brilliant abridgement of the political habits of Englishmen" (p. 53).

ciency of national politics; for what is destroyed by that very efficiency is the practical experience that must serve as a foundation for democracy. *Visible* rules and regulations set forth by national government can never truly have preeminence over the *invisible* practical experience of a people.[40] The scale of politics that alone admits the real preeminence of the invisible over the visible is local politics, the politics of the face-to-face:

> Feelings and ideas are renewed, the heart enlarged, and the understanding developed only by the reciprocal action of men upon one another.[41]

The meaning of the eminence of the political dimension, if you will, must be made clear here. Unlike Aristotle, for whom participation in the polis offers a site at which men may be who they are qua human,[42] or Arendt, for whom politics is the site where heroic action and utterance may break in upon a routinized society in order that immortality may be achieved,[43] for Tocqueville, politics offers a forum that may draw the self out of its self-enclosed world and unto the domain of direct hands-on experience that is so necessary for the success of democracy. Politics is crucial here because it offers a site for the development of a certain kind of knowledge. Tocqueville's argument about the eminence of the political dimension has little affinity with Aristotle or his heirs; it is trace-

40. Nevertheless, the natural tendency is to rely upon the visible signs. See Tocqueville, *Democracy in America*, vol. 2, part 5, chap. 3, p. 671: "[It is always difficult for men] to tear themselves away from their private affairs and pay attention to those of the community; the natural inclination is to leave only the *visible* and permanent representatives of collective interests, that is to say the state, to look after them" (emphasis added).

41. Tocqueville, *Democracy in America*, vol. 2, part 2, chap. 5, p. 515. See also Rousseau, *Emile*, bk. 3, p. 178: "[M]an has a good sense of what suits man only with respect to *those relations in which he himself has actually participated*" (emphasis added). Knowledge can be trusted, and yields beneficent results, only if it is based upon practical experience.

42. See Aristotle, *Ethics*, bk. 1, chap. 2, 1094a27–1094b12.

43. See Hannah Arendt, *The Human Condition* (Chicago: University of Chicago Press, 1958), pp. 54–55, where, in contradistinction to Augustine's impulse, "if the world is to contain a public space [that gathers men together and relates them to each other], it cannot be erected for one generation and planned for the living only; it must transcend the life-span of mortal men. Without this transcendence into the potentially earthly immortality, no politics, strictly speaking, no common world and no public realm, is possible." The Eternity that Christians sought is no substitute for the immortality of heroic deeds and words in the public space that politics offers.

able to Rousseau's epistemology and to Augustine's psychology. Upon these is his case for the importance of local government based.

3. THE INTERRELATION OF POLITICAL AND ECONOMIC PARTICIPATION

Precisely where the dividing line between political and economic participation lies is not always an easy matter to disentangle. Yet troubling though this issue may be, it did not seem to perplex Tocqueville. The "question of taking a road past [one's] property,"[44] while it draws citizens into the local political fray, is clearly also an economic affair. Tocqueville, however, treats it largely in political terms. In the preceding section local politics was treated as a site at which practical experience may come into play; here, however, the definition must be expanded. Beyond the promulgation of practical experience, local politics is where the self realizes that it is not sufficient unto itself, that it needs others:

> Thus, far more may be done by entrusting citizens with the management of minor affairs than by handing over control of great matters, toward interesting them in public welfare and convincing them that they constantly stand in need of one another in order to provide for it.[45]

Theologically, in local politics the realization that "it is not good for man to be alone"[46] may come firmly to mind. This allusion is, I think, helpful for understanding the meaning of the terms *political* and *civil* in Tocqueville's thinking, as well as for grasping the case he makes for the preeminence of political over civil associations. On the biblical account, Adam's encounter with Eve marks the original transition between solitary and social life; for Tocqueville, political association marks the preeminent occasion of being drawn unto social life. Once drawn out, the self can be more efficaciously drawn into the civil sphere. The civil sphere, while essential to the success of the American commercial spirit, does not confer upon the solitary citizen the habit of forming associ-

44. Tocqueville, *Democracy in America*, vol. 2, part 2, chap. 4, p. 511.
45. Tocqueville, *Democracy in America*, vol. 2, part 2, chap. 4, p. 511.
46. Gen. 2:18. See also Tocqueville, *Democracy in America*, vol. 1, part 2, chap. 6, p. 243: "[T]he inhabitants in some countries show a sort of repugnance in accepting the political rights granted to him by law; it strikes him as a waste of time to spend it on communal interests, and he likes to shut himself up in a narrow egoism, of which four ditches with hedges on top define the precise limits." The realization that "it is not good for man to be alone" is more likely to dawn upon the person long accustomed to bottom-up government.

ations as successfully as does the sphere of local politics. True, the relationship is not without its subtleties; civil associations, too, may form habits conducive to the formation of political associations. Yet the predominant catalyst is clearly political. A "culture of contentment" in which persons withdraw into their self-enclosed world even while they grow wealthy may for a time be sustained;[47] but ultimately it is politics that offers the most potent antidote against the tendency of the Augustinian self to withdraw.[48] Without this antidote, no commercial society can long endure.

> In civil life each man can, at a stretch, imagine that he is in a position to look after himself. In politics he could never fancy that. So when a people has a political life, the idea of associations and eagerness to form them are part of everybody's everyday life. Whatever natural distaste men may have for working in common, they are always ready to do so for the sake of a party.[49]

Here, as I have said, is a second way in which the preeminence of the political over the economic sphere shows itself in Tocqueville's thinking. In this place, the crux is not practical experience, but rather the basis of associations in general. Habits formed in this one sphere spill over into others:

47. See John Kenneth Galbraith, *The Culture of Contentment* (Boston: Houghton Mifflin, 1992), pp. 13–29, 174–83. Galbraith looks more to the national level for effective policies than to the local level for renewal through associational life. Augustine, too, worried about the pseudocontentment that the wealthy enjoy. " 'So long as it endures,' they say, 'as long as it prospers amid plenty and can boast of victories and enjoy the security of peace, what do morals matter to us? What concerns us more is that everyone should become richer and richer, so as to be able to bear the costs of his daily excesses, and to lord it over his economically weaker fellows' " (*City of God*, vol. 6, bk. 2, chap. 20, p. 104 (*CG*, p. 71).

48. Several caveats must be added here. Local politics is a necessary, but not sufficient, condition for the self to be drawn out. Other considerations that must be borne in mind are that there be no memory of servitude and mastery within the local community (Tocqueville, *Democracy in America*, vol. 2, part 2, chap. 4, p. 512); that there be a long-standing habit of bottom-up government (chap. 5, pp. 513–14); and that self-interest rightly understood be present. I will consider the relationship between self-interest rightly understood and Christian religion in section 3 of chapter 4.

49. Tocqueville, *Democracy in America*, vol. 2, part 2, chap. 7, p. 521. The French is *dans l'interet d'un parti*, which is more adequately translated as *in the interest of a party*.

In this way politics spread a general habit and taste for association. A whole crowd of people who might otherwise have lived on their own are taught *both to want to combine and how to do so*.[50]

While the policy implications of this will be spelled out in greater detail in section 3 of chapter 5, it should already be clear from this argument that if commerce is to be encouraged, if associations are key to healthy commerce, and if local politics singularly facilitates the development of associations, then the crisis of commercial society is not properly speaking an economic one. A healthy economy requires habits of association that devolve ultimately from political participation at the local level. The "competitiveness problem" has far more to do with the absence of habits that local politics singularly facilitates than with the distortions upon the market that subsidies, unions, trade restrictions, regulations, and so on produce. Eliminating these "inefficiencies" will not by themselves produce a healthier economy!

Commercial activity, the civil sphere, is not, in a word, self-sustaining; it has no internal logic of its own; it is not an autonomous sphere of activity. Commercial society withers without noncommercial foundations.

> When citizens have the faculty and habit of associating for everything, they will freely associate for little purposes as well as big. But if they are only allowed to associate for trivial purposes, they will have neither the will or the power to do so. To leave them entire liberty to combine in matters of trade will be in vain; they will hardly feel the slightest interest in using the rights granted; and having exhausted yourself in keeping them from forbidden associations, you will be surprised to find that you cannot persuade them to form those that are allowed.[51]

Once the self is drawn out of self-enclosure, commercial society not only becomes self-sustaining but may attain a feverish pitch. Theologically, the temptations of the world drive the self feverishly forward in the expectation that happiness may be attained through their satisfaction. This worldly temptation need not concern us here. The other, no

50. Tocqueville, *Democracy in America*, vol. 2, part 2, chap. 7, p. 521 (emphasis added).

51. Tocqueville, *Democracy in America*, vol. 2, part 2, chap. 7, p. 523. On this reading, (1) the failure of the Soviet economy was inevitable from the beginning, and (2) the commercial strength of the United States is likely to suffer a debilitating collapse should domestic policy continue to be guided by the empiricotheoretic models of economists rather than by the institutional analysis proffered by Tocqueville. Marx having been refuted, we blithely proceed as if the Smith of the Chicago school is the only remaining alternative.

less formidable, threat posed by the Augustinian self is at issue for the moment.[52] Self-enclosure, which withdraws the self from the world, needs its antidote. Local politics is uniquely suited.

The worry may be voiced, as it was during Tocqueville's time, that granting political liberties conduces to revolutionary politics. Yet this argument fails to attend to the close relationship between political and economic participation. While the question of whether identity is political or prepolitical has a profound bearing in this matter,[53] should identity not be politicized, then the effect of granting local political liberties is not the emergence of incommensurate differences, but rather the promulgation of habits conducive to the generation and maintenance of associations in all their forms. Commercial society can only benefit under these conditions:

> It is incontestable that the people often manage public affairs very badly, but their concern therewith is bound to extend their mental

52. Augustine's *Confessions* reveals precisely the double pattern of feverish participation and solitary withdrawal with which I am concerned here. Drawn to Rome, to the "world" in its most tempting aspects, much of the book also betrays a brooding self-enclosure and disengagement from the world. Interestingly enough, the first and second volumes, respectively, of *Democracy in America* convey this double pattern as well! Volume 1 conveys the success of the Americans in filling up the world; volume 2 conveys the brooding worry about the self-enclosed future of the democratic age. This pattern, this twin peril, may be also conflated so that society evinces both moments at the same time (see Galbraith, *The Culture of Contentment*) or sequentially (see Schlesinger, *Cycles of American History*).

53. See Tocqueville, *Democracy in America*, vol. 1, part 1, chap. 2, p. 47: "[I]n the moral world everything is classified, coordinated, foreseen, and decided in advance. In the world of politics everything is in turmoil, contested, uncertain. In the one case obedience is passive, though voluntary; in the other there is independence, contempt of experience, and jealousy of all authority." Because the identity of the American was prepolitical (religious),it could make politics an experimental realm. The possibility of its restless activity is predicated upon the disentanglement of the question of identity from political affairs. When identity becomes politicized, then the relationship between political and economic participation becomes more ambiguous: in these circumstances, while political participation may confer certain habits of association upon a people, questions of identity profoundly alter the valence of matters that would otherwise only be "in turmoil, contested, and uncertain." Differing interests that are scalar and mediable are overlaid by differing identities that are incommensurable and exclusive. See Tocqueville, vol. 2, part 1, chap. 1, p. 432: "[Because] the structure of religious life has remained entirely distinct from the political organization . . . [it has] been easy to change ancient laws without shaking the foundation of ancient beliefs."

horizon and shake them out of the rut of ordinary routine. Democracy does not provide a people with the most skillful of governments, but it does what the most skillful government often cannot do: *it spreads throughout the body social a restless activity, superabundant force, and energy never found elsewhere.*[54]

The energy produced by democratic politics is conservative rather than (politically) revolutionary. "Any revolution," Tocqueville says, "is more or less a threat against property."[55] Provided that citizens of a nation are preponderantly of the middle class (having neither too much to be genuinely concerned with their holdings nor too little to be tempted to risk what little they have for more), the encouragement of political participation at the local level nurtures order rather subverts it. The energy it unleashes, paradoxically, stabilizes political life rather than disrupts it. Above all, property loves *certainty*.[56] Marcuse was right: a society that "delivers the goods" has no room for revolutionary politics.[57]

54. Tocqueville, *Democracy in America*, vol. 1, part 2, chap. 6, pp. 243–44 (emphasis added).

55. Tocqueville, *Democracy in America*, vol. 2, part 3, chap. 21, p. 636. See also p. 637: "[T]rade is the natural enemy of all violent passions. Trade loves moderation, delights in compromise, and is most careful to avoid danger."

56. See Albert O. Hirschman, *The Passions and the Interests* (Princeton: Princeton University Press, 1977), for the view that Hobbes wished to found "a state so constituted that the problems created by passionate men are solved once and for all" (p. 31); and that Locke was concerned above all with eliminating the uncertainties of the passions. Identifying passion with uncertainty and interest with certainty, Hirschman claims that "although Locke does not appeal to interest to keep inconstancy at bay, there is clearly an affinity between the commonwealth he is attempting to construct and the 17th Century image of a world ruled by interest" (pp. 53–54). The modern project as a whole is concerned with quelling the unruliness of the passions and redirecting them toward more stable interests. See also Voltaire, *Letters on England*, trans. Leonard Tancock (New York: Penguin Books, 1980), letter 6, p. 41: "Go into the London Stock Exchange—a more respectable place than many a court—and you will see representatives from all nations gathered together for the utility of men. Here Jew, Mohammedan and Christian deal with each other as though they were all of the same faith, and only apply the word infidel to people who go bankrupt." Market relations transmute religious *passions* into rational *interest;* the market obliterates difference through the universal currency of money—a thought not lost to Marx, of course, or to Nietzsche. Tocqueville, too, grasped its meaning: "[T]here is no sovereign will or national prejudice that can fight for long against cheapness," he says (*Democracy in America*, vol. 1, part 2, chap. 10, p. 406).

57. Marcuse construed the problem of modernity as one in which the future is arrested because the dialectic is unable to proceed. His deepest worry was that in advanced capitalist society, "the space for the transcending historical

Whether the extraordinary energy that political participation unleashes in the form of commercial activity so tames citizens that they become incapable of impassioned action—and so blink when confronted with the call to greatness[58]—shall be considered in section 7 below.

4. OF ASSOCIATIONS

> Among democratic nations the only form of government that naturally comes to mind is a sole and central power [and] they are not familiar with the notion of intermediate powers.[59]

It would be correct, though somewhat abstruse, to say at the outset here that Tocqueville's social theory, like Catholicism, requires the mediation of the saints! Yet this is the case. Associations, as it turns out, are the functional equivalent of mediators who stand between the Sovereign and the all who are beneath him.

In order to understand how this might so, it is necessary to turn, first, to Tocqueville's understanding of the meaning of history. History, recall, evinces the movement toward the equality of all. Hierarchical relations give way—often reluctantly—to the historically inevitable condition of equality. The dawn of this movement, ironically, Tocqueville traces back to the Roman Catholic Church itself. In the beginning, he notes, landed property was passed from generation to generation, thus precluding any genuine prospect for social mobility, let alone equality:

> But then the political power of the clergy began to take shape and soon to extend. The ranks of the clergy were open to all, poor or rich, commoner or noble; through the church, equality began to insinuate itself into the heart of government, and a man who would have vegetated as a serf in eternal servitude could, as a priest, take his place among the nobles and often take precedence over kings.[60]

---

practice . . . is being barred by a society . . . that has its *raison d'être* in the accomplishments of its overpowering productivity" (*One-Dimensional Man*, p. 23). To be fair to Marcuse, he is less dogmatic about what the content of the future fulfillment will be than Marx, in part because he is less certain that the future would be genuinely different. Marcuse's overarching thought is already portended in Rousseau: society has become a total system. (This latter insight is something about which Tocqueville worries, as well. See Tocqueville, *Democracy in America*, vol. 1, part 2, chap. 7, pp. 254–56.)

58. See Nietzsche, *Thus Spoke Zarathustra*, prologue, pp. 17–18.
59. Tocqueville, *Democracy in America*, vol. 2, part 4, chap. 4, p. 675.
60. Tocqueville, *Democracy in America*, vol. 1, Author's Introduction, p. 10.

The irony of the historical narrative he proceeds to offer is that, in his view, (Catholic) Europe ultimately comes to be an arrest upon the overarching providential design; more specifically, because the Church aligned itself with the transient worldly powers that resisted the march toward equality, the Church, too, became an obstacle instead of an agent of that march. The Church aligned itself with an aristocracy that was to be overthrown. The misfortune of the Europeans was to be unable to forget their aristocratic past, as the Americans largely had.

While Roman Catholicism becomes bound up with the fate of aristocracy in Europe, across the ocean the (Protestant) Americans had no aristocratic past to overcome. In America the claim of Christianity (implicit in Roman Catholicism as well) that all are equal under God coincided with the absence of an aristocratic class, and so (Protestant) religion here was not an obstacle to the march of history that would leave aristocracy behind.[61]

Reading the movement of history denominationally, then, the march toward equality is helped along initially by the Roman Catholic Church but ultimately is handed over to the Protestant culture in America. To put it otherwise: America, the land where the Protestant insistence upon the equality of all under the One reigns supreme, is the future!

There is, however, a certain disposition that plagues the Protestant soul, one that is absent in the Catholic. To put it baldly, the Protestant is more independent than the Catholic,[62] and consequently more likely to be drawn toward an all-powerful state.[63] The theological pattern of the equality of all under the One (without mediators) habituates the Protestant mind to think in terms of the polarity of utter independence and resolute subservience to the One—in its political form, the state—and to oscillate back and forth between these two poles.

61. See Tocqueville, *Democracy in America*, Author's Introduction, p. 11: "Protestantism maintained that all men are equally able to find the path to heaven." See also p. 16: "Christianity which has declared all men equal in the sight of God, cannot hesitate to acknowledge all citizens equal before the law." The difficulty with historically rooted Roman Catholicism was that it could not articulate this *universal* aspiration within an aristocratic social structure that conduced toward recognizing only particular differences and not universal similarities.

62. See Tocqueville, *Democracy in America*, vol. 1, part 2, chap. 9, p. 288: "Protestantism in general orients men much less toward equality than toward independence."

63. See Tocqueville, *Democracy in America*, vol. 2, part 4, chap. 3, p. 671: "[W]hile in times of equality men readily conceive the idea of a strong central power, there is no doubt that both their habits and their feelings predispose them to accept and help it forward."

Parenthetically, Hegel recognized the problem and its antidote; and it is not by accident, I suggest, that this greatest of Protestant philosophers traverses the terrain from the "beautiful soul" dissevered from its moorings in the *Phenomenology*,[64] to the state as incarnate agent of salvation in the *Philosophy of Right*. The dispositions of Protestantism are bound up in his entire project.[65]

Hegel, however, is not the concern here; nor is the dialectic by which he reconciles these antinomies. What is of interest is Tocqueville's claim (a variant of which is to be found in Hegel) that mediating institutions are necessary for democracy to survive. In effect, what Tocqueville argues is that while the Protestant theological insight comported with the historical movement that overturned the social hierarchy of the aristocratic order, the social truth of Catholic theology—that there must be mediators—still stands!

So while Protestant America best comports with God's design of equality, "social Catholicism" offers the antidote to the excesses to which the Protestant soul is prone. Put another way: Protestantism may be the most efficacious carrier of equality; the form of the equality toward which it gravitates, however, is the form of *servitude*. "Social Catholicism" (the presence of mediary groups, or associations) is what helps to assure that the form of equality achieved will be free rather than servile. Protestants are prone to gravitate toward a strong state because they have not the habit of thinking that would allow a mortal intermediary. Roman Catholics, it would seem, have this habit of thinking and so turn out to be the best citizens of a democracy.[66]

On Tocqueville's view, what alone tempers this instinct to abandon

64. See Hegel, *Phenomenology*, secs. 632–59, pp. 383–401; *Philosophy of Right*, sec. 140, p. 103.

65. For Hegel, the state must contain the moment of self-consciousness (which may become the "beautiful soul" if lost in indeterminacy) for it to qualify as a state at all—as his discussion of oriental despotism suggests. "An oriental despotism is not a state, or at any rate the self-conscious form of the state which alone is worthy of mind, the form which is organically developed and where there are rights and free ethical life" (*Philosophy of Right*, sec. 270, p. 173). A state must contain the subjective freedom that is Protestantism's great discovery without that freedom going astray, as it is wont to do. Having said this, Hegel is quite clear on the need for intermediate levels of association—and in this respect his understanding accords with Tocqueville's. See Steven B. Smith, *Hegel's Critique of Liberalism* (Chicago: University of Chicago Press, 1989), especially pp. 98–131.

66. See Tocqueville, *Democracy in America*, vol. 1, part 2, chap. 9, pp. 288–89; vol. 2, part 1, chap. 6, pp. 450–51.

mediary bodies in America is a long experience with local freedoms.[67] Habits thus formed counteract the natural disposition of the Protestant soul; political participation confers the habit of forming associations that stand between the independent isolation of the "all" and the awesome power of state. (This much we have already covered.) The associations formed as a consequence of long experience with local freedoms are the theological analogue of the priests (or saints) who mediate between all merely mortal, fragile, Christians and the awesome God.

Another way to understand why intermediary associations are profoundly important in Tocqueville's thinking is to consider the general problem of authority. Since such a consideration will serve to elucidate the case made in *Democracy in America* for the need of newspapers most clearly, we will turn to it here. This analysis, too, will involve a consideration of the theology that informs Tocqueville's political thinking.

Recall, for a moment, that Luther's resolute confrontation with the Roman Catholic Church was predicated upon his rejection of the idea that the Church could mediate in matters of salvation. Faith alone would suffice; and faith was a matter between the Christian and God.[68] No priests or saints had the authority to intercede. In the Roman Catholic Church, of course, priests and saints did have such authority; and it is no mere coincidence that the aristocratic social structure of Europe reproduced this theological pattern (of mediation) in real life. Aristocrats, like priests and saints, stood between the "sovereign" and the people. They were, as well, a locus of authority.

Precisely why the absence of authority in a democratic age (which has dislodged the premodern complex of Roman Church and aristocratic order) might pose a problem for democratic freedom is not immediately clear. Yet Tocqueville argues that it does, in fact, pose a great danger. Theologically, there must always be a site of authorization toward which the many may be drawn, or else they lose themselves in their self-enclosed world.

> So people living in an aristocratic age are almost always involved with something outside themselves, and they are often inclined to forget about themselves. It is true that in these ages the general conception of human fellowship is dim and that men hardly ever think of devoting themselves to the cause of humanity, but men do often make sacrifices for the sake of certain men. In democratic ages, on the contrary,

67. See Tocqueville, *Democracy in America*, vol. 2, part 4, chap. 4, pp. 674–79.

68. See Martin Luther, "Temporal Authority: To What Extent It Should Be Obeyed," in *Luther's Works*, 45:108, where faith is referred to as that "secret, hidden, spiritual matter." Faith cannot be known by *the world* or its agents.

the duties of each to all are much clearer but devoted service to any individual much rarer. The bonds of humanity are wider but more relaxed.[69]

Transposed into a theological idiom, here Tocqueville is offering a criticism of Protestantism itself: there is no site of authorization (priest or saint) that pulls the self out of itself. Its protestations to the contrary, the self remains woefully the same: perversely, "unperturbed, like God himself."[70] Absent a site of authority, the self collapses in upon itself—both theologically and politically.[71]

Whether or not mediaries are truly authoritative does not concern Tocqueville. It is their standing above the many that accords them their authority, not the integrity of what they proffer. Because aristocrats *were* aristocrats was sufficient reason for their authority. So, too, we may presume, with the priests and saints. Locke reminds us, recall, that what Christ said was authoritative *because he said it.*[72]

In a democracy, however, no one has authority by virtue of who he or she is; indeed, it is almost correct to say that no one has authority because everyone is no one. This absence of authority, conjoined with the fact that "when social conditions are equal every man tends to live apart,

69. Tocqueville, *Democracy in America*, vol. 2, part 2, chap. 2, p. 507. See also Rousseau, *Emile*, bk. 1, p. 39: "[D]istrust those cosmopolitans who go to great lengths in their books to discover duties they do not deign to fulfill around them. A philosopher loves the Tartars so as to be spared having to love his neighbors." On these readings, the peculiar paradox of the democratic age is evinced by the growing cry for universal human rights at the very moment that particular associations between neighbors fall into abeyance. Put another way: the only community that is difficult to dismantle in the democratic age is the abstract, universal, community; local communities more readily give way.

70. Jean-Jacques Rousseau, *Reveries of a Solitary Walker*, trans. Charles E. Butterworth (New York: New York University Press, 1979), first walk, p. 5. The pathos of Rousseau's soul is revealed here all too clearly: dissevered from social relations, this beautiful soul suffers hubris in its most egregious form.

71. Robert P. Kraynak argues (in *History and Modernity in the Thought of Thomas Hobbes* [Ithaca: Cornell University Press, 1990]) that this is not a Protestant problem, but rather a modern one—inaugurated by the thought of Hobbes. Kraynak's analysis captures an important aspect of Hobbes's thinking, though he does not adequately attend to the theological aspects of Hobbes's entire project.

72. See Locke, *The Reasonableness of Christianity*, sec. 243, p. 180. See also Tocqueville, *Democracy in America*, vol. 2, part 2, chap. 5, p. 526: "[W]hen Aristocrats adopt a new idea or conceive a new sentiment, they lend it something of the conspicuous station they themselves occupy, and so the mass is bound to take notice of them, and easily influence the minds and hearts of all around."

centered in himself and forgetful of the public,"[73] makes it especially difficult to draw the self out, to forge links with others.[74] Aristocrats and priests had the authority to do this; but the democratic age has rejected these.

> As men grow more like each other, a dogma concerning intellectual equality gradually creeps into their beliefs, and it becomes harder for any innovator whosoever to gain and maintain influence over the mind of a nation. For taking the general view of world history, one finds that it is *less the force of an argument than the authority of a name* that has brought about great and rapid changes in accepted ideas.[75]

Luther himself, harbinger of the Protestant age in which the authority of mediators is rejected, could not have had the success that he did without "great territorial magnates and princes to listen to him."[76]

If authority pertains to a site, as Tocqueville suggests, then the absence of such sites in a democratic age jeopardizes freedom itself. The tyrant, Tocqueville says,

73. Tocqueville, *Democracy in America*, vol. 2, part 3, chap. 21, p. 645.

74. See Tocqueville, *Democracy in America*, vol. 2, part 2, chap. 2, p. 508: "[A]ristocracy links everybody, from peasant to king, in one long chain. Democracy breaks the chain and frees each link." For the theological analogue to this idea of linkage from the lowest to the highest level, see, for example, Thomas Aquinas, *Summa Theologica* (Garden City, N.Y.: Image Books, 1969), question 4, article 3 (Can Creatures Be Said to Resemble God?), pp. 94–95. "Creatures are said to resemble God . . . only analogically, inasmuch as God exists by nature, and other things partake existence." The scriptural passage Aquinas cites is Genesis 1:26, where man is said to be made "in our image, after our likeness." Protestant theology has emphasized the discontinuities between the realms much more than the continuities.

75. Tocqueville, *Democracy in America*, vol. 2, part 3, chap. 21, p. 641 (emphasis added).

76. Tocqueville, *Democracy in America*, vol. 2, part 3, chap. 21, p. 642. From Luther to J. S. Mill the Protestant impulse has been to defend the authority of personal experience alone. The doctrine of *sola fide* in its many guises betrays a deep suspicion of the world and the loci of power and authority residing there. While Mill admits that "it would be absurd to pretend that people ought to live as if nothing whatsoever had been known in the world before they came into it" ("On Liberty," in *Three Essays*, p. 72), his untiring efforts are nevertheless devoted to disclosing the awesome forces that confront conscience under the guise of authority. Theologically, Mill is concerned about the law that would obliterate Spirit. Spirit alone renews; the law—the purportedly authoritative proclamations *of others*—cannot offer "salvation." In this respect he is no different from Luther.

will lightly forgive his subjects for not loving him, provided they do not love one another. He does not ask them to help him guide the state; it is enough if they do not claim to manage it themselves. He calls those who try to unite their efforts to create a general prosperity "turbulent and restless spirits," and twisting the natural meaning of words, he calls those "good citizens" who care for none but themselves.[77]

It is not, then, simply that mediating bodies (which stand between the many and the sovereign) are necessary in all societies, democratic ones or otherwise; more precisely than this, what is necessary is that there be sites of authority toward which the many—themselves without the authority of station that the aristocrat possesses—may be drawn. Mediating bodies provide this.

This may seem a roundabout way of coming upon Tocqueville's apprehensions about the American situation; yet this has been necessary in order to understand precisely what is at issue in the next section. With a view to considering how the Americans have solved the twin problems of site and authority, we turn next to a treatment of newspapers: the functional equivalent (in America) of the aristocratic and religious mediators of the now-superseded European social order.

5. OF NEWSPAPERS: THE SOLUTION TO THE PROBLEM OF SITE AND AUTHORITY

> When no firm and lasting ties any longer unite men, it is impossible to obtain the cooperation of any great number of them unless you can persuade every man whose help is required that he serves his private interest by voluntarily uniting his efforts to those of all others.
>
> That cannot be done habitually and conveniently without the help of a newspaper. Only a newspaper can put the same thought at the same time before a thousand readers.[78]

The *habit* of forming associations, we have said, is what saves the Americans from falling into an equality of servitude. This habit, however, is sustained because there is a site that gathers together those who, alone, lack the authority to do so. This site is the newspaper.[79]

77. Tocqueville, *Democracy in America*, vol. 2, part 2, chap. 4, p. 509.

78. Tocqueville, *Democracy in America*, vol. 2, part 2, chap. 6, p. 517.

79. Lenin, too, seemed to have grasped this insight. In his words, "[W]hat we require foremost and imperatively is to broaden the field, establish real contacts between the towns on the basis of *regular, common* work; for fragmentation weighs down on the people and they are 'stuck in a hole' . . . not knowing what is happening in the world, from whom to learn, or how to acquire experience and satisfy their desire to engage in broad activities. I continue to insist that we

Newspapers are not, in this view, simply purveyors of undistorted information; nor are they effective avenues for the dissemination of those provocative ideas of the best minds in the country.[80]

> In France little space is given over to trade advertisements, and even news items are few; the vital part of the newspaper is that devoted to political discussion. In America three quarters of the bulky newspaper put before you will be full of advertisements and the rest will usually contain political news or just anecdotes; only at long intervals and in some obscure corner will one find one of those burning arguments which for us are the readers' daily food.[81]

While freedom of the press is crucial for the survival of democracy,[82] it would seem that the preeminent purpose of newspapers lies elsewhere. They are not preeminently *political*. "We should underrate their importance," Tocqueville says, "if we thought they just guaranteed liberty; they maintain civilization."[83] Logically prior to maintaining liberty,

---

can *start* establishing *real* contacts only with the aid of a common newspaper, as the only regular, All-Russian enterprise, one which will summarize the results of the most diverse forms of activity and thereby *stimulate* people to march forward untiringly along *all* the innumerable paths leading to revolution" (V. I. Lenin, *What Is to Be Done?* [New York: International Publishers, 1969], p. 163 [emphasis in original]). Lenin's reference to being "stuck in a hole" corroborates Tocqueville's worry about the self-enclosure of the Augustinian self. Beyond this point, it should be noted that Lenin's repeated allusions to the real and to the concrete belied their presence. Unlike newspapers in America, which sprang up locally and served as a site that promulgated concrete experience, Lenin's newspapers were merely a dream (pp. 166–67). His conviction that "without revolutionary theory there can be no revolutionary movement" (p. 25), and that "the Social-Democratic movement is in its very essence an international movement" (p. 26), betrays a commitment to abstract principles and a denial of the centrality of the face-to-face that, for a time at least, forestalls tyranny in America.

80. See Tocqueville, *Democracy in America*, vol. 1, part 2, chap. 3, pp. 185–86. The absence of administrative centralization assures that intellectual power remains geographically diffuse. America has no Paris.

81. Tocqueville, *Democracy in America*, vol. 1, part 2, chap. 3, pp. 183–84.

82. Tocqueville, *Democracy in America*, vol. 1, part 2, chap. 3, pp. 181–82. But see pp. 186–88, where political ideas are less renewed than reconfirmed by the press. The newspaper's genuine contribution to democracy must be found elsewhere. Put another way, to the extent that American newspapers tend toward the French model (fewer trade advertisements, more provocative political ideas, increased sway over the national consciousness), the *less* they serve democracy.

83. Tocqueville, *Democracy in America*, vol. 2, part 2, chap. 6, p. 517.

newspapers provide a site that gathers individuals together. Newspapers counteract the tendency of the Augustinian soul to withdraw into itself, into the darkness of its self-enclosed world. Without this site in a democracy, the absence of authority in this age of equality would conclude in tyranny:

> But in democratic countries it often happens that a great many men who both want and need to get together cannot do so, for all being very small and lost in a crowd, they do not see one another at all and do not know where to find one another. Then a newspaper gives publicity to the feeling or idea that had occurred to them simultaneously but separately. They all at once aim toward the light, and these wandering spirits, long seeking each other in the dark, at last meet and unite. [84]

Without newspapers, associations are unlikely to form; and without associations, equality in freedom secretly gravitates toward an equality in servitude. "[T]he more equal men become and the more individualism becomes a menace," Tocqueville says, "the more necessary are newspapers." [85] In the age of equality, "[F]ree association of the citizens [must] take the place of the individual authority of the nobles." [86] Without newspapers—more precisely, without a forum that gathers people together, face to face—associational life cannot prosper.

The matter must be pushed further, however. For while newspapers may provide a site of authority and may act as a necessary supplement to the formation of associations, they can only be efficacious for a literate society. [87] The intimate connection between Protestantism, which, like Judaism before it, was a religion of *the Book*, [88] and the place of intelli-

---

84. Tocqueville, *Democracy in America*, vol. 2, part 2, chap. 6, p. 518.

85. Tocqueville, *Democracy in America*, vol. 2, part 2, chap. 6, p. 517. To understand why individualism may "become a menace" see vol. 1, part 1, chap. 3, p. 57: "[W]hen citizens are all more or less equal, it becomes difficult to defend their freedom from the encroachments of power. No one among them being any longer strong enough to struggle alone with success, only a combination of forces of all is able to guarantee liberty. But such a combination is not always forthcoming."

86. Tocqueville, *Democracy in America*, Author's Introduction, p. 14.

87. See Neil Postman, *Amusing Ourselves to Death* (New York: Viking Penguin, 1985), pp. 30–43, for a discussion of the importance of literacy in America during the pre-Tocquevillian era.

88. See Postman, *Amusing Ourselves to Death*, p. 9: "[On the basis of the Second Commandment we may assume that] a people who are being asked to embrace an abstract, universal deity would be rendered unfit to do so by the habit of drawing pictures or making statues or depicting their ideas in any concrete, iconographic form. The God of the Jews was to exist in the Word and through

gence and education in America was duly noted by Tocqueville.[89] While he does contrast the literary character of the European newspapers with the more mundane concern for trade evinced in their American counterparts, he does not underrate the literacy of the Americans:

> Anyone trying to find out how enlightened the Anglo-Americans are is liable to see the same phenomenon from two different angles. If his attention is concentrated on the learned, he will be astonished how few there are; but if he counts the uneducated, he will think the Americans the most enlightened people in the world.[90]

Tocqueville does not, however, fully develop an argument about the effect the Protestant emphasis of the word has upon the American soul. A brief observation about this emphasis upon the word is helpful in setting up the problem.

> Generally speaking, the word, whether written or read or preached, has, because of its verbal form, a conceptual character, or at any rate a more conceptual character than belongs to the sacraments. The word is *heard*; and to be heard is to be *understood*. . . . The sacraments communicate on a much broader front. They too make use of words, but they also employ ritual acts which impinge upon the sight and other senses. . . . [In Protestantism generally] preaching has quite overshadowed the sacraments, and the type of Christian faith that has been developed has been intellectual, ethical, dependent upon the hearer's faith and comprehension, and thus inevitably a somewhat middle-class affair.[91]

---

the Word, an unprecedented conception requiring the highest order of abstract thinking." Martin Luther, too, recall, insisted upon returning to the Bible, to the *Word* of God, for guidance. See, for example, Martin Luther, "To the Christian Nobility of the German Nation concerning the Reform of the Christian Estate," in *Luther's Works*, 44: 123–217. His argument against the Roman Catholic Church is wholly based upon Scripture.

89. See Tocqueville, *Democracy in America*, vol. 1, part 1, chap. 2, p. 47: "[American] religion regards civil liberty as a noble exercise of men's *faculties*, the world of politics being a sphere intended by the Creator for the free play of *intelligence*" (emphasis added). See also part 2, chap. 9, p. 293: "I have known Americans to form associations to send priests out into the new states of the West and establish schools and churches there; they fear that religion might be lost in the depths of the forest and that the people growing up there might be less fitted for freedom than those from whom they sprang."

90. Tocqueville, *Democracy in America*, vol. 1, part 2, chap. 9, p. 302. See also p. 302: "[The American plunges] into the wilderness with his *Bible*, ax, and *newspaper*" (emphasis added).

91. John Macquarrie, *Principles of Christian Theology* (New York: Charles Scribner's Sons, 1977), pp. 450–51.

The word promotes *abstract thinking;* sacraments and rituals, on the other hand, are concrete enactments and reenactments that summon and announce the mystery of the Word made flesh. Tocqueville had noticed this relationship and insisted upon the need for both word and ritual:

> I believe firmly in the need for external ceremonies. I know that they fix the human spirit in the contemplation of abstract truths and help it grasp them firmly and believe ardently in them. I do not imagine that it is possible to maintain a religion without external observances.[92]

Notwithstanding the importance of concrete practices, however, "[D]ogma [is the] essence of religions, whereas ritual is only the form."[93] The word remains preeminent.

These brief remarks have not been without purpose. They are intended to underscore the importance of the fact that Protestant America was strongly oriented by the word; and that the social-theoretical import of this fact is that notwithstanding a comparatively low level of intellectual sophistication, a broadly disseminated orientation to the word made it possible for newspapers to act as a site that draws together those who are "lost in the crowd."

When this site loses its sway, when the temptation to circumvent the authority of the word (and sacrament) and to rely wholly upon "graven images" comes to prevail,[94] then newspapers may no longer serve their real purpose. The movement away from the word and toward the image is, moreover, more than a mere change of the medium through which information is conveyed.[95] Sustained attention to the word is invited by

92. Tocqueville, *Democracy in America*, vol. 2, part 1, chap. 5, p. 447. The French, *pratiques exterieures*, Lawrence translates as *external observances;* this is more adequately rendered as *external practices*.

93. Tocqueville, *Democracy in America*, vol. 2, part 1, chap. 5, p. 447. Recall that, in England, "absorption in *talk* about religion led to chaster mores" (vol. 1, part 1, chap. 2, p. 33 [emphasis added]). The mystery of the sacraments could not have served to institute the moral austerity the Puritans displayed, nor to maintain the political liberties they were capable of bearing.

94. Exod. 20:4–5. Reliance upon the word is an achievement, liable to be supplanted by the less demanding reliance upon the image. Theologically, reliance upon the word mitigates the prospect of confusing the utter transcendence of God, whereas the image solicits human beings to trust their mortal vision. Because human beings are prideful, that is, because they tend to confuse the difference between the Creator and the created, the image must be shunned.

95. See Joshua Meyrowitz, *No Sense of Place* (New York: Oxford University Press, 1985), p. 314: "[T]he sixteenth century saw a striking change in the sense of place and in the degree of 'permeability' of the domestic sphere. Historians have noted the new sense of 'boundaries' dividing public and private, domestic

the nature of the word itself, but images confer their content in a more circumscribed time frame, and conduce to short-term habits of thinking.[96] As Postman remarks,

> [In the contemporary period] we do not refuse to remember; neither do we find it exactly useless to remember. Rather, we are being rendered unfit to remember. For if remembering is to be something more than nostalgia, it requires a contextual basis—a theory, a vision, a metaphor—*something* within which facts can be organized and patterns discerned. . . . A mirror records only what you are wearing today. It is silent about yesterday. With television, we vault ourselves into a continuous, incoherent present.[97]

What seems to be at issue here is whether the associational life so necessary for a vigorous democracy to be maintained may be sustained in an epoch when the word is being supplanted by the image, when newspapers are being supplanted by video imagery. Undergirding the broadly disseminated literacy of the Americans, I have suggested, was the Protestant emphasis upon the book; and so, perhaps, we must consider whether the Protestant age, linked as it necessarily was to the dis-

---

and political, family and community in the transition between the premodern and modern age. In our time, we have found a dramatic reversal of this trend." Meyrowitz argues that the video age, unlike the age of print, tends to obliterate boundaries—a problem, Tocqueville would argue, that is acute in the democratic age.

96. The stronger emphasis upon the centrality of the sacraments within the Roman Church is not to be taken here as suggesting that Protestantism does, and Roman Catholicism does not, conduce to long-term habits of thinking. The tradition of the Roman Church clearly conduces to such thinking. See Macquarrie, *Principles of Christian Theology*, p. 474: "[T]he Eucharist . . . gathers into a unity the dimensions of past, present, and future. It reaches into the past, for it is done in remembrance of Christ and his work. It has its eschatological dimension, for it is done until his coming, and prefigures the heavenly banquet. But it is above all a making present, in which both the past and future events are, in a sense, realized in the moment." For further discussion of long-term thinking, see section 5 of the chapter 4.

97. Postman, *Amusing Ourselves to Death*, p. 137. See also George Steiner, *Real Presences* (Chicago: University of Chicago Press, 1989), p. 26: "[T]he genius of the age is that of journalism. Journalism throngs every rift and cranny of our consciousness. It does so because the press and the media are far more than technical instruments and commercial enterprise. The root-phenomenology of the journalistic is, in a sense, metaphysical. It articulates an epistemology and ethics of spurious temporality. Journalistic presentation generates a temporality of equivalent instantaniety. All things are more or less of equal import; all are only daily."

semination of literacy that *all* might come into the priesthood,[98] is indeed coming to a close, and whether the demise of that site where a crucial problem of the democratic age might be solved bespeaks a deeper breakdown that the evinced movement away from the word and toward the image only dimly intimates.

6. OF MODERATION AND MOTION: MOTHER NATURE AND FATHER INDUSTRIOUSNESS

> What we [Europeans] call love of gain is praiseworthy to Americans, and they see something cowardly in what we consider moderation of desires.[99]

We may wonder why Tocqueville, who well knew of the strenuous efforts throughout the history of Western political thought to instill virtue into a citizenry forever prone to the immoderation of desire, seems so little concerned with this problem in the American context. His claim that the human heart in the age of equality is ruled preeminently by self-interest figures prominently, of course, in his answer;[100] ancient virtue, he says, no longer offers an adequate language by which the human heart may be understood.

This postulate, however, does not take us far enough. More than language is at issue here. Consider, for example, the French Canadians:

> In France we regard simple tastes, quiet mores, family feeling, and love of one's birthplace as great guarantees for the tranquility and happiness of the state. But in America nothing seems more prejudicial to society than virtues of that sort. The French of Canada, who loyally preserve the tradition of their ancient mores, are already finding it difficult to live on their land.[101]

Here was a people who, unlike the Americans, had not forgotten their old, European, identity. Virtue, made necessary by the very proximity of persons in Europe, was transplanted to Canada without modification. Old lessons were retained. Plato's assault upon the appetites;[102] Aristo-

---

98. See Luther, "Christian Nobility," in *Luther's Works*, 44:134, where St. Peter gives to keys to the Church to all Christians.

99. Tocqueville, *Democracy in America*, vol. 1, part 2, chap. 9, p. 284.

100. See Tocqueville, *Democracy in America*, vol. 1, part 2, chap. 6, pp. 235–37, on the distinction between instinctive and well-considered patriotism; and vol. 2, part 2, chap. 8, pp. 525–28.

101. Tocqueville, *Democracy in America*, vol. 1, part 2, chap. 9, p. 284.

102. See Plato, *Republic*, bk. 2, 372d–373e, where the admission of luxury into the city set up in speech leads to war; and bk. 4, 442: "[Reason and spirit

tle's plea for moderation;[103] St. Paul's derogation of the flesh;[104] Augustine's petition to turn from the City of Man;[105] Hobbes's profoundly disturbing assessment of the depth of human pride;[106] Rousseau's entreaty to disentangle real from imaginary need[107]—these are calls for an austerity, for a constraint upon the expansive proclivities of desire. And these calls *were* appropriate for a geographical region long settled and, therefore, too easily unsettled. The history of Western political thought, in this light, may be understood as an effort by the intellect to limit desire in proportion to the limits of geography. Its *truth* cannot be disencumbered from the verities of space and density.[108] The French Canadians, in effect, never renounced their citizenship in that delimited world.

The Americans, on the other hand, began anew. In one of its valences this new beginning involved a different relationship to the world in

---

must] preside over the appetitive part which is the mass of the soul in each of us and the most insatiable by nature of wealth." Because the appetites are insatiable, they must invariably come into conflict, a conflict that the tyrant would purport to sidestep in his promise to the democratic soul that all its appetites may be sated, that he will be a friend of the people (bk. 8, 565d).

103. See Aristotle, *Nicomachean Ethics*, bk. 2, chaps. 6–9, 1106b37–1109b27.

104. See Gal. 5:19–21 ("Now the works of the flesh are manifest, which are these; Adultery, fornication, uncleanness, lasciviousness, Idolatry, witchcraft, hatred, variance, emulations, wrath, strife, seditions, heresies, Envyings, murders, drunkenness, revellings, and such like: of the which I tell you before, as I have also told *you* in time past, that they which do such things shall not inherit the kingdom of God").

105. See Augustine, *City of God*, vol. 7, bk. 14, chap. 4, pp. 353–56 (*CG*, pp. 552–54).

106. See Hobbes, *De cive*, chap. 1, p. 113: "[N]o society can be great or longlasting which begins with vainglory." So tenacious is human pride that there must be a "king of the children of pride," a need for a Leviathan, if there is to be peace at all.

107. See Rousseau, *Emile*, bk. 2, p. 81: "[T]he real world has its limits; the imaginary world is infinite. Unable to enlarge the one, let us restrict the other, for it is from the difference between the two alone that are born all the pains which make us truly unhappy."

108. Thus, it is not surprising that Smith should begin his defense of the appetites—and even more to the point, should oppose sumptuary laws (see *The Wealth of Nations*, vol. 1, bk. 2, chap. 3, p. 367)—at a moment when expanding markets made possible by empire effectively *enlarge* Europe. (See, for example, E. J. Hobsbawm, *Industry and Empire* [New York: Penguin Books, 1969], pp. 34–55.) No longer constrained by the finite resources within the European market, the appetites now could be allowed to expand; now their defense could appear to be plausible.

which they found themselves—an empty world that seemed to be "only waiting."[109] Here, the expansive proclivities of desire were not wholly chastised; the motion to which the immoderation of desire gave rise could be accommodated by the very extensiveness of the land; the motion of the Americans was proportional to the scale of the continent. For this reason, they alone would come to dominate the land.

> So, then, it must not be thought possible to halt the impetus of the English race in the New World. . . . No power on earth can shut out the immigrants from that fertile wilderness which on every side offers rewards to industry and a refuge from every affliction. . . . Thus, in all the uncertainties of the future, one event at least is sure. [The] Anglo-Americans alone will cover the whole of the immense area between the polar ice and the tropics, extending from the Atlantic to the Pacific coast.[110]

About the appropriateness among the Americans of what, from the European vantage, could only be considered an immoderation of desire, Tocqueville was quite clear. The industriousness of the Americans, their love of property, was not disruptive. Locke had captured the American mind and heart,[111] and it was good.

Let me now amplify these remarks. Recall that on Locke's account, property is of biblical origin and justification. In the beginning there was common property given to Adam—that is, to humankind as a whole. This property was, of course, to be used; for only through use could the earth *be for* humankind, as God had ordained in the beginning:

> God, by commanding to subdue, gave authority so far to *appropriate*. [And this] necessarily introduces *private Possessions*.[112]

---

109. Tocqueville, *Democracy in America*, vol. 1, part 1, chap. 1, p. 30. Tocqueville does recognize the presence of the Indians, yet notes at the same place that they did not take possession of the soil. In contrast, the Indians of South America did possess the soil; the conquests of the Europeans there, consequently, were even more bloody than in North America (see part 2, chap. 9, p. 280).

110. Tocqueville, *Democracy in America*, vol. 1, part 2, conclusion, p. 411.

111. The Locke who is often purported to have captured the American soul is purported to be the Locke of the *Second Treatise*, that is, the so-called secular Locke. (Hartz, in *Liberal Tradition in America*, takes this view.) Yet the Locke of *The Reasonableness of Christianity* was also taken at his word, as the American editor's comments to the 1811 edition indicates. See John Locke, *The Reasonableness of Christianity* (Boston: T. B. Wait, 1811), pp. iii–xix.

112. Locke, *Second Treatise*, chap. 5, sec. 35, p. 292 (emphasis in original). See Gen. 1:28.

Yet the matter cannot be left at that. (Mother) nature, too, figures into Locke's thinking.

> Though the Water running in the Fountain be every ones, yet who can doubt, but that in the Pitcher is his only who drew it out? His *Labour* hath taken it out of the hands of Nature, where it was common, and belong'd equally to all her Children, and *hath* thereby *appropriated* it to himself. [113]

"Nature and the Earth furnish only almost worthless materials," he says. Labor *"puts the greatest part of Value upon the Land."* [114] Put otherwise, Mother nature must be appended by industrious labor (which derives and is authorized by God the Father) for nature to be bountiful. Mother is passive; father is active. Nature, the "common mother of all," [115] and God the Father provide the wherewithal and justification for appropriation among the children of Adam.

This way of thinking about property, which requires for coherency the invocation of both active and passive aspects, is reproduced in Tocqueville's thinking about property as well. As we have noted already, the motion of the American soul, its activity, was peculiarly suited for the New World. Importantly, however, Tocqueville never imagined that the active aspect—the industriousness of the Americans—would supervene over the passive aspect. (Locke, in his own way, agrees.) [116] For all his praise of American activity, father industriousness was forever being received by mother nature, and he did not overwhelm her.

> The deep *silence* of the North American wilderness was only broken by the monotonous cooing of wood pigeons or the tapping of green woodpeckers on the trees' bark. Nature seemed completely left to herself, and it was far from my thoughts to suppose that the place had once been occupied. . . . I noticed [however] the traces of man. Then, looking closely at everything around, I was soon convinced that a European had come to seek a refuge in this place. But how greatly his work had changed appearance! The logs he had hastily cut to build a shelter had sprouted afresh; his fences had become live hedges, and his cabin had been turned into a grove. . . . For some time I silently

113. Locke, *Second Treatise*, chap. 5, sec. 29, p. 289 (emphasis in original).
114. Locke, *Second Treatise*, chap. 5, sec. 43, p. 298 (emphasis in original).
115. Locke, *Second Treatise*, chap. 5, sec. 28, p. 288.
116. See Locke, *Second Treatise*, chap. 5, sec. 37, p. 294: "[H]e, that incloses Land and has a greater plenty of the conveniences of life from ten acres, than he could have from an hundred left to Nature, may truly be said, to give ninety acres to Mankind." Mother nature retains her bounty not *in spite* of, but rather *because* of, father industriousness.

contemplated the resources of nature and the feebleness of man; and when I did leave the enchanted spot, I kept saying sadly: "What! Ruins so soon!" In Europe we habitually regard the restless spirit, immoderate desire for wealth, and an extreme love of independence as great social dangers. But precisely those things assure a long a peaceful future for the American republics. Without such restless passions the population would be concentrated around a few places. . . . What a happy land the New World is, *where man's vices are almost as useful to society as his virtues!*[117]

For all its activity, "the silence of the North American wilderness" was capable of containing the (clamorous) American soul. True, the Americans "clutch everything but hold nothing fast, and so lose grip as they hurry after some new delight."[118] Notwithstanding the immoderation of their activity, however, mother nature could receive father industriousness without violation; in North America, while the father had dominion, the mother was sovereign.

I have moved in this direction for reasons not directly pertinent to Tocqueville's view of property. A weightier matter is at issue than property alone, which a brief consideration of Tocqueville's view of the relationship between the sexes helps to make clear. That the pattern of thinking is similar is not, I think, merely a coincidence.

With respect to the relationship between the sexes, of course, Tocqueville believed that the purview of each must be separated:

> In America, more than anywhere else in the world, care has been taken to trace clearly distinct spheres of action for both sexes, and both are required to keep in step, but along paths that are never the same. . . . If the American woman is never allowed to leave the *quiet* sphere of domestic duties, she is also never forced to do so.[119]

Beyond, and in accordance with, this necessary separation, however, he understood that one aspect must have preeminence over the other—a view not unlike Augustine's and Rousseau's about the central place of the *silence* in the overall human economy of happiness:

> There have never been free societies without mores, and as I have observed in the first part of this book, it is woman who shapes these mores. Therefore everything which has a bearing on the status of

---

117. Tocqueville, *Democracy in America*, vol. 1, part 2, chap. 9, p. 284 (emphasis added).

118. Tocqueville, *Democracy in America*, vol. 2, part 2, chap. 13, p. 536.

119. Tocqueville, *Democracy in America*, vol. 2, part 2, chap. 12, p. 601 (emphasis added). See also Rousseau, *Emile*, bk. 5, p. 358: "[I]n the union of the sexes each contributes equally to the same end but in different ways."

woman, their habits, and their thoughts is, in my view, of great political importance. [120]

On Tocqueville's view, the passive aspect must have preeminence over the active. Without this relationship being honored, there can be no peace amid the turbulence of human life.

I will consider the all-important religious manifestation of the relationship between passivity and activity in sections 4 and 6 of chapter 4. There, too, the Americans' earnest separation between the active (worldly) and passive (otherworldly) domains makes possible the ongoing success of both a commercially strong democracy and a vital religion; the extraordinary worldly activity of the Americans, both civil and political, was made possible in large measure by a passivity before God.

There is, to be sure, reason to doubt the accuracy of Tocqueville's portrayal of these three manifestations of the relationship between passivity and activity during his visit more than a century and a half ago; he was, as I noted in the preface, a *moral* historian, concerned with what might be called the inner logic of these relationships. Notwithstanding his consolidation, as it were, of the historical evidence, his understanding of this inner logic is suggestive about these three relationships at the present moment. A few remarks are warranted.

To begin with, the attempt to distinguish between the active and passive aspects is being met with increasing resistance. This is an inevitable consequence of equality. Rather than grant each its due, what reigns is a kind of *preemptive androgyny*, [121] in which the difficult task of delineating rightful boundaries has given way to the enterprise of obliterating them all together. False universalism has come increasingly to

---

120. Tocqueville, *Democracy in America*, vol. 2, part, 1, chap. 9, p. 590.

121. See Meyrowitz, *No Sense of Place*, pp. 187–225. He links the obliteration of boundaries between men and women, between public and private, to the electronic media. In his words: "[E]lectronic media's invasion of the home not only liberates women from the home's informational confines but also tends to reintegrate the public and domestic spheres and to foster a 'situational androgyny.' Men are now able to 'hunt' for information at home computers and women can breast feed children while doing business on the telephone" (p. 224). Tocqueville would, I think, see the electronic media as an aspect of a larger movement within the democratic age that would obliterate all boundaries. See also Plato, *Republic*, bk. 6, 563b–c: "[Within a democracy there is a] spirit of freedom and equal rights in the relations of men to women and women to men." The philosophical claim out of which this particular articulation emerges is that only the just soul may "grant each its due." *All* others draw boundaries in the wrong place—or not at all.

prevail. Accompanying this development, however, is a paradoxical development (the reasons for which will be discussed in section 2 of chapter 4) wherein the obliteration of these differences has been accompanied by their resurrection in a caricatured form.

At the heart of this paradox—indeed, it may be the very cause—is the failure to recognize the manner in which the passive element may be preeminent. The three problems that increasingly frustrate us—the degradation of nature, the relationship between the sexes, and the question of the importance and place of religion in the world—are each instances of the passive aspect of human existence increasingly being derogated and being reestablished in anomalous and contrived ways.

The effort wholly to bring nature under the sway of a calculus that would render her accountable to the system of human activity,[122] for example, is coincident with what might be called the modern cult of nature. The mounting evidence that the "traditional" mother has no place in the contemporary world[123] has been attended by her elevation

---

122. Here even the effort to protect nature from industry with the buying a selling of "pollution credits" only further betrays the logic of subsuming nature within an economic calculus, the supposition behind which is that everything has its price. (See, further, Karl Marx, "Money," in *Marx's Concept of Man*, pp. 163–68.) There are, of course, environmentalists who wish to arrest this movement, but their good will alone cannot interrupt a logic that while manifesting itself as the environmental crisis, lies deeper still. In "Private Property and Communism," Marx soberly offers the suggestion that "the domination of material property looms so large [under capitalism] that it aims to destroy everything which is incapable of being possessed by everyone as private property" (p. 126).

123. See Freud, *Civilization and Its Discontents*, p. 59: "[W]omen soon come into opposition to civilization and display their retarding and restraining influence . . . [They] represent the interests of the family and of sexual love. The work of civilization has become increasingly the business of men. . . . Thus the woman finds herself forced into the background by the claims of civilization and she adopts a hostile attitude towards it." See also Hegel, *Philosophy of Right*, sec. 166, p. 114: "[T]hus one sex is mind in its self-diremption into explicit personal self-subsistence and the knowledge and volition of free universality, i.e. the self-consciousness of conceptual thought and the volition of the objective final end. The other sex is mind maintaining itself in unity as knowledge and volition of the substantive, but knowledge and volition in the form of concrete individuality and feeling." For both Hegel and Freud the domain of universality is the domain of men, the domain of particularity the domain of women. That the problem of the democratic age comes to be the reign of a false universalism that derogates the particular, as Tocqueville intimated, is profoundly suggestive.

to the status of an icon that is belied by the historical record.[124] The growing and increasingly dangerous voice of biblical literalism that purports to strengthen religion, too, has been accompanied by a New Age spiritualism as docile as it is vacuous; Calvinism and Unitarianism—the eternal American alternatives—in ever more unsettling guises. These three paradoxical trajectories each betray the diminution of the passive element and reestablishment of it in perverted form. The paradoxes that attend each site, moreover, are not accidental. The relationship between passivity and activity can never be obliterated; the manner in which it manifests itself can, however, become perverse.

The paradoxes that arise in conjunction with the effort to obliterate boundaries aside, however, Tocqueville, along with a host of other luminaries in the history of political thought concur that the effort to make the passive aspect *strong* by subsuming it wholly within the logic of the active aspect, by "empowering" it, betrays an underlying judgment against passivity. Strength is not, apparently, made perfect in weakness.[125] What such empowerment yields, Tocqueville warns, is a new and perhaps less salutary passivity.

Heidegger anxiously worries that the modern project involves "filling out the world."[126] Feminists contend that the concept of the self embed-

---

124. See Stephanie Coontz, *The Way We Never Were* (New York: Basic Books, 1992). Coontz's treatment of the traditional family suggests that the passive/active distinction between women and men arises out of the modern complex of capitalism and liberal ideology (p. 49). It is a *social construction*, rather than linked in some way to nature, and becomes prominent in the early nineteenth century (p. 58). This view is something of a caricature of liberal theory, in that it fails to recognize the rather qualified individualism proffered by liberal theory (see Mitchell, *Not by Reason Alone*, pp. 132–37), and also fails to grasp the deeper and long-standing philosophical pedigree of the relationship. Having said this much, however, I note that Coontz is helpful in pointing out that the *idea* of the traditional family reflects as much the verities of post–World War II affluence and culture in America as the facts of history. On the other hand, Bly offers an ethereal fabrication of primeval man that can exist nowhere but in disjointed fantasy. See Robert Bly, *Iron John: A Book about Men* (New York: Addison-Wesley, 1990).

125. Cf. 2 Cor. 12:9.

126. See Martin Heidegger, "The Essence of Truth," in *Basic Writings*, ed. David Farrell Krell (New York: Harper and Row, 1977), p. 134: "[T]he forgotten mystery of Dasein is not eliminated by forgottenness; rather, the forgottenness bestows on the apparent disappearance of what is forgotten a peculiar presence." Heidegger proceeds to note that this living amid errancy and refusing to grasp the Ground thrusts human beings into a certain kind of relationship with the world, one of proposing and planning, of using and using up. Errancy pro-

ded in liberal theory is suspiciously gender biased.[127] Defenders of faith righteously proclaim the need for religion to guide human life in a world that would wish to live without it. These insights are, properly understood, correct; and the wanton disregard against which they protest must be redressed. The wood pigeons that filled the "deep silence of the North American wilderness" are now extinct! Mother nature is less and less able to receive father industriousness without violation. What was unthinkable for Tocqueville, namely, that the passive element of nature, in the family, and of religion, would succumb to the active element, is increasingly becoming a contemporary verity. This verity, moreover, can only grow more acute without the once existing mechanisms of an awesome wilderness, differently structured family, and religious understanding that was capable of attenuating what, following thinkers from the writers of the Old Testament and Plato to Heidegger, may be a universal propensity to be drawn to the clamorous, the visible, and the illusory—the *active*.[128] The time of retrievable errors (to invoke Tocqueville's phrase), where circumstance favors the Americans' good fortune, is coming to a close.

---

duces a peculiar kind of relationship to the world. Standing before Being in passivity, *letting-be*, is the condition under which human life does not betray the errancy that is its restless activity and *evasion* of death. See also Rousseau, *Emile*, bk. 4, p. 282: "[T]he more [man] wants to flee [death], the more he senses it."

127. Although her claims were not directed toward political theory, Carol Gilligan's *In a Different Voice* (Cambridge, Mass.: Harvard University Press, 1982) served to focus attention in this direction. Kolberg's six-stage theory of moral development, she argues, supposes a psychological profile that can be traced (through Piaget) to Kant's privileging of reason and autonomy—historically masculine attributes. (See Jean Bethke Elshtain, *Meditations on Modern Political Thought: Masculine/Feminine Themes from Luther to Arendt* [New York: Praeger Publishers, 1986], pp. 21–35). It should be noted that Tocqueville does *not* privilege reason and autonomy, and that his "relegation" of women to their own sphere is a mechanism for combating the deleterious effects of both. Moreover, one of the odd paradoxes of the present situation is that while the woman's sphere is on the one hand being derogated, on the other hand the privatization of the life of *both* men and women is increasing. See Elshtain, *Meditations*, p. 116.

128. The passive aspect will always be present; the only question is *where*. Tocqueville worries that the form that passivity will take in the future for the Americans is the passivity of citizens before a tyrant. See Tocqueville, *Democracy in America*, vol. 2, part 4, chaps. 1–7, pp. 667–702. In Rousseau's view, the active element can only be appropriately quelled by women. "Each sex ought to keep to its own tone. A husband who is too gentle can make a woman impertinent; but unless a man is a monster, the gentleness of a woman brings him around and triumphs over him sooner or later" (*Emile*, bk. 5, p. 370).

7. WHEN BOUNDARIES ARE TRANSGRESSED

In one important respect, we have just considered three instances in which boundaries are being transgressed. There are, however, other ways to consider boundaries and their transgression, and to these I now turn.

The problem of boundary transgression is a formidable one in the history of political thought—from Plato [129] and Augustine [130] in more obvious ways; and in less obvious ways, perhaps, forward to Hobbes [131] and Rousseau. [132] Unless certain boundaries are observed, human life can only go astray. The irony of this verity, for Tocqueville, is that in the aristocratic age (now superseded) certain boundaries were observed; while in the democratic age the boundaries between human beings are largely obliterated. Boundaries, criteria of difference, break down. *Discrimination* becomes a term of derogation. True, the democratic soul is prone to withdraw into its own fortification, and for this reason associations are necessary to promote a redrawing of boundaries; yet the effacement of difference is an essential change that occurs in the movement toward democracy. It is, in fact, this very effacement (with its

---

129. See Plato, *Republic*, bk. 3, 414d–15c, where the city is to maintain a strict separation between those whose souls are composed of one metal and those composed of another. The general problem of justice is how to assure that "each is granted its due." Unhappiness is a consequence of not maintaining what is appropriate to each.

130. The fundamental problem for Augustine is the human propensity to confuse the demarcation between the Creator and the created, between God and humankind. This failure expresses itself as pride. See *City of God*, vol. 7, bk. 12, chap. 6, p. 253 (*CG*, p. 477).

131. See Hobbes, *Leviathan*, part 1, chap. 13, p. 101: "[In the state of nature there is no] *mine* and *thine* distinct" (emphasis in original). The state of nature— where the violation of boundaries abounds—can only be superseded by the *many* deferring to the *one* (Leviathan).

132. *Emile*, for example, is dedicated to the proposition that the boundary between childhood and adulthood has been transgressed by that education which prematurely draws the child into the adult world of learned knowledge and the fear of death—hence, the frontispieces to book 2 (p. 76: "Chiron training Achilles to run") and book 1 (p. ii: "Thetis dipping Achilles into the River Styx"), respectively. See p. 80: "[T]he man must be considered in the man and the child in the child"; and p. 90: "[N]ature wants children to be children before being men." The "famed societies" about which Rousseau speaks in the *First Discourse* are another instance of a boundary that must not be transgressed. There, knowledge must be *bounded*, kept within the purview of those capable of using knowledge *well*. See Rousseau, *First Discourse*, pp. 59–64.

concomitant obliteration of aristocratic sites of authority) that makes its possible for the soul in the modern age to withdraw into itself.[133]

A more thorough consideration of this matter of difference will wait until sections 2 and 3 of chapter 4. For present purposes we need only note that while boundaries break down in the democratic age, the effect of their effacement is equivocal. In the family, for instance, more *natural* bonds between members become possible when the conventions of the aristocratic order no longer exact their solemn price.[134] Beyond this, the obliteration of boundaries is not detrimental because the great leveling it accomplishes diminishes the magnitude of the transgressions possible within a democratic social order. While boundaries break down, the capacity of the solitary democratic soul—to accomplish either good or evil—dwindles:

> Therefore, as men become more alike and the principle of equality has quietly penetrated deep into the institutions and manners of the country, the rules of advancement become more inflexible and advancement itself slower. It becomes ever more difficult to reach a position of some importance quickly.[135]

And elsewhere,

> They have abolished the troublesome privileges of some of their fellows, but they have come up against the competition of all. The barrier has changed shape rather than place.[136]

Yet this is not the whole of the story. For while the very equality of the many keep most from rising above the level of the rest (which, paradoxically, reinstates the boundary upon thought and action that was ef-

133. Theologically, the supersession of the Catholic claim of the need for worldly mediators by the Protestant insistence that God the Son alone was a sufficient Mediator disposes the soul that has rejected God to fall into the self-enclosed world so in evidence in contemporary America, a phenomenon about which Bellah et al. protest in *Habits of the Heart*. Catholicism may not have aimed high enough in its choice of mediator, but should the High Ground of Protestantism give way, there is no fallback upon worldly mediators that may at least arrest the fall into solipsism. The self-enclosure of the American soul is not, on this reading, strictly a result of the "death of God." More than this, it is the result of Protestant *habits* that refuse to die *along with* the death of God. For a discussion of the Protestant habit of thinking about the equality of all under the One, see Mitchell, *Not by Reason Alone*, pp. 144–47.

134. Tocqueville, *Democracy in America*, vol. 2, part 3, chap. 8, pp. 584–89.

135. Tocqueville, *Democracy in America*, vol. 2, part 3, chap. 19, p. 630.

136. Tocqueville, *Democracy in America*, vol. 2, part 2, chap. 13, p. 537. See also Hobbes, *Leviathan*, part 1, chap. 13, p. 98: "[E]quality of ability produces equality of hope." Our likeness with our neighbor conduces to diffidence.

faced by the movement toward democracy), the few who do penetrate the boundary reinstated by the sheer numerical force of the many *encounter almost no restraint.* Once unbounded from the many, there is little to stop them. In *Emile*, Rousseau presents the problem well.

> The perpetual constraint in which you keep your pupils exacerbates their vivacity. The more they are held in check under your eyes, the more they are turbulent the moment they get away. They have to compensate themselves when they can for the harsh constraint in which you keep them. Two schoolboys from the city will do more damage in a place than the young of an entire village.[137]

The democratic soul is like the child from the city: "held in check" by competitive pressure from others like them, and "turbulent the moment they get away" from them.

Boundaries here are not as much institutionally drawn as imposed by the restrictive burden of numbers. The very absence of borders opens up the same field to all; yet the reach of *each* is diminished precisely because *all* may now play. The relative strength of each is reduced in proportion to the effacement of boundaries that stand in the way of all.[138] Reach extends while grasp, paradoxically, recedes.

This arrangement by which the very absence of boundaries constitutes them anew obtains, as I have said, for the many. Yet there are the few who penetrate this boundary that is not a boundary; and it is the puzzling juxtaposition in America of the few without borders and the many severely constrained *by the very absence of borders* about which something must be said here. The best way to comprehend the nature of the problem—for it is a problem—is to consider Tocqueville's observations about American monuments. Monuments, as it turns out, serve as a metaphor for the peculiar problem of boundary transgression in America.

> Nowhere else do the citizens seem smaller than in a democratic nation, and nowhere else does the nation itself seem greater, so that it is

---

137. Rousseau, *Emile*, bk. 2, p. 92.

138. See Rousseau, *Emile*, bk. 2, p. 84: "[S]ociety has made man weaker not only in taking from him the right he had over his own strength but, above all, in making his strength insufficient for him." Rousseau's concern here is with the question of how to supplement the natural weakness of children so that they might develop in such a way that their desires never outstrip their capacity to fulfill them (p. 80). The democratic soul, Tocqueville insists, desires to have no boundaries, yet it is precisely this condition that leads to their impotence—hence, the "secret longing" for a powerful state to stand over them in order that they might vicariously enjoy the strength that they lack.

easily conceived as a vast picture. Imagination shrinks at the thought of themselves as individuals and expands beyond all limits at the thought of the state. Hence people living cramped lives in tiny houses often conceive their public monuments on a gigantic scale. . . . Thus democracy not only encourages the making of a lot of trivial things but also inspires the erection of a very few large monuments. *However, there is nothing at all between these two extremes.*[139]

There are two distinctive (though related) moments here. On the one hand, there are a myriad of small projects that betray the isolation, relative weakness, and pedestrian concerns of the many. On the other hand, there are the few grand projects that starkly contrast with the first type, and that have no regard whatsoever for boundaries. The message here is clear: democracy is predisposed toward two, seemingly opposed, alternatives; enterprises are either stringently constrained or they know no boundaries. Ironically, the absence of boundaries in the democratic age gives rise to both conditions.

The social manifestation of this axiom is not difficult to discern. The democratic age bridles most; the remaining few have free reign. Both trajectories are pernicious. The many, whose seemingly unconstrained and laborious efforts yield little that their like-minded neighbor, too, might not attain, dimly intimate the limitations proffered by the democratic age—and are apt to resign themselves in defeat even while they rush impetuously forward.[140] The breathless and unceasing efforts of *this* democratic soul belie an impotence that can all too easily precipitate resignation.

On the other hand, the few who are unbridled, while they may have escaped the Charybdis of resignation, are wholly diverted by the Scylla of restlessness. *Their* desires are not discouraged. Here is the hyperambition of those who rise above the middling level to which most are relegated in the democratic age, a hyperambition the objects of desire of which, however, are in no way different than those who are incapable of acting with much effectiveness.

139. Tocqueville, *Democracy in America*, vol. 2, part 1, chap. 12, p. 469 (emphasis added). The city of Washington, built amid a swamp on a scale far too grand for the early American nation, is perhaps the most prominent example.

140. On Tocqueville's view, this limitation placed upon the many in civil life is precisely what makes the military so dangerous in a democracy. The military is the only avenue open to those who cannot overstep the boundaries imposed upon them in civil life—hence the great paradox of democratic societies: that its citizens want peace and its armies want war. See *Democracy in America*, vol. 2, part 3, chap. 22, pp. 645–51.

> They [men in democracies] are much *more in love with success than with glory.* . . . What they most desire is power. . . . As a result, very vulgar tastes often go with their enjoyment of extraordinary prosperity, and it would seem that their only object in raising to supreme power was to gratify trivial and coarse appetites more easily.[141]

Those few who come to ascend over the rest are, in a word, no less shortsighted (in their goals) than the many whom they have left behind. While they may resemble an aristocratic class, their tastes are democratic through and through.

On the basis of this peculiar configuration there are, in Tocqueville's view, unambiguous implications for how to structure incentives in a democratic society. This is made most clear, perhaps, in his discussion of pride. Recall that for Hobbes (not to mention Augustine), an antidote to human pridefulness must be found for there to be civil peace at all. Hobbes, of course, found a resolution to this problem in the figure of the *mortal-God* (while Augustine thought that only God the Son could arrest the debilitation of pride).

Tocqueville, however, thinks of pride less as an unwavering ontological fact of human life than as a sociohistorical composition. Pride was a problem in the aristocratic age, but in the democratic age the willfulness of pride has been supplanted by the reasonableness of self-interested calculation. In Nietzsche's idiom, the ascension of democracy is the victory of the prideless soul, the soul without any longing to be "a dangerous across, a dangerous on-the-way, a dangerous looking-back, a dangerous shuddering and stopping."[142] The prideless soul wants above all to keep its boundaries intact and diminutive enough that meager strength may defend its paltry claims. The will to self-overcoming is utterly absent here! So, too, is the prospect that boundaries will be overstepped.

Tocqueville, in his own way, agrees. Like Nietzsche, he worries that the "last man" of the democratic future will have neither great capacity nor inclination.

> People suppose that the new [democracies] are going to change shape daily, but my fear is that they will end by being too unalterably fixed with the same institutions, prejudices, and mores, so that mankind will stop progressing and will dig itself in. I fear that the mind may keep folding itself up in a narrower compass forever without produc-

141. Tocqueville, *Democracy in America*, vol. 2, part 3, chap. 19, p. 631 (emphasis added). The aristocratic soul, recall, desires glory (a passion); the democratic soul, in turn, desires commercial success (an interest).

142. Nietzsche, *Thus Spoke Zarathustra*, prologue, p. 14.

ing new ideas, that men will wear themselves out in trivial, futile activity, and that for all the constant agitation humanity will make no advance.[143]

There is, however, an aspect to the problem of the "last man" that Nietzsche did not surmise. Following Tocqueville, while the many may cease to "shoot their arrow of longing beyond themselves," the few do so with abandon. Their pridefulness knows no boundary. Their aspirations, it is true, do not become magisterial in virtue of their relative advantage; attending singularly to the *objects* of their aspirations, however, disregards a vital fact about the democratic soul. While both the many and the few may have similar objects of desire (while, that is, they are both "last men"), there is undoubtedly a difference between the many and the few in respect to their capacity to indulge their desires. Self-interest rather than glorious passion directs both; yet both are not equality bounded in virtue of the triviality of their longings. This, Nietzsche seemed not to have grasped.

Tocqueville's understanding of the pridelessness of the democratic soul is, I suggest, more nuanced than is Nietzsche's. While he would concur with Nietzsche (against Hobbes) that pride is not the principal obstacle to human peace,[144] the prideless few—the seemingly *noble ones* whose success outstrips the accomplishments of the many—are to be dramatically distinguished from the rest in respect to their capacities, but not in respect to their yearnings. In a democratic society pride must be encouraged; the longings of the heart must be nurtured wherever possible. Yet it is the pride of the many that must be fostered, not the pride of the few![145]

143. Tocqueville, *Democracy in America*, vol. 2, part 3, chap. 21, p. 645. Nietzsche, as I have said, has this worry as well; yet he wonders: "[M]ust the ancient fire not some day flare up much more terribly, after much longer preparation?" (*Genealogy of Morals*, first essay, sec. 17, p. 54).

144. See Hobbes, *De cive*, preface, p. 103. Contrast this to Nietzsche, for whom "a legal order thought of as sovereign and universal, not as a means in a struggle between power-complexes but as a means of *preventing* all struggle in general . . . would be a principle *hostile to life*, an agent in the dissolution and destruction of man, an attempt to assassinate the future of man, a sign of weariness, a secret path to nothingness" (*Genealogy of Morals*, second essay, sec. 11, p. 76 [emphasis in original]).

145. See Tocqueville's letter to Sophie Swetchine, September 10, 1856: "[H]ow I love to hear you speak so nobly against everything that resembles slavery! I am very much of your opinion that a more equal distribution of goods and rights in this world is the greatest aim that those who conduct human affairs can have in view" (*Selected Letters*, p. 337).

A paradox of the democratic age is that while the many will draw their boundaries closely around themselves, the few will overstep such boundaries with abandon. Both groups are prideless (in Nietzsche's idiom: self-interest, not passion, rules), yet *only the pride of the many is to be encouraged* in the age of democracy. Ambition must be fostered, but not in everyone. Both the few and the many are small-minded; yet the few will enjoy the bounty of their petty desires, while the many often will not. There is little need to foster the development of further desire among the few; among the many, however, the need is acute.

I have said repeatedly throughout these chapters that, in Tocqueville's view, the commercial success of the Americans must be understood on the basis of a calculus that is not, strictly speaking, economic. What may make economic sense may make social nonsense. Here is perhaps the most striking example. While it may be argued on economic grounds, for example, that reducing the tax burden upon the wealthy will produce enduring economic growth, the theory wholly disregards the peculiar way in which boundaries are imposed and transgressed in the democratic age.[146] Incentives structured to encourage the few merely give freer reign to those already relatively unburdened by boundaries; over time these incentives reinforce precisely the problem about which Tocqueville worried, namely, that the many become mortally frustrated with the gnawing sense of their relative impotence. The democratic age conspires to yield this habit of thinking anyway; social and economic policy that does not seek a remedy for it ultimately produces precisely the kind of malaise it is intended to inoculate against:

> The task should be to put, in advance, limits beyond which [ambition] would not be allowed to break. But we should be very careful not to hamper its free energy *within the permitted limits*.[147]

8. OF EMPIRE

What, precisely, is the relationship between democracy and empire? For Tocqueville, this is at once a historical and a sociological question requiring, on the one hand, an understanding of the psychological principles that predominate in each epoch of history and, on the other hand,

146. The Laffer curve, upon which important policy decisions were made during the past decade, is predicated upon logic alone and wholly disregards Tocqueville's insights about wealth in the democratic age.

147. Tocqueville, *Democracy in America*, vol. 2, part 3, chap. 19, pp. 631–32 (emphasis added).

an account of the social forces that conspire, paradoxically, to render democratic *peoples* peaceable and democratic *armies* pernicious. These two aspects, historical and sociological, operate at cross-purposes to one another.

The historical aspect of the question can be posed in the following way. If in the aristocratic age the predominant principle is glory, and in the democratic age it is comparatively innocuous self-interest; and if the aristocratic age has been superseded by the age of equality, as Tocqueville suggests, then has the very desire for empire become dormant,[148] if not expunged? Does the democratic soul, in other words, even have the capacity to overstep those boundaries that the desire for empire requires, or does self-interest preclude boundary transgressions of this sort in favor of a languid but secure fence around its fragile border? To put this another way, can it be concluded that the democratic age is one of general tranquility?[149]

If history truly evinces the transformation that Tocqueville imagines, then the democratic age would not seem to provide the inventory of attributes that empire seems to require. Indeed, war is antithetic to the democratic soul. War

> annoys and often drives to desperation that countless crowd of citizens whose petty passions daily require peace for their satisfaction.[150]

And elsewhere,

> If [as I fear] citizens continue to shut themselves up more and more narrowly in the little circle of petty domestic interests and keep themselves constantly busy therein, there is a danger that they may in the end become practically out of reach of those great and powerful pub-

148. Cf. Nietzsche, for whom the beast always lurks under the surface of the Judaic-Christian-democratic soul. No overlaying of civility and tame *self-interest* can wholly obliterate the trace of the barbarian who finds a "profound joy in all destruction" (*Genealogy of Morals*, first essay, sec. 11, p. 42). While the valence of Tocqueville's work is quite different from Nietzsche's, there are places where he seems to agree. See *Democracy in America*, vol. 1, part 2, chap. 10, p. 331 n. 18: "[W]hen [a European] does in the end return to civilized society [after a long hiatus], he confesses that the existence whose afflictions he has described has *secret charms which he cannot define*" (emphasis added). The American Indian represents the love of glory, honor, and ancestral ways—in short, all that will be overcome by the age of equality.

149. See Immanuel Kant, "Idea for a Universal History from a Cosmopolitan Point of View," in *On History*, ed. Lewis Beck (New York: Macmillan, 1963), theses 5–8, pp. 16–23.

150. Tocqueville, *Democracy in America*, vol. 2, part 3, chap. 22, p. 649.

lic emotions which do indeed perturb peoples but which also make them grow and refresh them. [151]

For Tocqueville, (aristocratic) glory and (democratic) interest are independent of one another historically and cannot be conjoined. (Does not the tragedy of the Indians in America confirm this?) The democratic *age* can, in fact, be spoken of only because glory has already given way. The great leveling has occurred; notwithstanding the residues of the arrest that still linger, glory is behind us. No great accomplishments may be expected in the future. This ought not to cause us to bemoan the relinquishment of noble passions.[152] They cannot, after all, be retrieved.[153] The future will display the ordered commotion of interest; glory and empire, however, will be unknown. The "end of history" is all but upon us;[154] citizens of such a world will prefer the market to the *Übermensch*.

151. Tocqueville, *Democracy in America*, vol. 2, part 3, chap. 21, p. 645. It was this worry that prompts him to remark several pages later: "I do not wish to speak ill of war; war almost always widens a nation's mental horizons and raises its heart. In some cases it may be the only factor which can prevent the exaggerated growth of certain inclinations naturally produced by equality and be the antidote needed for certain inveterate diseases to which democratic societies are liable" (chap. 22, p. 649). See also Augustine, *City of God*, vol. 6, bk. 1, chap. 30, p. 67 (*CG*, p. 42).

152. See Raymond Aron, *Main Currents in Sociological Thought* (New York: Doubleday Anchor, 1968), 1:259: "[Tocqueville] brought to democracy neither the enthusiasm of those who expected from it a transfiguration of the human lot nor the hostility of those who saw in it no less than the very decomposition of human society."

153. Beginning from the supposition that "modern political philosophy came into being through the conscious break with the principles established by Socrates," (*History of Political Philosophy*, ed. Leo Strauss and Joseph Cropsey [Chicago: University of Chicago Press, 1972], introduction, p. 2), much of Strauss's writing was dedicated to the proposition that ancient wisdom *could* be retrieved, that modernity had gone astray but could be redeemed if it returned to the ancients.

154. See Francis Fukayama, *The End of History* (New York: Free Press, 1991). Notwithstanding the *boredom* that the victory of economic liberalism carries in its wake, Fukayama supposes that such liberalism is stable (if not ossifying). Joseph A. Schumpeter argues (in *Capitalism, Socialism, and Democracy* [New York: Harper and Row, 1976]), on the contrary, that economic liberalism is *unstable*, that it is undermined and transformed by its very success. The secret hidden longing for a powerful state about which Tocqueville speaks—which may undo democratic freedom—corresponds to Schumpeter's worry about the emergence of the bureaucratic state. The logic by which democracy falls into the tyranny of the bureaucratic state for Tocqueville, however, is psychological rather than economic (as it was for Schumpeter).

The matter cannot be left at this monovalent understanding, however. The sociological aspect of the question of the relationship between empire and democracy suggests quite another outcome. In the previous section (sec. 7) I noted the paradox that accompanies the absence of boundaries within a democracy. The very absence of boundaries for the many serves to constrain their motion with respect to each other just as effectively as if they were stringently restrained by explicit borders. Effacing boundaries does not necessarily increase the degrees of freedom available.

The paradox that the absence of boundaries constitutes them anew is one that pertains, as we have discussed, to civil society. That domain, however, is enveloped, as it were, by another society that is responsible for maintaining the integrity of the territorial system within which civil society abides. This other society—the military—has peculiar attributes, however, which prompt it toward war rather than toward the peace that is so venerated in civil society.[155]

In the face of the stringent constraints upon advancement in civil society, the military serves as a kind of pressure release valve, one toward which the democratic soul is drawn precisely because there, the burden of sheer numbers is less acutely felt. Advancement is more likely.

> In democratic armies all the soldiers may become officers, and that fact makes desire for promotion general and opens *almost infinite doors* to military ambition.[156]

The conditions under which advancement is most prompt, however, are the conditions of war. While inactive, the military is perhaps only slightly less immune to the pressures felt in civil society. War, however, is an occasion to burst the bonds that are constituted by equality itself.

---

155. In this regard Kant was wrong in judging that republics, because of their peace-loving citizens in whom the right to declare war is vested, would be the only form of government that would assure peace among nations. See Immanuel Kant, "Perpetual Peace," in Beck, *On History*, p. 94: "[I]f the consent of the citizens is required in order to decide that war should be declared . . . nothing is more natural than that they would be very cautious in commencing such a poor game."

156. Tocqueville, *Democracy in America*, vol. 2, part 3, chap. 22, p. 647 (emphasis added). See also Hobbes, *Leviathan*, part 1, chap. 11, p. 81: "[N]eedy men, and hardy, not contented with their present condition; as also, all men that are ambitious of military command, are inclined to continue the causes of war; and to stir up trouble and sedition: for there is no honour military but by war; nor any such hope to mend an ill game, as by causing a new shuffle."

Therefore, all the ambitious minds in a democratic army ardently long for war, because war makes vacancies available and at last allows violations of the rule of seniority, which is the one privilege natural to democracy.[157]

The equality of all in civil society, it would seem, promotes the desire for war (among democratic souls) in the military.

The paradox that arises out of the conjunction of these two arguments (historical and sociological) is a sobering one indeed. The social equality that tends toward peace within civil society—and, in fact, conspires to build bonds between different democratic nations[158]—also carries with it the penchant to produce a military that stands ever more strongly in need of a foreign other.[159] We can only wonder on the basis of the paradox that Tocqueville grasps whether the future will betray the following somber scenario: while democratic nations will resist fighting one another because of their civil like-mindedness, the equality that gives rise to this disposition will yield a military society ever more eager for war.

Put another way, while the boundaries between different democratic nations will become more and more permeable and tenuous, the boundaries between democratic and nondemocratic nations will grow proportionally stronger. The mystification of the other, of the nondemocratic "aggressor," will be required by a military whose purpose of maintaining boundaries is less and less needed among the democratic federation of nations. Empire will not come to pass; like Nietzsche's ethic of no-

157. Tocqueville, *Democracy in America*, vol. 2, part 3, chap. 22, p. 647. See p. 648: "[M]aking [military honors] within the reach of all causes soldiers to dream of battlefields."

158. See Tocqueville, *Democracy in America*, vol. 2, part 3, chap. 26, p. 660: "[A]s the spread of equality, taking place in several countries at once, simultaneously draws the inhabitants into trade and industry, not only do their tastes come to be alike, but their interests come to be so mixed and intermingled that no nation can inflict on others ills which will not fall back on its own head." Democratic nations, in other words, will not wish to fight other democratic nations.

159. The disposition to constitute an other cannot be understood in social structural terms alone. See Vamik D. Volkan, *The Need to Have Enemies and Allies* (London: Jason Aronson, 1988), pp. 82–154, for a psychological account. Volkan's concern is with why conflicts based upon identities constituted in and through relations with an *other* "seem to defy all concerted efforts at resolution" (p. 6). His conclusions are coincident with Nietzsche's observations about the soul ruled by the ethic of resentment, though for Nietzsche such a soul is an historical creation, not a given datum of psychology.

bility, empire is expansive, bold, self-referential and needs no external enemy.[160] The alternative to empire, however, is not necessarily "perpetual peace." The spirit of equality—in Nietzsche's idiom, the ethic of resentment—requires an other. While this spirit may succeed in constituting an "us" that abrogates national boundaries between democracies,[161] this improvement upon the impulse toward empire may carry with it the need to draw lines of demarcation ever more strongly in other places. "They" are necessary; a democratic military will happily participate in this construction.[162]

9. OF PROPERTY AND RIGHTS

> It can never be too often repeated, that the time for fixing every essential right on a legal basis is while our rulers are honest, and ourselves united. From the conclusion of this war we shall be going down hill. . . . They will forget themselves, but in the sole faculty of making money, and will never think of uniting to effect a due respect for their rights. The shackles, therefore, which shall not be knocked off at the conclusion of this war, will remain on us long, will be made heavier and heavier, till our rights shall revive or expire in a convulsion.[163]

> Another instinct which is very natural for democracies, and very dangerous, is a tendency to despise individual rights and take little account of them. . . . Moreover, it happens, at the same time and among

160. See Nietzsche, *Genealogy of Morals*, first essay, sec. 10, pp. 36–39.

161. See Tocqueville, *Democracy in America*, vol. 2, part 3, chap. 1, p. 565: "[A]s a people become more like one another, they show themselves reciprocally more compassionate, and the law of nations becomes more gentle."

162. Cf. Schmitt, who argues that the problem with democratic regimes, constituted as they are by tamed souls, is that they will not have the strength or stamina to resist an incursion by a more virile neighbor. In his words, "[I]f a people no longer possesses the energy or the will to maintain itself in the sphere of politics, the latter will not thereby vanish from the world. Only a weak people will vanish" (Carl Schmitt, *The Concept of the Political* [New Brunswick, N.J.: Rutgers University Press, 1976], p. 53). One need only peruse the pages of Gray's *The Warriors* to see that "democratic man," like any other, is more than willing to fall in battle, and that all that is needed to do this is to demonize the enemy, make him wholly *other*. This the democratic man is eminently capable of doing. See also Freud, *Civilization and Its Discontents*, pp. 72–74. On his reading, Schmitt's error may have been in assuming that warfare is an extension of political *will* rather than being based on an aggressive *instinct* that would *more* wish to express itself upon another (society) as civilization becomes ever tamer.

163. Thomas Jefferson, Notes on the State of Virginia (New York: W. W. Norton, 1954), query 17, p. 161. See also Tocqueville, *Democracy in America*, author's preface to the twelfth edition, p. xiv.

the same peoples that have conceived a natural scorn for individual rights, that the rights of society are naturally extended and consolidated. This means that men become less attached to private rights just at the moment when it is most necessary to maintain and defend the few that still exist.[164]

Let us concede from the outset that rights are precarious. The call for rights may, no doubt, reach such a crescendo that apprehension about their durability, if not universality, seems suspect. The difference between rights as a rallying cry and rights in practice, however, is massive. To understand rights truly, the euphoric din of the rallying cry must be ignored, and the fragility of the practice attended to.

There are two aspects to the matter of why rights are tenuous. The first can be illuminated by considering Tocqueville's succinct remark: "[G]uided by [rights], we can each of us be independent without arrogance and obedient without servility."[165] The implication here, plainly enough, is that without rights the general disposition would be to gravitate in two opposite directions: toward arrogant independence *and* toward servile obedience. Tocqueville does not say that these two are coterminous with each other, yet within Augustinian psychology they clearly are. His remark,

[T]hat city which lusts to dominate the world and which, though nations bend to its yoke, *is itself dominated by its passion for dominion*,[166]

proffers the same insight, namely, that the arrogance of the seemingly independent soul that would wish to rule the world is necessarily complemented by a servile obedience. They are dialectically related; the latter is the internal contradiction of the former, and vice versa. The cycle will not end without an antidote.

The vicious polarity of independent arrogance and servile obedience can be overcome, in Augustine's view, only by God through his Son. While Tocqueville may be in agreement with Augustine in certain respects, he is quite insistent that the *use* of rights offers a powerful antidote to this unsavory polarity.

His disagreement with Augustine, such as it may be, would stem more from the fact that religion is faltering rather than that it is inadequate to the task in some ultimate sense. This, in fact, is the second source of the fragility of rights. In Tocqueville's words,

164. Tocqueville, *Democracy in America*, vol. 2, part 4, chap. 7, p. 699.

165. Tocqueville, *Democracy in America*, vol. 1, part 2, chap. 6, p. 238.

166. Augustine, *City of God*, vol. 6, bk. 1, preface, p. 18 (emphasis added) [*CG*, p. 5].

> Do you not see that religions are growing weak and that the concep-
> tion and sanctity of rights is vanishing? Do you not see that mores are
> changing and that the moral conception of rights is being obliterated
> with them?[167]

Religion here is the source of the *idea* of rights. That source (which
declares that each and every soul is consecrated in the eyes of God),[168]
however, is increasingly being disregarded. Rights, which allow human
beings to traverse the propitious territory between arrogant independence and servile obedience, must therefore also be linked to something other than God if they are to endure. Rights may originate from
God, but Tocqueville is not sanguine that that is enough. The theological analogue to this view—and here Tocqueville's Catholicism shines
through—is that human frailty requires that we have practices that instantiate in human life what mere ideas cannot.

> Do you not notice on all sides beliefs are giving way to arguments,
> and feelings to calculations? If amid this universal collapse you do not
> succeed in linking the idea of rights to personal interest, which pro-
> vides the only stable point in the human heart, what other means will
> be left you to govern the world, if not fear?[169]

Absent the instantiation of rights at a site of practical experience, it
would seem, rights will not endure. This is not to say, of course, that the
idea of rights is irrelevant, and that only the practical experience is necessary. A wholly "materialist" explanation will not suffice. *Both* the idea
and the practice are necessary; neither the rallying cry of rights absent
the site of their instantiation will secure them (the lesson of the French
Revolution, about which I will speak briefly in section 1 of the next
chapter), nor will the site where rights are practiced without the idea of
the universal dignity of humankind before God.

Rights, then, come from Christianity; but the possession of property

---

167. Tocqueville, *Democracy in America*, vol. 1, part 2, chap. 6, p. 239.

168. Tocqueville's observation, made at the outset of *Democracy in America*,
merits repeating here: "Christianity, which has declared all men equal in the
sight of God, cannot hesitate to acknowledge all citizens equal before the law"
(Author's Introduction, p. 16). The *declaration* may by the first cause, as it were,
but words are not sufficient; the practice is the necessary supplement.

169. Tocqueville, *Democracy in America*, vol. 1, part 2, chap. 6, p. 239. See
also Hegel, *Philosophy of Right*, sec. 153, p. 109: "[T]he right of individuals to be
subjectively destined to freedom is fulfilled when they belong to an actual ethical order, because their conviction of their freedom finds its truth in such an
objective order, and it is in an ethical order that they are actually in possession
of their own essence or their own inner universality."

grants to citizens the practical experience that allows them to make sense of rights. Possessing property constitutes a certain kind of person, the person capable of understanding the idea that mutual recognition is superior to the oscillation between "arrogant independence" and "servile obedience" that is the palpable alternative.[170] Without practical experience with property, the mutual recognition that is the essence of rights can be no more than a vacuous formalism.[171]

If these brief remarks have not made it clear already, property is, for Tocqueville, more than a economic datum. It is a prerequisite for the very health of a democratic society. The democratic soul is already prone to the twin excesses of utter independence and servile obedience (to the all-powerful state); rights, it seems, are a bulwark against falling into either form of errancy. Property is essential for this bulwark to be effective; it is less a condition of economic vitality than a precondition for the development of citizens capable of sustaining democratic freedom.

Locke (himself no defender of the wholly economic justification of property) would have it that possessing property is the condition under which the bounty of mother nature may be most fully developed and the boundary around the self preserved.[172] Property, for him, is the occasion for industriousness and reasonableness to emerge. Much of his defense, indeed, amounts to a plea to allow it to issue forth.

Tocqueville moves in a slightly different direction. Unlike Locke, and following Rousseau, industriousness and reasonableness are capacities that require above all practical experience for their development.

170. See Tocqueville, *Democracy in America*, vol. 1, part 2, chap. 6, p. 238: "[W]hen a baby first begins to move among things outside himself instinct leads him to make use of anything his hands can grasp; he has no idea of other people's property, not even that it exists; but as he is instructed in the value of things and discovers that he too may be despoiled, he becomes more circumspect, and in the end is led to respect for others that which he wishes to be respected for himself." The allusion to childhood and property is not one without precedence. See Rousseau, *Emile*, bk. 2, pp. 98–100. Rousseau concludes Emile's lesson with property with the injunction: "[R]emember that in everything your lessons ought to be more in actions than in speeches; for children easily forget what they have said and what has been said to them, but not what they have done and what has been done to them" (pp. 99–100). For both Rousseau and Tocqueville, practice has a kind of preeminence over ideas; or rather, without practice, ideas lack the referent they must have.

171. See Hegel, *Philosophy of Right*, sec. 217, p. 139. Tocqueville, too, recognizes that mutual recognition and the rule of law is possible in America because citizens possess property. (See *Democracy in America*, vol. 1, part 2, chap. 6, p. 238.)

172. See Mitchell, *Not by Reason Alone*, pp. 81–90.

Rousseau's disagreements with Locke would be shared by Tocqueville.[173] When children learn from practical experience that they may lose their possessions unless they respect the possessions of others, they become capable of independence without arrogance and obedience without servility. The fundamental lesson here is not what effect property has upon economic vitality but rather what it causes to be created within democratic citizens. Any democratic society wishing to sustain itself must recognize the difference between the two. They are not necessarily opposed, but one must be recognized as primary. Put another way, the psychological and political aspect of property must be granted preeminence over the economic aspect.

10. OF THE SUFFICIENCY OF POLITICS AND ECONOMICS

Emerson remarks,

> The antidote to [the] abuse of formal Government, is, the influence of private character, the growth of the Individual; the reappearance of the principle to supersede the proxy; the appearance of the wise man, of whom the existing government, is, it must be owned, but a shabby imitation.[174]

The argument about the relative standing of politics and economics is a longstanding one. Aristotle, it was, who first argued that quasi friendship based upon *use* can never be the basis for an enduring society,[175] and that higher than (economic) friendship is political friendship. In different guises this argument has appeared again and again.

Equally longstanding, as Emerson's passage indicates, is the debate about the sufficiency of politics or economics taken alone or together. About this question it was Plato who first argued that neither the love of politics nor the love of wealth will awaken the soul from its slumber.[176]

These two understandings, Plato and Aristotle's, accord in the view

173. See Rousseau, *Emile*, preface, p. 33: "[A]fter Locke's book [on education], my subject was still entirely fresh." Locke argued that reason must be developed in the child; Rousseau argues that *prior* to the education of reason must be practical experience.

174. Emerson, "Politics," p. 415.

175. See Aristotle, *Nicomachean Ethics*, bk. 9, chap. 9, 1169a9. Aristotle's argument is already implicit in Plato's *Republic*, bk. 8, 550c–555b. See also Karl Polanyi, *The Great Transformation* (Boston: Beacon Press, 1944), pp. 43–55, for a historical narrative predicated on the distinction Aristotle would wish to make.

176. See Plato, *Republic*, bk. 10, 611d–612a.

that the love of wealth is not a sufficient principle upon which to build an enduring society; and while the danger of oversimplification cannot be taken lightly, if not Smith, then certainly his heirs, who have intently built up the edifice of modern economic science, have moved in the opposite direction. Notwithstanding Tocqueville's deep appreciation of the American commercial spirit, in this regard his sympathies were more with Aristotle, for whom economics could not be the master science. He did not, as I have said in chapter 1, return from America and write an update to that portion of *The Wealth of Nations* from which the Chicago school has so exhaustively drawn.

Having made this distinction, however, we would be mistaken to rest satisfied with it. While politics may rank higher than economics (following Aristotle), religion ranks higher than both. In this regard, Tocqueville and Aristotle part company,[177] and the peculiar affinity between Tocqueville and Plato comes into view. Put another way, politics—construed as a *wholly immanent* affair—is not, for Tocqueville, the master science. Without taking into account the otherworldly dimension of human life, that place beyond the "cave" of transient pleasures that exists for us as hope and promise, both political and economic science will falter. Neither conventional political or economic science is sufficient. The next chapter is devoted to that suprapolitical and supra-economic dimension that is religion; here, however, I will offer a brief prolegomenon.

Convenient disciplinary boundaries offer an all-too-convenient answer to the question of whether the spiritual dimension is appropriately treated by political[178] or economic[179] science at all, as the scope of most

177. Aristotle recognizes that the philosophical life, the life of contemplation, is higher than the political life, the life of action, yet seems unable (or unwilling) to specify the relationship between the two. The well-known passages in the *Nicomachean Ethics* (bk. 10, chaps. 7–8, 1177a12–1179a32) where the philosophical life seems to *intrude* upon his discussion of politics confirm this awkwardness. I will argue, in chapter 4, that the nexus between politics and religion, for Tocqueville, is the (political) *character and habits of thinking* produced by Christian religion. The uneasy tension between contemplation and action in Aristotle does not readily map onto the terrain that Tocqueville explores.

178. In contrast see Eldon Eisenach, *The Lost Promise of Progressivism* (Lawrence: University of Kansas Press, 1994). Eisenach argues that universities were the church for social scientists during the Progressive Era. See especially pp. 98–103.

179. In contrast see Robert H. Nelson, *Reaching for Heaven on Earth* (Savage, Md.: Rowan and Littlefield, 1991). Nelson argues that economic theories are *disguised* theologies.

of its research indicates. Science, however, is knowledge adequate to its object; and Tocqueville, adhering to this understanding, insists on considering spiritual matters in his (new) political science. *Human* life—the real subject of science—is neither lived, nor can it be understood, as a wholly immanent affair.

The confirmation of this claim about human life is to be found, paradoxically, in Tocqueville's observations about the effect of trying to live wholly in the world: the more human beings embrace the world, the more explosive will be the demand to transcend it![180] Hence, in his view, the periodic cycles of spiritualism that irrupt in America, which are unknown in Europe. The Americans, a people rightly understood to love worldly wealth more than any other, are prone to extreme spiritualism because in focusing almost wholly on the world they disregard a vital part of their being. The more Americans throw themselves into material life, the more the demand emerges that that other portion of their being express itself.[181]

> Although the desire to acquire the good things of this world is the dominant passion among Americans, there are momentary respites when their souls seem suddenly to *break the restraining bonds of matter* and rush impetuously heavenward. . . . We should not be surprised at this. . . . The soul has needs which must be satisfied. Whatever pains are taken to distract it from itself, it soon grows bored, restless, and anxious amid the pleasures of the senses. If ever the thoughts of the great majority of mankind came to be concentrated solely on the

180. See Tocqueville's letter to Louis de Kergorlay, October 18, 1845: "[I]n my opinion, the march of time, the developments of well being, . . . have, in America, taken away from the religious element three-quarters of its original power. However, all that remains of it is greatly agitated" (*Selected Letters*, p. 193).

181. See Roger Finke and Rodney Stark, *The Churching of America, 1776–1990: Winners and Losers in Our Religious Economy* (New Brunswick, N.J.: Rutgers University Press, 1992), p. 237: "[S]ince at least 1776 the upstart sects have grown as the mainline American denominations have declined. And this trend continues unabated as new upstarts continue to push to the fore. . . . [This historical trend is not an oddity] of the American religious economy or of recent history—they are not new things under the sun. Rather, they reflect basic social forces that first cause successful religious firms to compromise their 'errand into the wilderness' and then lose their organization vigor, eventually to be replaced by less worldly groups, whereupon the process is repeated. That is, the *sect-church process is always under way*" (emphasis in original). In America, the more worldly churches become, the more they are supplanted by sects that purport to nourish the spirit in ways routinized religion cannot.

search for material blessings, one can anticipate that there would be a colossal reaction in the souls of men.[182]

Perhaps here, too, Rousseau speaks behind Tocqueville's insight and eloquence:

> The reasoning of materialists resembles that of a deaf man. They are indeed deaf to the inner voice crying out to them in a tone difficult not to recognize. . . . Something in you seeks to break the bonds constraining it. Space is not your measure; the whole universe is not big enough for you. [You] have another principle than this narrow body in which you sense yourself enchained.[183]

In both of these views human beings dwell in two worlds, as it were. The political and economic domains, important as they surely are, will forever remain only the "narrow body in which you sense yourself enchained" as they are presently understood. There will always be another *dimension*[184] that cannot be disavowed in existence—though from time to time, as the Americans demonstrate, the attempt will surely be made. This dimension cannot be discounted by fully adequate political and economic science.

There is other evidence to be adduced that Tocqueville thought human life must be comprehended in both spiritual and worldly terms. Here, too, there is a paradox. Above, it was suggested that episodic spirituality results from throwing oneself wholly into the world, and that the very triumph of worldly activity leads to a revolt against it. The second piece of evidence complements the first: without the presence of the spiritual dimension, which outstrips the physical world, human needs will not surpass animal needs, and so worldly activity will be reduced. As Hegel put it:

> An animal's needs and its ways and means of satisfying them are both alike restricted in scope. Though man is subject to this restriction too, yet at the same time he evinces his transcendence of it and his universality . . . *by the multiplication of needs and means of satisfying them.*[185]

---

182. Tocqueville, *Democracy in America*, vol. 2, part 2, chap. 12, pp. 534–35 (emphasis added). See also Augustine, *Confessions*, bk. 2, chap. 10, p. 34, where to wander from God is to create "a region of destitution."

183. Rousseau, *Emile*, bk. 4, p. 280.

184. Paul Tillich's use of the term "dimension" (*Systematic Theology* [Chicago: University of Chicago Press, 1951], 3: 15–30) is helpful here. He intends by it to allude to the way in which Spirit breaks in upon human life from a place not comprehendible, strictly speaking, from within the (worldly) domains of human life.

185. Hegel, *Philosophy of Right*, sec. 190, p. 127 (emphasis added).

In Tocqueville's words,

> [What makes us better than animals] is that we employ our souls to
> find those material benefits to which instinct alone directs them. *In
> man an angel teaches a brute how to satisfy its desires.* It is because man is
> able to raise himself above the things of the body and even to scorn
> life itself, a matter of which the beasts have not the least notion, that
> he can multiply these same good things of the body to a degree to
> which they have no conception.[186]

The spiritual dimension bestows on us our peculiar productive capacity
in the world. Contra Marx, the desire to produce beyond our needs as
beasts is not rooted in the immanence of human existence.[187]

Both of these examples, episodic spirituality and the spiritual roots
of desire, suggest to Tocqueville that human beings dwell in two worlds,
as it were, and that these worlds can neither be wholly disentangled in
concrete human life nor be circumscribed by the narrow disciplinary
borders set up by political and economic science.

Not to be underestimated, of course, is the capacity of human beings
to deny that they reside in two worlds. Dwellers in the "City of Man"
have always wished to think that that city is sufficient unto itself, as
Augustine pointed out long ago.[188] This judgment against the "City of
God" does not characterize the modern age alone; *all* epochs betray it!
Informed by this judgment, modern political and economic science will

---

186. Tocqueville, *Democracy in America*, vol. 2, part 2, chap. 16, p. 546 (emphasis added). It was precisely this propensity to multiply desires beyond natural need that Rousseau so wished to forestall. "The real world has limits," he says, "the imaginary world is infinite" (*Emile*, bk. 2, p. 81). In Tocqueville's language, if the angel is awakened too early, the human being can never be happy.

187. Marx remarks: "[A]n animal is one with its life activity. It does not distinguish the activity from itself. It is its activity. But man makes his life activity itself an object of his will and consciousness. He has a conscious life activity. It is not a determination with which he is completely identified. Conscious life actively distinguished man from the life activity of animals. . . . Only for this reason is his activity free activity. Alienated labor reverses the relationship, in that man because he is a self-conscious being makes his life activity, his *being*, only a means for his *existence*" ("Alienated Labor," in *Marx's Concept of Man*, pp. 101–2; emphasis in original).

188. See Augustine, *City of God*, bk. 1, preface, p. 18 (*CG*, p. 5): "I know, of course, what ingenuity and force of arguments are needed to convince proud men of the power of humility. Its loftiness is above the pinnacles of earthly greatness which are shaken by the shifting winds of time." Pride, *the* cardinal sin, is for Augustine the desire of human beings to construct a *totality* that disparages the Infinite.

claim their own sufficiency—and will yield opinion consonant with their assumptions rather than knowledge that *risks* to question them.[189] This procedure, at best, reflects prescientific judgment but fails to evaluate it.[190] There can be no wisdom in this.

Here it would be correct to say that insofar as this "scientific" course is pursued with steadfast resolve, and the other dimension of human existence disavowed, the "City of God" will more and more appear to be a "broken chain still occasionally dangling from the ceiling of an old building but carrying nothing,[191] an atavism unwittingly relied upon, but which no longer supports in the manner that it may. Whether such a course, which disavows the whole in preference for the visible and measurable parts, will contribute to a catastrophic reaction *against* "the world," or will diminish the very desire to be overly productive *in* the world, remains to be seen. Acting and thinking as if politics and economics are sufficient unto themselves will contribute, in Tocqueville's view, to bringing both alternatives to pass.

189. See Plato, *Republic*, bk. 6, 509d–511e, on the distinction between wisdom and opinion. Wisdom, as Plato suggests in the *Phaedrus* (in *Collected Dialogues of Plato*, 64a), risks philosophical death.

190. See Leo Strauss, *What Is Political Philosophy?* (Glencoe, Ill.: Free Press, 159), p. 16: "[A]ll knowledge of political things implies assumptions concerning the nature of things political, i.e., assumptions which concern not merely the given political situation, but political life or human life as such. One cannot know about a war going on at a given time without having some notion, however dim or hazy, of war as such and its place within human life as such. One cannot see a policeman as a policeman without having made an assumption about law and government as such. The assumptions concerning the nature of political things, which are implied in all knowledge of politics, have the character of opinion. It is only when these assumptions are made the theme of critical and coherent analysis that a philosophic or scientific approach to politics emerges." Strauss is of the view that social science *supposes already* what it must subject to inquiry.

191. Tocqueville, *Democracy in America*, vol. 1, part 1, chap. 2, p. 32.

4
Christianity and Democracy

We must begin here with a fundamental—and at once theological and historical—consideration without which Tocqueville's case for American exceptionalism would be incoherent, and the entire construction of *Democracy in America* would crumble to the ground: Providence has decreed that there will be equality.

Here is a pronouncement that, in Tocqueville's view, no human being or society may long violate. Just as Pharaoh could not successfully oppose the will of God,[1] so, too, those who might wish to countermand the movement toward equality cannot alter what has been ordained—either by overt actions[2] or by a more insinuating and subtle contempt that would shame us all into renouncing the great temptation of equality.[3] Equality has won; to battle against it now is to battle against God—as

1. Exod. 5:1–12:31. Every time Pharaoh opposes God's will his heart is hardened, he becomes more intransigent; yet his will is finally vanquished. This hardening and intransigence is pertinent to Tocqueville's discussion of race in America. There, in effect, the white race is charged with being Pharaoh, of resisting the equality that God has ordained. At the end of Tocqueville's discussion of the relationship between blacks and whites—a discussion that drives home the intractability of the problem—he says: "[W]ishing to have servitude, [the whites] have nevertheless been drawn *against their wills* or unconsciously toward liberty" (*Democracy in America*, vol. 1, part 2, chap. 10, p. 362). The whites have been hardened; notwithstanding their wish to maintain the *arrest* of servitude, however, equality (God's will) will prevail. I will discuss the problem of slavery in greater detail in sec. 2 below.

2. See Tocqueville, *Democracy in America*, vol. 2, Author's Introduction, pp. 417–18: "[T]he democratic revolution occurring before our eyes is an irresistible fact and . . . it would be neither desirable nor wise to try to combat it."

3. See Nietzsche, *Genealogy of Morals*, first essay, sec. 9, pp. 35–36: "[T]he people have won—or 'the slaves' or 'the mob' or 'the herd' or whatever you like to call them. . . . The 'redemption' of the human race is going forward; everything is becoming Judaized, Christianized, mob-ized (what do the words matter!)"

Nietzsche well knew. The human task is of a lower, though not undignified, order: establish an equality based in freedom rather than upon tyranny. The task of the new political science, in this light, is to comprehend the conditions under which this will be possible. Nothing less.

The significance of human agency—counterpoised, paradoxically, against the backdrop of the unalterable will of God—is confirmed by its multiple appearances throughout *Democracy in America*. Indeed, Tocqueville adjourns with this thought[4] and announces it at the outset of the Author's Introduction.[5] It is the master concept that informs his entire work. Equality will prevail; the only question for humankind to answer is what *kind* of equality will prevail. That is up to us, not God:

> To me the Christian nations of our day present an alarming spectacle; the movement that carries them along is already too strong to be halted, but is not yet so swift that we must despair of directing it; our fate is in our hands but soon may pass beyond our control.[6]

Notwithstanding Tocqueville's conviction that the Americans in the 1830s still had a time of retrievable mistakes, a period of time before their fate, too, might pass out of their hands, his occasionally insistent tone warns of the looming danger—a danger not just for the Americans, but for all of those who would forgo their responsibility to institute a beneficent form of equality. God has ordained that there will be equality; humanity will preside over its *content*—either by a dereliction of its duty or by performing it with integrity.[7] This is not co-creation, to

4. See Tocqueville, *Democracy in America*, vol. 2, part 4, chap. 8, p. 705: "The nations of our day cannot prevent conditions of equality from spreading in their midst. But it depends upon themselves whether equality is to lead to servitude or freedom, knowledge or barbarism, prosperity or wretchedness." The French, *lumières*, is better translated as *enlightenment* rather than as *knowledge*.

5. See Tocqueville, *Democracy in America*, Author's Introduction, pp. 11–12. "[Both defenders and detractors of equality] have been driven pell-mell along the same road, and all have worked together, some against their will and some unconsciously, blind instruments in the hands of God." While we may be blind instruments in the hands of God, however, human beings are charged with "[substituting] understanding of statecraft for present inexperience and knowledge of its true interests for blind instinct" (p. 12).

6. Tocqueville, *Democracy in America*, Author's Introduction, p. 12. Lawrence translates the French *sort* as *fate;* more accurate would be *lot* or *condition of life*. These renderings are faithful to Tocqueville's conviction that human beings are in some measure capable of directing their destiny.

7. Hence, the observation that his "whole book has been written in the impulse of a kind of religious dread" (Tocqueville, *Democracy in America*, Author's Introduction, p. 12). His worry is that humankind will abandon its charge of making good use of its freedom.

be sure; but here humankind is granted the freedom either to go astray (to live by instinct) or to live *meritoriously* in a community absent certain, but not all, harsh adversities and suffering.[8]

Tocqueville is unequivocal about what will be necessary for us to live under an equality of freedom rather than an equality under tyranny: for that, intelligence will be needed. In this regard, even the casual reader of *Democracy in America* will be struck by his elevation of the New England colonies and his depreciation of the Mid-Atlantic colonies. The reason is clear: he thought that the success of the American effort must have been due, in large part, to intelligence.[9] If America had succeeded in bringing about an equality in freedom, it is partially attributable to the substitution of knowledge for mere instinct.[10] His theology requires this conclusion and also directs his attention toward the New England colonies (where a reverence for ideas was most in evidence) in search of the democratic soul in America.[11]

8. This is a profoundly biblical notion, to be sure. Merit is the withstanding of the propensity toward errancy. See, for example, Martin Luther, "Lectures on Genesis," 1:145, where in answering why God should have allowed Eve to be tempted by Satan, he replies: "[I]t pleased the Lord that Adam should be tempted and should test his powers." See also p. 111. Rousseau offers the same idea in *Emile*, bk. 5, pp. 397–98; though there what is merited by those who, like *Emile*, have avoided errancy from nature is Sophie, or wisdom.

9. See Tocqueville, *Democracy in America*, vol. 1, part 1, chap. 2, p. 34, where those who had settled in Virginia were "gold seekers . . . men without wealth or standards whose restless, turbulent tempers endangered the infant colony." Those who settled in New England, on the other hand, came "in obedience to a purely intellectual craving; in facing the inevitable sufferings of exile they hoped for the triumph of *an idea*" (p. 36). See also chap. 1, p. 26, where the north is characterized as "the domain of intelligence," while the south is characterized as the domain "of the senses." Furthermore, if democracy is to survive in the future, education of a certain sort will be essential. "I see a time approaching in which freedom, public peace, and social stability will not be able to last without education," he says (vol. 2, part 2, chap. 8, p. 528). An analysis of the relationship between climate and disposition consistent in many respects with the one Tocqueville offers is to be found in Montesquieu, *Spirit of the Laws*, part 3, bk. 14, pp. 231–45.

10. See Tocqueville, *Democracy in America*, vol. 1, part 2, chap. 9, pp. 302–3: unlike the Europeans, who inherited their continent when they were steeped in "darkness and barbarism," the "Anglo-Americans were completely civilized when they arrived in the land which their descendants occupy; they had no need to learn, it being enough *that they should not forget*" (emphasis added).

11. More than this, Tocqueville offers a cultural-diffusion model of how the democratic soul in New England comes to occupy the whole of the nation. See Tocqueville, *Democracy in America*, vol. 1, part 2, chap. 9, p. 281: "[It is not the

These initial remarks about the relationship between God's providence and human responsibility, while not exhaustive, articulate the contours of the theological and historical framework within which Tocqueville's more subtle and substantive observations about Christianity and democracy find their place. To these I will now turn.

First, I will consider Tocqueville's forlorn assessment of the European arrest upon the plan of history. It is, in his estimation, the confluence of arrest and progress in Europe—in short, the ongoing influence of the aristocratic age that resists the new verities of history—that makes social revolution inevitable there and unnecessary in America; the aristocratic arrest in history America did not have. (The burden of the case for American exceptionalism rests here.) Yet another arrest America *did* have; and a consideration of the confluence of arrest and progress in Europe helps to establish the general form of the problem of which America supplies another instance: slavery.

Second, I will consider the social implications of the victory of the love of equality in this epoch, with a view to showing how *difference*— the beloved of postmodern thought—becomes both an infatuation and an intractable problem among a democratic people. Here, among other things, I will more fully develop Tocqueville's argument about the tragedy of slavery, which stems from the contradiction between an historically constituted identity in conflict with the verities of God's design of equality in history.

Third, I will consider how Christianity is, in effect, a palliative—perhaps the most powerful one available—to the peculiar afflictions of envy and of difference from which the democratic soul seems so much to suffer. Aristocracy, which countenanced distance (and so forestalled the envy that can only arise amid proximity of a certain sort), has receded; there must be some functional equivalent. Christianity, by orienting persons (now dwelling shoulder to shoulder) toward God, averts their gaze away from the fraternal order that is their source of security, object of affection, and occasion of their impotence.

Fourth, I will take up the question of the indirect effects of religion

recent immigrants, but rather the] Americans who are continually leaving their birthplace and going forth to win vast far-off domains"; and p. 293: "[To avoid the situation where] religion might be lost in the depths of the forest and the people growing up there might be less fitted for freedom than those from whom they sprang . . . New Englanders [have left] their native land in order to establish the fundamentals of Christianity and of liberty by the banks of the Missouri or on the prairies of Illinois." See also vol. 1, part 1, chap. 2, p. 35: "New England civilization has been like beacons on mountain peaks whose warmth is first felt close by but whose light shines to the farthest limits of the horizon."

upon politics. The great paradox turns out to be that religion is absolutely necessary for democratic politics to endure, and yet it must be overtly estranged from politics in order to offer the assistance that politics requires.

Fifth, I will indicate the importance of long-term goals for the democratic soul and consider how Christianity attenuates the dangerous disposition of the democratic soul to think and act irrationally; that is, only for the short term. In addition it will be possible there to consider why, on the basis of Tocqueville's understanding of the relationship between thought and real-life, a return to religion will be witnessed during this decade in which we have begun to intimate the worldly consequences of short-term thinking.

Sixth, I will consider the right relationship between religion and politics, not with a view to delineating the formal grounds of their separation, but rather with the intention of pointing out the danger of conflating the two domains. Irrespective of whether religion has or has not receded, we increasingly labor under the burden of a pantheism of sorts in which boundaries are violated, and religion and politics each serve the function of the other. Luther once noted that the carnal and the spiritual realms had been so confused that bishops ruled over cities while lords ruled over the human souls.[12] The contemporary problem bears some resemblance to the one over which he lamented. Here, the issue that increasingly pleads for our attention amid intensifying *political* conflicts about religion—the question of what the right forum for these wrenching problems may be—will be addressed.

Finally, the permanence of religion. As a social and political theorist, of course, Tocqueville could only view Christian religion from the vantage of its usefulness to society. Yet whatever its social attributions, these are necessarily outstripped by the condolence and hope it offers to the heart. In short, the empirical effect that is articulated, the *totality* conveyed and manifested by Christianity, cannot capture the infinite that opens up through the need of condolence and in abiding hope. Tocqueville the social scientist could only speak from the purview of totality, and yet he grasped that the power and stability of the totality articulated by Christianity stood unshakably upon that hidden foundation which alone can answer the heart's call.[13]

This distinction between Christianity as totality and Christianity as

12. Luther, "Temporal Authority," 45:109; see also 45:115–16.
13. Cf. Pascal, *Pensées*, sec. 110, p. 58: "[I]t is through [the heart] that we know first principles, and reason, which has nothing to do with it, tries in vain to refute them. . . . It is on [the knowledge coming from the heart] that reason has to depend and base all its argument."

infinity cannot be overlooked by social theorists who wish to educe policy implications from Tocqueville's thinking—for in these Christianity plays a part. Christianity as totality is lifeless; the effort to establish order by "bringing Christianity back in" can only more hastily bring about the death that one would wish to be averted—unless, that is, theorists grasp the difference between totality and infinity and the place where the one gives way to another. *This place is not politics.*[14] The lifelessness that has gripped one totality cannot simply be supplanted by the lifelessness of another totality—more dangerous still because it claims a higher authority for itself. Only the infinite can renew. About this something will be said in this last section, and again in the final chapter.

1. THE PROGRESS OF HISTORY AND ITS ARRESTS: THE DEPTH OF IDENTITY

God has ordained that there will be equality. Perhaps necessarily obscure until recently, but now clear,[15] this movement toward equality *is* the answer to the riddle of history.[16]

14. Mill argues that Marcus Aurelius committed the error to which human beings in all ages are susceptible, namely, that of trying to reestablish order by holding onto the religion of our ancestors. In his words, "[E]xisting society [Aurelius] knew to be in a deplorable state. But such as it was, he saw, or thought he saw, that it was held together, and prevented from being worse, by belief and reverence for the received divinities" ("On Liberty," p. 34). In the name of maintaining order Aurelius persecuted Christians, the new religion that sought to establish the ties between human beings on a different basis than had the ancient world. The lesson is clear: the health and vitality of a society cannot be maintained by the *imposition* of a *system* of thought, venerable or novel.

15. See Tocqueville, *Democracy in America*, Author's Introduction, p. 12: "God does not Himself need to speak for us to find sure signs of his will." Cf. Augustine, *City of God*, vol. 6, bk. 4, chap. 33, p. 237 (*CG*, p. 176), where history proceeds "by a divine disposition of events and dates which is unknown to us."

16. Cf. Karl Marx, "Manifesto of the Communist Party," in *The Marx-Engels Reader*, ed. Robert C. Tucker (New York: W. W. Norton, 1978), p. 473: "[T]he history of all hitherto existing society is the history of class struggles." Marx supposes that history is the record of the overcoming of the original opposition between humankind and nature. Social antagonism—class struggle—is predicated upon this original opposition. The end of history is a dialectical advance, a return to the communism of the beginning now superseded by the suffering that comes to discover a "Paradise within thee, happier far." From Eden to Exodus to the Heavenly Home Within. Tocqueville's history, in spite of its more overtly Christian references, is *less* patterned upon biblical history than is Marx's.

There are, however, fateful consequences of this coming equality, and these will play themselves out in Europe in peculiar ways that the Americans, *because they have not the burden of history upon their shoulders,*[17] will not have to endure. Several references already in the Author's Introduction to "the ruins [democracy] has itself created,"[18] and to "we [Europeans who] obstinately keep our eyes fixed on the ruins still in sight on the bank, while the stream whirls us backward—facing toward the abyss,"[19] alert the reader that the case for American exceptionalism may rest in no small degree with the good fortune of its new beginning, with the absence of ties that must be overcome in order for equality to reign peaceably in Europe.[20]

The difficulty can be phrased in the following way: how, in the face of a movement of history that conspires to constitute a new and democratic soul, can the arrests of nondemocratic identity (which were constituted in earlier moments of history) be superseded without violence? All things constituted in time have duration and are not easily expunged. They have, as it were, a memory that does not readily give way. The ineffable will of God cannot be impeded by the efforts of mere mortals, but older and deeper currents continue to swirl, erode, and ma-

---

There is the prospect of errancy, to be sure; but there is no awaiting in the desert of the soul (late capitalism) for the Eschaton. God's intentions are clear; human responsibility in the history God has ordained is to grasp and guide the multiplex reality of social and political life toward an equality in freedom. "For my part," he writes, "I hate all those absolutist systems that make all the events of history depend on great first causes linked together by the chain of fate and thus succeed, so to speak, in banishing men from the history of the human race" (*The Recollections of Alexis de Tocqueville*, ed. J. P. Mayer, trans. George Lawrence [Garden City, N.Y.: Doubleday, 1970], p. 62).

17. The good fortune of the Americans is to have been spared the tribulation of renouncing the residual feudal identity that delays the arrival of democracy in Europe; but that is not enough to assure that it will remain immune from the coming European conflagration. What more is needed is a refusal to enter into ongoing European history—hence Tocqueville's praise for the disinclination of Washington and Jefferson to be drawn into the fray of foreign wars. See Tocqueville, *Democracy in America*, vol. 1, part 2, chap. 5, pp. 226–30. An America that stands away from Europe is not obliged "to take the past into account and adapt it to the present; nor need it, like them, accept a vast heritage of mixed glory and shame, national friendships and hatreds, bequeathed by its ancestors" (p. 228).

18. Tocqueville, *Democracy in America*, Author's Introduction, p. 12.

19. Tocqueville, *Democracy in America*, Author's Introduction, p. 13.

20. Tocqueville, *Democracy in America*, vol. 2, part 3, chap. 21, p. 634.

lign what God brings forth. The trace of the past plagues a present that would like to forget but cannot.[21]

In America, however, the arrests that would plague Europe were absent. Because the feudal identity had been left behind, no atavisms haunted the Americans' ongoing effort to live in accordance with the design of history.[22] Whatever residuals of the European past did remain—the emphasis upon local government brought over from England, the existence of a lawyer class, and Christian mores, for example—conduced toward God's providential plan; they ameliorated the instabilities of democracy rather than obstructed its progress. Forces that in Europe brought wrenching upheaval, in America brought repose; the body through which they surged was differently constituted in America and, so, had different ramifications:

21. About this Augustine has much to say (*Confessions*, bk. 8, chap. 5, pp. 139–41). In his view, life is habitual, and newness is made possible only by a Mediator who "saves the world." The ethics of Aristotle, too, grasps that life is *mimetic*, though "the world" so constituted by it need not lead to unhappiness. There, moral virtue is the result of habituation (*Nicomachean Ethics*, bk. 2, chap. 1, 1103a14–b25). Rousseau takes a more nuanced view: submit children to constant change to avert the dominion of habit (*Emile*, bk. 1, pp. 61–64), so that adults thus formed will have the habits that allow them to use their freedom well. Nietzsche, too, recognized the enduring power of the past and the extraordinary phenomenon of forgetfulness that allows human beings to "have done" with their past. See Nietzsche, *Genealogy of Morals*, second essay, sec. 1, p. 58: "[T]here could be no happiness, no cheerfulness, no hope, no pride, no *present*, without forgetfulness" (emphasis in original). See also René Girard, *Violence and the Sacred*, trans. Patrick Gregory (Baltimore: Johns Hopkins University Press, 1977), p. 146, *passim*. Here, mimesis leads to violence, which must be circumvented through ritual violence—a thought not lost to St. Paul, for whom earthly blood could atone for the sins of a *particular* people, but heavenly blood alone could atone for the *universal* sin of all in Adam. "For if the blood of bulls and of goats, and the ashes of an heifer sprinkling the unclean, sanctifies to the purifying of the flesh: How much more shall the blood of Christ, who through the eternal Spirit offered himself without spot to God, purge your conscience from dead works to serve the living God? (Heb. 9:13–14).

22. The massive exception to this is, as I have said, is slavery. Slavery is the arrest of identity that must be superseded yet, because of the *depth* of identity, cannot be easily overcome. The profound paradox and tragedy of this situation is captured in Tocqueville's remark that "Christianity had destroyed servitude; the Christians of the sixteenth century reestablished it" (*Democracy in America*, vol. 1, part 2, chap. 10, p. 341). God had ordained that there would be equality, yet the ostensible agents of that equality introduced an arrest upon God's plan!

[A] democratic revolution has taken place in the body of [French] society without those changes in laws, ideas, customs, and mores, which were needed to make the revolution profitable.[23]

Equality has come, but the Europeans have remained woefully the same. Europe is caught between a present with which it must accord and a past that shadows the blossoming claim of democracy.

Examples abound. The distinction between instinctive and well-considered patriotism is instructive. Like so many of the antinomies Tocqueville constructs, these are fully comprehensible only within the context of the historical narrative he invokes. European history evinces a movement away from the enchanted world of instinctive patriotism; enchantment gives way to disenchantment. (Max Weber's ideas, not surprisingly, occur in *this* historical context!)

> [When enchantment fades,] men see their country only by a weak and doubtful light; their patriotism is not centered on the soil, which in their eyes is just inanimate earth; nor upon the customs of their ancestors, which they regard as a yoke; nor upon their religion, which they doubt.[24]

The disposition of the Europeans is to fall into a narrow egoism that cannot easily be prompted toward healthy patriotism. Instinctive affiliation in which the self is caught up, almost mystically, into something greater than itself gives way to nearsighted self-interest. An autonomy of sorts is the yield, but moderate politics is the casualty; primitive unity is supplanted by an incessant standing apart. Theologically, Adam, his eyes now opened, recognizes his own separation from God.[25]

The question, theologically, is how to get Adam to again become a-part-of, now that he recognizes himself to be separate. Politically, the question is how to move from instinctive patriotism beyond the self-enclosure of separateness. In America, Tocqueville argues, the political world never was enchanted in the way Europe's had been and so was not subject to its attendant alternative: disenchantment. Politics was the realm of the free play of intelligence,[26] created and sanctioned by God,

23. Tocqueville, *Democracy in America*, Author's Introduction, p. 13.

24. Tocqueville, *Democracy in America*, vol. 1, part 2, chap. 6, p. 236.

25. Gen. 3:7–8. Another alternative to standing apart is to attempt to go back to the first innocence, so to speak. Having grasped the emptiness of standing apart, the soul gravitates toward the alternative that is firmly ensconced in memory, but that is not a genuine possibility.

26. See Tocqueville, *Democracy in America*, vol. 1, part 1, chap. 2, p. 47. In insisting that reason cannot comprehend the mystery of faith, the labor of reason is directed in Protestant thought entirely and with legitimacy toward the "world."

it is true; but it never was an enchanted realm. The either-or of Edenic unity and utter dissolution arises only when the memory of the enchantment of the aristocratic age confronts a providential history that has already superseded it. The confluence of past and present yields the alternatives, neither of which can now (in this democratic age) sustain a community in Europe. Eden has receded; Adam should not be alone; yet once out of the Garden he is disoriented.

Not having had their eyes opened, however, not having to face the cessation of a social order that no longer comported with God's design, the situation for the Americans was different. Patriotism here could supersede the dangerous opposition from which Europe could not disengage itself precisely because the notion of an enchanted politics had no hold on the memory of the Americans. Right from the beginning they knew self-interest rather than egoism and so could construe patriotism in those terms. Self-interest superseded the antinomies of enchanted instinctual patriotism and egoism that constitute the parameters of the European experience.[27] Rather, guided by the religious *habit of thinking* that freedom was made possible by virtue of obedience,[28] the American comes to recognize that patriotism involves a giving over of some free-

---

For an exposition of this thesis with respect to Luther, see B. A. Gerrish, *Grace and Reason: A Study in the Theology of Luther* (Oxford: Clarendon Press, 1962). Luther's insistence that reason cannot understand salvation frees reason from a burden it is not capable of bearing. Tocqueville remarks about the peculiar way in which Christian faith and reason can work together, and argues that, unlike Islam, Christianity and Enlightenment are not contradictory impulses precisely because Christian faith demands that reason defer *only in matters of salvation* (see *Democracy in America*, vol. 2, part 1, chap. 5, p. 445). Reason is not the disenchanted offspring of religion here.

27. See Carl Schmitt, *The Crisis of Parliamentary Democracy* (Cambridge, Mass.: MIT Press, 1985). Commenting on Marxism's response to bourgeois rationalism, Schmitt notes, "[A]s Trotsky justly reminded the democrat Kautsky, the awareness of relative truths never gives one the courage to use force and to spill blood" (p. 64). (See also Rousseau, *Emile*, bk. 3, p. 183: "[I]n vain does tranquil reason make us approve or criticize; it is only passion which makes us act." Rousseau's comment, however, pertains to the stage in the development of the soul where reason begins to be awakened by the right exercise of the body, after which we become adults.) Schmitt's opposition to liberalism stems from his assumption that self-interest is weak and unable to make sacrifices. Community must be based on enchantment, not reason and self-interest. Tocqueville would, I think, see in Schmitt further evidence of European categories of thought that do not map onto the American experience.

28. Tocqueville, *Democracy in America*, vol. 1, part 1, chap. 2, pp. 46–47.

dom in order that true freedom be attained.[29] True self-interest involves a giving up that gains. The natural disposition to conceive of self-interest narrowly is counterpoised in America by religious habits become political that are rooted in a memory that did not have to be overcome as it did in Europe: The American

> has nothing to forget and has no need to unlearn, as Europeans must, the lessons of his early education.[30]

There is also the matter of rights. This has been discussed in another context in chapter 3 (sec. 9); its bearing upon the issue of history and its arrests, however, was not considered earlier and so warrants some attention here.

The idea of rights, recall, can take hold in the event that there is a forum in which rights may be exercised; and in the American context, that forum is property.[31] Practical experience with property promotes the idea of rights in general, and this serves to counteract the diminishing *moral* force of rights that Christianity, presently in abeyance, proffers. Experience serves as a substitute for injunction.

In Europe, however, the idea of rights could not easily take hold. History conspired against any new beginnings. In Paine's words:

> So deeply rooted were all the governments of the old world, and so effectually had the tyranny and the antiquity *of habit* established itself over the mind, that no beginning could be made in Asia, Africa, or Europe, to reform the political condition of man.[32]

---

29. I have explored the theological dimensions of this notion elsewhere. See Joshua Mitchell, "The Equality of All under the One in Luther and Rousseau: Thoughts on Christianity and Political Theory," *Journal of Religion* 72, no. 3 (1992): 351–65. See also Macquarrie, *Principles of Christian Theology*, chap. 3, p. 82: "[I]nsistence upon one's autonomy is more typically the mark of adolescence than of maturity."

30. Tocqueville, *Democracy in America*, vol. 1, part 2, chap. 9, p. 286.

31. Tocqueville, *Democracy in America*, vol. 1, part 2, chap. 6, p. 238.

32. Thomas Paine, *The Rights of Man* (New York: Penguin Books, 1984), part 2, introduction, p. 159 (emphasis added). Elsewhere, in his attack upon Burke, he objects that the dead—the past—should not hold sway over the living (part 1, p. 45). Oakeshott characterizes this as the *rationalist* attitude in his essay, "Rationalism in Politics" (in *Rationalism in Politics*, pp. 5–42). He notes the affiliation there (pp. 9–10, passim) between rationalism and universalism. The particular habits of the past are invariably shunned by the rationalist in favor of a *technique* applicable to all situations. This hidden tendency of rationalism corresponds to Tocqueville's "inner secret" of the democratic soul, namely, that it would wish to defer to a powerful state that stands over all citizens and views them without regard for their particular differences.

The inevitable paroxysm, the irruption of the claims of universal rights in the French Revolution,[33] however, gave way to "the *fury* of destruction"[34] during the Terror because the idea of rights was unable to be embodied in a society subject, as all are, to the empire of habit.[35] Society as it stood could not have been other than unresponsive to the new social verity of equality. Hence the fall into abstract universalism. Having no experiential referent or forum, its claims could only go astray. Rights, instantiated in the form of property, are a stabilizing force in the democratic age; yet the faltering aristocracies of Europe could not peacefully accommodate this verity. Where "in America the people were invested with political rights at a time when it was difficult to make ill use of them,"[36] in Europe the crumbling of the old order conferred powers onto a people yet without the experience to make good use of them.[37]

33. Tocqueville remarks that the French Revolution was Christian religion in disguise; it sought to supplant a "particularist" social structure with a "universal" one, something unprecedented in political history—yet something still being played out in the ecumenical political movements of today. See Old Régime, part 1, chap. 3, pp. 10–13. See also *Democracy in America*, vol. 2, part 1, chap. 4, pp. 441–42, where the French are taken by general ideas, but the Americans seek to embody particular ideas in existing social practices; and also vol. 1, part 2, chap. 8, p. 267, where the American and English jurists "look for judgments [while] the [French look] for reasons." The law of precedent looks to existing practice, to which the law of reason *may* not accede.

34. Hegel, *Phenomenology of Spirit*, sec. 589, p. 359 (emphasis in original).

35. The "slaughter bench" about which Hegel writes (see G. W. F. Hegel, *Reason in History*, trans. Robert S. Hartman [Indianapolis, Ind.: Bobbs-Merrill, 1953], p. 27) is made necessary because of the enduring power, yet inadequacy, of the forms that arise in history. *Geist* reveals itself to itself only on the slaughter bench of history. Theologically, *habit* forms a world that must (and can) be annulled by dying to "the world" through the Spirit—as both Augustine and Luther knew. See also Hegel, *Phenomenology of Spirit*, preface, p. 19: "[The life of spirit] wins its truth only when, in utter dismemberment, it finds itself."

36. Tocqueville, *Democracy in America*, vol. 1, part 2, chap. 6, p. 239.

37. See Edmund Burke, *Reflections on the Revolution in France*, ed. Connor Cruise O'Brien (New York: Penguin Books, 1968), pp. 150–55. Burke argues against the abstract notion of rights; these must always be rooted in existing practice. The present cannot step blithely over the practices and institutions that come from the past. Hegel notes that "in England, [unlike France,] every parish, every subordinate division and association has its own part to perform. Thus the common interest is concrete, and particular interests are taken cognizance of and determined in view of that common interest. These arrangements, based on particular interests, render a general system impossible. Consequently, abstract and general principles have no attraction for Englishmen" (*Philosophy of History*, part 4, sec. 3, chap. 3, p. 454). This "bottom-up" arrangement, as Tocqueville later noted, was carried over to America.

Burke and Paine, then, were both right—and wrong! Burke saw the need of an ongoing past in the present, yet failed to grasp that a new moment in history had arrived; Paine saw the new moment, yet failed to understand that without a way to embody the new truth of equality and universal rights in certain social arrangements, the yield could only have been bad infinity. Tocqueville comprehends their insights without their deficiencies, something that cannot be done without attending to the progress of history and its arrests. The institution of property in America did not need to overcome a past that would oppose it,[38] and so rights could take hold there.

The progress of history and its arrests need not eternally clash; formidable disruptions may, in time, give way to placidity. With a mind fixed upon showing his fellow Europeans that democracy need not be feared, Tocqueville addresses the matter of whether unquenchable ambition is the inevitable denouement of a democratic revolution.

Ambition, he argues, is not unleashed by democracy, but rather by democratic *revolutions*. At the moment that the arrest of history (the old order) is overthrown, the memory of the grandeur once attainable there is firmly fixed in the minds of the citizens:

> Longings on a vast scale remain, though the means to satisfy them become daily less. The taste for huge fortune persists, though such fortunes in fact become rare, and on all sides there are those who eat out their hearts in secret, consumed by inordinate and frustrated ambition.[39]

Democratic revolutions efface the visible markings of the past in an effort to start anew, but the invisible markings firmly ensconced in memory can be overcome only by more time. The present revolutionary moment, which purports to issue an unencumbered future, retains the past in memory; arrest and progress conjoin in a surreal overlap that does not yet move *beyond* but cannot go *back*.

> But little by little the last *traces* of the battle are wiped out and the *relics* of aristocracy finally vanish. . . . Longings once more become proportionate to the available means. Wants, ideas, and feelings again

---

38. Tocqueville notes that other factors contributed to sustain property as well: in the North the soil could not support a landed aristocracy (*Democracy in America*, vol. 1, part 1, chap. 2, p. 33); the law of primogeniture had been abolished (chap. 3, pp. 51–53); and above all, perhaps, "[B]y handing a limitless continent over to [the Americans, God] gave them the means of long remaining free and equal" (part 2, chap. 9, p. 279).

39. Tocqueville, *Democracy in America*, vol. 2, part 3, chap. 19, p. 628.

learn their limits. Men find their level and democratic society is finally firmly established.[40]

Democratic revolutions are tumultuous; democratic conditions, however, are not. Here is an answer to the reticence of Hobbes,[41] of Rousseau,[42] and of generations of thinkers who have witnessed that slow revolution in thought and in deed during the modern age: the ambition unleashed was transitional, due to the confluence of arrest and progress—bound, perhaps, to give way to the weariness and mediocrity of which Nietzsche warned and Tocqueville worried.[43] *The brilliance and massive achievements of the modern age are due to the confluence of arrest and progress.*
The resistance of the arrest does not, however, always give way through the explosive shedding of blood or gradually upon the erasure of memory. The arrest may itself be implicated in the perpetual use of the sword. In such a case the shedding of blood *in the name of revolution* serves only to confirm the intractability of a people's identity anew.

40. Tocqueville, *Democracy in America*, vol. 2, part 3, chap. 19, p. 628 (emphasis added). Cf. Nietzsche, *Genealogy of Morals*, first essay, sec. 9, p. 36: "[T]he progress of this poison [democracy] through the entire body of mankind seems irresistible, its pace and tempo may from now on even grow slower, subtler, less audible, more cautious—there is plenty of time."

41. The central problem for Hobbes was how to arrest the pridefulness of the many. His extraordinary answer was that this would be possible only if the many submit to "that great Leviathan, or rather to speak more reverently, of that mortal god to which we owe . . . our peace and defense" (*Leviathan*, part 2, chap. 17, p. 132 [emphasis in original]).

42. The *First Discourse* offers its own solution to the corruption of society by the many. Famed societies are institutions that instantiate the virtue of which only a few human beings are capable but to which many aspire. These institutions "serve as a check." Those admitted are worthy because of their "useful works and irreproachable morals" (Rousseau, *First Discourse*, p. 59). These societies are the light amid the darkness; a supplement of virtue that provides the antigen necessary to keep the vice of the many at bay, but not eradicate it. Famed societies can revive "love of virtue in the hearts of citizens" and "disseminate throughout the human race not merely pleasant enlightenment but also salutary teachings" (pp. 59–60). The few who possess the "strength to walk alone" (p. 63), who have the requisite virtue, hallow the halls of the famed societies. These few provide the light by which the many may be guided.

43. See Nietzsche, *Thus Spoke Zarathustra*, prologue, pp. 16–19, on the "last man" of modern Europe, of which mention was made in the previous chapter (sec. 7); and Tocqueville, *Democracy in America*, vol. 2, part 3, chap. 21, p. 645.

Here are the Russians.[44] Alternatively, the arrest may resist confrontation with what would supersede it. The conflict between arrest and progress is circumvented by recourse to a spatial segregation of the two—bloody, to be sure, but ultimately yielding mutual detachment. Here are the Indians.[45] Finally, an arrest may "mix without combining."[46] An erasure of any memory but servitude yields an arrest anathema to democratic freedom that stands in relationship, as servitude must. Here are the slaves.[47]

44. See Tocqueville, *Democracy in America*, vol. 1, part 2, chap. 10, p. 413: "[T]he American fights against natural objects; the Russian is at grips with men. The former combats wilderness and barbarism; the latter, civilization with all its arms. America's conquests are made with the plowshare, Russia's with the sword." On this reading communism was the old pattern in a new guise; on this reading the fall of communism will yield yet another version of the same. For a somber view of the intransigencies of the Russian past yet to be overcome (which perhaps cannot be overcome) see Peter Reddaway, "Russia on the Brink?" *New York Review of Books*, January 28, 1993, pp. 30–35.

45. The Indians retain the memory of their past; and this memory is of a self-sufficiency akin to what Rousseau describes when he writes of the noble savage in the early portions of the *Second Discourse*. See Tocqueville, *Democracy in America*, vol. 1, part 2, chap. 10, p. 319: "[T]he pretended nobility of his origin fills the whole imagination of the Indian." It was this almost aristocratic aloofness (p. 328) of the Indians that kept them from *needing* to mingle with the white race. "Living in freedom in the forest, the North American Indian was wretched but felt himself inferior to no man," Tocqueville says (p. 331).

46. Tocqueville, *Democracy in America*, vol. 1, part 2, chap. 10, p. 317. For corroboration see James Fenimore Cooper, *The American Democrat* (Indianapolis, Ind.: Liberty Press, 1981), p. 222: "[T]he time must come when American slavery shall cease, and when that day shall arrive, (unless early and effectual means are devised to obviate it,) two races will exist in the same region, whose feelings will be embittered by inextinguishable hatred, and who *carry on their faces*, the respective stamps of their factions" (emphasis added). Cooper, like Tocqueville, saw that the tragedy of modern slavery, unlike its ancient form, was that an external mark served to remind persons in perpetuity of the past relationship of servitude. Albert O. Hirschman's *Exit, Voice, and Loyalty* (Cambridge, Mass.: Harvard University Press, 1970) provides the categories by which the historical responses of black political thought to this "mixing without combining" can be understood. Malcolm X (*The Autobiography of Malcolm X* [New York: Grove Press, 1965]) endorses exit; W. E. B. Du Bois (*The Souls of Black Folks* [New York: Fawcett Publications, 1961]) solicits voice; and Booker T. Washington (*Up from Slavery* [New York: Doubleday, 1963]) countenances loyalty.

47. See Tocqueville, *Democracy in America*, vol. 1, part 2, chap. 10, p. 317: "[I]n one blow oppression has deprived the descendants of the Africans of almost all the privileges of humanity. The United States Negro has lost even the *memory* of his homeland" (emphasis added). About Tocqueville's view of the

Ironically, tragically, this memory of slavery, itself coincident with the effacement of memory, cannot easily be erased: skin color is the ever-present reminder. "Memories of slavery disgrace the race, and the race perpetuates memories of slavery,"[48] Tocqueville says. This reminder, which insinuates itself again and again, from generation to generation, is the ongoing obstruction to the erasure of a memory that impedes the arrival of equality to America. Providence has ordained that America is the land of the future, the land where equality is most firmly ensconced! Yet a memory of servitude gone by remains, unrelinquished—and perhaps indelible:

> Our children see this [commerce between master and slave], and learn to imitate it; *for man is an imitative animal.* This quality is the germ of all education in him. From his cradle to his grave he is learn-ing to do what he sees others do. . . . The parent storms, the child looks on, catches the lineaments of wrath, puts on the same airs in the

---

slaves something should be said. Unlike Montesquieu, for whom Negroes were not human beings (*Spirit of the Laws*, part 3, bk. 15, chap. 5, pp. 250), Tocque-ville does not link biological attributes to social standing or moral worth. Bernal locates Tocqueville within an nineteenth-century tradition suffused with a spirit that would wish to erase nonwhite attributes from Western history and offers Tocqueville's friendship with Gobineau (an avowed racist) for corroboration (Martin Bernal, *Black Athena* [New Brunswick, N.J.: Rutgers University Press, 1987], 1:238, 344, 352, 354, 482n). Aron suggests that this association had no real bearing upon Tocqueville's thought (*Main Currents*, vol. 1, p. 239). (See also Aron's chronology of Tocqueville's life [p. 294]. From 1839–51 Tocqueville was a spokesman for the abolition of slavery in the colonies.) The servitude of the slaves is an arrest of history, not an attribute linked to their biological makeup, as Gobineau would have insisted. "I believe absolutely none of it," he wrote of Gobineau's theories, "and yet I believe that in each nation, whether it comes from the race or rather the education of centuries, there is something very te-nacious, perhaps even permanent, which ties into all the events of its destiny and can be observed throughout every turn of fortune, in every epoch of his-tory" (letter to Beaumont, November 3, 1853, in *Oeuvres complètes*, 8:164). See also David Hume, "Of National Character," in *Essays*, p. 208 n. 10; Jefferson, *Notes*, query 14, pp. 137–43.

48. Tocqueville, *Democracy in America*, vol. 1, part 2, chap. 10, p. 341. Hence the need for a history that counters the forgetfulness of identity. Cf. Arthur M. Schlesinger Jr., *The Disuniting of America* (Knoxville, Tenn.: Whittle Communi-cations, 1990), p. 52: "[T]he use of history as therapy means the corruption of history as history." Schlesinger's objections are to the teaching of separate his-tories of any particular ethnic group. "Low self-esteem," he observes, "is too deep a malady to be cured by hearing nice things about one's own ethnic past" (p. 58). Schlesinger misapprehends the bearing of history upon identity.

circle of smaller slaves [and] cannot but be stamped by it with odious peculiarities.[49]

2. THE PROBLEM OF DIFFERENCE IN A DEMOCRACY

The intransigence of the problem of the arrest of servitude, however, cannot be attributed wholly to the memory that refuses erasure. Tocqueville does note that there are three aspects of this intransigence: "the prejudice of the master, the prejudice of race, and the prejudice of the white."[50] Yet even here, in these occasions that entrench the arrest of servitude amid freedom, what bestows upon these seemingly self-sufficient aspects the powerful valence they bear is the condition of social equality that profoundly affects human judgment:

> When inequality is the general rule in society, the greatest inequalities attract no attention. When everything is more or less level, the slightest variation is noticed.[51]

49. Jefferson, *Notes*, query 18, p. 162 (emphasis added). To seemingly move far afield, see Rupert Sheldrake, *The Presence of the Past* (New York: Random House, 1988), p. 159: "[T]he hypothesis of formative causation provides a radical interpretation of the nature of memory. It proposes that memory is inherent in all organisms in two related ways. First, all organisms inherit a collective memory of their species by morphic resonance from previous organisms of the same kind. Second, individual organisms are subject to morphic resonance from themselves in the past, and this self-resonance provides the basis for their own individual memories and habits." The implications of Sheldrake's work for social science are immense but cannot be explored here. See pp. 239–69.

50. Tocqueville, *Democracy in America*, vol. 1, part 2, chap. 10, p. 342. The prejudice of the master is the "natural prejudice [that] leads a man to scorn anybody who has been his inferior, long after he has become his equal" (p. 341); the prejudice of race is the external mark that serves as a reminder of past servitude; and the prejudice of the white is "[the] pride of origin, which is natural to the English" (p. 357). See Joseph R. Washington Jr. *Anti-Blackness in English Religion, 1500–1800* (New York: Edwin Mellon Press, 1984), pp. 3–22, for the claim that the origin of the "prejudice of the white" may be attributed in some measure to the Old Testament accounts of blackness that were read in earnest by the Puritans. Tocqueville remarks: "[O]f all the Europeans, the English have least mingled their blood with that of the Negroes" (*Democracy in America*, vol. 1, part 2, chap. 10, p. 356). See Gen. 9:25–27, where Ham, the progenitor of the Africans, is a "servant of servants" to Japheth, the progenitor of the Greeks, Romans, and Europeans. Cf. Gal. 3:28.

51. Tocqueville, *Democracy in America*, vol. 2, part 2, chap. 13, p. 538. See also part 4, chap. 3, p. 672: "[M]en's hatred of privilege increases as privilege becomes rarer and less important."

Here, strangely perhaps, Tocqueville and Nietzsche are in agreement: the "pathos of distance"[52] has receded; the victory of Christianity was so complete that it has become almost impossible to comprehend just how different the state of affairs was before its ascension.[53] Where difference now only offends, it offered certain comforts in the past. In Tocqueville's words:

> When royal power supported by aristocracies governed the nations of Europe in peace, society, despite all its wretchedness, enjoyed several types of happiness which are difficult to appreciate *or conceive* today.[54]

All that has changed. When the spirit of equality has won, difference becomes an obstruction and an affront.[55] All efforts are directed against it. (The postmodern fascination with difference confirms that it is indeed the heir to the biblical tradition. The problem of difference emerges only to a people perturbed by latent differences that resist the Judaization, the Christianization, the democratization of the world.[56] Heirs of Nietzsche indeed!) Strictly speaking, it is due to the victory of equality that the prejudice of the master, of race, and of the white can be found to be offensive:

52. See Nietzsche, *Beyond Good and Evil,*, part 9, sec. 257, p. 201. See also Tocqueville, *Democracy in America*, vol. 2, part 3, chap. 1, p. 562: "[In the Middle Ages, the aristocrats] did not form a clear idea of the sufferings of the poor [and] took but a feeble interest in their fate."

53. So complete has been the victory of the spirit of equality that the only trace of the age of nobility that remains is to be found in the etymological record (Nietzsche, *Genealogy of Morals*, first essay, sec. 4, pp. 27–28).

54. Tocqueville, *Democracy in America*, Author's Introduction, p. 13 (emphasis added).

55. Drescher suggests that Tocqueville's failure was not to have seen that the middle class cannot serve as a model for a society like America, which already had massive social differentiation when *Democracy in America* was written, and which would be further differentiated by the complexities of late-nineteenth- and twentieth-century life. Tocqueville, he suggests, had no adequate theory of social change (Seymour Drescher, *Dilemmas of Democracy* [Pittsburgh: University of Pittsburgh Press, 1968], p. 278). Yet Tocqueville's claim was less to explain social change than to give an account of the paradoxes that the age of equality produces, one of which is that as equality comes to prevail, the differences about which Drescher speaks will come to greatly affront democratic sensibilities. The conditions of equality conspire to imbue difference with a peculiar valence.

56. Nietzsche, *Genealogy of Morals*, first essay, sec. 9, p. 36; *Beyond Good and Evil*, part 5, sec. 202, p. 116: "[T]he *democratic* movement is the heir of the Christian movement" (emphasis in original).

It is not exercise of power or habits of obedience which deprave men, but the exercise of power which they consider illegitimate and obedience to a power which they think usurped and oppressive.[57]

There are, in fact, two psychological principles at work here, which operate at cross-purposes. They may be stated as simple propositions: (1) persons who see in their neighbor someone like them will want them to remain the same; (2) persons who see in their neighbor someone unlike them will want them to remain different. The brother is drawn closer while the foreigner is propelled farther away. What is most striking, here, is the second principle; for it seems to violate the spirit of equality that reigns in the modern age. The principle that "the same want sameness" has much support—both in Tocqueville[58] and, indeed, throughout the whole of political philosophy.[59] Sameness, while it invites invidious comparison, has its secret comforts.

The principle that "the different want difference" is no less conspicuous, however; and, in fact, comes to prominence precisely when conditions of equality conspire to overcome long-standing difference—which now increasingly resides only in memory. Consider the following remark:

The southern American has two active passions which will always lead him to isolate himself: he is afraid of resembling the Negro, *once a slave,* and he is afraid of falling below the level of his white neighbor.[60]

And elsewhere:

[After a democratic revolution] those who once held the highest ranks in the subverted hierarchy *cannot forget* their ancient greatness at once and for a long time feel themselves strangers in the new society. They regard all those whom society now makes their equals as oppressors whose fate could not concern them. . . . But those formerly at the bottom of the social scale and now brought up to the common level

---

57. Tocqueville, *Democracy in America*, Author's Introduction, p. 14.

58. See Tocqueville, *Democracy in America*, vol. 1, part 1, chap. 3, p. 57: "[T]he human heart also nourishes a debased taste for equality, which leads the weak to want to drag the strong down to their level and which induces men to prefer equality in servitude to inequality in freedom."

59. The whole of Western thought was, for Nietzsche, confirmation of the victory of this impulse toward equality; violated briefly during the Renaissance (and later by Napoleon), but ultimately coming to triumph during the Reformation (see *Genealogy of Morals*, first essay, sec. 16, pp. 53–54).

60. Tocqueville, *Democracy in America*, vol. 1, part 2, chap. 10, p. 357 (emphasis added).

by a sudden revolution cannot enjoy their newfound independence without some secret uneasiness: there is a look of fear mixed with triumph in their eyes if they do meet one of their former superiors, and they avoid them.[61]

However this principle is construed—as a consequence of memory or as the modern equivalent of the revolt against God's will—difference does not always yield and pronounces itself ever more forcefully in the face of the democratization of the world.[62] The yield of the effort to efface difference, to bring *into proximity* the different, is not unequivocal acquiescence. Laws designed to institute equality may also serve to re-constitute the claim of difference at another site.

> I plainly see that in some parts of the country the legal barrier be-tween the two races is tending to come down, but not that of mores: I see that slavery is in retreat, but the prejudice from which it arose is immovable.
>
> In that part of the Union where the Negroes are no longer slaves, have they come closer to the whites? Everyone who has lived in the United States will have noticed just the opposite.[63]

Longstanding differences come to be supported even more strongly by mores—perhaps even by science[64]—when laws conspire to eliminate them. Race emerges as an immovable foundation precisely at the mo-ment when equality is professed evermore strongly; race is, in a word,

61. Tocqueville, *Democracy in America*, vol. 2, part 2, chap. 3, pp. 508–9 (em-phasis added).

62. See Benjamin R. Barber, "Jihad vs. McWorld," *Atlantic*, March 1992, pp. 53–63. Barber suggests that both tendencies are unfriendly to democracy, though by democracy he, unlike Tocqueville, does not mean equality.

63. Tocqueville, *Democracy in America*, vol. 1, part 2, chap. 10, pp. 342–43. See also p. 356: "[T]he freer the whites in America are the more they will seek to isolate themselves."

64. See, for example, Herbert Spencer, *On Social Evolution* (Chicago: Uni-versity of Chicago Press, 1972), for an early post-Darwin formulation that perti-nent social difference is rooted in biology. "Any one variety of creature in the course of many generations acquires a certain constitutional adaptation to its particular form of life, and every other variety acquires its own special adapta-tion. The consequence is that, if you mix the constitutions of two widely diver-gent modes of life, you get a constitution which is adapted to the mode of life of neither . . . my advice is [therefore] strongly conservative in all directions, and I end by saying as I began—*keep other races at arm's length as much as possible*" (part 4, chap. 24, p. 257, emphasis in original). Cf. R. C. Lewontin, Steven Rose, and Leon J. Kamin, *Not in Our Genes* (New York: Pantheon Books, 1984), pp. 119–27.

less a cause than a consequence of a difference (not rooted in nature)[65] that refuses to be forgotten.

This proliferation of difference occurs in less sinister forms as well. When equality reigns, a person's natural pride will wish to establish a mark by which to be distinguished from the rest:

> In democracies, where there is never much difference between one citizen and another . . . a multitude of artificial and arbitrary classifications are established to protect each man from the danger of being swept along in spite of himself with the crowd.[66]

Already existing similarity, in a word, leads to the proliferation of difference. Here is a prophetic thought for the next century. Difference in an aristocratic age may have been preestablished and immovable; it was, nevertheless, bounded.[67] The victory of equality, however, effaces those differences and consecrates others anew. The site that *authorizes* new distinctions shifts away from the aristocrat of the old order, to be sure;[68]

---

65. A difference that is partially rooted in nature is the difference between men and women. Tocqueville follows Rousseau (*Emile*, bk. 5, pp. 357–58) and Plato (*Republic*, bk. 5, 451c–57c) in the view that there are respects in which men and women are the same, and respects in which they are not. In Europe, Tocqueville suggests, the spirit of equality has not yet insinuated itself into the relations between the sexes; there a man "makes himself a woman's slave [but] he never sincerely thinks her his equal" (*Democracy in America*, vol. 2, part 3, chap. 12, p. 602). Not having grasped the points of equality, women are alternatingly slave and master of men—as Baron de Montesquieu had made clear in the early eighteenth century with his hugely influential *Persian Letters* (trans. C. J. Betts [New York: Penguin Books, 1973]). In America, on the other hand, equality prevails—but not to the point where the logic of equality supplants *natural* differences. The relations between the sexes were healthy precisely because the similarity of, and the difference between, men and women was respected. It is worth pondering whether the argument that applies to the relations between the races also applies to the relations between the sexes, namely, does the attempt to efface difference *completely* lead to its reestablishment— perhaps in caricatured form—at another site?

66. Tocqueville, *Democracy in America*, vol. 2, part 3, chap. 13, p. 605.

67. See Tocqueville, *Democracy in America*, vol. 2, part 3, chap. 17, p. 614: "[I]n aristocracies each man is pretty firmly fixed in his sphere, but men are vastly dissimilar; their passions, ideas, habits, and tastes are basically diverse. Nothing changes, but everything differs."

68. See Tocqueville, *Democracy in America*, vol. 2, part 2, chap. 5, pp. 514– 16. See also, part 3, chap. 21, pp. 641–42, where the authority of a *name* authorizes new ideas in the aristocratic age; ideas have no authority in themselves. This has grave implications for the authority of new ideas in the age of democracy— as Mill grasped in "On Liberty."

but the production of difference remains. Its locus is now the citizen—at once an utterly independent agent and at the same time completely beholden to the opinion of the majority.[69]

The problem of difference in a democracy, then, takes two forms. On the one hand there is the demand to level all difference; on the other hand there is the wish to retain difference in the face of the democratization of the world. The first aspect produces the affliction of envy; the second, the promulgation of difference that manages to maintain distance. In the following section I consider Tocqueville's view that Christianity can ameliorate but never wholly arrest both of these intransigent problems, and that democracy requires this palliative in order to avert these twin perils.

3. CHRISTIANITY AS PALLIATIVE FOR ENVY AND DIFFERENCE

> In democracies private citizens see men rising from their ranks and attaining wealth and power in a few years; that spectacle excites their astonishment and their envy; they wonder how he who was their equal yesterday has today won the right to command them.[70]

The distrust of government, about which much is written today, is peculiarly acute within a democracy at all times. This is not simply because the competency of its elected officials is suspect; rather, in a democracy

---

69. This paradox can be traced to the absence of intermediary powers capable of standing between the solitary person and society as a whole. See, for example, Tocqueville, *Democracy in America*, vol. 2, part 4, chaps. 1–3, pp. 667–74. The theology of this cannot be overlooked. Without the mediation of the "priesthood" there can be no "salvation." Tawney's characterization of the dilemma of Protestantism is apropos here: "[Protestantism contained] a dualism which, as its implications were developed, emptied religion of its social content, and society of its soul. Between light and darkness a great gulf was fixed. Unable to climb upwards plane by plane, man must choose between salvation and damnation. If he despairs of attaining the austere heights where alone true faith is found, no human institution can avail to help him" (R. H. Tawney, *Religion and the Rise of Capitalism* [London: John Murray, 1936], p. 101). Translated from theology to social theory: the "priesthood" of intermediaries makes possible a middle ground between a "salvation" that takes the form of being drawn into the awesome body-social and a "damnation" of isolation and solipsism, both of which forms are suffered by the Protestant culture in America. See Tocqueville, *Democracy in America*, vol. 2, part 1, chap. 6, p. 450.

70. Tocqueville, *Democracy in America*, vol. 1, part 2, chap. 5, p. 221. See also vol. 2, part 2, chap. 4, p. 512: "[What is wanted of the rich by the poor] is not the sacrifice of their money but of their pride."

the social distance between the rulers and ruled has collapsed.[71] Corruption is no more pervasive here than in an aristocracy; it is, however, *transparent* in a democracy. Proximity makes for visibility. The one who rises above the rest is like the rest, but set apart from them. Here is the prerequisite of envy: that the self attend with great interest to the distance between itself and the other who is akin. As Augustine put it:

> [There is a] kind of temptation [that] has not ceased to trouble me, nor during the whole of this life can it cease. The temptation is to wish to be feared and loved by people for no reason other than the joy derived from such power, which is no joy at all. It is a wretched life, and vanity is repulsive. This is the main cause why I fail to love you and fear you in purity.[72]

Envy in its political form seems most to confirm Augustine's apprehension. Politics is a worldly affair into which the Americans have wholly thrown themselves.[73] And so thrown, their point of orientation tends to be other human beings with whom they compare themselves.[74] The envy that ensues may be attenuated without recourse to drawing the invidious soul away from the created world and toward the Creator, to be sure. (Think here of Tocqueville's claim that moderate property holdings can arrest envy,[75] Rousseau's assertion that envy can be attenuated if learning is institutionally circumscribed and left to members of famed societies,[76] and Hobbes's conflated theology, which arrests the pride of the many by shifting the citizen's gaze to the powerful sovereign.)[77] The question, however, is whether these correctives can serve

71. See Nietzsche, *Genealogy of Morals*, second essay, sec. 12, p. 78: "[T]he democratic idiosyncrasy . . . opposes everything that dominates and wants to dominate [and a] modern *misarchism* (to coin an ugly word for an ugly thing) has permeated the realm of spirit" (emphasis in original).

72. Augustine, *Confessions*, bk. 10, chap. 36, pp. 213–14.

73. Tocqueville, *Democracy in America*, vol. 2, part 2, chap. 6, pp. 242–43.

74. See David Hume, *A Treatise of Human Nature* (Oxford: Clarendon Press, 1978), ed. L. A. Selby-Bigge, bk. 2, part 2, sec. 8, p. 372: "[S]o little are men govern'd by reason in their sentiments and opinions, that they always judge more of objects by comparison than from their intrinsic worth or value."

75. Tocqueville, *Democracy in America*, vol. 2, part 3, chap. 21, p. 636.

76. See Rousseau, *First Discourse*, p. 64.

77. See Hobbes, *De cive*,, author's preface, p. 103, where "it is better that matters of justice be left to the laws of the realm, [for then] you will no longer suffer ambitious men through the streams of your blood to wade to their own power." For a brief discussion of the theological elements in Hobbes's thinking see Joshua Mitchell, "Hobbes and the Equality of All under the One," in *Political Theory* 21, no. 1 (1993), pp. 78–100.

as adequate substitutions for what Augustine insists only the humble recognition of the distinction between Creator and created fosters.

Tocqueville, like Augustine, recognizes the danger of abrogating the distinction. Ironically, democracy, linked in essential ways to Christianity, creates the conditions under which this distinction may be dissolved. In one of its valences democracy erases difference. The real-life movement toward unity inclines the soul away from the distinction between Creator and created; it wants only a One, it wants pantheism. Moving in this direction, however, disavows the claim of the radically Other over human life. Thus unfettered, human beings now erroneously think themselves wholly sufficient unto themselves and answerable to no one—precisely the picture of the disengaged soul about which Tocqueville so worries.[78]

There is a further irony, one not lost to Tocqueville. The seemingly self-sufficient soul knows in its heart its own impotence, *and for that reason is drawn to the idea of a unity that outstrips its impotence.*

> [The system of pantheism,] although it destroys human individuality, *or rather because it destroys it,* will have secret charms for men living under democracies.[79]

I will consider below how this intimated impotence contributes to a secret longing for a strong state (in sec. 4). Here I will only note that Tocqueville seems to be well aware of the paradox of power and weakness about which Plato,[80] St. Paul,[81] Augustine,[82] Luther,[83] and (in a

---

78. See Tocqueville, *Democracy in America*, vol. 2, part 1, chap. 7, p. 452: "[Pantheism] fosters pride and soothes the laziness of their minds." Pride and laziness serve to keep persons self-enclosed.

79. Tocqueville, *Democracy in America*, vol. 2, part 1, chap. 7, p. 452 (emphasis added).

80. See Plato, *Republic*, bk. 9, 579d–e. Appearances to the contrary, the tyrant is in fact the least happy human being. Love of the Good is the only foundation upon which human existence can participate in plenitude.

81. See 1 Cor. 1:25 ("Because the foolishness of God is wiser than men; and the weakness of God is stronger than men"); and 2 Cor. 12:9 ("And he said unto me, My grace is sufficient for thee: for strength is made perfect in weakness. Most gladly therefore will I rather glory in my infirmities, that the power of Christ may rest upon me").

82. See Augustine, *Confessions*, bk. 2, chap. 6, p. 31: "[P]ride imitates what is lofty; but you alone are God most high above all things." God on the Cross, the contemptible Nazarene, is the Wellspring.

83. See Luther, "Freedom of a Christian," 31:333–77. True freedom, he argues, is made possible through Christ by human passivity toward God the Father. See also "Lectures on Galatians," in *Luther's Works*, 26:5: "[H]uman rea-

heartfelt idiom very much his own) Rousseau[84] speak. A pretended self-sufficiency not grounded upon a true foundation exposes an impotence that will seek absolution in the wrong place.

Envy and the impulse toward pantheism, both of which bespeak an impotence[85] of the soul that, paradoxically, both stands alone and yet is akin to others close by, must be circumscribed. Institutional mechanisms, as important as they surely are, will not suffice by themselves—and indeed, eventually fall away. They may successfully reduce proximity at the outset of a democratic revolution (think, again, of Hobbes's and Rousseau's attempts to avert the gaze of the demos), but when its victory is complete, the barriers that keep envy in abeyance topple; now all must be seen; now everyone must be a neighbor; now everyone's gaze must be unobstructed. Everything is unconcealed.[86] Envy now re-

---

son cannot refrain from looking at active righteousness, that is, *its own righteousness*; nor can it shift its gaze to passive, that is, Christian righteousness" (emphasis added). I will only mention in passing here the resemblance between Luther and Heidegger's thinking in "The Essence of Truth" (p. 134). Heidegger there suggests that "filling up the world" intimates a hiding-from-Being. Luther has the same insight, namely, that the terror of conscience, the terror of looking below the everyday world of works, leads Christians to "look at nothing except . . . works." See also Rousseau, *Emile*, bk. 4, pp. 229–30.

84. See Rousseau, *First Discourse*. Among the many provocations offered there is to be found the intimation that the brilliance of the visible is only apparent: real brilliance is invisible, is prior to enlightenment. Bringing to presence before the light of the mind betrays already the loss of all that is vital. "The Romans had been content to practice virtue," he says; "all was lost when they began to study it" (p. 45).

85. See John Rawls, *A Theory of Justice* (Cambridge: Harvard University Press, 1971), pp. 530–41. Rawls notes the relationship between envy and impotence (p. 535) but reverses Tocqueville's insight that envy becomes acute precisely when social distance is diminished. Rawls argues that the general condition of equality established by the original condition circumscribes the envy that would arise were there gross inequalities (p. 536). (See Tocqueville, *Democracy in America*, vol. 1, part 2, chap. 10, p. 355, on the principle of "relative justice.") The temporal horizon invoked by Rawls in his *Theory* is the one with which the American is most at home. The past, for the American, is not constitutive. Moving in this direction offers, in Oakeshott's words, "a technique which puts all minds on the same level [and makes them] incapable of appreciating the concrete detail of their total inheritance" (*Rationalism in Politics*, p. 23). Such a move is an aspect of the victory of rationalism, which substitutes the rule for the particular and sacrifices the sullied past and its ongoing burdens in the name of creating a (purportedly) pristine future.

86. See Plato, *Republic*, bk. 8, 557b–58c, for a view of the democratic city. Here appetites long harbored emerge into view; the injunction of justice—to

quires a palliative that no worldly (institutional) construction may offer; the democratic *demand* that there be no difference in the world makes such constructions unendurable.

This line of thinking, I recognize, pushes the logic of Tocqueville's argument to its farthest point—toward Plato's less than charitable view of the democratic soul. Yet this has been done only to make clear his claim, echoing Augustine, that there must be an orientation toward the transcendent if the temptations of the world are to be ameliorated:

> Every religion places the object of man's desires outside and beyond worldly goods and naturally lifts the soul into regions far above the realm of the senses.[87]

Put another way, an enduring community in a democratic age is possible only when its members are oriented *to* one another *through* a transcendent God. Proximity begets invidiousness if one's gaze is perpetually directed toward the neighbor *in our face*. In Augustine's words,

> [A true friendship] is not possible unless you bond together those who cleave to one another by love which "is poured into our hearts by the Holy Spirit who is given to us" (Rom. 5:5).[88]

Tocqueville's presentation is not so explicit, to be sure; yet the need to avert one's gaze in order that vision be subsequently more clear, that envy be attenuated, remains: only a (creator) God may draw the (created) soul away from the comparative and toward the absolute. As social conditions become ever more equal, the need for God becomes ever more acute.[89]

---

grant each its due—is violated. The whole of book 8 can be understood as a story of the progressive unconcealment of the tyranny that lurks in all souls who are not oriented by a love of the Good.

87. Tocqueville, *Democracy in America*, vol. 2, part 1, chap. 4, p. 444.

88. Augustine, *Confessions*, bk. 4, chap. 4, p. 75. Cf. Aristotle, *Nicomachean Ethics*, bk. 9, chap. 8, 1168b6: "[A]ll friendly feelings toward others are an extension of the friendly feelings a person has for himself."

89. See Plato, *Republic*, bk. 6, 500c: "[T]he man whose mind is truly fixed on eternal realities has no leisure to turn his eyes downward upon the petty affairs of men, and so engaging in strife with them to be filled with envy and hate." The democratic regime spoken of in book 8 is, like the tyrannical regime that follows, in dire need of this orientation toward the Eternal. In Augustine's words, "[W]hat has satisfied them is their own imaginings, not your [God's] truth. This they thrust away from them, and so bounce back and forth into their own emptiness" (*The Trinity*, bk. 4, prologue, sec. 1, pp. 152–53).

W here envy emanates from a proximity of those who are akin, difference is engendered by an intimation of a kinship that would
be rebuffed. The movement toward democracy is history's ever more
vocal proclamation that all are equal; yet this voice is muffled by another
voice within that revolts against the impotence that such leveling accomplishes. This other voice wishes to elevate the soul above the rest
and cries all the louder as equality commutes all difference, legal or
otherwise.

> There is a tendency in democracy not to draw men together, but
> democratic revolutions make them run away from each other and per-
> petuate, in the midst of equality, *hatred originating in inequality.*[90]

The extraordinary proliferation of difference occurs just at the moment
when the soul intimates its kinship with others. However this is understood—as an arrest that cannot yet be forgotten; as the result of the
demise of an aristocratic authority capable of circumscribing the range
of difference; as a repercussion of the absence of mediating institutions
that must take their stead in a democratic age; as a consequence of an
egoism that cannot be vitiated—the forces that engender difference
seem to be diametrically opposed to the equality that is forgone, yet are
actually a ramification of it.[91] The envy of the one who always faces the
other is coincident with the withdrawal into oneself and keeping the
other at bay.

The bearing of politics upon this matter deserves some attention
here. For Tocqueville, recall, this tendency to withdraw was *the* principle problem that politics attenuates. I have commented earlier (in sec.
1 of chap. 3) that politics works well, not when it *represents*, but rather

---

90. Tocqueville, *Democracy in America*, vol. 2, part 2, chap. 3, p. 509 (emphasis added). See vol. 1, part 2, chap. 10, p. 342, where speaking of slavery in
America, Tocqueville remarks, "[F]or my part, remembering the extreme difficulty with which aristocratic bodies, of whatever nature they be, mingle with
the mass of people, the excessive care they take to preserve down the centuries
the artificial barriers that keep them apart, I despair of seeing an aristocracy
founded on visible and indelible signs vanish." Also see vol. 2, part 3, chap. 19,
p. 632: "[In one of the valences of pride,] everyone thinks himself better than
his neighbor and dislikes obeying a superior."

91. Consider, in this light, Julien Benda, *The Treason of the Intellectuals* (New
York: W. W. Norton, 1969). Benda recognizes the proliferation of political passions that proclaim difference (pp. 3–29) yet identifies the "clerks" as the
source of this proliferation (pp. 43–177). More precisely, the clerks are implicated by virtue of the renunciation of their historical role as disinterested ideal-
ists. Tocqueville would argue that the intellectual class is not at the root of this
proliferation of difference; rather, it is occasioned by democracy itself.

when it draws persons out of their self-enclosed worlds. What is note-worthy about the Americans is that they were largely able to solve this problem by political participation at the local level.

> Citizens who are bound to take part in public affairs must turn from the private interests and occasionally take a look at something other than themselves. As soon as common affairs are treated in common, each man notices that he is not as independent of his fellows as he used to suppose and that to get their help he must often offer his aid to them.[92]

Local, not national, politics is the forum for attenuating the difference that is born of self-enclosure. Here, unlike the national forum, self-in-terest—the "only stable point in the human heart"[93]—may serve and be served. Unlike national politics, local politics pertains palpably to one's immediate affairs, and it is palpability, not principle, that moves the American. Should this arena be lost, should the secret hidden long-ing for a strong central government emerge, then the problem of differ-ence is thrust into an arena incapable of ameliorating it. Strong central government is the product of the longing for unity; any unity produced at that site can only be heteronymous.[94] Difference cannot be elimi-nated; at the local level, however, when conjoined with the give and take of self-interest rightly understood, its valence may be modified.

Tocqueville's profound insight about the site at which difference may be attenuated ought to be closely heeded as the question of unity be-comes ever more momentous in this democratic age. Even were his un-derstanding to be taken seriously, however, local politics alone could not allay the difficulty, for the site of local politics is of no avail without persons of a certain sort who are capable of arriving at the compromises that this forum makes possible. Politics may be the stage, but without certain kinds of actors on hand, there can be no performance.

There are, significantly, prepolitical foundations necessary for the success of local politics, and these must be attended to here. To come

92. Tocqueville, *Democracy in America*, vol. 2, part 2, chap. 4, p. 510.
93. Tocqueville, *Democracy in America*, vol. 1, part 2, chap. 6, p. 239.
94. See Tocqueville, *Democracy in America*, appendix 1, Y, pp. 734–35: "[M]en think that the greatness of the idea of unity lies in means. God sees it in the end. It is for that reason that the idea of greatness leads to a thousand mean actions. To force all men to march in step toward the same goal—that is a human idea. To encourage endless variety of actions but to bring them about so that in a thousand different ways all tend toward the fulfillment of one design—that is a God-given idea." To make the central government that one unity is bad theology, for it asks of the state what only God can do. Lawrence translates the French, *introduire*, as *encourage*, which is too strong; more accurate is *introduce*.

right to the point, self-interest rightly understood is *not* political in origin. It is religious. The problem of difference, which can be assuaged but not eliminated at the level of local politics, returns Tocqueville to a consideration of Christianity.

> If the doctrine of self-interest properly understood were concerned with this world only, this would not be nearly enough. For there are a great many sacrifices which can only be rewarded in the next. However hard one may try to prove that virtue is useful, it will always be difficult to make a man live well if he will not face death.[95]

Worldly activity, in a word, will always comport with the economy of salvation.[96]

A lengthy digression about the massive difference between Tocqueville and Nietzsche's understanding of the kernel of Christianity would be fitting here, were space not at a premium. For Tocqueville, the inner truth of Christianity is not the "awe-inspiring *catastrophe* of two thousand years of training in truthfulness that finally forbids itself the *lie involved in belief in God.*"[97] Christianity is not a dialectic that unconceals the true ground of the will's purity amid the wilderness of Judea—as it was from Luther to Nietzsche. Rather, following Pascal,[98] Christianity is a training in self-interest rightly understood. Christianity speaks to reason, not to the will; it teaches forbearance, not inner perspicuity. Its capacity to arrest the immediacy of desire is its great social asset; without that, there is cause to wonder whether self-interest rightly understood (which must involve forbearance) is possible at all.

I will consider this matter of forbearance further below (in sec. 5). Something more needs to be said here, however, about the problem of difference.

95. Tocqueville, *Democracy in America*, vol. 2, part 2, chap. 9, p. 528. If the temporal horizon of human life is bounded by its short span, then the soul is likely to say, with Augustine, "I found myself heavily weighed down by a sense of being tired of living and scared of dying" (*Confessions*, bk. 4, chap. 6, p. 59).

96. See Tocqueville, *Democracy in America*, vol. 2, part 1, chap. 5, p. 442: "[T]here is hardly any action, however private it may be, which does not result from some very general conception men have of God, of His relations with the human race, of the nature of their soul, and of their duties to their fellows." It is no wonder, then, that Tocqueville follows up his discussion of self-interest rightly understood (vol. 2, part 2, chap. 8, pp. 525–28) with a chapter on the bearing of religion upon self-interest (chap. 9, pp. 528–30).

97. Nietzsche, *Genealogy of Morals*, third essay, sec. 27, p. 160 (emphasis in original).

98. Pascal, *Pensées*, sec. 418, pp. 149–53; Tocqueville, *Democracy in America*, vol. 2, part 2, chap. 9, p. 529.

While local politics is the arena within which difference may be attenuated but not annulled, and Christianity forms persons capable of diminishing distance within this forum through self-interest rightly understood, the theoretical problem of difference and equality remains and requires an articulation that comprehends these two moments without glorifying or decrying either one. Where Nietzsche would give us difference and Rawls would make us essentially the same, Tocqueville's Christianity embraces both moments. Difference cannot be erased; yet beneath all difference is the authoritative claim of unity that countenances neither a prurient aggrandizement of difference nor a complacent, imaginative fiction that largely ignores it.

> Only the Christian ethos solves the problem of equality and inequality, since it neither glorifies force and accident in the sense of a Nietzschean cult of breed, nor outrages the patent facts of life by a doctrinaire egalitarianism. It recognizes differences in social position, power, capacity, as a condition which has been established by the inscrutable Will of God; and then transforms this condition by an inner building of personality, and the development of a mutual sense of obligation, into an ethical cosmos.[99]

These are Troeltsch's words, but the sentiment is to be found already in Augustine:

> [It should be remembered that Adam was created] for the precise purpose of reminding us to preserve unity in a multitude of men.[100]

Tocqueville, too, is no less aware of the capacity of Christianity to redress the twin perils of envy (by averting the soul's gaze toward heaven) and difference (by insisting upon an underlying unity).

> Every religion places the object of man's desires outside and beyond worldly goods and naturally lifts the soul into regions far above the realm of the senses. Every religion also imposes on each man some obligations toward mankind, to be performed in common with the

99. Troeltsch, *Social Teachings*, 2:1005. See also Helmut Schoeck, *Envy: A Theory of Social Behavior* (Indianapolis, Ind.: Liberty Press, 1987), p. 160: "[I]n the West, the historical achievement of this Christian ethic is to have encouraged and protected, if not to have been actually responsible for the extent of, the exercise of human creative powers through the control of envy."

100. Augustine, *City of God*, vol. 7, bk. 12, chap. 28, p. 296. The Bettenson edition has: "[It should be remembered that Adam] was created by God with this intention: that from that one individual a multitude might be propagated, and that this fact should teach mankind to preserve unity in plurality (*CG*, p. 508).

rest of mankind, and so draws him away, from time to time, from thinking about himself.[101]

The natural tendency is to fall into the irrationalities of envy and the proliferation of difference. Theologically, the flesh would have its way and must be countered with strong measures.[102] While local politics may provide the site that can ameliorate these problems,[103] without certain authoritative proclamations against the irrationalities of envy and difference, this site would be of no avail. Feuerbach was wrong: the insurmountable distance between humankind and God does not bespeak a loss of the true ground of human community,[104] but rather the opposite. And Marx? He was half right; Christianity *is* the "opium of the

101. Tocqueville, *Democracy in America*, vol. 2, part 1, chap. 5, pp. 444–45. The whole of the law and the prophets, it is said in Matt. 22:37–40, hang on the twin command to love God and one's neighbor. As Augustine notes, these commandments are necessarily linked, just as the (natural tendency of) turning away from God is linked to (natural) hatred of the neighbor when the human gaze is wholly immanent. In his words, "[W]hen therefore we love our brother out of love, we love our brother out of God; and it is impossible that we should not love especially the love that we love our brother with. Thus we infer that those two commandments cannot exist without each other: because God is love, the man who loves love certainly loves God; and the man who loves his brother must love love" (*The Trinity*, bk. 8, chap. 5, sec. 12, pp. 253–54.

102. Luther put it quite starkly: there is a need for a salutary fear that draws human beings away from their more egregious tendencies. "If anyone attempted to rule the world by the Gospel and abolish all temporal law and sword . . . he would be loosing the ropes and chains of the wild savage beast and letting them bite and mangle everyone" ("Temporal Authority," 45:91). See also Calvin, *Institutes of Christian Religion*, vol. 1, bk. 2, chap. 7, p. 362, sec. 14: "[T]he law has power to exhort believers. . . . [It serves to] shake off sluggishness, by repeatedly urging them, to pinch them awake to their imperfection."

103. See Tocqueville, *Democracy in America*, vol. 2, part 2, chap. 4, p. 511: "[L]ocal liberties . . . bring men constantly into contact, despite the instincts which separate them, and force them to help one another."

104. See Feuerbach, *The Essence of Christianity*, trans. George Eliot (New York: Harper and Row, 1957), p. 270: "[W]e have shown that the substance and object of religion is altogether human; we have shown that divine wisdom is human wisdom; that the secret of theology is anthropology; that the absolute mind is the so-called finite subjective mind." "Love of man," he continues, "must be no derivative love; it must be original. . . . The relations of child and parent, of husband and wife, of brother and friend—in general, of man to man—in short, all the moral relations are *per se* religious" (p. 271). Karl Barth's introductory essay (pp. x–xxxii) insists upon the same distinction Tocqueville makes, namely, between the Creator and the created. Feuerbach's *Essence*, on Tocqueville's reading, succumbs to the pantheist temptation.

people"[105] in that it averts the gaze of envy. Yet it is also a stimulant that would roust the soul from its complacent self-enclosure by demanding that it attend to others—not because they are different, but because underneath their difference is an essential similarity that must be accorded a place in the moral economy.

4. THE INDIRECT EFFECTS OF CHRISTIANITY UPON DEMOCRACY

> Of all the dispositions and habits which lead to political prosperity, religion and morality are indispensable supports. In vain would that man claim the tribute of patriotism, who should labor to subvert these great pillars of human happiness, these firmest props of the duties of men and citizens. . . . And let us with caution indulge the supposition, that morality can be maintained without religion. Whatever may be conceded to the influence of refined education on minds of peculiar structure, reason and experience both forbid us to expect that national morality can prevail in exclusion of religious principle.[106]

The objectionable alignment of the Christian Church with ephemeral political powers during the transition to the democratic age in Europe culminated, as Tocqueville notes, in the rejection of Christianity itself. Whether this rejection took the form of the effort wholly to supplant religion with reason or to demonstrate that its inner truth accorded with reason, the effect was the same: the *scandal* of Christian religion—that it demands a deference to a God whom unaided reason alone cannot grasp[107]—was renounced. About the capacity of the trajectories of thought seeking to escape from the Christian orbit to furnish an adequate foundation for human freedom Tocqueville was unequivocal. They are inadequate to the task.

> I am informed that on the other side of the ocean freedom and human happiness lack nothing but Spinoza's belief in the eternity of the

105. See Karl Marx, "Contribution to the Critique of Hegel's Philosophy of Right: Introduction," in *The Marx-Engels Reader*, p. 54. The abolition of religion, of required illusions, would direct the human gaze wholly upon the world.

106. George Washington, "Farewell Address," in *George Washington: A Collection*, ed. W. B. Allen (Indianapolis, Ind.: Liberty Press, 1988), p. 521.

107. Consider, for example, Luther's view of circumcision. See Gerrish, *Grace and Reason*, part 1, chap. 1, p. 19: "[C]ircumcision made the Jews a laughing-stock, so utterly pointless did the practice seem. Luther replies that the point of circumcision is precisely to offend reason, to force it to surrender its vanity. If God had given a token which reason could approve, then man's arrogance would have remained."

world and Cabinas's contention that thought is a secretion of the brain. To that I have really no answer to give, except that those who talk like that have never been in America and have never seen either religious peoples or free ones.[108]

The reason Tocqueville takes this stance must be made clear. Where Plato seeks to demonstrate that reason must rule in order for persons to be truly happy,[109] Tocqueville's efforts are directed toward elucidating the paradox of freedom and obedience. Plato is concerned with right rulership; Tocqueville, with rightful obedience. Following Augustine, human freedom and the happiness that is accorded in this life are not possible without divine assistance. Plato's error—the philosopher's error—is to suppose that human faculties alone are sufficient to the task.[110] For Tocqueville (and Augustine) happiness involves an acquiescence, a passivity, before God. The great paradox is that precisely by passively acquiescing before God it becomes possible actively and wholesomely to participate in the world. As with his view of the division of labor between men and women outside the home and in it,[111] by separating passivity and activity, by distinguishing what is owed to the Creator and what is owed to the world, freedom and happiness become possible. Not the existence of the two domains,[112] but rather the confusion about what is proper to each, is the source of human affliction.

> In the moral world [of the American] everything is classified, coordinated, foreseen, and decided in advance. In the world of politics everything is in turmoil, contested, and uncertain. In one case obedience is passive, though voluntary; in the other case there is independence, contempt of experience, and jealousy of all authority. Far from

108. Tocqueville, *Democracy in America*, vol. 1, part 2, chap. 9, p. 294. Worth pondering, in this light, is Acts 17:15–18:17. In Athens, where philosophy ruled, St. Paul's proclamation of the Good News was received with derision; in Corinth, where commerce prevailed, Christianity was received more favorably.

109. See Plato, *Republic*, bk. 4, 441d–42d.

110. See Augustine, *City of God*, vol. 7, bk. 10, chap. 31, pp. 177–78 (*CG*, pp. 419–20); bk. 11, chap. 2, pp. 188–89 (*CG*, pp. 430–31); bk. 14, chaps. 2–5, pp. 348–58 (*CG*, pp. 548–55).

111. See Tocqueville, *Democracy in America*, vol. 2, part 3, chap. 12, p. 601: "[T]he Americans have applied to the sexes the great principle of political economy which now dominates industry. . . . Care has been taken constantly to trace clearly distinct spheres of action for the two sexes."

112. See Hobbes, *Leviathan*, part 3, chap. 39, p. 340: "[T]here is therefore no other government in this life, neither of *state*, nor *religion*, but *temporal*" (emphasis added). Hobbes's efforts were directed against the claim that political and theological matters are separate. Christ did not come into the world to sow the seeds of division. Cf. Matt. 12:25; Mark 3:24–25; Luke 11:17–22.

harming each other, these two apparently opposed tendencies work in harmony and seem to lend mutual support.[113]

The theoretical issue, for Tocqueville, is whether humans will accord what is due to each domain. In practical terms, this devolves onto the question of whether obedience will be accorded to an earthly or to the heavenly sovereign! "If [a man] has no faith he must obey," he says, "and if he is free he must believe."[114] The passive and active aspects will always appear, the significant question is whether they will appear in such a way that they yield freedom or servitude. Servitude before God in Heaven makes possible the freedom of humankind on earth.

Should there be a passivity toward God, then the mind is held firm; and this makes possible the free play, the extraordinary activity, in the world. Should this passivity toward God be absent, then it will ensconce itself in the political world—in the form of passivity before a worldly sovereign! For this reason Tocqueville is able to say,

> Religion, which never intervenes directly in the government of American society, should therefore be considered as the first of their political institutions, for although it did not give them the taste for liberty, it singularly facilitates their use thereof.[115]

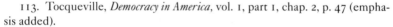

113. Tocqueville, *Democracy in America*, vol. 1, part 1, chap. 2, p. 47 (emphasis added).

114. Tocqueville, *Democracy in America*, vol. 2, part 1, chap. 5, p. 444. Arendt would later speak not about the crisis of passive obedience, but rather of the crisis of authority. In her words, "Authority, resting on a foundation in the past as its unshakable cornerstone, gave the world the permanence that human beings need precisely because they are mortals—the most unstable and futile beings we know of. Its loss is tantamount to the loss of the groundwork of the world, which indeed since then has begun to shift, to change and transform itself with ever-increasing rapidity from one shape to another, as though we were living and struggling with a Protean universe where everything at any moment can become almost anything else" (*Between Past and Future*, p. 95).

115. Tocqueville, *Democracy in America*, vol. 1, part 2, chap. 9, p. 292. In *The Closing of the American Mind*, Bloom chides Max Weber's view that Nietzsche destroyed once and for all the naive belief in reason and suggests that America, up to the time of the invasion of Nietzsche's thought, still shared the "rationalist dream" (p. 195). Bloom seems unable to comprehend that the only alternative to the purported *rational* foundations of the American experiment is not a führer (p. 212), that *deeper* than reason may be a conviction of the heart that religion articulates that nevertheless comports with the conclusions of reason—as Tocqueville suggests. See *Democracy in America*, vol. 1, part 2, chap. 9, p. 294, where Tocqueville asks, "[W]hat can be done with a people master of itself if it is not subject to God?"

Holding of mind within firm bounds in a democracy requires nonpolitical foundations;[116] the true ground of beneficent activity is passivity.[117]

Theologically, citizens must be Jews who acquiesce before God in the wilderness of the soul in order to enter into the promised land of worldly freedom. Murmuring against God in that wilderness,[118] insisting upon the sufficiency of human agency, can lead only to the Egyptian captivity—to the "flesh pots"[119] of Pharaoh's "single central power" toward which Tocqueville so worries the democratic soul is imperceptibly drawn.[120] Tocqueville's citation of Mather's *Magnalia Christi Americana* is portentous;[121] it captures the insight essential to the success of American freedom: liberty is made possible through obedience.[122] Here, in

116. See Marvin Zetterbaum, *Tocqueville and the Problem of Democracy* (Stanford: Stanford University Press, 1967), p. 117: "Democracy, it seems, is impossible without such a sanctuary above and beyond democratic inquiry; and all of Tocqueville's efforts are bent on preserving this sanctuary from the impious and destructive onslaughts of the many." Zetterbaum worries that religion is not strong enough to arrest the fall into mediocrity and materialism toward which the democratic soul naturally gravitates (p. 123), and that, following Leo Strauss, society must foster the myth of religion even while political philosophy revolts against the delusion it perpetrates (p. 160). Why this violates the spirit of Tocqueville's inquiry will be considered in section 7 below.

117. In gendered terms, the passive, feminine aspect (while less visible) has a certain preeminence over the active, masculine aspect. Without the former, the latter cannot subsist. The feminine aspect in America can—and must always—contain the masculine aspect, whether in terms of the family (Tocqueville, *Democracy in America*, vol. 1, part 2, chap. 9, p. 291) or in terms of the relationship between Mother nature and Father industriousness (pp. 283–84). I have considered these two relationships briefly in section 6 of chapter 3. Jane P. Tompkins has argued (in *West of Everything: The Inner Life of Westerns* [New York: Oxford University Press, 1992]) that it was precisely the feminization and evangelization of America in the nineteenth century that prompted the production of Western genre that has so captured the twentieth-century mind. This analysis, which suggests the magnitude of *resistance* against passivity, is consistent with aspects of Tocqueville's thinking.

118. Exod. 15:24, 16:2–3,8, 17:3; Num. 14:27, 16:11; John 6:43. See Walzer, *Exodus and Revolution*, pp. 43–70.

119. Exod. 16:3; Num. 11:4–5.

120. Tocqueville, *Democracy in America*, vol. 2, part 4, chap. 2, p. 668.

121. Tocqueville, *Democracy in America*, vol. 1, part 1, chap. 2, p. 46. While Tocqueville does not cite this passage in the French edition, note Winthrop's reference to *murmuring* in the sentence that ends the passage in the Lawrence translation.

122. John Macquarrie, *Principles of Christian Theology*, p. 346: "[T]he strange paradox is that the man who asserts his freedom and autonomy loses it through

what religion countenances to the soul *outside* of the domain of politics, is the crucial support for what transpires within politics. Here, and here alone, may religion regulate politics. Religion is the central support for politics; but that effect must always be indirect if it is not to be destructive of politics and self-destructive of religion.[123]

5. OF LONG-TERM GOALS

[I look forward to] moving not towards those future things what are transitory but to "the things which are before" me, *not stretched out in distraction* but extended in reach, not by being pulled apart but by concentration. So I "pursue the prize of the high calling" where I "may hear the voice of praise" and "contemplate your delight" (Ps. 25:7, 26:4) which neither comes nor goes.[124]

The supposition of rational action presupposes a coherent relationship between means and ends and therefore presupposes not only a temporal horizon of past, present, and future, but also a being capable of coherently uniting these modes through memory (of the past), attentativeness (to the present), and expectation (of the future).[125] It is in the mind where these modes are to be found;[126] and in the Augustinian view, the mind that has strayed from the Eternal Ground that underlies these three temporal modes is bound to vacillate between them, restlessly searching for an anchor that cannot be found there:

---

his self-idolatry; while the man who lives in obedience and dependence toward God is set free from the very things that are most oppressive and distorting, and becomes most responsibly his true self." See also Augustine, *Confessions*, bk. 3, chap. 3, p. 38, where, while errant from God, the freedom he enjoyed was "merely that of a runaway." The "green pastures" and "still waters" of the Lord's Prayer (Ps. 23:2) come only by way of being shepherded obediently by God. A pertinent New Testament passage is Mark 8:35 ("Whoever would save his life shall lose it, and whoever loses his life for my sake and the gospel's will save it").

123. See Tocqueville's letter of January 1, 1839 to Paul Clamorgan: "I honor the priest in church, but I will always put him outside of government, if I have any influence whatsoever in affairs" (*Selected Letters*, p. 132).

124. Augustine, *Confessions*, bk. 11, chap. 19, p. 244 (emphasis added). See also 1 Cor. 9:24; Phil. 3:13–14.

125. Augustine, *Confessions*, bk. 11, chap. 28, p. 243. See also chaps. 11–19, pp. 228–44, for an extensive discussion of the modes of temporality and their relationship to Eternity.

126. Cf. Immanuel Kant, *Critique of Pure Reason*, trans. F. Max Müller (New York: Doubleday Anchor, 1966), 1, first part, secs. 4–7, pp. 46–58.

I am scattered in times whose order I do not understand. The storms of incoherent events tear to pieces my thoughts, the inmost entrails of my soul.[127]

The American manifestation of being torn between past, present, and future is a restless but never satisfied or satisfiable dream of a better future,[128] conjoined in a painful paradox with a myopic but never fully attentive focus upon the present moment. In this latter manifestation, the democratic soul is fickle and easily dissuaded from its course. (Is not the fatuous democratic lawmaker proof enough?)[129] Consoled by the promise of the future, it neglects the present; incapable of forgoing the shifting enticements of the present, it forfeits the future.

The brilliant failure of Rousseau's alluring portrayal of the startling development in the state of nature of the ability to think ahead and of Nietzsche's strident depiction of how the capacity to make promises arose notwithstanding,[130] the problem of how an orderly relation of the three temporal modes may be fostered at all remains an acute one for Tocqueville. The issue, however, is not the prehistory of this development, as it was for Rousseau and Nietzsche (both of whom confidently assume that the stability of these relations was established in *a time gone by*); rather, what worries Tocqueville—again, following Augustine—is the inherent instability of these relations *at all times*, but especially during the democratic age.

127. Augustine, *Confessions*, bk. 11, chap. 19, p. 244. Macquarrie observes: "[A]s selfhood develops, one becomes less and less a creature of the instant, subject to the passing circumstances or desires, and one attains more and more a unified existence that transcends mere successiveness and integrates past, present, and future" (*Principles of Christian Theology*, p. 363). Eternal life, on this reading *is* the attainment of a selfhood that has transcended successiveness and the temptation of merely transient goods. Consider, also, Augustine's anticipation of the postmodern insight about the incoherency of the self—in his view, something bound to occur when the soul turns from God: "[B]y forsaking the one above itself with regard to whom alone it could keep its strength and enjoy him as its light, [the soul] became weak and dark, with the result that it was miserably dragged down from itself to things that are not what it is and are lower than itself by loves that it cannot master and confusions it can see no way out of" (*The Trinity*, bk. 14, sec. 18, p. 385).

128. See Tocqueville, *Democracy in America*, vol. 1, part 2, chap. 9, p. 285; vol. 2, part 2, chap. 13, pp. 535–38.

129. See Tocqueville, *Democracy in America*, vol. 1, part 2, chap. 5, pp. 226–30; chap. 6, pp. 231–35; and chap. 7, p. 250, on prison projects adopted and abandoned with haste.

130. Rousseau, *Second Discourse*, pp. 117–19; Nietzsche, *Genealogy of Morals*, second essay, sec. 3, pp. 60–62.

Consider the temporal horizon of the aristocrat: "being master of [himself], and not subject to transitory impulses,"[131] he is both able fully to attend to the present and plan for the future. What makes this possible is never fully articulated, yet it is clear that the peculiar relationship of the aristocrat to the land facilitates both present sobriety and a long-term efficacy.

> [For the aristocrat] family feeling finds a sort of physical expression in the land. The family represents the land, and the land the family, perpetuating its name, origin, power, and virtue. It is an imperishable *witness to the past and a precious earnest of the future.*[132]

And elsewhere:

> Among aristocratic nations families maintain the same station for centuries and often live in the same place. . . . A man always knows about his ancestors and respects them; his imagination extends to his grandchildren, and he loves them. He freely does his duty by both ancestors and descendants and often sacrifices personal pleasures *for the sake of beings who are no longer alive or are yet to be born.*[133]

Contrast this with democratic nations:

> Among democratic peoples new families continually rise from nothing while others fall, and nobody's position is quite stable. The woof of time is forever being broken and the track of past generations lost. Those who have gone before are easily forgotten, and no one gives a thought to those who will follow.[134]

The short-term thinking of the democratic soul must be displaced, yet the aristocratic age in which this problem had an earthly palliative (landed property) has reached its end, and so can no longer be of assistance.

Tocqueville, however, does not hastily abandon the verities of the aristocratic age; for they form the basis upon which the social-theoretic problem of the democratic age must be understood. I have spoken of the pertinence of the aristocratic class in the previous chapter (secs. 4–5). Associations and newspapers fill the vacuum left by the absence of

131. Tocqueville, *Democracy in America*, vol. 1, part 2, chap. 6, p. 232. See also Tocqueville's characterization of the Indian as possessing a long-term memory (chap. 10, p. 338).

132. Tocqueville, *Democracy in America*, vol. 1, part 1, chap. 3, p. 52 (emphasis added).

133. Tocqueville, *Democracy in America*, vol. 2, part 2, chap. 2, p. 507 (emphasis added).

134. Tocqueville, *Democracy in America*, vol. 2, part 2, chap. 2, p. 507.

the aristocratic class in the democratic age. The aristocratic element, the mediative element, must be present for society to function, no matter what the age! In the context of the problem of long-term thinking, the aristocratic element that attenuates the democratic impulse must reside somewhere as well; only here, the locus is religion. God performs the same social function as did the aristocratic class; religion is the functional equivalent of the aristocratic element during the democratic age. It is not by accident, I suggest, that Tocqueville characterizes the aristocratic element in the religious terms that he does:

> The nobles, placed so high above the people, could take the calm and benevolent interest in their welfare which a *shepherd takes in his flock*.[135]

The aristocrat once was the shepherd; now the aristocrat has no place; now God is the shepherd, is the site through which habits of long-term thinking are encouraged. Religion takes on a burden in the democratic age that in the past was left to the aristocrat but is now unthinkable there. As with the victory of Protestantism over Catholicism, so, too, with the victory of the democratic over the aristocratic age: God the Sovereign supplants the earthly, mediary, priestly-aristocratic class! The forum for the thinkability of long-term goals is now preeminently religious:

> The view of heaven and hell will cast a slight upon the short pleasures and pains of this present state, and give attractions and virtues, which reason and interest and the care of ourselves cannot but allow and prefer.[136]

Tocqueville is quite clear about what is likely to happen without a shepherd toward whom the democratic flock turns its gaze: memory, attentiveness, and expectation collapse into a present "torn this way and that."

> As soon as they have lost the way of relying chiefly on distant hopes, they are naturally led to want to satisfy their least desires at once; and

135. Tocqueville, *Democracy in America*, Author's Introduction, p. 13 (emphasis added). See also vol. 2, part 2, chap. 8, p. 525, where the nobles once acted toward the people "without self-interest, as God himself does"; and part 4, chap. 6, p. 692, where in the future *government* shall be the shepherd and the people shall be the tame flock. Cf. Ps. 23:1.

136. Locke, *The Reasonableness of Christianity*, sec. 245, p. 185. See Tocqueville, *Democracy in America*, vol. 2, part 1, chap. 5, p. 444, where in contrast to the natural tendency of the democratic soul to get caught up in the moment, "[T]he greatest advantage of religions is to inspire diametrically contrary urges."

it would seem that as soon as they despair of living forever, they are inclined to act as if they could not live for more than a day. [137]

Religion, then, is an essential palliative for the democratic soul that is prone to attend singularly but without satisfaction to the immediacy of desire. When its influence begins to languish, however, effort must be made to imbue salutary habits with the assistance of government— that analogue of the Shepherd on high. Long-term goals established by government are the only remaining bulwark. "That is [government's] most important business," Tocqueville says.[138]

Should government be moderately successful at this mission, however, should it produce the real-life conditions that dispose thinking toward long-term goals, then not only will it have supplemented the Shepherd on high, but it also will have served to redirect the gaze of the citizens toward him. In a transitional age without the support of the aristocrat-mediary, and in which aversion to Christianity has not receded from memory, there is a need for government—that necessary though dangerous supplement which points beyond itself—to stand in for God:

> I have therefore no doubt that, in accustoming the citizens to think of the future in this world, they would gradually be led without noticing it themselves toward religious beliefs. [139]

In analogical fashion, and in accordance with a longstanding tradition of thinking within the Catholic Church, government serves to point be-

---

137. Tocqueville, *Democracy in America*, vol. 2, part 2, chap. 17, p. 548. See also Rousseau, *Emile*, bk. 4, p. 229: "[T]he restlessness of desire produces curiosity and inconstancy."

138. Tocqueville, *Democracy in America*, vol. 2, part 2, chap. 17, p. 548. The purpose of government, on this reading, is not to *represent*, but rather to attenuate an irrationality in the human soul. Needless to say, such long-term goals cannot be justified solely on the basis of a so-called cost-benefit analysis; their true yield is the development of certain attributes necessary but not naturally conspicuous in a democratic society. I note in passing that one of the worst things that a government can do is sanction lotteries; these promote habits of thinking that silence the already quiet (and moderate) voice that would countenance patience and perseverance. The economic benefits of lotteries do not outweigh the deleterious habits of thinking they engender. Theologically, lotteries are the functional equivalent to grace, which simply breaks in upon the soul as a *gift*. The labor made necessary by accepting the lifelong terms of the *wager* is abrogated by the plenitude of the *Nunc-stans*. I will consider lotteries in greater detail in section 3 of chapter 5.

139. Tocqueville, *Democracy in America*, vol. 2, part 2, chap. 17, p. 549.

yond itself; an institution is the trace of God, not sufficient in itself, but capable of directing attention on High.[140] The modern problematic: how can government be representative, so evident in the thinking of Hobbes (which is comprehensible as yet another Reformation attempt to search the Old Testament for models helpful in illuminating the present travail)[141] has no place here. The central issue is how to instill salutary habits in an age that conspires against their easy formation, not the subtleties of right representation upon which Protestant thought has focused to this day.

6. THE RIGHT RELATIONSHIP BETWEEN RELIGION AND POLITICS

> Any alliance with any political power whatsoever is bound to be burdensome for religion. It does not need their support in order to live, and in serving them it may die.[142]

I have already spoken of the connection between passivity and activity (in sec. 4, above). The passive aspect, recall, though deferential, has a preeminence over the active aspect. This paradox is not only at the heart of Tocqueville's understanding of the relationship between the sexes but underscores the metaphysical principle that orients his thinking elsewhere—the masterful way in which he demonstrates how the indirect effects of Christianity upon democracy are superabundant over the direct ones being perhaps the most important illustration.

In order to comprehend Tocqueville's argument about the right relationship between religion and politics, it will be necessary to make some further observations about the preeminence of the deferential, passive aspect over the boisterous, active aspect. For this, Rousseau's thinking is perhaps most helpful—partly on its own merits, and partly because of the avowed influence he had on Tocqueville's thinking.

The silent, the hidden from view, has a kind of substantive preeminence over the explicated in the *First Discourse* and the *Second Discourse* and in *Emile*.

140. See the bull *Unam Sanctum*, of Boniface VIII, written in 1302. "The way of religion is to lead the things which are lower to the things which are higher through the things which are intermediate. According to the law of the universe all things are not reduced to order equally and immediately; but the lowest through the intermediate, and the intermediate through the higher" (cited in Tawney, *Religion and Capitalism*, pp. 20–21).

141. The model of representation is, I suggest, the covenant between the Moses and the Israelites. Hobbes makes much of this covenant in *Leviathan*. Of special importance to Hobbes is Exodus 20:19.

142. Tocqueville, *Democracy in America*, vol. 1, part 2, chap. 9, p. 298.

[I give my pupil] the art of being ignorant, for the science possessed by him who believes that he knows *only what he does in fact know* amounts to very little. You give science—splendid. I busy myself with the instrument fit for acquiring it. [143]

The concealed is the real; the hidden from view is the ground out of which all brilliance appears. (Did not God create the light from the midst of the darkness?) The transitory and dazzling artifacts of human effort mask an antecedent that we are tempted to forgo, even though, like the Good spoken of in the *Republic,* it is "the cause of knowledge, and of truth in so far as known." [144] For both Rousseau and Plato the hidden appears weak and frail, appears to be nothing next to artifacts that exude a kind of strength and potency.

Yet this is deceiving; for while "the stronger appears to be master [it] actually depends on the weaker." [145] Here is the metaphysical position embedded in the relationship of Pharaoh to Moses; Plato's tyrant to the philosophical soul who, by contrast, appears impotent; Augustine's City of Man to the City of God; Luther's active righteousness to passive righteousness; Hegel's master to slave; Nietzsche's ancient noble soul to the Jew/Christian/democrat—the list is not exhaustive.

The truth that appears insubstantial, worried and restive about the prospect for its own confirmation, is alluded to over and over again by Rousseau in the *First Discourse* and the *Second Discourse* in the antinomies that he invokes: reality and appearance, inner and outer, freedom and servitude, action and thought, and natural goodness (not to be confused with virtue) and vice. And in *Emile:* conscience, the voice of nature, "is timid, it likes refuge and peace. The World and noise scare it," [146] he says. The heart alone can hear; it listens and may receive sus-

143. Rousseau, *Emile,* bk. 2, p. 126 (emphasis added).

144. Plato, *Republic,* bk. 6, 508e. In Plato's idiom, the apparent brilliance and appeal of the tyrant can only be *seen through* when the Good, the source of all things, illuminates the soul. Then, and only then, do appearances reveal themselves as they truly are and does the philosophic life appear to be the most substantial of all.

145. Rousseau, *Emile,* bk. 5, p. 360. The quote is a description of the relationship between the sexes. Man *appears* stronger than woman but is actually weaker. The one who does not write (in the history of Western political thought, say) is the silent measure that no writing can comprehend. Writing betrays impotence, not potency. Nietzsche correctly posed the question that most terrifies the philosopher: "[S]upposing truth is a woman—what then?" (*Beyond Good and Evil,* preface, p. 2).

146. Rousseau, *Emile,* bk. 4, p. 291. See also bk. 5, p. 362n, where Sophie (wisdom), too, is timid; *Second Discourse,* p. 107: "[N]othing is so timid as man in the state of nature"; and 1 Kings 19:11–14, where God addresses Elijah not amid wind, earthquake, and fire, but as "a small voice."

tenance in a place far from the din of the world.[147] Appearances notwithstanding, the invisible is always superabundant over the visible.

The difficulty surrounding the question of the right relationship between religion and politics—about which Tocqueville seems well aware—is that human beings have a natural tendency to be deceived by appearances, to think that visible powers are preeminent over invisible powers, that politics, not God, is the wellspring of power. *Decipimur specie recti.*[148] Theologically, while human beings are *of* God, their errancy *from* him has averted their gaze wholly toward the world.[149]

Within the confines of this self-deception, the temptation will be to try to empower religion. (Here are the Roman Catholics of Tocqueville's Europe.) Yet behind this impulse already lies the supposition that the power of God is not sufficient in the face of worldly power, that the God who comes to presence in the heart does not outstrip all worldly power.[150] In a word, the attempt to secure religion through an alignment with government betrays a secret disavowal of God's power—for the attempt supposes that "the world" *could* do without him.[151] The anxiety that religion is losing its sway is falsely assuaged by the promptings of the Christian who would tether religion to political power.

147. With this Augustine, too, would agree. The world seems graspable with the mind, and so the mind of the person who succumbs to its temptation is attuned to the noise of the world and their heart is silenced. Writing of his earlier (preconversion) years, Augustine says, "I wrote [of] fictitious physical images [that were] strident noise in the ears of my heart (*Confessions*, bk. 4, chap. 12, p. 68).

148. Rousseau begins his *First Discourse* (p. 34) with this phrase from Horace.

149. Gen. 3:7–8. See also Isa. 59:1–2 ("your iniquities have separated you from your God; and your sins have hidden His face from you, so that He will not hear").

150. Cf. Macquarrie, *Principles of Christian Theology*, p. 80: "[H]uman existence makes sense if [God] grants what [he] commands, that is to say, if there are resources beyond our human resources to help fulfill the claims that our very existence lays upon us." The impulse to secure a place for religion in the world supposes that these resources do not exist. See Rom. 8:31 ("If God *be* for us, who *can be* against us?").

151. See Jürgen Moltmann, *The Crucified God* (New York: HarperCollins, 1991), p. 19: "[H]e who is of little faith looks for support and protection for his faith, because it is preyed upon by fear. Such a faith tries to protect its 'most sacred things,' God, Christ, doctrine and morality, *because it no longer believes that these things are sufficiently powerful to maintain themselves.* When the 'religion of fear' finds its way into the Christian church, those who regard themselves as the most vigilant guardians of the faith do violence to faith and smother it" (emphasis added).

In gender terms, the theological principle at issue has already been considered: the masculine and feminine, the active and passive aspects, must not be confused; they each have their own realm: politics is the active principle; religion, the passive. The passive, though less overt, is always superabundant over the restless and ultimately ephemeral, active, political domain.

> Some trust in chariots, and some in horses: but we will remember the name of the LORD our GOD. [152]

The victory of the active, worldly element over the passive other-worldly element seems forgone to the one who has already renounced the passive aspect; religion cannot, however, be won back through such a stance. The weapons by which it may be won are not the weapons of the world, tempting as it might be to rely upon them. Religion, like a woman, finds its voice in its proper sphere! The Americans, unlike the Europeans, have accorded a place to both the active and passive, masculine and feminine, elements; and for this reason religion (and women) hold sway over American society.

> Religion, being free and powerful within its own sphere and content with the position reserved for it, realizes that its sway is all the better established because it relies only on its own powers and rules men's hearts *without external support*. [153]

Politics will forever be a realm for the play of interest. Religion defames itself when it betrays the human heart and enters into the political fray; for the heart has no *interests*, properly speaking. What Rousseau said of the danger of drawing the inner truth of the heart out into the daylight

152. Ps. 20:7.

153. Tocqueville, *Democracy in America*, vol. 1, part 1, chap. 2, p. 47 (emphasis added). See also vol. 2, part 2, chap. 15, pp. 545–46: "I am so deeply convinced of the almost inevitable dangers which face beliefs when their interpreters take part in public affairs, and so firmly persuaded that at all costs Christianity must be maintained among the new democracies that I would rather shut priests up within sanctuaries than allow them to leave them." For Jefferson's agreement see *Notes*, query 17, pp. 160–61. It should be added that the effort to "bring religion back in" is akin to the movement among feminists to "bring women in" to a world dominated by men. Both crusades grasp that the active, masculine aspect has overrun the passive, feminine aspect. The question to be asked is whether the redress sought merely reinforces the imbalance. The censure of women and religion in the world are linked, and cannot be revoked simply by granting them a place *along side of* men and other *values*. That Tocqueville notes a kinship between women and religion (*Democracy in America*, vol. 1, part 2, chap. 9, p. 291) is suggestive. Their power is maintained through "discrimination."

of language, Tocqueville would later say about of the danger of drawing religion into the daylight of politics: the site where the eternal may come to presence becomes a battleground where the multiplicity of interests, not eternity, prevails:

> As soon as peoples took it into their heads to make God *speak*, each made him speak in its own way and made Him say what it wanted. If one had listened only to what God says to the heart of man, there would never have been more than one religion on earth.[154]

The site where the One God may come to presence yields faction rather than unity, produces wounds rather than heals them. In Tocqueville's words,

> There has never been a government supported by some invariable disposition of the human heart or one founded upon some *interest* that is immortal.[155]

The right relationship between religion and politics, then, is, on the one hand, that the two should be utterly separated and, on the other hand, that politics must be undergirded by religion. American democracy will not survive should it—as the Europeans did—*mix* politics and religion; but neither will it survive unless religion is the indirect support for politics. The paradox of freedom, of beneficent activity, is that it requires an obedience, a passivity, before God. Political freedom rests upon nonpolitical foundations. This is the cornerstone of Tocqueville's seemingly peculiar liberalism.[156]

154. Rousseau, *Emile*, bk. 4, p. 295 (emphasis added). See also Matt. 5:8, 6:21.

155. Tocqueville, *Democracy in America*, vol. 1, part 2, chap. 9, p. 297 (emphasis added).

156. Tocqueville identifies himself as a "liberal of a new kind," to be sure (letter to Eugène Stoffels, July 24, 1836, in *Memoir, Letter, and Remains of Alexis de Tocqueville*, translated from the French by the translator of *Napoleon's Correspondence with King Joseph* [Boston: Ticknor and Fields, 1862], 1:381); with respect to the bearing of Christianity upon liberal politics, however, his divergences with early modern thinkers are not great. See, for example, Locke, *The Reasonableness of Christianity*, sec. 241, p. 170, where prior to the coming of Christ societies were held together, but only in subjection. Christ supplemented the natural light of reason granted by God to Adam and made it possible, after the incarnation, for all citizens (who are one in Adam) to form political communities based in freedom—that is, communities ruled by the law that reason's light may grasp. See Mitchell, "John Locke and the Theological Foundation of Liberal Toleration: A Christian Dialectic of History," in *Review of Politics* 52, no. 1 (1990): 64–83. See also James Tully, "Governing Conduct," in *Conscience and*

The remaining question, of course, is how politicians, whose charge it is to respect this utter separation between, yet undergirding of, religion and politics, are to act. Tocqueville's answer is as unequivocal as it is salutary for our day:

> I think the only effective means which governments can use to make the doctrine of the immortality of the soul respected is daily to act as if they believed it themselves.[157]

7. THE PERMANENCE OF RELIGION

"Religion," Hobbes says, "can never be abolished out of human nature."[158] By this he meant that no matter how brightly the light of reason

---

Casuistry in Early Modern Europe, ed. Edmund Leites (Cambridge: Cambridge University Press, 1988), p. 59: "[In Locke's view] God spreads Christianity by the same mode of governance as other opinions are spread." Christianity is the true religion, ascertainable by the light of reason, to be sure; yet the light of reason acquires its brightness by being guided by the *practices* in a Christian commonwealth. "Christian philosophers have come closer to demonstrating ethics than the pre-Christians, but this is not because, as they assume, they have an independent rule of reason to test moral principles. It is rather because their first principles are derived from Revelation. We grow up with the Gospel from the cradle. It seems 'natural' to us and we take it for 'unquestionable truths.' Rationalists think they have discovered the foundations of morality, but they only 'confirm' Revelation. We would be lost without it. Revelation is the foundation of reason, of what we take to be 'self-evident' " (p. 59). Locke's liberalism, like Tocqueville's, presupposes that Christianity is the foundation upon which politics of a certain sort may be built.

157. Tocqueville, *Democracy in America*, vol. 2, part 2, chap. 15, p. 546.

158. Hobbes, *Leviathan*, part 1, chap. 12, p. 94. See Tocqueville, *Democracy in America*, vol. 1, part 2, chap. 9, p. 295: "[E]ighteenth-century philosophers had a very simple explanation for the gradual weakening of beliefs. Religious zeal, they said, would die down as enlightenment and freedom spread. It is tiresome that the facts do not fit the theory at all." The so-called secularization of the world, about which Tocqueville was not unaware, is the result of massive historical shift from aristocracy to democracy—subject to abandonment when, by Providential hand, equality comes to prevail! For a recent discussion of the inappropriateness of the secularization paradigm to the American religious experience see R. Stephen Warner, "Work in Progress toward a new Paradigm for the Sociological Study of Religion in the United States," *American Journal of Sociology* 98, no. 5 (March 1993): 1044–93. In his words, "[T]he newer paradigm stems not from the old one which was developed to account for the European experience, but from an entirely independent vision inspired by American history" (p. 1045).

shines, there will always be a boundary to reason's luminescence—and a beyond that can neither be abolished nor ignored without peril. It is this beyond, which reason cannot illuminate, that religion directs the soul to encounter in the hope and longing of the heart.

> Religion is the vision of something which stands beyond, behind, and within, the passing flux of immediate things; something which is real, and yet waiting to be realized; something which is a remote possibility, and yet the greatest of present facts; something that gives meaning to all that passes, and yet eludes apprehension; something whose possession is the final good, and yet is beyond all reach; something which is the ultimate ideal, and the hopeless quest.[159]

"The short space of sixty years can never shut in the whole of man's imagination,"[160] Tocqueville says. The world may captivate human attention, but only for so long. The "instinctive sense of another life without difficulty"[161] makes itself known—and in proportion (if only periodically) to the effort to deflect its call and to evade the coincidence of finitude and infinity that the "short space of sixty years" serves to underscore.[162]

The need is there, Tocqueville insists; yet the temptations of the world often intercede and cannot be underestimated. Evading the call from beyond the short space of sixty years may be understood in many idioms: the psalmist's mocked cry for God;[163] Plato's shackled cave dwellers who resist the light that nurtures and burns unto death;[164] St. Paul's "stumbling block" of the worldly wise;[165] Augustine's Romans

159. Alfred North Whitehead, *Science and the Modern World* (New York: Macmillan, 1925), pp. 192–93. See also Heb. 11:1. Whitehead, like Hobbes, carves out the domain graspable by reason and then speaks of what reason cannot grasp and can only be "known" through *worship*.

160. Tocqueville, *Democracy in America*, vol. 1, part 2, chap. 9, p. 296.

161. Tocqueville, *Democracy in America*, vol. 2, part 2, chap. 9, p. 300.

162. Because "life is more than meat" (Matt. 6:25), the unswerving focus upon the material world and upon the conditions of finite human life must lead to spiritual eruptions. The fervor and unboundedness of American spirituality, which so perplexes the Europeans, is inevitable in a nation like America that is so oriented by the love of the world. See Tocqueville, *Democracy in America*, vol. 2, part 3, chap. 12, pp. 534–35. Zetterbaum (*Tocqueville*, p. 160) is incorrect: religion is a permanent aspect of human life, not a deception.

163. "All they that see me laugh me to scorn: they shoot out their lip, they shake the head, saying, He trusted on the LORD that he would deliver him: let him deliver him, seeing he delighted in him" (Ps. 22:7–8).

164. Plato, *Republic*, bk. 7, 514b–17a.

165. 1 Cor. 1:23. See also 2 Tim. 1:8 ("Be not therefore ashamed of the testimony of our Lord").

tempted by the City of Man who "are shaken by the shifting winds of time"; [166] Luther's errant Christians beguiled by the *active* righteousness of works [167] that conceals the Byss (Böhme's term for the ground beneath the apparent groundlessness of the world) where Christ may come to presence; Rousseau's "respectable man" [168] who dimly intimates that he is caught up wholly in an alluring world without substance; Tocqueville's restless Americans whose very acquisitiveness betrays a knowledge of the insufficiency of the world; [169] or Heidegger's Dasein whose very constitution entails being almost wholly lost to its ground. [170] These formulations bespeak the paradox of the world's errancy from *the way*.

In a word, the human capacity for self-deception, for wishing to confine itself within the short space of sixty years, is enormous, and cannot easily be overridden. [171]

Tocqueville is aware of the difficulty. For all his reverence for Rousseau, on the question of how to draw the soul away from its imaginative projections in the world Tocqueville would have no commerce with the remedy he proposes. The self-deception, the imaginative projections, of an errant one, cannot, as Rousseau suggested in *Emile*, be arrested simply by constructing a world of mental somnolence for early childhood; nor by imploring us, as he did in the *Second Discourse*, to listen attentively to the voice of nature. Tocqueville offers no endorsement of Rousseau's not-too-veiled proposal to supplant religious education with one that ostensibly has a more generous view of the human capacity for freedom and happiness. For Tocqueville, religion alone has the authority to call the soul toward the transcendent source from which it perennially strays, and to circumscribe the imagination of the one bemused by the bad infinity, the hubris, that attends errancy from God:

166. Augustine, *City of God*, vol. 6, bk. 1, preface, p. 18 (*CG*, p. 5).

167. See Luther, "Lectures on Galatians," 26:5.

168. Rousseau, *First Discourse*, p. 39.

169. See Tocqueville, *Democracy in America*, vol. 2, part 2, chap. 13, pp. 535–38. Of the Americans, Augustine would ask: "With what end in view do you again and again walk along the difficult and laborious paths? There is no rest where you seek for it. Seek for what you seek, but it is not where you are looking for it. You seek the happy life in the region of death; it is not there. How can there be a happy life where there is not even life?" (*Confessions*, bk. 4, chap. 12, p. 64).

170. See Martin Heidegger, *Being and Time*, trans. John Macquarrie and Edward Robinson (New York: Harper and Row, 1962), pp. 219–224, passim.

171. See also Aldous Huxley, *Brave New World* (New York: Harper and Row, 1946), pp. 236–47. Mustapha Mond there commends his world for confining the imagination of its citizens, for keeping death and the questions about God it raises *at bay*.

> Enter ye in at the strait gate; for wide *is* the gate, and broad *is* the way,
> that leadeth to destruction, and many there be that go in thereat: Be-
> cause strait *is* the gate, and narrow *is* the way, which leadeth unto life,
> and few there be that find it.[172]

The Americans, Tocqueville says, "never see an unlimited field before
[them]."[173] In order to draw them back from the temptations of the
world, Rousseau's philosophy (and that of all others) will never be sufficient. Without God, as Locke put it,

> [It was] too hard a task for unassisted reason, to establish morality, in
> all its parts, upon its true foundation; with a clear and convincing
> light.[174]

Philosophers, assisted by a natural reason "make but a slow progress and
little advance in the world,"[175] he says. The great majority of human
beings do not have the leisure to enlarge their knowledge; hence, they
cannot know but must *believe*.[176] And because belief is predicated on

---

172. Matt. 7:13–14. See also Gen. 6:5–7, where God found it necessary to
send a flood in order to begin anew. The imagination of humanity in the ante-
diluvian period could not be quelled of its own accord.

173. Tocqueville, *Democracy in America*, vol. 1, part 2, chap. 9, p. 292.

174. Locke, *The Reasonableness of Christianity*, sec. 241, p. 170. Augustine,
much earlier, expressed the same thought in his *City of God*. The heading of bk.
2, chap. 7 reads: "Apart from the authority of the gods, the theories of philosophers are of no value, because every man's natural proneness to evil inclines him
to act according to the examples set by the gods rather than according to the
words of men" (vol. 6, p. 3). The Bettenson edition has: "The conclusions of
the philosophers are ineffective as they lack divine authority. Man is easily corrupted and the God's examples influence him more than the argument of man"
(*CG*, p. 54). Montesquieu gives an interesting twist to this view. "The Christian
religion," he says, "succeeding philosophy fixed, so to speak, ideas for which
[philosophy] only cleared the way" (*Spirit of the Laws*, part 4, bk. 23, chap. 21,
p. 448). That is, Christianity does not more fully authorize what philosophy had
discovered, but rather *ossifies* a pattern of worldly renunciation.

175. Locke, *The Reasonableness of Christianity*, sec. 241, p. 171.

176. Locke, *The Reasonableness of Christianity*, sec. 243, p. 179. Hobbes notes,
as well, that "it is impossible that the multitude should ever learn their duty,
but from the pulpit and upon holidays" (*Behemoth*, dialogue 1, p. 39). What the
multitude really learned was disobedience, and this because those who preached
were themselves taught at the universities set up by the pope. Hence, his claim
in *Leviathan*, review and conclusion, pp. 510–11, that his work is the antidote
that ought to be taught in the universities. Elsewhere he says, "I despair of any
lasting peace amongst ourselves, till the Universities here shall bend and direct
their studies to the settling of it, that is, to the teaching of absolute obedience
to the laws of the King" (*Behemoth*, dialogue 1, p. 56).

authority,[177] even the law of reason discovered by the philosophers could not be disseminated.

To all this Tocqueville would have acceded. In his words,

> Fixed ideas about God and human nature are indispensable for the conduct of daily life, and it is daily life that prevents them from acquiring them.[178]

The human need to defer to a transcendent authority that would quell the imagination is so strong, in fact, that once the need has been felt at all the soul so inclined will be drawn toward the Roman Catholic Church.[179] Perhaps this is because Protestantism, which "in general orients men much less toward equality than toward independence,"[180] tends to decompose into a form of solipsism in which the method and object of love cease to correspond.[181] The *longing* for an escape from this condition leads the soul invariably toward the Roman Church, which alone may fully satisfy it. While Catholics may be resigning their faith because of the unholy alliance between Church and worldly powers, Protestants, when they reach the abyss of independence and impotence, are being drawn back toward it.[182]

---

177. In this instance both Locke and Hobbes agree: authority is essential for belief. See Locke, *The Reasonableness of Christianity*, sec. 238, pp. 165–66, where rational men did worship the one true God "in their own minds . . . [but reason could not] prevail upon the multitude." For Locke, Christ provides the authority; for Hobbes the Leviathan, that mortal-god, *is* the authority. Cf. Matt. 7:29; Mark 1:22.

178. Tocqueville, *Democracy in America*, vol. 2, part 1, chap. 5, p. 443.

179. Tocqueville, *Democracy in America*, vol. 2, part 1, chap. 6, pp. 450–51.

180. Tocqueville, *Democracy in America*, vol. 1, part 2, chap. 9, p. 288.

181. The problem is endemic to Protestantism. See, for example, Friedrich Schleiermacher, *On Religion: Speeches to Its Cultured Despisers*, trans. Richard Crouter (Cambridge: Cambridge University Press, 1988), second and third speeches, pp. 96–161; Hegel, *Phenomenology of Spirit*, sec. 658, pp. 399–400; Karl Barth's introductory essay in Feuerbach, *The Essence of Christianity*, p. xix; Ernst Troeltsch, *Protestantism and Progress* (Philadelphia: Fortress Press, 1986), pp. 95–99; Max Weber, *The Protestant Ethic and the Spirit of Capitalism*, trans. Talcott Parsons (New York: Charles Scribner's Sons, 1958), pp. 180–83; Bellah et al., *Habits of the Heart*, pp. 243–48, passim. In contemporary social science, the "rational choice" paradigm is the latest incarnation. Here, theologically, there is no intermediary between the soul ("actor") and God (the "good" desired); each person *chooses* on the basis of their own conscience ("values"); and the locus of authority is the self. The method ("rationality") has become disembodied from the original Protestant theological insight. The self-reflective method no longer leads to God, but rather to strictly human "values."

182. See Hegel, *Philosophy of Right*, addition to sec. 141, pp. 258–59:

Our grandchildren will tend more and more to be divided clearly between those who have completely abandoned Christianity and those
who have returned to the Church of Rome. [183]

"Faith is the only permanent state of mankind," [184] Tocqueville says.
Those who expressly reject its call are those still dwelling with the
memory of the Church's collusion and collision with the world; in time,
they and the rest will quietly make their way back.

On this reading the permanent, religious, needs of human beings can
be met only by the Roman Catholic Church. The truth of this insight
will not be able to be seen for quite some time, to be sure, for revolutionary transitions are times of great uncertainty and suspicion; yet
when the memory of the old alignment does pass, when democracy finally and fully comes to reign, the Roman Church, too, will prevail.

This prediction, however, is for a distant future that we will never
know. Of more pressing interest is the transitional period in which we
live. Here, Tocqueville's worries are acute:

> I do not know what is to be done to give back to European Christian-
> ity the energy of youth. God alone could do that, but at least it de-
> pends on men to leave faith the use of all the strength it still retains. [185]

Religion is in abeyance; the foundation upon which habits conducive to
an equality in freedom are maintained is collapsing; without the support
of the salutary fear religion instills, these habits cannot long endure.

These habits will, nevertheless, abide for some considerable length
of time before they recede altogether. Tocqueville, indeed, is fascinated
with the persistence of habit throughout *Democracy in America*.

> If we could go right back to the elements of societies and examine
> the very first records of their histories, I have no doubt that we should
> there find the first cause of their prejudices, habits, dominant pas-
> sions, and all that comes to be called the national character. We should
> there be able to discover the explanation of customs which now seem

"[M]any Protestants have recently gone over to the Roman Catholic Church,
and they have done so because they found their inner life worthless and grasped
at something fixed, at a support, an authority, even if it was not exactly the
stability of thought which they caught." See also Hegel, *Philosophy of History*,
part 4, sec. 3, chap. 1, p. 425: "[T]he self-tormenting disposition [of Protestant-
ism] in the present day has induced many persons to enter the Catholic pale,
that they might exchange this inward uncertainty for a formal broad certainty
based upon the imposing totality of the Church."

183. Tocqueville, *Democracy in America*, vol. 2, part 1, chap. 6, p. 451.
184. Tocqueville, *Democracy in America*, vol. 1, part 2, chap. 9, p. 297.
185. Tocqueville, *Democracy in America*, vol. 1, part 2, chap. 9, p. 301.

contrary to the prevailing mores, of laws which seem opposed to recognized principles, and of incoherent opinions still found here and there in society *that hang like broken chains still occasionally dangling from the ceiling of an old building but carrying nothing.*[186]

Religious faith may fade, but the habits it once engendered are tenacious. The empire of habit is not easily overthrown; habits endure.[187] Here we have the present age: religious habits, the arrests of a history gone by, "dangle from the ceiling but carry nothing." Religion recedes focally, but not tacitly.[188] In Nietzsche's succinct phrase: "[I]t is the church, and not its poison, that repels us."[189]

It may be argued, of course, that the modern age is legitimate on its own terms, that the distortions left in the wake of Christian categories that could not be expunged (even while the answers to which they pointed were renounced) in fact gave rise to our present difficulties, and that the Enlightenment need only further purge itself of these residual habits of thinking in order truly to find its own voice.[190]

On Tocqueville's reading, however, the effort to disencumber the Enlightenment of its Christian habits should not be met with commendation. The transitional stage, the present age, in which can be found religious habits of thinking now only tenuously linked to their former substance,[191] is bound to be a confused one. Like Blumenberg, Tocqueville would insist that the residual habits that "dangle from the ceiling

186. Tocqueville, *Democracy in America*, vol. 1, part 1, chap. 2, pp. 31–32 (emphasis added).

187. Again, see Augustine, *Confessions*, bk. 8, chap. 5, pp. 139–41. Weber's *Protestant Ethic* can be understood as putting forward this thesis as well; faith gives rise to a habit of thinking that then endures long after faith has receded.

188. See Michael Polanyi and Harry Prosch, *Meaning* (Chicago: University of Chicago Press, 1975), pp. 22–45, for a discussion of the relationship between focal and tacit knowledge.

189. Nietzsche, *Genealogy of Morals*, first essay, sec. 9, p. 36.

190. See Hans Blumenberg, *The Legitimacy of the Modern Age*, trans. Robert M. Wallace (Cambridge, Mass.: MIT Press, 1983). Blumenberg would wish that the Enlightenment project disentangle itself form the categories it inherited from the Middle Ages.

191. Think here, for example, of the application of the Calvinist notions of purity and *stain* to "the world." John Muir, a central figure in the ecological movement in America, was, recall, the son of a Calvinist minister. The *righteousness* embedded in the call of certain environmentalists to entirely eliminate stain from the world can be understood as a manifestation of a religious habit of thinking. See Frederick Turner, *Rediscovering America: John Muir in His Time and Ours* (New York: Viking Press, 1985), p. 12: "[John Muir] had to wear the harness of [his father's] beliefs; [his mother] showed [him] how to wear it in some comfort."

but carry nothing" are distortions upon the present; yet Tocqueville would alert us that these habits, feeble as they may be, are all that remain of a religion now repudiated in places *by thought*. Should these, too, fall into disuse, should they be cast off by the final radicalization of the Enlightenment project, then and only then shall we finally see the awful consequences of Christianity truly superseded.

Of the philosophers Rousseau once equivocally said: "[T]o bring them to the foot of the altars it would suffice to send them among atheists."[192] Tocqueville would say the same—only with profound earnestness. The permanence of religion may indeed by recognized by future eyes. It may, unfortunately, require that "our eyes be fully opened"[193] to a world without religion before this can be seen. Theologically, Adam and Eve must fall into errancy and concealment from God before a mode of atonement becomes necessary and then finally appears. To put it otherwise, the City of God, as Augustine's *Confessions* attests, is revealed only on that sorrowful journey through the deceptive brilliance of Rome.[194] In Tocqueville's own perhaps prophetic words, which only slightly transpose the Augustinian insight:

> Sometimes I think that the only chance that remains for seeing a lively taste for liberty reborn in France is in the tranquil and, on the surface, final establishment of despotism.[195]

192. Rousseau, *First Discourse*, p. 50. See also Rousseau, *Second Discourse*, p. 170: "[H]uman governments needed a basis more solid than reason alone [could provide, and therefore it became necessary] for public repose that divine will intervened to give sovereign authority a sacred and inviolable character which took from the subjects the fatal right of disposing of it."

193. Gen. 3:7.

194. See Augustine, *Confessions*, bk. 5, chap. 8, p. 81: "[You] put before me the attractions of Rome to draw me there, using people who love a life of death.... To correct my steps you secretly made use of their and my perversity."

195. Tocqueville, letter to Gustave de Beaumont, February 27, 1858 (in *Selected Letters*, p. 367). See also *Democracy in America*, vol. 1, part 2, chap. 9, p. 314.

5
Conclusion

1. THE NEW POLITICAL SCIENCE

> [In any] discussion of [politics] . . . we must be satisfied to indicate the truth with a rough and general sketch. . . . [We must be satisfied with] that degree of precision in each kind of study which the nature of the subject at hand admits: it is obviously just as foolish to accept arguments of probability from a mathematician as to demand strict demonstrations from an orator.[1]

Having now assayed the general contours of Tocqueville's thinking, it is worth pondering at the outset of these concluding remarks whether democratic freedom, fragile as it surely is, is nourished by the extant political science that purports to comprehend it, or whether, in fact, the search for certainty—indeed, the *need* for it—in contemporary political science rather reflects a moment of the democratic soul that most threatens such freedom. To be sure, the search for scientific certainty may well find its most profound expression in the modern age in the thought of Descartes,[2] yet the motive behind such a search is not peculiar to the age of equality or its dawning theoretical foundations. That Aristotle should have insisted already at the onset of epistemological inquiry that the quest for truth should not subordinate substance to method suggests the pervasiveness, if not the amplitude, of the wish for certitude—a wish strong enough, occasionally, that we ardently forgo the nuance and incertitude that must accompany all investigations into the most human of things. Regretfully, when at the threshold of that knowledge most needful for human conduct and understanding, we are forever faced

---

1. Aristotle, *Nicomachean Ethics*, bk. 1, chap. 3, 1094b18–1094b28. See also Eric Voegelin, *The New Science of Politics* (Chicago: University of Chicago Press, 1952), pp. 3–8, passim.

2. If this is so, then America is the most modern nation. See Tocqueville, *Democracy in America*, vol. 2, part 1, chap. 1, p. 429: "[O]f all countries in the world, America is the one in which the precepts of Descartes are least studied and best followed." The deleterious effects I shall discuss shortly.

with articulations that, in Plato's words, "are hard to accept, but also hard to reject."[3] As Tocqueville put it:

> It is not that there are not some truths that merit man's complete conviction, but be sure that they are very few in number. Concerning the immense majority of points that it is important for us to know, we have only probabilities, almosts. *To despair of its being so is to despair of being a man, for that is one of the inflexible laws of our nature.*[4]

The modern age, however, seems to have an inordinate longing for certainty. The logic of this development in our time was noticed, not surprisingly, by Tocqueville, who understood that, in one of its valences, the democratic soul has a peculiar need for certainty.[5] Notwithstanding his praise of the Americans for their emphasis upon practical experience rather than theory,[6] upon the perpetual flux of experiment and contingency rather than the quiet repose of order;[7] notwithstanding these,

3. Plato, *Republic*, bk. 7, 532d.

4. Tocqueville, letter to Charles Stoffels, Oct. 22, 1831, in *Selected Letters*, p. 64 (emphasis added).

5. Consider, in light of this claim, a passage from the opening paragraph of Descartes's Discourse on the Method: "[T]he power of judging well and of distinguishing the true from the false . . . is naturally equal in all men, and consequently . . . the diversity of our opinions does not arise because some of us are more reasonable than others but solely because we direct out thoughts along different paths and do not attend to the same things" (René Descartes, *Discourse on the Method*, in *The Philosophical Writings of Descartes*, trans. John Cottingham, Robert Stoothoff, and Dugald Murdoch [Cambridge: Cambridge University Press, 1985], 1:111). Descartes's epistemological speculations are imbued with democratic sensibilities.

6. See Tocqueville, *Democracy in America*, vol. 2, part 1, chap. 4, p. 442: "[C]itizens of democracies are greedy for general ideas because they have little leisure, and such conceptions save them from wasting time considering particular cases. That is true, but it should not be understood to cover matters which are the *habitual and necessary* subject of their thoughts" (emphasis added). Tocqueville here notes that practical experience attenuates the temptation to allow (universal) thought to supervene over (concrete and particular) experience. Without a site where practical experience may reign, the bad infinity toward which thought is disposed cannot be countermanded.

7. Recall that for Tocqueville, it was only by virtue of keeping the mind within bounds that restless activity within the world was possible. Should the mind be unbound, the democratic soul would renounce its willingness to confront a world unbound and contingent. See Tocqueville, *Democracy in America*, vol. 2, part 1, chap. 5, p. 444: "[W]hen there is no authority in religion or in politics, men are soon frightened by the *limitless* independence with which they are faced. They are worried and worn out by the constant restlessness of everything" (emphasis added).

the conditions of equality bring forth countervailing tendencies. The democratic soul, as Nietzsche observed, is a tame soul; security is its greatest interest.[8] Uncertainty, the incommensurability of life, unnerves it; the urge to encompass all disparate instances within a universal rule is unrelenting.[9]

I have discussed elsewhere how this injurious tendency may be offset (notably in sec. 2 of chap. 3). Here I only add that the tendency toward universality and the derogation of the merely particular may well be linked—or perhaps exacerbated—by Protestantism. Hegel, the great Protestant theoretician, duly noted this connection,[10] though he, like

8. For Nietzsche, security was precisely what the healthy soul does not want. See *Genealogy of Morals*, first essay, sec. 12, p. 43: "*not* fear; rather that we no longer have anything left to fear in man; that the maggot 'man' is swarming in the foreground; that the 'tame man,' the hopelessly insipid man, has already learned to feel himself as the goal and zenith, as the meaning of history." See also *Beyond Good and Evil*, part 1, sec. 10, p. 16: "[The modern European prefers] even a handful of 'certainty' to a whole carload of beautiful possibilities." See also Theodore J. Lowi, *The End of Liberalism: The Second Republic of the United States*, 2d ed. (New York: W. W. Norton, 1979), pp. xi–xii (Articles 1 and 2 of the Constitution of the Second Republic). Lowi's claim is that the purpose of the Second Republic of the United States is to reduce risk. Tocqueville would agree. The antidote that Lowi propounds—juridical democracy (pp. 295–313)—does not, however, relieve the democratic soul of its secret hidden longing for a powerful state that pacifies its uncertainty and dispels its emptiness.

9. See Oakeshott, *Rationalism in Politics*, chap. 1, p. 16: "[T]he heart of the matter is the pre-occupation of the [modern] Rationalist with certainty. Technique and certainty are, for him, knowledge which does not require to look beyond itself for certainty; knowledge, that is, which not only ends with certainty but begins with certainty and is certain throughout." Oakeshott locates the decisive turn toward certainty with Descartes and Bacon (pp. 17–25). He traces epistemological changes rather than the changing conditions of equality that are so central in both Tocqueville and Nietzsche's thinking. See also David Tracy, *The Analogical Imagination* (New York: Crossroads Publishing, 1989). Tracy suggests that the need for certainty in the human sciences yields either an ossified interpretation of "the tradition" or the positivist rejection of the very idea of a tradition. In both cases, "[W]e are left with our cherished, if formal and increasingly private, autonomy unchallenged, unprovoked, untransformed by the effort and risk of entering into a conversation with the text" (p. 105). A tradition comes to life, and can give life, only when we *risk* interpretation, when we are willing to accept uncertainty, when we are willing to be drawn outside of ourselves into a community of discourse. Here, as in Tocqueville, mediational sites are a source of human vitality.

10. See Hegel, *Philosophy of History*, part 4, sec. 3, chap. 1, pp. 419–21. There Hegel considers why Protestantism did not sweep through the Christian world without impediment. "The Englishman," he says, "attaches his idea of

Tocqueville, saw that the original of this tendency is to be found in the Roman world, not in modernity.[11] "Equality leads men to very general and very vast ideas," Tocqueville says.[12] And it was in Rome that equality was presaged.[13]

Irrespective of its origin, the logic of equality, which subsumes difference under the general rule, has not failed to insinuate itself into modern thinking about politics. The abstruse fixation upon "rationality" is, to be sure, an aspect of this universalizing trend. Here, abiding differences between persons are effectively disregarded (treated as scalar *quantities*

---

liberty to the special, as opposed to the general" (p. 421). This is a prescient observation; it was the Englishman in the American identity who is enamored of the *particular* site of local government that, as Tocqueville reminds us, saves the American soul from gravitating toward the powerful and overarching state that applies its *universal* rule to all. The Englishman in the American saves the Americans from the fully exposed logic of Protestantism. (The great Anglican achievement, recall, was the Book of Common Prayer, which is concerned with the *practice* of worship rather than with the purifications of Spirit about which Protestantism has always been concerned.) For a recent example of the Englishman attempting to save liberty by shielding the local level from the state, see T. S. Eliot, "Notes towards the Definition of Culture," in *Christianity and Culture* (New York: Harcourt Brace Jovanovich, 1977), pp. 123–40.

11. See Hegel, *Philosophy of History*, part 3, pp. 278–79.

12. Tocqueville, *Democracy in America*, vol. 2, part 1, chap. 5, p. 445. See also chap. 3, p. 439: "[T]he democratic citizen sees nothing but people more or less like himself around him. . . . Truths applicable to himself seem equally applicable, *mutatis mutandis*, to his fellow citizens and to all men. Having acquired a taste for generalizations in matters which most closely take up his attention and touch his interests, he carries it with him when dealing with everything else." Nietzsche suggests that the development of the very idea of universal laws which science can discover in the natural world is attributable to the now reigning democratic impulse. In his words, "'[N]ature's conformity to law' [is] only a naïvely humanitarian emendation and perversion of meaning, with which [scientists] make abundant concessions to the democratic instincts of the modern soul! 'Everywhere equality before the law; nature is no different in that respect, no better off than we are' " (*Beyond Good and Evil*, part 1, sec. 22, p. 30). Nietzsche's observations apply no less to the social scientist.

13. See Tocqueville, *Democracy in America*, vol. 2, part 1, chap. 5, p. 446. See also Michael Oakeshott, "The Tower of Babel," in *Rationalism in Politics*, pp. 465–86. On his view, it was the need of Christianity to respond in a self-conscious manner to the Roman world that established a permanent tension in the West between customs of behavior, which are essentially particular, and reflective thought, which tends toward universalism. Christianity is both saved by customs of behavior that attenuate a destructive universalism and implicated in the development of that dangerous propensity. See especially pp. 484–86.

rather than irreconcilable *qualities*), subsumed by the enveloping category of "rational maximizer," and policy implications are educed that need not consider the obtrusions of habit or passions—in short, the arrests and irrationalities that constitute human identity as it is lived rather than merely fabricated. The entire sophisticated enterprise, vacuous as it may be, however, offers a philosophical epiphany for the democratic soul; in few other places does the messiness of the flesh encroach so little upon the spirit of the age.

That this approach to political science would be one to which the Americans might succumb was anticipated by Tocqueville. Twentieth-century commentators have elaborated on his anticipation. As one has observed:

> The early history of the United States of America is an instructive chapter in the history of the politics of Rationalism. . . . The founders of American independence had both a tradition of European thought and a native political habit and experience to draw upon. . . . [They were] a plain and unpretentious people, not given over-much to reflection upon the habits of behavior they had in fact inherited, who, in frontier communities, had constantly the experience of setting up law and order for themselves by mutual agreement, were not likely to think of their arrangements except as the creation of their own unaided initiative; they seemed to begin with nothing, and to owe to themselves all that they had come to possess. A civilization of pioneers is, almost unavoidably, a civilization of self-made men. . . . They were disposed to believe, and they believed more fully than was possible for the inhabitant of the Old World, that the proper organization of a society and the conduct of its affairs were based upon abstract principles, and not upon a tradition.[14]

Tocqueville, as I have said, was aware of this disposition of the Americans. Consider, for example, his remark that the Americans

> treat *tradition* as valuable for information only [and] accept existing facts as no more than a useful sketch to show how things could be done differently and better.[15]

14. Oakeshott, *Rationalism in Politics*, pp. 31–32.

15. Tocqueville, *Democracy in America*, vol. 2, part 1, chap. 1, p. 429 (emphasis added). See vol. 1, part 2, chap. 9, p. 283: "[The Americans'] desire for well-being has become a restless, burning passion which increases with satisfaction. They broke the ties of attachment to their native soil long ago and have not formed new ones since." See also chap. 10, p. 404: "[The American] is not attached to one way of working rather than another; he has no preferences for old methods compared to a new one; he has created no habits of his own, and he can easily rid himself of any influence foreign habits might have over his mind,

He was, additionally, cognizant of the necessary link between equality and the unbounded optimism about reason's capacity to "improve" the human condition. In his words,

> [W]hen castes disappear and classes are brought together, when men are jumbled together and habits, customs, and laws are changing, when new facts impinge and new truths are discovered, when old conceptions vanish and new ones take their place, *then the human mind imagines the possibility of an ideal but always fugitive perfection.* [16]

Notwithstanding these insights, however, he was aware that certain institutional arrangements might counter this tendency to think in certain ways. The breadth of his argument need not be rehearsed; here I only need repeat that, aside from the place God must hold in the democratic soul, the way to arrest reason's tendency to be drawn toward abstract universalism, toward the general rule that obliterates rather than accommodates particularity, is to embody it in a local associational life, with all its peculiarities, inefficiencies—and, yes, "prejudices." [17]

The task of political science is, in fact, first, to grasp the logic of this equality that gravitates (theoretically) toward universalism and (politically) toward servitude; and second, to understand the *habits* of a people that can be enlisted to develop and nurture the institutions that may

---

for he knows that his country is like no other and that his situation is something new in the world." Contrast this tendency, however, with the American legal system, which, like its English counterpart, is based on precedent rather than principle. See Tocqueville, *Democracy in America*, vol. 1, part 2, chap. 8, pp. 263–70.

16. Tocqueville, *Democracy in America*, vol. 2, part 1, chap. 9, p. 453 (emphasis added).

17. In contrast, see Benjamin Barber, *Strong Democracy* (Berkeley and Los Angeles: University of California Press, 1984), p. 235: "[L]ocal institutions can indeed be a crucial training ground for democracy. But to the extent that they are privatistic, or parochial, or particularistic, they will also undermine democracy. Parochialism enhances the immediate tie between neighbors by separating them from alien 'others,' but it thereby subverts the wider ties required by democracy—ties that can be nurtured only by an expanding imagination *bound to no particular sect or fraternity*" (emphasis added). Barber's "strong democracy" supposes that the face-to-face of local politics yields only self-enclosure and resistance to the other. While this tendency is not to be underestimated, the antidote he offers magnifies the very problem he seeks to overcome, namely, that the democratic soul, in seeking to absolve its impotence, aligns itself in its secret heart with the overarching state—which then undercuts participation. Democracy cannot be saved from the top down.

attenuate these propensities. "A new political science is needed for a world itself quite new," Tocqueville says.[18]

Sadly, Tocqueville's remains a bold yet solitary venture into this new territory. The discipline of political science as a whole has become captive to the very impulse it must strive to overcome, namely, the thoroughly democratic impulse that relentlessly disavows *enduring* particularities. Conceptually, as I have said, this takes the form of thinking almost exclusively in terms of disembodied "rational actors" who possess "interests." Theoretically, this takes the form of adopting a view of justice that is without any appreciation of the habits that shape human identity in history.[19] (Only for Americans could such a theory receive the measure of attention it has; for only here does the burden of history weigh less heavily upon a people's shoulders than elsewhere.)[20] Practically, this has too often resulted, as Rousseau long ago anticipated, in "a nondescript scientific jargon, even more despicable than ignorance, [which has] usurped the name of knowledge."[21]

The quest for scientific certainty, which, ironically, has yielded precious little these past many decades, unremittingly requires that differences be reduced to scalar quantities (comprehendible by mathematical equations rather than through the laborious and inexact inquiries of historians and philosophers who yet remain insulated from the ever-increasing pressures to conform with the "standards of the discipline"), but these efforts can only serve to reinforce rather than counter the tendency Tocqueville thought it was the responsibility of political science to help avert.

The need for certainty that animates the discipline of political science less helps us to understand the conditions under which democracy may thrive than reinforces, by a secret complicity, its weakest aspect. By a circuitous route, democracy is undermined by a political science that

18. Tocqueville, *Democracy in America*, Author's Introduction, p. 12.

19. Rawls recognizes the problem and tries to circumvent it by recurring to "the public culture of a democratic society" (John Rawls, "Justice as Fairness: Political not Metaphysical," *Philosophy and Public Affairs* 14, no. 3 [1985]: 250).

20. The massive exception, of course, is slavery. Notwithstanding this fact (which has scarcely penetrated the armor of academic life), however, Tocqueville's remark about Jefferson's foreign policy may be taken as an indicator of his more general understanding of the Americans' relationship to history. The American, he says, is not obliged "to take the past into account and adapt it to the present; nor need [he], like [the European], accept a vast heritage of mixed glory and shame, national friendships and hatreds, bequeathed by [his] ancestors" (*Democracy in America*, vol. 1, part 2, chap. 5, p. 228).

21. Rousseau, *First Discourse*, p. 35.

insists that only quantities that can be measured using the methods of natural science are to be regarded. In the democratic age, prone as it is to offer the false hope of a future unburdened by the dead weight of history, of tradition, and of philosophy, the belief that we should only take account of the things we can measure refutes our tacit claim to have achieved a level of insight superior to what Aristotle long ago achieved and to what Tocqueville fortunately still possessed.

> [There are those] whose object is to make men materialists, to find out what is useful without concern for justice, to have science quite without belief and prosperity without virtue. Such men are called champions of modern civilization, and they insolently put themselves at its head, usurping a place which has been abandoned to them, though they are utterly unworthy of it. [22]

The machinations of abstract reason cannot serve democratic freedom. The politics of reason alone will never be sufficient to understand, let alone maintain, a polity, important as it surely is when not disembodied. As Rousseau put it:

> [T]he human race would have perished long ago if its preservation had depended only on the reasoning of its members. [23]

In Tocqueville's words,

> I am quite convinced that political societies are not what their laws make them, but what sentiments, beliefs, ideas, habits of the heart, and spirit of the men who form them. [24]

A fateful issue before us, then, is whether the momentum of the present age, which makes of us all "blind instruments [in the service of equality]," [25] will yield a political science that is infatuated with disembodied reason and that *reflects* rather than reflectively evaluates the present condition and probable future. At the outset of this study I noted that Tocqueville knew himself to be a stranger in America; whether the science that truly takes the measure of the age of equality must suffer the same fate is a portentous question.

22. Tocqueville, *Democracy in America*, Author's Introduction, p. 17.

23. Rousseau, *Second Discourse*, p. 133.

24. Tocqueville, letter of Claude-François de Corcelle, Sept. 17, 1853, in *Selected Letters*,, p. 294. See also Hennis, "In Search Of," p. 46: "[M]en's feelings [are] more important, more fundamental to their life together than their thinking, i.e., than their rationally considered rights and interests."

25. Tocqueville, *Democracy in America*, Author's Introduction, pp. 11–12.

2. ASKING TOO MUCH OF GOVERNMENT, ASKING TOO MUCH OF "THE WORLD"

There is a peculiar irony involved in the depreciation of a religious orientation and in the defense of a seemingly purely political one. Tocqueville recognized the problem; Rousseau, who greatly influenced him, may not have. Here, I would like to venture some thoughts about "the politico-theological problem," if you will, which are informed by Tocqueville's thinking.

Consider, by way of introduction, Rousseau's effort to disentangle Christianity from politics. What use could Christianity serve, he asked, in the political arena?

> But I err in speaking of a Christian Republic; for each of these terms contradicts the other. Christianity preaches only servitude and submission. Its spirit is too favorable to tyranny for tyranny not to take advantage of it. True Christians are made to be slaves; they know it and they hardly care; this life has too little value in their eyes. [26]

What was needed, he thought, was a civil religion that could be distinguished from the purely inward worship of God in the heart—a thought that has reverberated forward into the present day.

This seemingly straightforward conclusion, however, misses the mark. For while it is true that such a depreciation may serve to focus allegiance, it may also unwittingly draw into the sphere of politics longings that can in no way be satisfied there. Emerson's luminous remark, "[O]nly the finite suffers . . . the infinite lies stretched in smiling repose," [27] is pregnant with implications for Rousseau's view. Human beings, because they are finite beings, suffer. [28] It is, however, a massive

26. Rousseau, *The Social Contract*, bk. 4, chap. 8, p. 184.

27. Ralph Waldo Emerson, "Spiritual Laws," in *Emerson's Essays* (New York: Harper and Row, 1951), p. 93. See also Niebuhr, "The Tower of Babel," p. 29: "[Human life] touches the fringe of the eternal." The human temptation is to confuse the fringe for the center; all our efforts and understandings, consequently, are prone to be enterprises of the sort described in the story of the building of the Tower of Babel (Gen. 11:1–9).

28. Freud, in his own way, even confirms this. If God is construed from the vantage of the biological aspects of the psyche alone and rejected as a mere infantile projection, if human happiness is equated with the pleasure principle alone, then we can only hope to *cope* with the vicissitudes of the world. With Freud, there will always be suffering; only the mechanisms by which we adjust to it are variable. See Freud, *Civilization and Its Discontents*, p. 34: "[T]he programme of becoming happy, which the pleasure principle imposes on us, cannot be fulfilled; yet we must not—indeed, we cannot—give up our means to bring it nearer to fulfillment by some means or other."

and unwarranted leap that we increasingly make today when we seek wholly to alleviate suffering through political means.[29] This historically novel disposition toward worldly suffering asks of politics what it is incapable of offering. The elimination of suffering ultimately requires that we turn away from finitude in the recognition that smiling repose cannot be delivered by political institutions or, indeed, by any other means available to mere mortals.[30]

This is not to say that politics has no responsibility for the amelioration of suffering; rather, ironically, that to the extent to which we ask

29. Oakeshott, to whom I alluded earlier, speaks of this as the rationalist impulse. In his words, "[T]he modern history of Europe is littered with the projects of the politics of Rationalism. The most sublime of these is, perhaps, that of Robert Owen for a 'world convention to emancipate the human race from ignorance, poverty, division, sin and misery.' [Akin to this, however, is] the diligent search of the present generation for an innocuous power which may safely be made so great as to be able to control all other powers in the human world" (*Rationalism in Politics*, pp. 10–11). The reliance upon technical solutions to human problems in the political realm, which is evidence of a peculiarly modern kind of rationalism, would, for Tocqueville, be evidence of the breakdown of face-to-face politics that occurs at the local level and the unconcealment of the secret longing for a powerful state that recognizes only universal principles, not particular and local differences. As I noted earlier, Oakeshott's Rationalism would not, on Tocqueville's reading, be the fruit of the ruminations of Bacon and Descartes, as he suggests, but rather the intellectual propensity of the unfettered democratic soul whose origins long antedate Bacon and Descartes. Nevertheless, Oakeshott clearly grasps the political implications of this movement: "[A] beneficent and infallible technique replaced a beneficent and infallible God; and where Providence was not available to correct the mistakes of men it was all the more necessary to prevent such mistakes" (p. 23). National (and perhaps ultimately transnational) politics comes to be the site that promises to eliminate suffering.

30. Alternatively, if finite creatures accept their finitude, then a purely political orientation can avoid the bad theology of seeking smiling repose in the world. The most powerful articulation of this view in the twentieth century remains Weber's "ethic of responsibility." See Max Weber, "Politics as a Vocation," in *From Max Weber*, trans. H. H. Gerth and C. Wright Mills (New York: Oxford University Press, 1946), pp. 77–128. Weber asks that we bear the burden of our finitude in politics and effectively denies the possibility of smiling repose at all. (With Nietzsche before him, he might say: "How much truth does a spirit *endure*, how much truth does it *dare?* More and more that became for me the real measure of value" (Friedrich Nietzsche, *Ecce Homo*, trans. Walter Kaufman [New York: Random House, 1967], preface, sec. 3, p. 218 [emphasis in original.]) Tocqueville accepts that smiling repose is possible only through the religious *hope* that belongs wholly *outside* of politics. Both see the danger of conflating politics with ultimate concerns.

that it provide more than it is capable of offering it becomes paralyzed and incapable of offering any diminution of our burden. We confuse finite with infinite, partial with ultimate, when we seek smiling repose in the domain of worldly politics. Seeking it there alone can only lead to further suffering. In Plato's idiom: only the city oriented by the Good, by the infinite, can be happy in mortal measure. Such a city is

> far different from most cities today whose inhabitants are ruled darkly as in a dream by men who will fight each other over shadows and use faction in order to rule, as if that were some great good.[31]

Human suffering is a consequence of looking in the wrong place for repose. Locke, in his own way, agrees. He noted in the late seventeenth century that government must be a judge on earth, which partially stands in for God's judgment in Heaven.[32] To seek smiling repose in the world is to ask of government something that would have been inconceivable for him, namely, that it be judge in all cases.

The problem—at once so patently political and yet profoundly theological as well—is not the suffering of finite beings. There has always been suffering; we will "have the poor with [us] always."[33] Rather, the problem is that suffering, diremption, alienation, negativity, lack, void, darkness, errancy, privation—the words matter very little—point beyond themselves to a lost unity that is never wholly forgotten, and which is promised in the future. Biblically, the Egyptian captivity of the soul always points beyond itself to the promised land of Israel:

> For the children of Israel walked forty years in the wilderness, till all the people *that were* men of war, which came out of Egypt, were consumed, because they obeyed not the voice of the LORD: unto whom the LORD sware that he would not shew them the land, which the LORD sware unto their fathers that he would give us, a land that floweth with milk and honey.[34]

Most importantly for our purposes here, the promised land of milk and honey is not achieved by *human* artifice alone; those lost in the Egyptian bondage of the soul, in that world wholly unto itself and incapable of "obeying the voice of the LORD," do not pass over. The overcoming of suffering entails an irruption of the Infinite into the finite world, and not the ever more sophisticated and efficient workings of human reason. Again: "Only the finite suffers. . . . the infinite lies stretched in smiling repose."

31. Plato, *Republic*, bk. 7, 520c–d.
32. Locke, *Second Treatise*, chap. 14, sec. 168, pp. 379–80.
33. Mark 14:7.
34. Jos. 5:6.

Augustine's *Trinity*, too, is helpful in illuminating the problem. Precisely because human beings carry within them an *image* of God, they seek a repose of which merely finite creatures can neither conceive nor for which they can long. Human beings suffer in a way that other finite creatures do not.[35] The trace of God they possess prompts them in their suffering toward a sufficiency of which only God is truly capable: a smiling repose that is without deficiency. "All who desert you and set themselves up against you merely copy you in a perverse way," Augustine says.[36]

If Augustine is correct, then the problem behind the growing political impasse (which must arise once all suffering seeks an immanent appeasement) is not simply that human beings have turned away from the Infinite in favor of a purely political orientation; rather, it is that in so doing they cannot but carry the trace of what they have abandoned into the "City of Man" with them.

The overwhelming fascination with unity, which consumes the democratic soul who so loves the world, is certainly evidence of this trace.[37]

35. See C. S. Lewis, *The Problem of Pain* (New York: Macmillan, 1962), p. 20: "[W]hen man passes from physical fear to dread and awe, he makes a sheer jump, and apprehends something which could never be *given*, as danger is, by the physical facts and logical deductions from them" (emphasis in original). Pain and suffering in the human being, unlike in animals, point always to questions that cannot be answered by the conditions that occasioned them. See also p. 107: "My own experience [with suffering] is something like this. I am progressing along the path of life in my ordinary contentedly fallen and godless condition, absorbed in a merry meeting with my friends for the morrow or a bit of work that tickles my vanity today, a holiday or a new book, when suddenly a stab of abdominal pain that threatens serious disease, or a headline in the newspaper that threatens us all with destruction, sends this whole pack of cards tumbling down. At first I am overwhelmed, and all my little happiness looks like broken toys. Then, slowly and reluctantly, bit by bit, I try to bring myself into the frame of mind that I should have been in at all times. . . . But the moment the threat is withdrawn, my whole nature leaps back to the toys: I am even anxious, God forgive me, to banish from my mind the only thing that supported me under the threat because it is now associated with the misery of those few days. Thus the terrible necessity of tribulation is only too clear." Human pain, for Lewis, directs attention toward the God from whom we have strayed and hence may be salutary.

36. Augustine, *Confessions*, bk. 2, chap. 6, p. 50.

37. See Tocqueville, *Democracy in America*, appendix 1, Y, pp. 734–35. I have alluded to this passage earlier, in sec. 3 of chap. 3. In a democratic age, Tocqueville says, "[T]he concept of unity becomes an obsession" (vol. 2, part 1, chap. 7, p. 451).

(How Nietzsche, in his own way, would agree!) So, too, is the so-called secularization of the world.[38]

If Augustine's analysis is correct, moreover, then the democratic soul's search for the redress of suffering in the world it so loves will reach its end when it finds a mortal-God, one who, in Tocqueville's words, would be "the repairer of all ills suffered, the supporter of just rights, defender of the oppressed, and founder of order."[39] Here God comes down to earth; the religious incarnation is rejected and the political incarnation adored. I leave it to the reader to consider how close we are to such an arrangement.

Consistent with this view, Tocqueville notes that we naturally defer to the state because we wish it to fulfill our *longings*. "The older the democratic society," he says, "the more centralized will its government be."[40] The hidden logic by which it arrives at that condition is, however, theological rather than political. Said otherwise, our longings in the sphere of politics do not betray a merely political impulse. Because the theological dimension of the problem is unrecognized, however, the democratic soul grows less satisfied—though not less demanding—as the sphere of politics is increasingly vested with the reserves purportedly necessary to bring about that smiling repose which comfortingly divests it of its suffering, both declared and concealed.

Politics, however, can never fulfill—notwithstanding that our hunger seems to grow ever more gnawing as we perceive that we are not well fed by it. "The more one starves of [the food that does not perish,] the more unpalatable it seems," Augustine says.[41] To this we may add his

38. See Karl Löwith, *Meaning in History* (Chicago: University of Chicago Press, 1949). The notion that the "philosophy of history [that] originates with the Hebrew and Christian faith . . . ends with the secularization of its eschatological pattern" (p. 2) does not at all suggest a *new* relation to God obtains in the modern age. Augustine's *Trinity* offers the same argument already in the fifth century, namely, that human beings tend to apply in the finite realm a pattern that originates in Heaven.

39. Tocqueville, *Democracy in America*, vol. 1, part 2, chap. 6, p. 240. See Hobbes, *Leviathan*, part 2, chap. 20, pp. 157–58: "[T]he greatest objection [to a Leviathan] is, that of practice; when men ask, where, and when, such power has by subjects been acknowledged. But one may ask them again, when, or where has there been a kingdom *long free* from sedition and civil war" (emphasis added). On this reading, the long experiment with democracy will lead, in good time, to sedition and civil war; only then will we finally accede to the One who overawes us all.

40. Tocqueville, *Democracy in America*, vol. 2, part 4, chap. 3, p. 672.

41. Augustine, *Confessions*, bk. 3, chap. 1, p. 55.

pertinent corollary: avoid "visionary foods on which [we may be fed] but not sustained."[42] The verse "The Lord *is* my shepherd; I shall not want"[43] cannot be transposed into political form without the incapacitation of government! If Tocqueville is correct in thinking that the impulse toward pantheism is the great theological temptation in the democratic age, then there is reason to believe that the *bad theology* that passes for good government, that fails to distinguish between Creator and created, between the domain of smiling repose and finite suffering, is an ominous political threat to the future.

There is a second consideration as well, which I shall only touch upon briefly in the compass of these remarks about the limitations of government: the problem of evil. Consider the parable of the wheat and the tares in Matthew, chapter 13.

> The kingdom of heaven is likened unto a man which sowed good seed in his field: But while men slept, his enemy came and sowed tares among the wheat, and went his way. But when the blade was sprung up, and brought forth fruit, then appeared the tares also. So the servants of the householder came and said unto him, Sir, didst not thou sow good seed in thy field? from whence then hath it tares? He said unto them, An enemy hath done this. The servants said unto him, Wilt thou then that we go and gather them up? But he said, Nay: lest while ye gather up the tares, ye root up also the wheat with them. Let both grow together until the harvest: and in the time of harvest I will say to the reapers, Gather ye together first the tares, and bind them in bundles to burn them: but gather the wheat into my barn.[44]

In this parable what is extraordinary, among other things, is the injunction *not* to gather the tares; for if uprooted they will disrupt the good seed. Evil—the tares—will be with be us always, until the end, until the harvest. It cannot be eradicated by mortal effort.

This is a lesson not easily learned by the democratic soul, which so yearns for unity. The interpenetration of good and evil profoundly disturbs it. Wishing to live in an unambiguously good world, it ferrets out evil without pausing to consider that the good seed may be uprooted by its seemingly beneficent efforts. There is, here, a blindness to the ambiguity of all temporal goods, an impatience in the democratic soul that wants to reap the harvest early—for its barn is empty! "If the tares are the seed of evil," it pronounces, "then let us simply tear them out." And immediately after that: "Why have we waited so long?" Theologically,

---

42. Augustine, *Confessions*, bk. 3, chap. 6, p. 61.

43. Ps. 23:1.

44. Matt. 13:24–30.

the root of these pronouncements is the belief that we need no longer wait in hope and "in steadfast patience,"[45] for the long march of history has, indeed, brought us to the end of the season. We are the harvester!

This phenomenon cannot be understood as a purely political one. The desire to eradicate evil *in politics* can, I think, best be understood within a theological context. Again, what masquerades as good government may simply be bad theology.

These theological musings about the relationship between finitude and the Infinite, and about the problem of evil, do not exhaust the matter. There is another dimension of this problem; theological, to be sure, but practical as well. While the soul's orientation must be toward the transcendent in patience, such an orientation alone will not solve the problem; for while the human soul is in the world, its *gaze* must be directed somewhere. That place, for Tocqueville, must be first and foremost local politics, where the face-to-face of associational life may attenuate the bad infinity of the rationalist impulse. Associations, in a word, are central to the health of a democratic regime:

> Among laws controlling human societies there is one more precise and clearer, it seems to me, than all the others. If men are to remain civilized or to become civilized, the art of association must develop and improve among them *at the same speed as equality of conditions spreads.*[46]

Equality of conditions, recall, produces both the extreme isolation of individuals, one from another, and the compulsive drive toward unity. Associations, however, draw persons out of themselves and ameliorate the logic of unity.

Of the first salutary aspect of associations, Tocqueville notes: "[A]s soon as common affairs *are treated* in common, each man notices that he is not as independent of his fellows as he used to suppose."[47] The basis for the unity of the isolated many is not theoretical, but rather practical. In the actual face-to-face machinations of politics is forged a measure of common life.

The question, however, is at what level of aggregation may the (approximate) unity that politics offers be forged? For Tocqueville, the answer is clear: only at the local level is this possible. Unity cannot be a top-down affair without sacrificing freedom. Nor on his view, I suspect,

---

45. Augustine, *City of God*, vol. 6, bk. 1, preface, p. 18 (*CG*, p. 5).

46. Tocqueville, *Democracy in America*, vol. 2, part 2, chap. 5, p. 517 (emphasis added).

47. Tocqueville, *Democracy in America*, vol. 2, part 2, chap. 4, p. 510 (emphasis added).

can the local level be reinvigorated from above![48] A political program designed *by a powerful state in whom we trust* to redress the problems caused by its ascension is itself implicated in the predicament it seeks to remedy![49] Worse than this seeming impasse, however, would be the results if the state would forge the basis of political unity! As Tocqueville put it:

> the best possible corrective [to the extravagance of general ideas] is to make the citizens pay daily, practical attention to it. That will force them to go into the details, and the details will show them the weak points of the theory. The remedy is often painful but always effective. That is how democratic institutions which make each citizen take a practical part in government moderate the excessive taste for general political theories which is prompted by equality.[50]

This passage brings us to the truly salutary aspect of associations. Here and here alone, at the level of aggregation between the solitary individual and the powerful state, is it possible to forge a semblance of unity that is neither overarching nor overawing, but that works. This is the best we ought to hope for—and the most we can truly expect without eradicating differences.

---

48. See Joshua Cohen and Joel Rogers, "Secondary Associations and Democratic Governance," *Politics and Society* 20, no. 4 (December 1992): 427: "[Associations] are themselves in part a product of opportunities and incentives that are induced by the structures of political institutions and the substance of political choice and so can be changed through public policy." Paul Q. Hirst responds: "[N]o matter how accurate Cohen and Rogers's diagnosis of the problems, it does not follow that a political mechanism is available to solve them in a liberal capitalist state like the United States" ("Comments on 'Secondary Association and Democratic Governance,'" *Politics and Society* 20, no. 4 [December 1992]: 477). Tocqueville's view, which anticipates Hirst's cautions, was that the habit of forming associations was there already to be drawn upon in the American experience. He made no recommendations that they be constructed, for he was of the mind that human beings would be drawn into associational life, provided the site for its emergence was not effaced by a powerful state.

49. Writing of efforts to combat rationalism in politics, Oakeshott remarks: "[T]he main significance of Hayek's *Road to Serfdom* [lies not in] the cogency of his doctrine, but [in] the fact that it is a doctrine. A plan to resist all planning may be better than its opposite, but it still belongs to the same style of politics. And only in a society already deeply infected with Rationalism will the conversion of the traditional resources of resistance to the tyranny of Rationalism into a self-conscious ideology be considered a strengthening of those resources" (*Rationalism in Politics*, pp. 26–27).

50. Tocqueville, *Democracy in America*, vol. 2, part 1, chap. 4, p. 442.

This insight is perhaps Tocqueville's most brilliant, one that we fail to heed at our peril. Only when "common affairs are *treated* in common," when there is a concrete site where differences may be actually worked through, can a measure of unity emerge.

Yet the increasing abandonment of this mediating site between the impotent democratic soul and the powerful state in our time makes it ever less likely that a common ground will be found between a self-enclosed and solitary unity that is vacuous, and an overarching and abstract unity that becomes vicious, exclusionary, pretentious, righteous, and unremitting—no matter how well intended at first blush.

About this latter tendency, increasingly in evidence today, consider Hegel on negative freedom.

> Only in destroying something does this negative will possess the feeling of itself as existent. Of course it imagines that it is willing some positive state of affairs, such as universal equality or universal religious life, but in fact it does not will that this shall be positively actualized, and for this reason: such actuality leads at once to some sort of order, a particularization of organizations and individuals alike; while it is precisely out of the annihilation of particularity and objective characterization that the self-consciousness of this negative freedom proceeds. Consequently, what negative freedom intends to will can never be anything in itself but an abstract idea, and giving effect to this idea can only be the fury of destruction.[51]

Without the mediating capacity of a vital associational life we are condemned to vacillate between a pseudo-self-reliance that countenances angelic tolerance from the comfort of our insularity[52] (the fruit of the "individualism" about which Tocqueville speaks), *and a frenzied effort to establish the abstract content of the American character at the level of national politics* (the result of the absence of a concrete site where, to transpose Hegel's idiom, the word may become flesh). Neither alternative absolves the difficulty of establishing a unity of the different; both alternatives prophetically anticipate a future in which equality reigns yet where freedom has been renounced.

Tocqueville, as I have suggested, fully understood this logic and was deeply troubled about the prospect of maintaining the mediating institutions of associational life:

51. Hegel, *Philosophy of Right*, sec. 5, p. 22.

52. In Mill's words: "[N]atural to mankind is intolerance in whatever they really care about" ("On Liberty," p. 13). Human toleration, he says, is more apt to be a consequence of indifference.

> I think that in the dawning centuries of democracy individual independence and local liberties will always be the product of art. Centralized government will be the natural thing.[53]

And elsewhere,

> I think democratic peoples have a natural *taste* for liberty; left to themselves, they will seek it, cherish it, and be sad if it is taken from them. But their *passion* for equality is ardent, insatiable, eternal, and invincible.[54]

A passion for equality, a taste for liberty. The passion to obliterate differences, it would seem, is more powerful than the taste for liberty that can only be sated at the level of associational life.

This does not bode well for the effort to forestall servitude. The passion to obliterate difference, to subsume all particularity under a general rule, can only lead—by a hidden logic—to the emergence of a powerful state. Here the site of national politics is asked to be the common ground. Yet this move invites nothing but the lethargy of solipsism and the fury of destruction animated by the need for unity.

There have, of course, always been contentions in American political life; there has never been *a* unity. Now, however, as the site of the face-to-face increasingly falls away, the only place these tensions, these difference, can emerge is at the national level. Difference has always been with us; now, however, the valence of difference is increasingly becoming either wholly neutral or thoroughly supercharged. Politics is being apathetically renounced within the closed comfort of the four walls that surround us at the same moment all politics becomes inflammatory national politics.

Absent a site where differences can be treated in the inefficient, oft-times blundering, manner that is the hallmark of local politics, we are left only to oscillate between brooding despair and asking of government that it recreate a nation with planned efficiency in one image or another. And insofar as we do this, we ask not more than what our representatives promise, but much more than they can deliver. The entire complex of bitter renunciation and vehement hope that would remake the world through politics is—you have guessed it—evidence of the Augustinian self gone astray, unshackled from the moorings that only mediating institutions can provide.

53. Tocqueville, *Democracy in America*, vol. 2, part 4, chap. 3, p. 674.
54. Tocqueville, *Democracy in America*, vol. 2, part 2, chap. 1, p. 506 (emphasis added).

3. WHAT IS TO BE DONE?

There is a certain incongruity in posing the question as I have, for it supposes the need for a plan—a plan, moreover, of broad scope to avert a systemic disorder. Tocqueville's theology, which insists that we work within the given historical conditions, does not, however, countenance such a view.[55] The centrality of mediating institutions, which themselves can only be vital when they emerge and are maintained through face-to-face relations *that have no predetermined outcome*, also suggests that Tocqueville would not have endorsed any such project. In a passage that bears repeating, he declares:

> [F]eelings and ideas are renewed, the heart enlarged, and the understanding developed *only* by the reciprocal action of men upon one another.[56]

This is not the stuff that fills up the world with proposing and planning, to be sure; yet neither does his view sanction a kind of resoluteness in the face of a destiny wholly beyond human guidance. Tocqueville adopts a more moderate position, several applications of which I wish to explore briefly below.

A. Affirmative Action

The contemporary rhetoric of affirmative action has moved away from the notion of redressing the intransigencies of habit that have perpetuated injustice, and toward the view that all *voices* must be heard. I would like to suggest, however, that this rhetoric conceals the problem of habit and memory, of which slavery is the most intractable instance, and for that reason remains oblivious to the nature of the problem and to the measures necessary truly to attenuate it. Other instances, other "voices," confirm the depth of the problem to greater or lesser extents. Here I will focus on affirmative action in light of slavery in America. The memory of servitude, unfortunately, illuminates the difficulty all too well.

The theoretical problem of which affirmative action is a highly charged instance is the contradiction between an historical movement that conspires toward the equality of conditions and ongoing identities that are rooted in memories that cannot be easily erased. The con-

---

55. Recall that for Tocqueville, God has ordained that there will be equality; the human task is to establish the form it will take—either an equality in servitude or an equality in freedom. The human task is not to remake the world.

56. Tocqueville, *Democracy in America*, vol. 2, part 2, chap. 5, p. 515 (emphasis added).

tradiction is, if you will, between habit and the logic of history, between enduring differences and the spirit of equality. I make no pretense that this formulation captures the agony of slavery, only that this is the most theoretically succinct expression of what I take to Tocqueville's understanding of the problem. "Christianity had destroyed servitude," he says; "the Christians of the sixteenth century reestablished it."[57] Providence declared that there would be equality; Christians fixed a durable identity in time that is still with us and that—ironically, not to say tragically—contradicts the logic of history.

Tocqueville, it is true, was more concerned with the tyranny of equality than with the burden of marginalization. This was so not because he was unaware of the problem, but rather because he thought it would be confined to an ever-smaller geographical region: the Deep South.[58] Because of this (inaccurate) prognostication, his acumen was focused elsewhere, and he was able to say with some justification, of that large portion America to which he most closely attended, that because

> men equal among themselves came to people the United States, there is as yet no natural or permanent antagonism between the interests of the various inhabitants.[59]

Notwithstanding this important oversight, however, his understanding of the nature of the problem of slavery remains unrivaled—and for four reasons.

First, because he understood the remarkable durability of habit, he knew that the relationship between master and slave would not be overcome by the mere alterations of a law that reason can comprehend—no matter how severe or well meaning. This debilitating relationship insinuates itself deeply into the soul of both participants, and whatever measure of freedom is attained or granted is purchased slowly, at great cost, and with considerable backsliding along the way. The passage from the relationship of lordship and bondage to freedom takes time and is played out on a field where reason is not the most formidable player.

In Exodus, recall, Moses withdraws to Sinai to receive God's injunctions. While the Israelites—who are long accustomed to their Egyptian bondage—wait, they fashion a golden calf,[60] an idol of Egyptian descent

---

57. Tocqueville, *Democracy in America*, vol. 1, part 2, chap. 10, p. 341.

58. See Tocqueville, *Democracy in America*, vol. 1, part 2, chap. 10, p. 351: "[T]he great question of the [the Negro race's] future concerns a limited area, which makes it less frightening but no easier to solve." I will not consider Tocqueville's thinking about the marginalization of the Indians here.

59. Tocqueville, *Democracy in America*, vol. 1, part 2, chap. 7, p. 248.

60. Exod. 32:4.

that no free soul could truly worship. Pharaoh had (unwillingly) renounced his hold, yet the Israelites themselves could not yet let go. The
lesson, with which Tocqueville's understanding of freedom is consistent, is that the servitude of the soul cannot be easily surmounted, that
so powerful was the logic of servitude that it was necessary *for God himself* to intervene—and not once, but many times!

Hegel's dialectic of lordship and bondage,[61] too, conveys the strength
of servitude's hold on the soul; it is so strong, in fact, that only by a kind
of "death" can it be overcome:

> The individual who has not yet risked his life may well be recognized
> as a *person*, but he has not attained the truth of this recognition as an
> independent self-consciousness.[62]

Notwithstanding the differences between these two understandings,
however, neither suffers from the contemporary delusion that the relationship of mastery and servitude can be overcome by the manipulations of law. Servitude is deeper than law, and cannot be rescinded by
the machinations of reason.

Second, as I mentioned above, Tocqueville understood that the logic
of equality is massively in contradiction with the arrest of slavery. Not
only, then, is there a recalcitrance to throw off the yoke of slavery and
the embarrassment of mastery that is deeply woven into the fabric of
American life, and which is scarcely touched by law, but there is also an
utterly contrary force, as well. It is, moreover, the tension between the
two that so supercharges the debate about affirmative action. On the one
hand, the memory of slavery that won't go away impedes the progress
toward equality—and will continue to do so until the memory is obliterated.[63] On the other hand, there is the legitimate and unwavering demand, in this age, that these differences be surmounted. The problem

61. Hegel, *Phenomenology of Spirit*, secs. 178–96, pp. 111–19.
62. Hegel, *Phenomenology of Spirit*, sec. 187, p. 114.
63. That this may even be impossible is suggested by Tocqueville in his
discussion of ancient and modern slavery. Because modern slavery was linked
to the physical attribute of skin color, which serves as a constant reminder of
slavery gone by, modern slavery is more intractable than the ancient form. See
Tocqueville, *Democracy in America*, vol. 1, part 2, chap. 10, pp. 341–42. See Derrick Bell, *Faces at the Bottom of the Well: The Permanence of Racism* (New York: Basic
Books, 1992), p. 199: "[Our choice is not] between the pragmatic recognition
that racism is permanent no matter what we do, or an idealism based on the long-
held dream of attaining a society free of racism. Rather, it is a question of *both,
and. Both* the recognition of the futility of action—where action is more civil
rights strategies destined to fail—*and* the unalterable conviction that something
must be done, that action must be taken" (emphasis in original).

is far deeper than the political stage upon which this reluctant and tragic drama is played out can fathom.

Third, conjoin this already explosive contradiction with the fact that national politics seems increasingly to be the only site where such differences may be surmounted, and the stage is set for a "fury of destruction" that belies the ostensibly peaceful disposition that the democratic soul possesses. This matter I have already considered in the previous section and will return to shortly. Here I only note that Tocqueville was well aware of the danger of looking for unity in the world.

Fourth, and perhaps most important for any effort to defuse the explosive pressure that disregarding these insights portends, Tocqueville understood the relative weight of laws, mores, and religion, in any equation of stability or change—something to which political science, with its perverse fixation upon "rationality," has been quite oblivious. "I see that slavery is in retreat, but the prejudice from which it arose is immovable," he says.[64] Laws may change, but without a change in the mores of a people such laws are of little consequence.

Deeper still than mores, as I have said, is religion,[65] with its practices that shape the very habits of a people, and whose proclamations about the radical equality of all human beings before God may, in the end, be the most powerful means of overcoming the historically constituted disposition *not to* "love thy neighbor as thy self."[66]

> The profoundest and most wide-seeing minds of Greece and Rome never managed to grasp the very general but simple conception of the likeness of all men and of the equal right of all at birth to liberty. They were at pains to show that slavery was natural and would always exist. . . . All the great writers of antiquity were either members of the aristocracy of masters or, at the least, saw that aristocracy in undisputed possession before their eyes. . . . *Jesus Christ had to come down to Earth to make all members of the human race understand that they were naturally similar and equal.*[67]

The idea of equality is not, as Nietzsche reminds us, self-evident; biblical religion has profoundly insinuated itself into the habits of thinking,

---

64. Tocqueville, *Democracy in America*, vol. 1, part 2, chap. 10, p. 343. See also ibid.: "In antiquity the most difficult thing was to change the law; in the modern world the hard thing is to alter the mores, and our difficulty begins where theirs ends."

65. See Tocqueville, *Democracy in America*, vol. 1, part 1, chap. 2, p. 47.

66. Lev. 19:18; Matt. 22:39.

67. Tocqueville, *Democracy in America*, vol. 2, part 1, chap. 3, p. 439 (emphasis added).

the mores, of a civilization. Tocqueville agrees—though he would enlist its support rather than seek to overcome it.

These four insights of Tocqueville's do not make it possible to assemble a plan, yet they do point to certain possibilities and at the same time foreclose others.

What is not possible, clearly, is to solve the residual problem of slavery at the national level by legal means alone. Habit and memory are the problem, and these are resistant (though not wholly immune) to legal manipulations. Law cannot appreciably change the habit of seeing the other as different. While from the comfort and isolation of our living rooms we are apt to have great faith in the human capacity for tolerance, the lessons of history suggest otherwise: charity and brotherly love have been commandments precisely because they are not natural. Law does not readily alter these natural dispositions; and what may occur in the wake of such attempts to do so is a relocation of the abundant human capacity for intolerance and hatred. If Tocqueville is correct about the relative standing of law, mores, and religion, then notwithstanding the barbarous offenses that may be done in its name, religion is a more powerful antidote for the tragedy of slavery than is law alone. Religion, it is, that invites us to honor the mysterious proclamation that below the differences that sense may observe and reason may with innocence or malevolence confirm, we are all of one origin, of one family. In an important letter to Gobineau two years before his death, Tocqueville made this clear:

> As for the letter [of Christianity], what is more clear in Genesis than the unity of mankind and the emergence of all men from the same man? As for the spirit of Christianity, is not its distinctive trait having wanted to abolish all distinctions of race that the Jewish religion had continued to allow to subsist and making one human species, all of whose members were equally capable of perfecting themselves and becoming alike.[68]

This does not mean, however, that law is irrelevant to the relations between the races. The question is not whether law is pertinent, but rather how extensive its hold really can be. Without recognizing that there are deeper levels than law may penetrate, changes at one site that are due to the intervention of the law are simply, inexorably, bound to be offset at another.

The contemporary disposition, unfortunately, is to reverse Tocqueville's insight about the relative weight of laws, mores, and religion.

68. Tocqueville, letter to Arthur de Gobineau, Jan. 24, 1857, in *Selected Letters*, p. 343.

Law, after all, offers a general rule, and general rules always placate the (Democratic) soul that is averse to the messy business of sorting through the peculiar valences of habit. To the extent that this misunderstanding continues, the conscience of the nation may be appeased by policies that comport with the spirit of equality. Yet such appeasement is belied by the ongoing verities of isolation, contempt, and misunderstanding. Legal "advances" have not solved the problem, nor can they.

The lesson here is not that laws are wholly ineffective, but that they can never wholly release this nation from the dread of slavery, and may in fact exacerbate it. The real problem lies elsewhere:

> [The Americans] have opened their ranks to their slaves, but when they tried to come in, they drove them out with ignominy. Wishing to have servitude, they have nevertheless been drawn against their will or unconsciously toward liberty, without the courage to be either completely wicked or entirely just. [69]

To ask of government that it pass laws in the grand hope that the affliction of slavery will abate by that singular course is a dreamy diversion from which we may all someday awake in horror—the purity and majesty of the effort notwithstanding.

The parable of the wheat and the tares, about which I spoke in the previous section, is also apropos here, for it illuminates the dilemma of working to eradicate the seeds of evil, the residue of slavery, before the harvest. Might the consequence—unintended, to be sure—of national efforts to eliminate the residues of servitude, which seemed so deeply rooted at the local level, be the nationalization of questions of identity from which we will all surely suffer in the future? In the service of the principle of unity we have disrupted the sites at which democracy may alone be sustained[70] and have nourished the secret longing of the democratic soul for a powerful state that expiates all suffering. The entire inefficient enterprise of local life—which cannot make such promises—is jettisoned as an anachronism in the age of efficiency:

> A very civilized society finds it hard to tolerate attempts at freedom in a local community; it is disgusted by its numerous blunders and is apt to despair of success before the experiment is finished. [71]

69. Tocqueville, *Democracy in America*, vol. 1, part 2, chap. 10, p. 362.

70. See Robert D. Putnam, *Making Democracy Work: Civic Traditions in Modern Italy* (Princeton: Princeton University Press, 1993). Putnam's provocative empirical study of northern and southern Italy over the past two decades confirms Tocqueville's view that bottom-up rather than top-down civic traditions are essential for the survival of a healthy democracy.

71. Tocqueville, *Democracy in America*, part 1, chap. 5, p. 62.

We are, here, on the threshold of an issue of imposing stature: whether the hidden agenda of modernity, if I may,[72] involves, in fact, a wish to substitute a false universalism for particularism. In America, I suggest, the logic of this agenda is being played out, among other places, on the field of affirmative action. Indeed, this logic shows every sign of including ever more participants. The question, however, is not whether equality will prevail against the conservative forces of darkness, but rather whether the equality that will come to pass honors the particular along with the universal, or whether the bald disregard of the particular by those whose passion for equality exceeds their taste for liberty will, in the end, unwittingly be party to a cataclysmic reaction against the politicization of this or that identity at the national level. The wheat and the tares cannot be separated without uprooting both; in theoretical rather than theological terms, the particular cannot coexist with the universal without a site of mediation that stands somewhere between the solitary person and the overawing state. The local level, where alone associational life may thrive, offers such a site; we cannot dispose of the profound ambiguity that attends all good things simply by planting wheat in state-owned fields.

It is our fate as a nation to wrestle with the vestiges of slavery; that is *our* history, from which we cannot hide. While the nationalization of the issue may absolve certain local inefficiencies and weed out the tares, it sows other seeds that may yield bitter fruit in the future. That, too, may be the unwitting fate of a nation in which "two races are bound one to

---

72. See Stephen Toulmin, *Cosmopolis: The Hidden Agenda of Modernity* (Chicago: University of Chicago Press, 1990). Toulmin argues that one aspect of modernity involves the movement from the oral to the written; from the particular to the universal; from local to the general; and from the timely to the timeless (pp. 31–35)—all of which developments Tocqueville, too, observed. He also notes, however, that another aspect, inaugurated by Montaigne and the sixteenth-century humanists, has coexisted along with the decontextualized rationalism that has been responsible for the trends enumerated above. More importantly, this other tradition *may be drawn upon still* as we approach the end of the twentieth century and move into the next. We may, in other words, return to the oral; to the particular; to the local; to the timely (pp. 186–90). To this view Tocqueville would not, I believe, accede. The logic of equality is what has driven forward the modern project, not Descartes and other seventeenth-century philosophers. Because this logic shows no signs of abating, there is every reason to suspect that the hidden agenda of modernity will continue to go forward, notwithstanding certain eddy currents of resistance. This is, to be sure, a bleak view; yet it is one that accords with Augustine's prognostications about the City of Man written so many centuries ago. Tocqueville writes in the shadow of Augustine; Toulmin, in the shadow of Aristotle!

another without mingling," and where "it is equally difficult for them to separate completely or to unite."[73]

B. *"Empowerment" and Practical Experience*

The theoretical problem here is the nature and extent of the relationship between the logic of equality, which would subsume all difference under a universal rule, and the diminution of *practical experience* that is so necessary for a healthy democracy and economy. In the conventional language of economics the term often used to designate this experiential dimension that resists attempts to quantify it is *social capital*. This dimension is receiving renewed attention these days by economists who have rediscovered that the relationship between efficiency and productivity is a subtle one—an insight Tocqueville already had grasped in the early nineteenth century.[74]

Tocqueville, recall, pointed out that the industrial enterprise of the Americans was predicated upon the priority they granted (prearticulate) practical over (articulate), theoretical knowledge. Moreover, he noted that there was an intimate relationship between the extensiveness of practical knowledge in America *and the associational life through which it proliferated*. In his words,

> In democratic countries knowledge of how to combine is the mother of all other forms of knowledge; on its progress depends that of all others.[75]

Without a strong associational life, without mediational sites, practical experience languishes.[76]

---

73. Tocqueville, *Democracy in America*, vol. 2, part 2, chap. 10, p. 340.

74. See also Schumpeter, *Capitalism, Socialism, and Democracy*, pp. 131–34. The entrepreneur, who possesses a wealth of practical experience, is, in the course of the evolution of capitalism, superseded by the efficiencies of technical rationality within the marketplace. "Since capitalist enterprise, by its very achievements, tends to automatize progress, we conclude that it tends to make itself superfluous—to break to pieces under the pressure of its own success. The perfectly bureaucratized giant industrial unit not only ousts the small and medium-sized firm and 'expropriates' its owners, but in the end it also ousts the entrepreneur and expropriates the bourgeoisie as a class which in the process stands to lose not only its income but also what is infinitely more important, its function" (p. 134).

75. Tocqueville, *Democracy in America*, vol. 2, part 2, chap. 5, p. 517.

76. This insight I take to be an advance upon Rousseau's provocative epistemological musings in Emile, which suggest that the premeditated knowledge that must antedate mediated knowledge can—and indeed must—develop without participation in a life with others. Not having grasped the intimate re-

The problem, on Tocqueville's view, is that the logic of equality militates against the development and maintenance of mediational sites—ironically, to the detriment of the health of a democracy. I have noted elsewhere (more extensively in section 2 of chapter 3, but also in section 6 of chapter 4) the relative importance Tocqueville granted to the invisible and the visible. Appearances notwithstanding, the invisible (whether religion, woman, or, in this case, practical experience) has a more primordial standing than does the visible (whether "the world," man, or theoretical knowledge).

We are, however, often deceived by appearances. The inefficiency of local politics, which above all else accomplishes the priceless task of drawing persons out of their self-enclosed world and offering a forum for practical experience to proliferate, seems to be eclipsed by the efficient, top-down, politics of national government. In certain respects, of course, it is; but only as long as the reservoir of (invisible) practical experience that is promulgated by that inefficient forum of associational life remains full.

> The predicament of our time is that the rationalists have been at work so long on their project of drawing off the liquid in which our moral ideals were suspended (and pouring it away as worthless) that we are left only with the dry and gritty residue which chokes us as we try to take it down.[77]

Sooner or later the well that is drawn upon in secret, as it were, will dry as mediational sites are abandoned in the rush toward that visible, national forum that alone seems to exude potency. Then, and only then, will the incompetency of national government that is run in accordance with efficient rules become clear. No longer nourished by that training in practical experience on the basis of which the application of such rules can be at all efficacious, the entire efficient edifice will come to a grinding halt—or worse. As one critic of this tendency to disregard, if not repudiate, practical experience has put it:

> By destroying traditional social habits of the people, by dissolving their natural collective consciousness into individual constituents, by licensing the opinions of the most foolish, by substituting instruction

---

lationship between practical experience and the face-to-face of associational life, Rousseau could not have come upon a thought that informs the entirety of Tocqueville's thinking, namely, that mediational sites alone provide the epistemological, political, and theological wherewithal to exempt the (democratic) soul from a relentless oscillation between being a solitary walker, if I may, and an obedient servant to a general will that seemingly absolves all impotence.

77. Oakeshott, *Rationalism in Politics*, p. 41.

for education, by encouraging cleverness rather than wisdom, the upstart rather than the qualified . . . Liberalism can prepare the way for
that which is its own negation: the artificial, mechanized or brutal control which is a desperate remedy for its chaos.[78]

The language here may be overly harsh, yet the general thread of the
argument accords with Tocqueville's own: practical experience and the
logic of equality, which instinctually draws the democratic soul into
the orbit of the powerful state and toward discomforting solitude, are at
odds with one another. Only practical experience can save equality in
freedom from decaying into equality in servitude.[79] Social capital is de-
generated by the very efficiency that promises to enhance human life:

> It is easy to see the time coming in which men will be less and less
> able to produce, by each alone, the commonest bare necessities of
> life. The tasks of government must therefore perpetually increase,
> and its efforts to cope with them must spread its net ever wider. *The
> more the government takes the place of associations, the more will individuals
> lose the idea of forming associations and need the government to come to their
> help.*[80]

About this matter we must be clear: when the mediational sites of
associational life are abandoned there are debilitating consequences *that
cannot be immediately measured* but that are no less real in their effect upon
the long-term health of a democratic nation that has long relied on them.
Regrettably, the rhetoric of "empowerment" does not accord with efficiency; it is an eddy that forms and dissipates in a river whose current
cannot be altered without changing the very passions that govern the
democratic soul. The prospect in the late twentieth century of saving
associational life from being overcome by a force that Tocqueville recognized was formidable already in his own day, however, is not bright.[81]

78. T. S. Eliot, "The Idea of a Christian Society," in *Christianity and Culture*,
p. 12.

79. This is, recall, a crucial aspect of the case for American exceptionalism
in *Democracy in America*. Unlike the weary Europeans, the Americans privileged
prearticulate knowledge.

80. Tocqueville, *Democracy in America*, vol. 2, part 2, chap. 5, p. 515 (emphasis added).

81. A people with a long habit of forming associations may be able to resist
this force. While this offers solace to those with such habits, those without them
will be little comforted. This painful conclusion is one with which Putnam wres-
tles. See *Making Democracy Work*, p. 183: "[O]ne able reformist regional presi-
dent in an uncivic region exclaimed when he heard our conclusions: 'This is a
counsel of despair! You're telling me that nothing I can do will improve our
prospects for success. The fate of the reform was sealed centuries ago.'"

The profound paradox that attends this relationship between practical experience and the logic of equality ought to be made clear. What is at issue, to put it starkly, is the diminution of the stability of a democracy by the logic of equality itself. While this logic tends to obliterate all obstacles to its progress along the way, it may end without vitality, devoid of a liveliness that can emanate only from the particularities of the associational life it supersedes. History ends, not with overawing energy, but rather with the impotence of an historically novel form of despotism that has poisoned the wellspring from which its vigor once issued.

Tocqueville was quite concerned about this possibility, about what might be called the parched landscape of the democratic future. Ironically, the river that now carries the resistant rhetoric of empowerment along with unstoppable force will, on this reading, run dry before it reaches the sea. What alone can invigorate equality is associational life—the very thing that the logic of equality overruns.

The hazard to which the rhetoric of empowerment is exposed is not, then, simply attributable to a failure of will in the face of certain clearly malevolent forces. Rather, it is that, notwithstanding vehement protestations to the contrary, without habits that direct it otherwise, the democratic soul will believe in its secret heart that empowerment worthy of the name comes only through the overawing state. Truly modern despotisms isolate not by the sword but by catering to the passions of its citizens—by drawing upon their need for unity, efficiency, security, and the like. (How Nietzsche would agree!)[82] It is in this discomforting light that Tocqueville's remarks about despotism must be understood:

> Despotism sees the isolation of men as the best guarantee of its own permanence. So it usually does all it can to isolate them.[83]

The new despotism will isolate by yielding to deep-seated need. The contemporary rhetoric that unabashedly announces the necessity of "making America competitive again" is, in one of its valences, a euphemism that masks those needs. Bombs and bullets, Huxley said, are so inefficient.[84]

So we arrive at the bedrock of the paradox. The democratic soul knows its impotence and so calls out for empowerment. Secret longings,

82. See Nietzsche, *Thus Spoke Zarathustra,* first part, "On the New Idol," pp. 48–51.

83. Tocqueville, *Democracy in America,* vol. 2, part 2, chap. 4, p. 509.

84. See Huxley, *Brave New World,* pp. xiv–xv: "[G]overnment by clubs and firing squads, by artificial famine, mass imprisonment and mass deportation, is not merely inhumane, it is demonstrably inefficient and in the age of advanced technology, inefficiency is the sin against the Holy Ghost. A really efficient totalitarian state would be one [in which a people] love their servitude."

however, direct its unobstructed gaze and unchanneled energy wholly toward the state, which simultaneously assuages its heart and redoubles its solitude—a vicious polarization of melancholy and delight, to be sure. If there is any comfort to be found in all of this it lies in the fact that our habits (conjoined with certain theological practices and understandings to be discussed in section 4 below), rather than any *plan* to redress the problem with legislation, may yet be drawn upon.

C. Lotteries and Long-Term Goals

The theoretical problem of which lotteries and long-term goals are an instance devolves from the exceedingly abbreviated temporal horizon of the democratic soul, which must be extended in order for self-interest rightly understood to rule. Prone to be taken in by the immediacy of the moment, the contingency of the Fates (or, if still biblically inclined, the *free gift* of God's grace) seems best to comport with its often erratic course. The discontinuities between the past, present, and future are self-evident to such a soul; a methodical course of action that draws together these disparate temporal moments, on the other hand, must be achieved—and can be only with continuous effort.

The very conditions of equality, however, conspire against an extension of the naturally truncated temporal horizon of the democratic soul. The longings of the democratic soul are, recall, established within the unbounded horizons that the age of equality bestows. The capacities of such a soul, however, are always exceeded by the scope of its imagination in this unbounded age. Lacking constraints, but nevertheless restrained by its own weakness and the sheer amplitude of others who are alike, the democratic soul secretly awaits a reprieve that *breaks in*, that belies all methodical planning—which it intimates, perhaps correctly, will never consummate its longings.

Lotteries nurture this dangerous disposition. They are the modern equivalent of the Fates, or perhaps of God's grace—only tidier; without terror or inconvenience they promise to deliver the soul from an unremitting sameness unto a life of the blessed that no somber plan may achieve. The damage this false promise incurs far exceeds any pecuniary benefit that lotteries might confer.[85] However noble may be the cause

---

85. See Richard T. Ely, *Social Aspects of Christianity, and Other Essays* (New York: Thomas Y. Crowell, 1889), p. 58: "[M]any a Christian cannot grasp the sinfulness of lotteries, does not grasp that it is trying to get something for nothing—the essence of theft." Ely, one of the founding members of the American Economic Association, believed that the purpose of economic analysis was "to advocate no opinions, but simply to strive to find out the underlying principles of industrial society, and to diffuse information among the working classes and

toward which the revenues are directed, they foster an indigence of soul that must be overcome if democratic liberty is to thrive. In the service of revenue, they undermine the very idea of an extended temporal horizon—without which rational action becomes wholly inconceivable.

While lotteries must be shunned in order that whatever measure of long-term thinking that resides in the democratic soul not be further reduced, long-term goals ought to be established by government in order to develop and fortify this habit of thinking. Moreover, whereas lotteries, in spite of their pecuniary return, cannot be justified, long-term goals ought not to be rejected simply because they fail to meet certain pecuniary criteria. Profoundly more important than their "costs and benefits" are the effect they have on the temporal horizon of the democratic soul. This should not, of course, be taken to mean that we should countenance fiscal frivolity. This said, however, efforts aimed at extending the temporal horizon with a "costly" program will yield far more beneficent results than will raising money to "benefit" a worthy cause should what is really purchased to finance it be the invisible and fragile capital upon which the rational action—and so economic power—is predicated.

Religion, Tocqueville reminds us, is that powerful institution which seems singularly capable of extending the temporal horizon of the soul, democratic or otherwise; when religion ceases to hold sway over the soul, however, government must shoulder that responsibility—if only as an interim measure. "That is [its] most important business," he says.[86] At a time when the irresponsibility of government fiscal practices is, ironically, conjoined with a deep and abiding fixation upon a perverse cost-benefit calculus, it would serve us well to attend more fully to the limited but not insignificant capacity of government to shape certain habits without which well intended expenditures will be futile and seemingly prudent fiscal restraint debilitating.

D. Property

The theoretical problem of which property is an instance is the need in a democratic age for a mediational site on the basis of which certain thoughts and habits necessary for the survival of liberty *become broadly conceivable*. I need only briefly rehearse Tocqueville's argument about the effect property has upon the soul. The possession of property is the

---

all classes. Briefly stated, its purpose is to study seriously the second of the two great commandments on which hang all the law and the prophets, in all its ramifications, and thus to bring science to the aid of Christianity" (pp. 24–25).

86. Tocqueville, *Democracy in America*, vol. 2, part 2, chap. 17, p. 548. For further discussion see sec. 5 of chap. 4.

basis for the *plausibility* of the idea of rights, as well as the wellspring of respect for law. The idea of rights achieves concrete form through the living possession of property. So embodied, the soul that retains it more easily comprehends the abstract idea of rights of which property is the specific and familiar instance. The idea of rights is, so to speak, made flesh through the substantiation of property. From that site can derive a healthy understanding of rights, as well as of the law that safeguards them.[87]

To be sure, this justification of property offers little in the way of defense (or criticism) of private appropriation or the mode of production of which it is a part. Property is not justified or condemned for economic reasons. How it figures in the equation of wealth has scant relevance here. The arguments of Locke, Smith, and Marx about property converge not at all with Tocqueville's own—notwithstanding his profound understanding of the commercial spirit in America. Rather, the true value of property lies in its capacity to develop certain essential attributes in the souls of citizens in the democratic age.

This justification of property, nowadays, receives little attention amid the rhetorical din of the post–cold war world. Yet we disregard it at our peril. Property is essential to the health of a democratic nation, but not only because of the wealth it generates. Great wealth may, after all, be generated when property is concentrated in the hands of a few—something about which Tocqueville worried in his dense but prophetic chapter on the new aristocracy.[88] Property must be defended because when working citizens of middling rank possess property, a stable citizenry is formed that is tethered to a particular site that averts both abject despair and the false hope of disembodied universal freedom. One need not be a professing Marxist to be suspicious that when the love of wealth is mistaken for the highest good, the distance between rich and poor will only be magnified and middling property holders cast into the ranks of the destitute.[89]

Every effort must therefore be made to assure that citizens have the

87. By contrast, an unhealthy understanding of rights would derive from the unmediated idea of rights in general. From this bad infinity can only come a proliferation of rights that knows no boundaries, and which encumbers any and all finite political systems with burdens they are incapable of bearing.

88. Tocqueville, *Democracy in America*, vol. 2, part 2, chap. 20, pp. 555–58.

89. See, for example, Plato, *Republic*, bk. 8, 551d: "[A city ruled by the love of wealth is of necessity] not one, but two, a city of the rich and a city of the poor, dwelling together, and always plotting against one another." The latter portions of Rousseau's *Second Discourse* convey the same thought, namely, that when the love of wealth comes to rule, there shall eventually be only two classes—a thought not lost, subsequently, to Marx.

opportunity to become property holders. It is not, after all, clear that economic efficiency in a world economy and broad-based property holdings are compatible—or if they are, whether this has been more for reasons of circumstance than of logical necessity. The sheer bounty and expanse of the American wilderness has certainly made for a comfortable alliance of middling property holders and economic expansion for several centuries. "Prosperity," Tocqueville says, "quenches the fires of faction."[90] Like democratic liberty, however, the future of such holdings may well depend upon human artifice rather than the purportedly beneficent invisible hand of the market.[91]

E. The Present Political Impasse

The theoretical problem of which the present political impasse provides evidence is the confusion—at once theological, epistemological, and political—about how the relationship between particularity and universality may be mediated such that each is granted its due. The difficulty, I suggest, is that without mediation the two aspects can only become viciously polarized; we are bound to arrive at an impasse in which each truth stands in desperate need of attention while at the same time, ironically, each becomes an empty caricature—as all half-truths must. Here are the two classes of knowledge and the two political parties that represent them: those who would push the frontier of principle and those who emphasize the habitual. The former are occasionally "ugly, rude, and disagreeable people, very progressive, it may be, but very aggressive to boot."[92] Unless annexed by forces that would plan a return to the past, the former are for the most part peaceable. As Emerson put it,

90. Tocqueville, *Democracy in America*, vol. 1, part 2, chap. 9. p. 306.

91. In this regard see Hilaire Belloc, *The Servile State* (Indianapolis, Ind.: Liberty Press, 1977). Contrary to Marx, the invisible hand in capitalism does not inexorably disenfranchise smaller property holdings. Rather, this logic proceeds only when property has *already* been appropriated and established severe maldistribution—as was the case in England during the Reformation. (See pp. 85–105.) Property relations here are less consequence than cause of capitalism's development. On this view, it is possible to circumvent the inexorable logic of capitalism of which Marx spoke through redistribution of property. Belloc, however, never fully developed his thinking on how this might be possible. Of additional interest are numerous pregnant remarks throughout *The Servile State* that intimate the complicity of the Reformation in the developments he deplores. It is not perhaps merely an accident that Belloc sees France and Ireland as countries most resistant to the trend toward servility (p. 203).

92. Samuel Butler, *Life and Habit*, in *The Shrewsbury Edition of the Works of Samuel Butler*, ed. Henry Festing Jones and A. T. Bartholomew (New York: AMS Press, 1968), 4:27.

"[O]f the two great parties . . . one has the best cause and the other the best men."[93]

There can be no political resolution to this antinomy.[94] More precisely, any attempt *at the national level* to make one aspect stand for the whole will only lead to further polarization, periodic vacillation—and ultimately, perhaps, to violence.

To grant each aspect its due, to circumvent the present political impasse, requires not a redoubling of efforts at the national level but rather the *resubstantiation* of that site which stands between the solitary soul and the overawing state. What appears, in short, to be a national political impasse demanding greater effort at the national level to be overcome is actually a consequence of the nationalization of all politics and the abandonment of the site of mediation between the solitary many and the overawing one. The impasse is not resolvable by reason, rhetoric, legislation, or power at the national level. Only a mediational site can save us now. The theology embodied in this thought I shall attend to more fully below.

4. CONCLUDING REMARKS

The notion that all human beings are, in essential ways, equal is not, as Nietzsche pointed out, self-evident. It has a history. Notwithstanding the advances toward this notion that the Greeks and Romans may have made, it remained for Judaism, and for Christianity, "that love that grew out of its crown,"[95] to reshape a world in which democracy—by which I mean a political order whose principles accord with this notion—could reign.

Equality has been a long time in coming, to be sure; about this both Tocqueville and Nietzsche agree. The protracted historical record of inequality, of disenfranchisement, offers no refutation; discord has invariably amplified rather than diminished the movement toward equality.[96]

93. Emerson, "Politics," p. 406.

94. Mill is more generous. "Each of these modes of thinking derives its utility from the deficiencies of the other; but it is in great measure the opposition of the other that keeps each within the limits of reason and sanity" ("On Liberty," p. 59). Mill does not understand that while his dialogical theory of truth has great merit, the site at which discourse takes place is crucial to its success. He seems unaware of the problem of bad infinity, about which Hegel and Tocqueville were deeply concerned.

95. Nietzsche, *Genealogy of Morals*, first essay, sec. 9, p. 35.

96. Schlesinger notes: "[T]he crimes of the West have produced their own antidotes. They have provoked great movements to end slavery, to raise the

Contradictions and difficulties have not forced the abandonment of the notion itself, but rather occasioned different formulations of it that betray an unrelenting effort to continue to comprehend the vagaries of experience in its terms. Democracy, as Nietzsche suggested, is the open declaration of the innermost principle of biblical religion—the radical equality of all persons (under God)! In his view, democracy, the spirit of equality, has won; only skirmishes remain.

Yet as Nietzsche pointed out, in that economical aphorism that bears repeating, "[I]t is the church, and not its poison, that repels us."[97] And in the same place: "Which of us would be a free spirit if the Church did not exist?" The proclamations and practices of the Church have been rejected, but the habits of thinking of those with "truly modern taste"[98] have not disengaged wholly from what offends them.

This, I take to be the condition in which we remain more than a century after Nietzsche first described it. The democratic habit of thinking, now in ways disencumbered from its religious substrate, took time to develop and will abide even if the scandalous injunction that gave rise to it falls wholly into disrepute.

Here, in this peculiar relationship, we are confounded by the strange paradox of belief in the late twentieth century: the habit of thinking that drives democracy forward at a frenzied pace both belies and confirms its religious origin. Because habits of thinking are deeper than the ideas they give rise to, no "mere" thought can effectively challenge democracy; yet because the religious ground of the habit has been weakened, there is an uneasy sense that democracy is drifting and without foundation. The durability of habit currently sustains democracy, even as the idea of the permanent alliance between Christianity and democracy, about which Tocqueville spoke, is increasingly disavowed—and this, by a world enamored, ironically, by the call unto universalism that itself arises out of biblical religion!

We dwell amid the lag, fortunate yet foreboding, that habit has bestowed. So situated, with security that renders the gravity of the situation opaque, and with anxiousness about the dangerous precipice upon which we dimly intimate we stand, there is an odd admixture of naïveté

---

status of women, to abolish torture, to combat racism, to defend freedom of inquiry and expression, to advance personal liberty and human rights. Whatever the particular crimes of Europe, that continent is also the source—the unique source—of those liberating ideas . . . to which most of the world today aspires" (*The Disuniting of America*, p. 76 [emphasis in original]).

97. Nietzsche, *Genealogy of Morals*, first essay, sec. 9, p. 36.
98. Nietzsche, *Genealogy of Morals*, first essay, sec. 9, p. 36.

and urgency in contemporary accounts whose intentions are to plumb the depths of the current American situation and establish the rock upon which democracy may stand in the century to come.

As to whether any of the many philosophic projects aimed at bolstering democracy on the basis of reason alone can be successful, Tocqueville offers this caution that is unheeded by all but a few democratic theorists:

> Did [the modern moral philosophers] really establish new foundations, or even new explanations, for human duties? . . . Through all the darkness all I think I can recognize is this: to me it is Christianity that seems to have accomplished the revolution—you may prefer the word *change*—in all the ideas that concern duties and rights; ideas which, after all, are the basic matter of all moral knowledge. . . . Thus Christianity put in grand evidence the equality, the unity, the fraternity of all men.[99]

Nor, in his view, can the greatness of the American legal system—and, by extension, the Constitution—substitute for what only Christianity can provide:

> A great part of the success of democratic government must be attributed to . . . good American laws, but I do not think that they are the main cause. While I think that they have more influence on American social happiness even than the nature of the country, I still have reasons for thinking *that mores are even more important.*[100]

The founding fathers, wise and prudent as they surely were, only provided laws for a people whose habits made them capable of bearing the

99. Alexis de Tocqueville, *The European Revolution and Correspondences with Gobineau*, trans. John Lukacs (Gloucester, Mass.: Peter Smith, 1968), pp. 190f. Consider also Locke. Prior to Christ's first coming, he argues, societies continued with just enough of this cement to "tie [them] together in subjection" (Locke, *The Reasonableness of Christianity*, sec. 241, p. 170). Lacking a foundation in Christian virtue, they were held together—but not in freedom. The illuminative truth of reason *did* rule the minds of a few human beings prior to Christ, notably the philosophers, "[but it was] too hard a task for unassisted reason, to establish morality, in all its parts, upon its true foundation; with a clear and convincing light (p. 170). Moreover, philosophers, assisted by a natural reason which "makes but a slow progress and little advance in the world" (p. 171), had no way to make the laws of reason authoritative. The great majority of human beings do not have the leisure to enlarge their knowledge; hence, they cannot know, but must *believe* (sec. 243, p. 179). And because belief is predicated on authority (see sec. 238, pp. 165–66), even the law of reason discovered by the philosophers could not be disseminated.

100. Tocqueville, *Democracy in America*, vol. 1, part 2, chap. 9, p. 307 (emphasis added).

weight of worthy laws and an aspiring spirit.[101] Deeper than law is habit. Deeper still, is religion:

> The [materialists who object to Christian belief] should hasten to call religion to their aid, for they must know that one cannot establish the reign of liberty without that of mores, and mores cannot be firmly founded without beliefs.[102]

Neither philosophic ruminations about the capacity of reason to ennoble democracy,[103] legal and historical scholarship designed to recover its adequate basis in the founding, nor any other effort to establish an authoritative narrative or narratives of the Unitarian sort will, however, provide democracy, or rather democratic freedom, with the foundation

---

101. See Montesquieu, *Spirit of the Laws*, part 1, bk. 1, chap. 3, p. 8: "[T]he government most in conformity with nature is one whose particular arrangement best relates to the disposition of the people for whom it is established."

102. Tocqueville, *Democracy in America*, Author's Introduction, p. 17. The relationship between beliefs and the habits of a people was not lost to Rousseau either. See Rousseau, *The Social Contract*, bk. 2, chap. 7, p. 87: "[The lawgiver] must have recourse to an authority of another order, one which can compel without violence and persuade without convincing." The lawgiver must, in other words, recur to God if he is to successfully found a people.

103. See Thomas L. Pangle, *The Ennobling of Democracy: The Challenge of the Postmodern Age* (Baltimore: Johns Hopkins University Press, 1992). With steely soberness Pangle unveils the strange situation of the postmodern movement: its "rush to escape the depths (in every sense) of Heidegger while preserving something of his philosophic and literary pyrotechnics" (p. 56), the fruits of which are as ripe as we might expect from the Last Man studying Nietzsche amid the bourgeois comforts of his study—or with a wry grin and resplendent white suit peaceably on his patio. *Anti*rationalism has consequences, Pangle warns us, that are belied by the innocent language of "play." In Tocqueville's language, real revolutions become rare as conditions of equality come to prevail—though that does not stop the imagination from wandering. The massive preoccupation with difference; the truncated and discontinuous temporal horizon of the democratic soul; the wanton disregard and revolt against reason in a world where the freedom of all, paradoxically, imposes harsh restrictions upon the field in which reason may operate: these "postmodern" impulses that frantically declare their freedom from the burden of "modernity" even while they admit its inescability are, through and through, articulations of the kind of soul Tocqueville thought would come to prevail as equality triumphed. It is not postmodern at all; it is democratic. Nevertheless, for all Pangle's cogency and critique, and notwithstanding the veracity of his thoughts on the liberating quality of dialectical thinking (pp. 183–218) to which all teachers in higher education should earnestly attend, it is not clear that democratic liberty can be maintained by the means he suggests. Philosophy, on Tocqueville's view, does not animate the springs of a nation.

it needs. While this thought may offend the philosophic, conservative-legal, and ecumenical spirit, Tocqueville was clear about the matter:

> I do not know if all Americans have faith in their religion—for who can know the secrets of the heart?—but I am sure that they think it is necessary to the maintenance of republican institutions. That is not a view of one class or party among the citizens, but of the whole nation; it is found in all ranks. [104]

This is not to say that conditions of equality will never arrive without Christianity; rather, that without it—without the salutary fear it authorizes, the long-term thinking it instantiates, the envy it palliates, the desire to "fill up the world" it averts, the neighborliness it commands, the kind of servitude it approves and countervails, [105] the unity it defers, the notion of mediation it countenances—there is reason to wonder if

104. Tocqueville, *Democracy in America*, vol. 1, part 2, chap. 9, pp. 292–93. See also Edwards, "Necessity of Belief," pp. 1187–1216. Edwards is less intent there upon establishing the truth of Christianity than its social benefit. Additionally, he is aware of what, in the contemporary idiom, might be called the "path dependency" of Christianity in America. In his words: "[S]ome religion then, and some belief of a future state is necessary to our political prosperity. But what religion shall we adopt? and what system concerning a future state is most useful to the state? It is not possible to introduce and give a general spread through the state, to Mahometanism or paganism; *and it would be a work of time and of great difficulty*, to lead the citizens in general into a belief of deism or what is called the philosophical religion. Therefore we seem necessitated to have recourse to Christianity" (p. 1191 [emphasis added]). See also Eliot, "Notes towards Definition," p. 200: "I do not believe that the culture of Europe could survive the complete disappearance of Christian faith. . . . If Christianity goes, the whole of our culture goes. Then you must start painfully again, and you cannot put on a new culture ready made. You must wait for the grass to grow to feed the sheep to give the wool out of which your new coat will be made. You must pass through many centuries of barbarism."

105. See Tocqueville, *Democracy in America*, vol. 2, part 1, chap. 5, p. 444: "I doubt whether man can support complete religious independence and entire political freedom at the same time. I am led to think that *if he has no faith he must obey, and if he is free he must believe*" (emphasis added). There will always be obedience, Tocqueville says; the only question is whether obedience will be toward God or toward the (human) tyrant. This is a venerable biblical theme. See Augustine, *Confessions*, bk. 11, chap. 29, p. 278: "[God] has upheld me in many ways and through many trials, in order that through him I may win the mastery, as he has won mastery over me." See also bk. 6, chap. 11, p. 128: "[F]ool that I was, I did not know that no man *can be master of himself, except of God's bounty*, as your Bible says" (emphasis in original). In Tocqueville's words, "[W]hat can be done with a people master of itself if it is not subject to God" (*Democracy in America*, vol. 1, part 2, chap. 9, p. 294).

the ever increasing measure of equality that looms over the horizon will favor liberty rather than servility. "Every religion has some political opinion linked to it by affinity," Tocqueville says.[106] Christianity forms the soul, shapes the habits of citizens in ways that make democratic freedom possible; servility, on the other hand, will arrive effortlessly absent countervailing effort. Providence, or the invisible hand of history, will gently take us there. "Despotism may be able to do without faith," Tocqueville says, "but freedom cannot."[107]

In his introduction to *Democracy in America*, Tocqueville suggests that "instinctual democracy [would] submit like [a slave] to its least desires."[108] Plato would say no less.[109] Augustine's citation of Cato—if further evidence is needed—is also instructive.

> In allies, in our citizens, in armaments, in horses, we have greater resources than [our ancestors] enjoyed. But it was other causes which made them great, causes that with us have ceased to exist: energy in our own land, a rule of justice outside our borders; in forming policy, a mind that is free because not at the mercy of criminal passions. Instead of these we have self-indulgence and greed, public poverty and private interest. We praise riches; we pursue a course of sloth. . . . When at home you are slaves to your appetites, and to money and influence in your public life. The consequence is that an attack is being launched on a republic left without defenses.[110]

While we casually speak of the "transitions to democracy" in other lands, it would behoove us to remember that democracy is not a stable regime type, that it tends to decompose without certain nonpolitical

---

106. Tocqueville, *Democracy in America*, vol. 1, part 2, chap. 9, p. 287. See also Hegel, *Philosophy of History*, part 4, sec. 3, chap. 1, p. 417: "States and Laws are nothing else than Religion manifesting itself in the relations of the actual world."

107. Tocqueville, *Democracy in America*, vol. 1, part 2, chap. 9, p. 294.

108. Tocqueville, *Democracy in America*, Author's Introduction, p. 13.

109. While the oligarchic soul would "gratify only his own most necessary appetites and desires, withholding expenditures for anything else and suppressing those appetites he deem[s] vain and unprofitable" (*Republic*, bk. 8, 554a), the democratic soul "yields to each appetite as it makes its presence felt so that it appears to be a matter of random choice. Then he gives himself over to it until he is satisfied. After that, he turns to some other pleasure, rejecting none and treating all as equally enjoyable" (561b). The democratic soul, Plato says, has been fed by the lotus eaters (560c), who have made it forget about its journey home—to the Good.

110. Augustine, *City of God*, vol. 6, bk. 5, chap. 13, p. 271 (*CG,*, p. 200). The political virtues of Rome, he argues, were a *gift* from God, even if the Romans had not yet turned to the worship of the one, true, God.

supports that it is the task of the new political science to comprehend. It cannot be repeated too often that Tocqueville's theology supposes that God has ordained that equality will come; human beings will determine the form that equality will take. Without certain institutional supports that human beings must nurture, the victory of democratic freedom that Tocqueville tentatively celebrated—now without religion to attenuate certain maleficent dispositions of the democratic soul—is short-lived; the beacon of democracy grows dim when not oriented by a heavenly light:

> Religious peoples are naturally strong just at the point where democratic peoples are weak. And this shows how important it is for people to keep their religion when they become equal.[111]

Democracy in America ends in the morass of envy, an insoluble fascination with and reprehension of difference, and a short-sightedness that no philosophic recovery may alter, legal intervention may arrest, or ecumenical narrative may propitiate.[112]

The lesson of the Jews, Hobbes was quick to point out, was that when they instituted a king who would "judge them like all other nations," their passion-clouded reason received no corrective. A "secular" state, one ruled by Saul, offers no antidote for the inevitable errancy of its subjects. To forestall this, the Jews had to be reminded of their obligation to God—hence, in Hobbes's view, the need for the New Covenant.[113] Without correctives, "[E]very man [will do] that which [is]

---

111. Tocqueville, *Democracy in America*, vol. 2, part 1, chap. 5, p. 445. See also Tocqueville's letter of Dec. 1, 1859: "[O]nly freedom (I mean, moderate and regular) and religion, in a joint effort, can pull men out of the swamp into which democracy casts them as soon as one of these supports is missing."

112. Worth pondering is Tocqueville's observation that "surprising though this seems at first sight . . . in our day it is the most anti-democratic element in the nation which gives the best example of the moral standards one can rationally expect from democracy" (*Democracy in America*, vol. 2, part 3, chap. 11, p. 600). As Christian religion recedes in Europe and America, by an ironic twist of history the Europeans will be better able to cope with the political consequences because the *residual* aristocratic elements there counter the short-term tendencies of the democratic soul; this residual trace is the functional equivalent to religion for the Americans: something that arrests one of the irrationalities of the democratic soul.

113. In his words: "[T]he end of Christ's coming was to renew the covenant of the kingdom of God, and to persuade the elect to embrace it, which was the second part of his office. If then Christ, while he was on earth, had no kingdom

right in his own eyes."[114] Tocqueville, while not resorting to Hobbes's austere proposals, saw in the self-enclosure of the democratic soul he observed, in self-interest wrongly understood, a massive threat to democratic freedom.[115]

Taking religion seriously within the confines of social science is discomforting, I recognize. Training, if not disposition, speaks against it. The enlightened mind, which has been battered by the events of the twentieth century but which still holds sway in many quarters, often finds this kind of thinking archaic; and yet Nietzsche would argue that while the articulated thoughts of religion are a scandal to the enlightened mind, the habits of thinking that biblical religion has engendered are precisely what the enlightened mind now seeks to promulgate around the world: the universal truth of democracy. Here is a dialectical puzzle as perplexing as any in the closing years of the twentieth century.

Democracy, however, like Christianity, "works" only through mediation. Dissevered from their respective sites of mediation, both succumb to the easy temptation of bad infinity, of false universalism. Whether the rejection of the one disposes the enlightened mind to reject the other is an interesting question. Nevertheless, what is clear is that there are provocative parallels between the two sites of mediation (Christian and democratic), which Tocqueville's defense of associational life, perhaps inadvertently, recapitulates. With these parallels, finally, I will conclude, in the hope that a *theological* understanding of mediation may serve to illuminate, in an allegorical fashion, the contemporary *political* dilemma. If, as Tocqueville suggests, Christianity and democracy are linked, then perhaps the exercise may be instructive.

First, in the mediational site of the Son, who stands between the powerful One (Father) and the exquisitely differentiated many, the mystery of the unity of the different is made manifest; there alone,

---

in this world, to what end was his first coming? It was to restore unto God, by a new covenant, the kingdom, which being his by the old covenant, had been cut off by the rebellion of the Israelites in the election of Saul" (Hobbes, *Leviathan*, part 3, chap. 41, p. 355 [emphasis in original]).

114. Judg. 21:25.

115. Like Hobbes, Tocqueville also believed that a site of mediation was necessary to avert the peril he foresaw. Where Hobbes would give us the mediation of a mortal-god who stands between the One (God) and the prideful many in order for there to be genuine liberty, Tocqueville would give us the mediation of associational life that stands between the one (powerful state) and the isolated many, and the mediation of God the Son who stands between the isolated many and God the Father. I shall consider this matter of mediation shortly.

face-to-face, may we "say the peace" to our neighbor with an open hand:

> There is neither Jew nor Greek, there is neither bond nor free, there is neither male nor female: for ye are all one in Christ.[116]

There alone, through mediation, may differences be, for a time, rendered oblique, though not obliterated. Only "under the shadow of [Christ's] wings"[117] are we safe from the One (Father) who would condemn us, even while we love him. Politically, only in the face-to-face of associational life, where we meet the other as a neighbor with an open hand, may there be the awkward but manageable peace we need, which averts the danger of our own identity being condemned by the overawing state that we love. "Under the wing" of associational life we are protected from the One that stands over us all.

Second, in the mystery of the Word made flesh the universal becomes particular, thought becomes embodied, and suffers the fate of all creatures. Spirit is drawn down into a world; it loses itself in the details that arrest its flight from the world.[118] The finitude of this mediational site points beyond itself to a unity with the One (God) that can exist *through hope*, to be sure; but unity with the One cannot exist in the world until the End Time. A mediational site renders such hope constructive rather than destructive. The soul can come unto the unity of the One (God) only through the mediational site of the Son.[119] Without this

---

116. Gal. 3:28.

117. Luther, "Lectures on Galatians," 26:231–32 (emphasis added). See also Ps. 17:8. God the Son, in effect, protects the soul from wrath of God the Father.

118. Again, see Tocqueville, *Democracy in America*, vol. 2, part 1, chap. 4, p. 442: "[T]he best possible corrective [to the extravagance of general ideas] is to make the citizens pay daily, practical attention to it. That will force them to go into the details, and the details will show them the weak points of the theory. *The remedy is often painful but always effective*. That is how democratic institutions which make each citizen take a practical part in government moderate the excessive taste for general political theories which is prompted by equality" (emphasis added).

119. See also Emmanuel Levinas, "Loving the Torah more than God," in *Difficult Freedom: Essays on Judaism*, trans. Seán Hand (London: Athlone Press, 1990), p. 144: "[T]he link between God and man is not an emotional communion that takes places within the love of a God incarnate, but a spirit or intellectual [*esprits*] relationship which takes place through an education in the Torah. It is precisely a word, not incarnate, from God that ensures a living God among us." Here, too, mediation prevails.

grounding in the concrete practices of associational life—the analogue to religious ritual—the unity we seek will only be a destructive fancy of the imagination.[120] Politically, the unity of the overawing state for which we long, which dares to supersede the face-to-face of associational life, is a false hope that can yield only "death."

Third, the mediational site is one that admits of weakness rather than strength; or rather, it is only through apparent weakness that true strength is admitted.[121] Precisely in our weakness, in turning away from the things that falsely exude a kind of potency, does the ground of our life together truly emerge. In Luther's idiom, in the abyss of powerlessness, when we turn from works in the world we heretofore had intimated would bring us salvation, we discover the ground, the Byss, upon which we may be grasped by God the Son, the true Source of power. In that "place," we see through his eyes and reenact the divine mystery of power coming to presence precisely where it is not expected.

Understood as an allegory about mediational sites in democracy, this is the most important yet difficult lesson to learn. It is, moreover, the key to revitalizing democracy—as Tocqueville seems to have intimated in the last portions of *Democracy in America*. Only by turning away from the thing that falsely exudes a kind of potency, does the true ground of our life together emerge. Precisely where power is not expected, where we intimate that the void we seek to fill cannot be filled—there we will find a power that offers the solace that the unmediated power of the state promises but, in fact, cannot deliver.

Upon the prospect of this turn rests the future of democracy. Whether the democratic soul, prone as it is to being unremittingly confronted in its secret heart by its own impotency, will be willing to accept the apparent impotence of associational life in place of the "expected" kingdom of the visible power of the state, remains an open question. For it to do so will require the political equivalent to the insight granted the centurion, who was not disposed to look for the wellspring of power where it had been expected:

---

120. See Hobbes, *Leviathan*, part 2, chap. 26, pp. 213–14: "[I]n a commonwealth, a subject that has no certain and assured revelation to himself concerning the will of God, is to obey as such, the command of the commonwealth, for if men were at liberty, to take for God's commandments, their own dreams and fancies, or the dreams and fancies of private men; scarce two men would agree upon what is God's commandment." Although Hobbes's understanding of *who* the mediator must be is peculiar, the general form of his insight is quite consonant with biblical religion as a whole, namely, that without a site of mediation the One God is obscured by the multiple projections of the human mind.

121. See 2 Cor. 12:9.

And when the centurion, which stood over against him, saw that he so cried out, and gave up the ghost, he said, Truly this man was the Son of God.[122]

The centurion, the one who did not expect the Messiah at all, was the only person who came to recognize Christ; all the rest failed to understand because they were looking with great expectation in some other place.[123]

Understood allegorically, something like this must occur for democratic freedom to thrive. Through this site that is not "expected," difference may be saved, bad infinity averted, and genuine power achieved. Without it we are condemned to oscillate back and forth between the immoderate positions toward which the democratic soul is naturally prone: between envy that wants no "discrimination" and pride that desperately wants to retain difference; between an insular concrete personal life that is abstracted from community and a substantive community that abides only as an empty and dangerous, even if imaginative, abstraction; between the solemn impotence of self-enclosure and the euphoric identification with a national forum of politics that promises to fill the void in our souls but simply cannot.

122. Mark 15:39. See also Leon Kass, "What's Wrong with Babel," *American Scholar* 58, no. 1 (winter 1989): 57–59. Kass suggests that it might be significant that the story of Abram's election follows directly upon the story of Babel. "The universal city [Babel] of self-made men," he says, "will not be a pious, moderate, just, thoughtful, or dignified home for human life, notwithstanding its ability to improve man's material conditions through technology. To have discovered the moral and political sufficiency of human artfulness opens one to the possibility of something beyond artifice, to something real and truly satisfying" (p. 57). Abram responds to the call from God to be his particular and chosen people after it has become clear that the universalist aspiration of Babel is a faulty one. Might the willingness to eschew the universalist aspiration require that we witness its failure? That "Abram went" (Gen. 12:4) without quarrel is suggestive.

123. The Gospel of Mark originally ended with 16:8 ("And they went out quickly, and fled from the sepulcher; for they trembled and were amazed: neither said they any thing to any man; for they were afraid."), not with 16:20 ("And they went forth, and preached everywhere, the Lord working with *them*, and confirming the word and signs following. Amen.") as it is in King James. In the original version those who awaited the expected Messiah *never* understood him when he came. *They* ended in isolation and fearfulness.

Bibliography

Aquinas, Thomas. *Summa theologica*. Garden City, N.Y.: Image Books, 1969.

Arendt, Hannah. *Between Past and Future*. New York: Viking Press, 1961.

———. *The Human Condition*. Chicago: University of Chicago Press, 1958.

Aristotle. *Nicomachean Ethics*. Translated by Martin Ostwald. New York: Macmillan, 1986.

———. *Politics*. Translated by Ernest Barker. New York: Oxford University Press, 1958.

Aron, Raymond. *Main Currents in Sociological Thought*. Vol. 1. New York: Doubleday Anchor, 1968.

Augustine, Saint. *City of God*. Translated by Demetrius B. Zema, S.J., and Gerald G. Walsh, S.J. In *The Fathers of the Church*. Edited by Roy Joseph Deferrari, vols. 6–8. New York: Fathers of the Church, 1950.

———. *City of God*. Translated by Henry Bettenson. New York: Penguin Books, 1972.

———. *Confessions*. Translated by Henry Chadwick. New York: Oxford University Press, 1991.

———. *Confessions*. Translated by R. S. Pine-Coffin. New York: Penguin Books, 1961.

———. *Confessions*. Translated by F. J. Sheed. New York: Sheed & Ward, 1943.

———. *The Trinity*. Translated by Edmund Hill. New York: New City Press, 1991.

Bacon, Francis. *The New Organon*. Edited by Fulton H. Anderson. New York: Macmillan, 1960.

Barber, Benjamin R. "Jihad vs. McWorld." *Atlantic*, March 1992, pp. 53–63.

———. *Strong Democracy*. Berkeley and Los Angeles: University of California Press, 1984.

Bell, Derrick. *Faces at the Bottom of the Well: The Permanence of Racism*. New York: Basic Books, 1992.

Bellah, Robert, et al. *Habits of the Heart*. New York: Harper and Row, 1985.

Belloc, Hilaire. *The Servile State*. Indianapolis, Ind.: Liberty Press, 1977.

Benda, Julien. *The Treason of the Intellectuals*. New York: W. W. Norton, 1969.

Bernal, Martin. *Black Athena*. Vol. 1. New Brunswick, N.J.: Rutgers University Press, 1987.

Bloom, Allan. *The Closing of the American Mind.* New York: Simon and Schuster, 1987.

Blumenberg, Hans. *The Legitimacy of the Modern Age.* Translated by Robert M. Wallace. Cambridge, Mass.: MIT Press, 1983.

———. *Work on Myth.* Translated by Robert M. Wallace. Cambridge, Mass.: MIT Press, 1985.

Bly, Robert. *Iron John: A Book about Men.* New York: Addison-Wesley, 1990.

Bork, Robert. "Neutral Principles and Some First Amendment Problems." *Indiana Law Journal* 47, no. 1 (1971): 1–35.

Brauer, Jerald C. *Protestantism in America.* Philadelphia: Westminster Press, 1965.

Brunner, Karl. "The Perception of Man and the Conception of Society: Two Approaches to Understanding Society." *Economic Inquiry* 25, no. 3 (1987): 367–88.

Burke, Edmund. *Reflections on the Revolution in France.* Edited by Connor Cruise O'Brien. New York: Penguin Books, 1968.

———. "Thoughts on the Cause of the Present Discontents." In *Burke's Politics.* Edited by Ross J. S. Hoffman and Paul Levack. New York: A. A. Knopf, 1949.

Butler, Samuel. *Life and Habit.* In *The Shrewsbury Edition of the Works of Samuel Butler.* Edited by Henry Festing Jones and A. T. Bartholomew, vol. 4. New York: AMS Press, 1968.

Calvin, John. *Institutes of Christian Religion.* Edited by John T. McNeill. Translated by Ford Lewis Battles. 2 vols. Philadelphia: Westminster Press, 1960.

Cohen, Joshua, and Rogers, Joel. "Secondary Associations and Democratic Governance." In *Politics and Society* 20, no. 4 (December 1992): 393–472.

Connolly, William E. *Political Theory and Modernity.* New York: Basil Blackwell, 1988.

Coontz, Stephanie. *The Way We Never Were.* New York: Basic Books, 1992.

Cooper, James Fenimore. *The American Democrat.* Indianapolis, Ind.: Liberty Press, 1981.

Dahl, Robert A. *Polyarchy.* New Haven: Yale University Press, 1971.

Derrida, Jacques. *Of Grammatology.* Translated by Gayatri Spivak. Baltimore: Johns Hopkins University Press, 1976.

———. "Plato's Pharmacy." In *Dissemination.* Translated by Barbara Johnson. Chicago: University of Chicago Press, 1981.

Descartes, René. *Discourse on the Method.* In *The Philosophical Writings of Descartes.* Translated by John Cottingham, Robert Stoothoff, and Dugald Murdoch. 2 vols. Cambridge: Cambridge University Press, 1985.

Drescher, Seymour. *Dilemmas of Democracy.* Pittsburgh: University of Pittsburgh Press, 1968.

Du Bois, W. E. B. *The Souls of Black Folks.* New York: Fawcett Publications, 1961.

Edwards, Jonathan. "The Necessity of the Belief of Christianity by the Citizens of the State, in Order to Our Political Prosperity." In *Political Sermons of the American Founding Era, 1730–1805,* 1187–1216. Edited by Elis Sandoz. Indianapolis, Ind.: Liberty Press, 1991.

Eisenach, Eldon. *The Lost Promise of Progressivism.* Lawrence: University of Kansas Press, 1994.

————. *Two Worlds of Liberalism: Religion and Politics in Hobbes, Locke, and Mill.* Chicago: University of Chicago Press, 1981.

Eliade, Mircea, *The Myth of the Eternal Return.* Princeton: Princeton University Press, 1954.

Eliot, T. S. "The Idea of a Christian Society." In *Christianity and Culture.* New York: Harcourt Brace Jovanovich, 1977.

————. "Notes towards the Definition of Culture." In *Christianity and Culture.*

Elshtain, Jean Bethke. *Meditations on Modern Political Thought: Masculine/Feminine Themes from Luther to Arendt.* New York: Praeger Publishers, 1986.

Ely, Richard T. *Social Aspects of Christianity, and Other Essays.* New York: Thomas Y. Crowell, 1889.

Emerson, Ralph Waldo. "Experience." In *Emerson's Essays.* New York: Harper and Row, 1951.

————. "Nominalist and Realist." In *Emerson's Essays.*

————. "The Over-Soul." In *Emerson's Essays.*

————. "The Poet." In *Emerson's Essays.*

————. "Politics." In *Emerson's Essays.*

————. "Spiritual Laws." In *Emerson's Essays.*

Etzioni, Amitai. *The Moral Dimension: Toward a New Economics.* New York: Free Press, 1988.

Feuerbach, Ludwig. *The Essence of Christianity.* Translated by George Eliot. New York: Harper and Row, 1957.

Filmer, Sir Robert. *Patriarcha.* In *Patriarcha and Other Writings.* Edited by Johann P. Sommerville. Cambridge: Cambridge University Press, 1991.

Finke, Roger, and Rodney Stark. *The Churching of America, 1776–1990: Winners and Losers in Our Religious Economy.* New Brunswick, N.J.: Rutgers University Press, 1992.

Freud, Sigmund. *Civilization and Its Discontents.* Edited and translated by James Strachey. New York: W. W. Norton, 1989.

Fukayama, Francis. *The End of History.* New York: Free Press, 1991.

Galbraith, John Kenneth. *The Affluent Society.* Boston: Houghton Mifflin, 1984.

————. *The Culture of Contentment.* Boston: Houghton Mifflin, 1992.

Gerrish, B. A. *Grace and Reason: A Study in the Theology of Luther.* Oxford: Clarendon Press, 1962.

Gilligan, Carol. *In a Different Voice.* Cambridge, Mass.: Harvard University Press, 1982.

Girard, René. *Violence and the Sacred.* Translated by Patrick Gregory. Baltimore: Johns Hopkins University Press, 1977.

Goldstein, Doris S. *Trial of Faith: Religion and Politics in Tocqueville's Thought.* New York: Elsevier Press, 1975.

Gray, J. Glenn. *The Warriors.* New York: Harper and Row, 1970.

Hancock, Ralph. "The Uses and Hazards of Christianity." In *Interpreting Tocqueville's "Democracy in America,"* 348–93. Edited by Ken Masugi. Savage, Md.: Rowan and Littlefield, 1991.

Hartz, Louis. *The Liberal Tradition in America.* New York: Harcourt Brace Jovanovich, 1955.

Hatch, Nathan O. *The Democratization of American Christianity.* New Haven: Yale University Press, 1989.

Hegel, G. W. F. *The Phenomenology of Spirit.* Translated by A. V. Miller. London: Oxford University Press, 1977.

———. *Philosophy of History.* Translated by J. Sibree. New York: Dover Publications, 1956.

———. *Philosophy of Right.* Translated by T. M. Knox. Oxford: Oxford University Press, 1967.

———. "The Positivity of the Christian Religion." In *Early Theological Writings.* Edited by Richard Kroner. Philadelphia: University of Pennsylvania Press, 1971.

———. *Reason in History.* Translated by Robert S. Hartman. Indianapolis, Ind.: Bobbs-Merrill, 1953.

———. "The Spirit of Christianity and Its Fate." In *Early Theological Writings.*

Heidegger, Martin. *Being and Time.* Translated by John Macquarrie and Edward Robinson. New York: Harper and Row, 1962.

———. "The Essence of Truth." In *Basic Writings.* Edited by David Farrell Krell. New York: Harper and Row, 1977.

———. "Nur ein Gott Kann Uns Retten." *Der Spiegel,* May 31, 1976, 193–219.

———. *The Question concerning Technology.* Translated by William Lovitt. New York: Harper and Row, 1977.

Hennis, Wilhelm. "In Search of the 'New Science of Politics.'" In *Interpreting Tocqueville's "Democracy in America,"* 27–62. Edited by Ken Masugi. Savage, Md.: Rowan and Littlefield, 1991.

Hirschman, Albert O. *Exit, Voice, and Loyalty.* Cambridge, Mass.: Harvard University Press, 1970.

———. *The Passions and the Interests.* Princeton: Princeton University Press, 1977.

Hirst, Paul Q. "Comments on 'Secondary Association and Democratic Governance.'" *Politics and Society* 20, no. 4 (December 1992): 473–80.

Hobbes, Thomas. *Behemoth.* Chicago: University of Chicago Press, 1990.

———. *De cive.* In *Man and Citizen.* Translated by Bernard Gert. Gloucester, Mass.: Humanities Press, 1978.

———. *Leviathan.* Edited by Michael Oakeshott. New York: Macmillan, 1962.

Hobsbawm. E. J. *Industry and Empire.* New York: Penguin Books, 1969.

Hood, F. C. *The Divine Politics of Thomas Hobbes.* Oxford: Clarendon Press, 1964.

Hume, David. "Of National Character." In *Essays, Moral, Political and Literary.* Indianapolis, Ind.: Liberty Press, 1985.

———. "Of Superstition and Enthusiasm." In *Essays, Moral, Political, and Literary.*

———. *A Treatise of Human Nature.* Edited by L. A. Selby-Bigge. Oxford: Clarendon Press, 1978.

Huxley, Aldous. *Brave New World.* New York: Harper and Row. 1946.

James, William. *The Varieties of Religious Experience.* New York: Vintage Books, 1990.

Jefferson, Thomas. *Notes on the State of Virginia.* New York: W. W. Norton, 1954.

Kant, Immanuel. *Critique of Pure Reason*. Translated by F. Max Müller. New York: Doubleday Anchor, 1966.

———. "Idea for a Universal History from a Cosmopolitan Point of View." In *On History*. Edited by Lewis Beck. New York: Macmillan, 1963.

———. "Perpetual Peace." In *On History*.

Kass, Leon. "What's Wrong with Babel." *American Scholar* 58 (winter 1989): 41–60.

Katz, David S. *Philo-Semitism and the Readmission of the Jews to England, 1603– 1655*. Oxford: Clarendon Press, 1982.

Kierkegaard, Søren. *The Sickness unto Death*. Translated and edited by Howard V. Hong and Adna H. Hong. Princeton: Princeton University Press, 1980.

Kraynak, Robert P. *History and Modernity in the Thought of Thomas Hobbes*. Ithaca: Cornell University Press, 1990.

Lawler, Peter Augustine. *The Restless Mind: Alexis de Tocqueville on the Origin and Perpetuation of Human Liberty*. Lanham, Md.: Rowan and Littlefield, 1993.

Lenin, V. I. *What Is to Be Done?* New York: International Publishers, 1969.

Levinas, Emmanuel. "Loving the Torah More Than God." In *Difficult Freedom: Essays on Judaism*. Translated by Seán Hand. London: Athlone Press, 1990.

———. *Totality and Infinity*. Translated by Alphonso Lingis. Pittsburgh: Duquesne University Press, 1969.

Lewis, C. S. *The Problem of Pain*. New York: Macmillan. 1962.

Lewontin, R. C., Steven Rose, and Leon J. Kamin. *Not in Our Genes*. New York: Pantheon Books, 1984.

Locke, John. "Can Anyone by Nature Be Happy in This Life? No." In *Essays on the Law of Nature*. Edited by W. von Leydon. Oxford: Clarendon Press, 1954.

———. *An Essay concerning the True Original, Extent, and End of Civil Government*. In *Two Treatises of Government*. Edited by Peter Laslett. Cambridge: Cambridge University Press, 1988.

———. *The Reasonableness of Christianity*. Edited by George W. Ewing. Washington: Regnery Gateway, 1965.

———. *The Reasonableness of Christianity*. Boston: T. B. Wait, 1811.

Lowi, Theodore J. *The End of Liberalism: The Second Republic of the United States*. New York: W. W. Norton, 1979.

Löwith, Karl. *Meaning in History*. Chicago: University of Chicago Press, 1949.

Luther, Martin. "Bondage of the Will." In *Luther's Works*. Edited by Jaroslav Pelikan, vol. 33. Saint Louis: Concordia Publishing House, 1958.

———. Luther, Martin. "The Freedom of a Christian." In *Luther's Works*, vol. 31.

———. "Lectures on Galatians." In *Luther's Works*, vol. 26.

———. "Lectures on Genesis." In *Luther's Works*, vol. 1.

———. "Temporal Authority: To What Extent It Should Be Obeyed." In *Luther's Works*, vol. 45.

———. "To the Christian Nobility of the German Nation concerning the Reform of the Christian Estate." In *Luther's Works*, vol. 44.

Machiavelli, Niccolò. *The Discourses*. Edited by Bernard Crick. Translated by Leslie J. Walker, S.J. New York: Penguin Books, 1970.

————. *The Prince*. Translated by Harvey C. Mansfield. Chicago: University of Chicago Press, 1985.

Macquarrie, John. *Principles of Christian Theology*. New York: Charles Scribner's Sons, 1977.

Malcolm X. *The Autobiography of Malcolm X*. New York: Grove Press, 1965.

Marcuse, Herbert. *One-Dimensional Man*. Boston: Beacon Press, 1964.

Martinich, A. P. *The Two Gods of Leviathan*. Cambridge: Cambridge University Press, 1992.

Marx, Karl. "Alienated Labor." In *Marx's Concept of Man*. Edited by Erich Fromm. New York: Frederick Ungar, 1978.

————. "Contribution to the Critique of Hegel's *Philosophy of Right:* Introduction." In *The Marx-Engels Reader*. Edited by Robert C. Tucker. New York: W. W. Norton, 1978.

————. "German Ideology." In *Marx's Concept of Man*.

————. "Manifesto of the Communist Party." In *The Marx-Engels Reader*.

————. "Money." In *Marx's Concept of Man*.

————. "Private Property and Communism." In *Marx's Concept of Man*.

Marx, Karl, and Fredrick Engels. *Marx-Engels Correspondence*. Moscow: Progress Publishers, 1955.

Meyrowitz, Joshua. *No Sense of Place*. New York: Oxford University Press, 1985.

Mill, J. S. "Considerations on Representative Government." In *Three Essays*. Oxford: Oxford University Press, 1975.

————. "On Liberty." In *Three Essays*.

Mitchell, Joshua. "The Equality of All under the One in Luther and Rousseau: Thoughts on Christianity and Political Theory." *Journal of Religion* 72, no. 3 (1992): 351–65.

————. "Hobbes and the Equality of All under the One." *Political Theory* 21, no. 1 (1993): 78–100.

————. "John Locke and the Theological Foundation of Liberal Toleration: A Christian Dialectic of History." *Review of Politics* 52, no. 1 (1990): 64–83.

————. "Luther and Hobbes on the Question, Who Was Moses, Who Was Christ? *Journal of Politics* 53 (August 1991): 676–700.

————. *Not by Reason Alone: Religion, History, and Identity in Early Modern Political Thought*. Chicago: University of Chicago Press, 1993.

Moltmann, Jürgen. *The Crucified God*. New York: HarperCollins, 1991.

Monaghan. Henry. "Our Perfect Constitution." *New York University Law Review* 56, nos. 2–3 (1981): 353–96.

Montesquieu, Baron de. *Persian Letters*. Translated by C. J. Betts. New York: Penguin Books, 1973.

————. *The Spirit of the Laws*. Translated and edited by Anne M. Cohler, Basia Carolyn Miller, and Harold Samuel Stone. Cambridge: Cambridge University Press, 1989.

Nelson, Robert H. *Reaching for Heaven on Earth*. Savage, Md.: Rowan and Littlefield, 1991.

Niebuhr, Reinhold. "The Tower of Babel." In *Beyond Tragedy: Essays on the Christian Interpretation of History*. New York: Charles Scribner's Sons, 1951.

Nietzsche, Friedrich. *Beyond Good and Evil.* Translated by Walter Kaufman. New York: Random House, 1966.

———. *Daybreak: Thoughts on the Prejudices of Morality.* Translated by R. J. Hollingdale. Cambridge: Cambridge University Press, 1982.

———. *Ecce Homo.* Translated by Walter Kaufman. New York: Random House, 1967.

———. *On the Genealogy of Morals.* Translated by Walter Kaufman. New York: Random House, 1967.

———. *Thus Spoke Zarathustra.* Translated by Walter Kaufman. New York: Penguin Books, 1978.

———. *Twilight of the Idols.* Translated by R. J. Hollingdale. New York: Penguin Books, 1968.

Oakeshott, Michael. "Political Education." In *Rationalism in Politics.* London: Methuen 1962.

———. "Rationalism in Politics." In *Rationalism in Politics.*

———. "The Tower of Babel." In *Rationalism in Politics.*

Orwin, Clifford. "Civility." *American Scholar* 60 (autumn 1991): 553–64.

Paine, Thomas. *The Rights of Man.* New York: Penguin Books. 1984.

Pangle, Thomas. *The Ennobling of Democracy: The Challenge of the Postmodern Age.* Baltimore: Johns Hopkins University Press, 1992.

———. *The Spirit of Modern Republicanism.* Chicago: University of Chicago Press, 1988.

Pascal, Blaise. *Pensées.* Translated by A. J. Krailsheimer. New York: Penguin Books, 1966.

Pitkin, Hanna Fenichel. *The Concept of Representation.* Berkeley and Los Angeles: University of California Press, 1972.

Plato. *Phaedo.* Translated by Hugh Tredennick. In *The Collected Dialogues of Plato.* Edited by Edith Hamilton and Huntington Cairns. New York: Bollingen Books, 1961.

———. *Phaedrus.* Translated by R. Hackforth. In *The Collected Dialogues of Plato.*

———. *Philebus.* Translated by R. Hackforth. In *The Collected Dialogues of Plato.*

———. *Republic.* Translated by Paul Shorey. In *The Collected Dialogues of Plato.*

Polanyi, Karl. *The Great Transformation.* Boston: Beacon Press, 1944.

Polanyi, Michael. *Personal Knowledge.* Chicago: University of Chicago Press, 1958.

Polanyi, Michael, and Harry Prosch. *Meaning.* Chicago: University of Chicago Press, 1975.

Postman, Neil. *Amusing Ourselves to Death.* New York: Viking Penguin, 1985.

Putnam, Robert D. *Making Democracy Work: Civic Traditions in Modern Italy.* Princeton: Princeton University Press, 1993.

Rawls, John. "Justice as Fairness: Political Not Metaphysical." *Philosophy and Public Affairs* 14, no. 3 (1985): 223–251.

———. *A Theory of Justice.* Cambridge, Mass.: Harvard University Press, 1971.

Reddaway, Peter. "Russia on the Brink?" *New York Review of Books,* January 28, 1993, 30–35.

Reventlow, Henning Graf. *The Authority of the Bible and the Rise of the Modern World.* Philadelphia: Fortress Press, 1985.

Rorty, Richard. *Contingency, Irony, and Solidarity.* New York: Cambridge University Press, 1989.

Rousseau, Jean-Jacques. "Discourse on the Origin and Foundations of Inequality among Men." In *The First and Second Discourses.* Translated by Roger D. Masters. New York: St. Martin's Press, 1964.

———. *Emile.* Translated by Allan Bloom. New York: Basic Books, 1979.

———. "Has the Restoration of the Sciences and Arts Tended to Purify Morals." In *The First and Second Discourses.*

———. *Reveries of a Solitary Walker.* Translated by Charles E. Butterworth. New York: New York University Press, 1979.

———. *The Social Contract.* Translated by Maurice Cranston. New York: Penguin Books, 1968.

Sahlins, Marshall. *Stone Age Economics.* Chicago: Aldine-Atherton, 1972.

Schleiermacher, Friedrich. *On Religion: Speeches to Its Cultured Despisers.* Translated by Richard Crouter. Cambridge: Cambridge University Press, 1988.

Schlesinger, Arthur M., Jr. *The Cycles of American History.* Boston: Houghton Mifflin, 1986.

———. *The Disuniting of America.* Knoxville, Tenn.: Whittle Communications, 1990.

Schmitt, Carl. *The Concept of the Political.* New Brunswick, N.J.: Rutgers University Press, 1976.

———. *The Crisis of Parliamentary Democracy.* Cambridge, Mass.: MIT Press, 1985.

Schoeck, Helmut. *Envy: A Theory of Social Behavior.* Indianapolis, Ind.: Liberty Press, 1987.

Schumpeter, Joseph A. *Capitalism, Socialism, and Democracy.* New York: Harper and Row, 1976.

Sheldrake, Rupert. *The Presence of the Past.* New York: Random House, 1988.

Smith, Adam. *The Wealth of Nations.* Chicago: University of Chicago Press, 1976.

Smith, Steven B. *Hegel's Critique of Liberalism.* Chicago: University of Chicago Press, 1989.

Spencer, Herbert. *On Social Evolution.* Chicago: University of Chicago Press, 1972.

Steiner, George. *Real Presences.* Chicago: University of Chicago Press, 1989.

Strauss, Leo. Introduction to *History of Political Philosophy,* 1–6. Edited by Leo Strauss and Joseph Cropsey. Chicago: University of Chicago Press, 1972.

———. *Natural Right and History.* Chicago: University of Chicago Press, 1953.

———. *What Is Political Philosophy?* Glencoe, Ill.: Free Press, 1959.

Tarcov, Nathan. *Locke's Education for Liberty.* Chicago: University of Chicago Press, 1984.

Tawney, R. H. *Religion and the Rise of Capitalism.* London: John Murray, 1936.

Thucydides. *History of the Peloponnesian War.* Translated by Rex Warner. New York: Penguin Books, 1972.

Tillich, Paul. *Systematic Theology.* Vol. 3. Chicago: University of Chicago Press, 1951.

Tocqueville, Alexis de. *Democracy in America.* Edited by J. P. Mayer. Translated by George Lawrence. New York: Harper and Row, 1968.

————. *The European Revolution and Correspondences with Gobineau.* Translated by John Lukacs. Gloucester, Mass.: Peter Smith, 1968.

————. *Memoir, Letter, and Remains of Alexis de Tocqueville.* Translated from the French by the translator of *Napoleon's Correspondence with King Joseph.* 2 vols. Boston: Ticknor and Fields, 1862.

————. *Oeuvres complètes.* Edited by J. P. Mayer. 28 vols. Paris: Gallimard, 1977.

————. *The Old Régime and the French Revolution.* Translated by Stuart Gilbert. Garden City, N.Y.: Doubleday, 1955.

————. *The Recollections of Alexis de Tocqueville.* Edited by J. P. Mayer. Translated by George Lawrence. Garden City, N.Y.: Doubleday 1970.

————. *Selected Letters on Politics and Society.* Edited by Roger Boesche. Berkeley and Los Angeles: University of California Press, 1985.

Tompkins, Jane P. *West of Everything: The Inner Life of Westerns.* New York: Oxford University Press, 1992.

Toulmin, Stephen. *Cosmopolis: The Hidden Agenda of Modernity.* University of Chicago Press, 1990.

Tracy, David. *The Analogical Imagination.* New York: Crossroads, 1989.

Troeltsch, Ernst. *Protestantism and Progress.* Philadelphia: Fortress Press, 1986.

————. *The Social Teachings of the Christian Churches.* Translated by Oliver Wyon. 2 vols. New York: Harper and Row, 1960.

Tully, James. "Governing Conduct." In *Conscience and Casuistry in Early Modern Europe,* 12–71. Edited by Edmund Leites. Cambridge: Cambridge University Press, 1988

Turner, Frederick. *Rediscovering America: John Muir in His Time and Ours.* New York: Viking Press, 1985.

Turner, Frederick Jackson. "The Significance of the Frontier in American History." In American Historical Association, *Annual Report for the Year 1893,* 199–227. Washington, 1894.

Voegelin, Eric. *The New Science of Politics.* Chicago: University of Chicago Press, 1952.

Volkan, Vamik D. *The Need to Have Enemies and Allies.* London: Jason Aronson, 1988.

Voltaire. *Letters on England.* Translated by Leonard Tancock. New York: Penguin Books, 1980.

Walker, Graham. *Moral Foundations of Constitutional Thought: Current Problems, Augustinian Prospects.* Princeton: Princeton University Press, 1990.

Walzer, Michael. *Exodus and Revolution.* New York: Basic Books, 1985.

Warner, R. Stephen. "Work in Progress toward a new Paradigm for the Sociological Study of Religion in the United States." *American Journal of Sociology* 98, no. 5 (March 1993): 1044–93.

Washington, Booker T. *Up from Slavery.* New York: Doubleday, 1963.

Washington, George. "Farewell Address." In *George Washington: A Collection.* Edited by W. B. Allen. Indianapolis, Ind.: Liberty Press, 1988.

Washington, Joseph R., Jr. *Anti-Blackness in English Religion, 1500–1800.* New York: Edwin Mellon Press, 1984.

Weber, Max. "Politics as a Vocation." In *From Max Weber.* Translated by H. H. Gerth and C. Wright Mills. New York: Oxford University Press, 1946.

———. *The Protestant Ethic and the Spirit of Capitalism.* Translated by Talcott Parsons. New York: Charles Scribner's Sons, 1958.

Weil, Simone. "Gravity and Grace." In *Gravity and Grace.* London: Routledge and Kegan Paul, 1963.

———. "Imagination Which Fills the Void." In *Gravity and Grace.*

West, Thomas G. "Misunderstanding the American Founding." In *Interpreting Tocqueville's "Democracy in America,"* 155–177. Edited by Ken Masugi. Savage, Md.: Rowan and Littlefield, 1991.

Whitehead, Alfred North. *Science and the Modern World.* New York: Macmillan, 1925.

Wiessberg, Robert. "Collective vs. Dyadic Representation in Congress." *American Political Science Review* 72, no. 2 (1978): 535–47.

Wilson, James Q. "Human Nature and Social Progress." Bradley Lecture, American Enterprise Institute, May 9, 1991.

Zetterbaum, Marvin. *Tocqueville and the Problem of Democracy.* Stanford: Stanford University Press, 1967.

Index